COMPUTER-HARDWARE
EVALUATION OF
MATHEMATICAL FUNCTIONS

COMPUTER-HARDWARE EVALUATION OF MATHEMATICAL FUNCTIONS

Amos Omondi

Zed Consultants, Canada

Imperial College Press

Published by

Imperial College Press
57 Shelton Street
Covent Garden
London WC2H 9HE

Distributed by

World Scientific Publishing Co. Pte. Ltd.

5 Toh Tuck Link, Singapore 596224

USA office: 27 Warren Street, Suite 401-402, Hackensack, NJ 07601

UK office: 57 Shelton Street, Covent Garden, London WC2H 9HE

Library of Congress Cataloging-in-Publication Data
Omondi, Amos R., author.
  Computer-hardware evaluation of mathematical functions / Amos Omondi, Zed Consultants,
Canada.
     pages cm
  Includes bibliographical references and index.
  ISBN 978-1-78326-860-3 (hardcover : alk. paper)
  1. Computer arithmetic. 2. Computer arithmetic and logic units. 3. Computer algorithms.
4. Integrated circuits--Verification. 5. Computer architecture. I. Title.
  QA76.9.C62O464 2015
  005.1--dc23
                                        2015034747

British Library Cataloguing-in-Publication Data
A catalogue record for this book is available from the British Library.

Printed in Singapore

To Anne, Miles, and Micah

Preface

Lo, the enraptured arithmetician. Easily satisfied, he asks for no Brussels lace, or a coach and six. To calculate contents his liveliest desires, and obedient numbers are within his reach.

ELIE DE JONCOURT, 1762

This book deals primarily with the methods used in the computer-hardware evaluation of some elementary transcendental functions and some algebraic functions: trigonometric functions and their inverses, hyperbolic functions and their inverses, exponentials, logarithms, reciprocals, and square roots and their inverses. Nevertheless, a great deal of what is discussed is equally applicable to numerous other functions. Of necessity, some material on multiplication and division is also included.

Titles of technical books are always quite straightforward and rarely require explanation. But, on the basis of some remarks from two people who looked at parts of the manuscript, I believe a few words on the "hardware" are in order; the "few words" are also a good starting point for a more detailed explanation on what this book is about and what background is required of the reader. The main point is this: contrary to what the title might suggest to some, this book does not contain numerous diagrams of logic circuits, gate-diagrams, diagrams that depict "hardware blocks", etc., and discussions of such. On the other hand, leaving out the "hardware" could, perhaps, have led the reader to expect a much wider coverage than is the case. This book is not about hardware in the aforementioned sense, but it is also not about software algorithms, even though the algorithms given may be implemented in software. Perhaps the following remarks will be clarifying.

At the level of *architecture*, hardware for the evaluation of the functions listed above will consist of relatively simple "functional units"—adders, multipliers, shifters, multiplexors, and so forth—and the challenge is how best to put these together. At its highest level, that "putting together" is largely about the choice of methods, and the considerations are different from those in software implementation. Three examples will give some idea of the differences:

- The evaluation of a polynomial approximation for a given function: The basic hardware required for the evaluation of any polynomial is an adder, a multiplier, and some memory to hold the polynomial-coefficients; and these, perhaps with some replication, can be put together in fairly straightforward ways. The basic issue is then that of which (or what type of) polynomial, and the considerations for hardware implementation are different from those for software implementation. For example, in the former, the degree of the polynomial is very important, and even a single term—going from degree n to degree $n + 1$—can make a substantial difference, especially in high-performance implementations.

- Sharing hardware: For hardware implementation, cost-effectiveness is critical; so it is helpful if the same hardware can be used for different functions. One therefore strives for methods that are very similar. On the other hand, the software-writer is unlikely to be particularly concerned with, say, whether one "subroutine" is used for both division and square-root evaluation, or whether there is one "subroutine" per function.

- Basic operations: Consider rational functions, which are quotients of polynomials. These can provide very good approximations for many functions and have been used routinely in software implementations, but their implementation requires division. In hardware, however, division is about as hard as the evaluation of the functions of interest and is therefore undesirable as a basic operation. This limits the range of algorithms that may usefully be considered for hardware evaluation.

The emphasis of this book is therefore on those *methods* that are suitable for hardware evaluation, rather than on nitty-gritty hardware details that will mostly be straightforward for the well-prepared reader: *the primary issues are how the methods have been derived, how they work, and how well they work*. The reader who is familiar with the design of basic arithmetic units will be able to readily see how the methods can be implemented; we do not dwell on such matters but do make particular points as necessary. Therefore, a background in computer arithmetic, while helpful, is not strictly necessary. (On the other hand, the reader who requires details of implementations will readily find a good supply of descriptions in the published literature; however, many of the best are also particular to specific technologies.)

A brief explanation of the origins of the book might perhaps help in giving the reader a better idea of what to expect as well as what background is expected: Some years ago, when I was with the School of Electrical and Electronic Engineering at Yonsei University (Seoul), I taught a course on computer arithmetic; this book is made up of the lecture notes—updated and given some polish—for the "function evaluation" half of that course. The readership I have in mind is largely similar to the students who took that course: postgraduate students in computer science, computer engineering, and electrical and electronic engineering. Nevertherless, none of the material is beyond an advanced undergraduate student. This book might also be useful, as an introduction to the subject matter, to professionals engaged in designing and building arithmetic units and to prospective researchers in the field. Indeed, the subject matter is so fascinating that even the merely-curious should find this book quite enjoyable.

The aforementioned course was a complete one on computer arithmetic, and by the time function-evaluation came along, basic arithmetic-unit design had all been done. The ideal background for this book therefore consists of a reasonable understanding of digital logic, some knowledge of arithmetic-unit design, and a level of mathematics that one may reasonably expect of a well-equipped undergraduate student in science or engineering. The first two are not strict requirements. Some aspects of the basic arithmetic-unit algorithms are indeed essential and have been included in Chapter 2. Beyond that, what is covered in this book does not require much knowledge of arithmetic units, provided one is prepared to accept that adders, multipliers, dividers, and so forth can be realized in digital logic, as indeed is the case; it might even be that the reader already has in mind such building blocks and simply wishes to know how best to put them together for the evaluation of some function. There are a few places where statements are made on the comparative cost and performance of hardware; the reader who does not have the requisite background may simply take those on faith and proceed.

The level of detail and choice of material (beyond the obvious) were largely determined by feedback from the original course, but I believe they are appropriate for similar readership elsewhere. On detail, there are places where, in response to students, I covered much more than I initially intended to; for example, what is Chapter 6 was originally just a few pages summarizing some basic results. And there are other places where faith seemed sufficient as the main ingredient. What all this means is that the "atypical" reader might consider the coverage somewhat uneven. I beg the forbearance of the reader who is unhappy with that, but the primary purpose and target-readership should be kept in mind. That applies as well to another possible source of minor irratations: the repetition, in a few places, of one or two short paragraphs. This is a "left-over habit" from the original lecture notes that shows up wherever it is necessary to draw the reader's attention to a significant explanation that has already been given, but I have considered that it would be helpful to not have him or her search back over a hundred pages or so to find the first instance.

For the material, I did not cover only "state-of-the-art" methods. There are two main reasons for that. First, I considered that a (very) slightly "historical" view of how the state of the art came about would be helpful to the students—not just in understanding the current current algorithms and their implementations but also in preparing them to understand and appreciate future advances. Second, it seemed to me unwise to make any assumptions about what one might be interested in putting to use and in what ways. For example, the assumption of existing building blocks (such as are to be found in FPGAs) will limit choices in what to implement, and it might well be that "old" methods are more suitable than the "very best"; on the other hand, the situation is very different if the assumption is that everything can be done "from scratch" (as in custom ASIC). At the other extreme, from both the "historical" and the "current" (in practical terms), I have included a very small number of methods whose practicality is probably "shaky" and which best belong in the "to-be-continued" category. These methods embody novel ideas, and it is not unreasonable to expect that the situation will change with advances in technology and refinements. I considered it important that, say, students who might be interested in undertaking research in the field should be aware of such methods.

Chapter 1 is on *errors, range reduction*, and *rounding*. Error-control is obviously important in any numerical computation, and the general concerns are how to keep errors low, how to determine error bounds for a given algorithm, and what the bounds are in particular cases. Range reduction—

the conversion of an evaluation on one argument range into one on a smaller range—is necessary because most of the algorithms of interest work only for arguments in limited ranges, and others work better (e.g. converge faster) when the argument ranges are sufficiently constrained. And proper rounding is generally problematic for transcendental functions; in contrast with the case of basic arithmetic operations and algebraic functions in general, a great deal of effort and care are necessary in rounding for the transcendental functions.

Redundant number-representation systems, in which a single number can have several representations, play a significant role in the design and implementations of algorithms for high-speed arithmetic. Chapter 2 consists of an introduction to such systems and their use in high-speed *multiplication* and *division*. Algorithms for division, whether or not they use such number systems, are very significant in relation to several algorithms that are discussed in this book: many of the latter algorithms have their origins in division algorithms and are very similar. In implementation, this means that essentially the same hardware can be used for all, and it should be noted that division will usually be implemented as a "standard and required" operation. The reader who has a good background in basic computer arithmetic may skip this chapter and return to particular sections according to references elsewhere.

Chapter 3 covers the *CORDIC* algorithms, which are based on the idea of rotation in a geometric space. These algorithms are among the most-studied for the evaluation of elementary functions. Their chief merit is that they facilitate the use of essentially the same hardware for a large number of functions, and so implementations will have excellent cost:performance ratios if several functions are to be evaluated. Chapter 4 extends the material in Chapter 3, by including, for high-performance implementations, the use of redundant number representations and radices larger than two.

Chapter 5 is on *normalization*, in which a function-evaluation consists of the computation of two sequences, such that as the values of one are driven to some constant, those of the other are driven to the value to be computed of the function at hand. The technique is a uniform approach to the direct evaluation of the functions covered in the CORDIC approach and of other functions that are evaluated only indirectly through CORDIC. Also included in the chapter are discussions on the use of redundant number representations and large radices for high performance.

Chapter 6 covers *polynomial evaluation* in some generality. Although Taylor and Maclaurin series will be familiar to all students in science and engineering, their practical limitations in numerical computation, especially for hardware evaluation, sometimes constitute a gap that must be filled; and familiarity with, say, Chebyshev polynomials and their applications might not be standard. For hardware evaluation, the polynomials are generally low-order ones, combined with some form of table lookup. Chapter 7 is on such *table lookup* and *polynomial approximations*.

The last chapter is on the evaluation of *reciprocals*, *square roots*, and *inverse square roots*. These functions are especially important given the frequency with which they are used, and this is especially so for the square root, which is included in the IEEE standard on floating-point arithmetic. The first appearance of these functions is halfway through this book, but this chapter comes at the end because many of the methods described are based on those in the preceding chapters: normalization, polynomials and table lookup, and the use of redundant number representations.

Comments, notification of errors, and so forth: I shall be grateful and indebted if any reader can spare the time to communicate these, to *amos.omondi.ca@ieee.org*

Sir,

In your otherwise beautiful poem ("The Vision of Sin") there is a verse that reads—

> *Every moment a man dies,*
> *Every moment one is born.*

It must be manifest that if this were true, the population of the world would be at a standstill. In truth the rate of birth is slightly in excess of that of death. I would suggest that in the next edition of your poem you have it read—

> *Every moment a man dies,*
> *Every moment* $1\frac{1}{16}$ *is born.*

Strictly speaking, this is not correct, the actual figure is so long that I cannot get it into a line, but I believe the figure $1\frac{1}{16}$ will be sufficiently accurate for poetry.

I am, Sir, yours, etc.

CHARLES BABBAGE TO TENNYSON

LETTER, 1842

Acknowledgments

All Thanks and Praise to The Almighty

I was very fortunate in the staff at Imperial College Press that I worked with, and I am grateful for their high levels of professionalism. Alice Oven, commissioning editor, made sure that the initial phase went smoothly and quickly. Catharina Weijman, production editor, similarly made sure that the subsequent phases were as pain-free possible and also carried out thorough and helpful final checks. And Maia Vaswani is an author's dream of a copy editor: she was fast, completely thorough, and managed to catch several non-trivial technical errors.

My friend Clare Davidson was kind enough to proof-read the first draft of the manuscript. I am indebted to her for that.

Contents

Chapter 1

Errors, Range Reduction, and Rounding

The first section of this chapter is on *errors*. In general, for a given function we seek a good hardware-implementable approximation that, ideally, will be computable with only simple operations: table lookup, addition, and multiplication.[1] Evidently, this will involve some errors—from both the mathematical nature of the approximation and various machine limitations—and we shall consider how to derive bounds on such errors. The general manner in which such bounds are obtained in the book is such that in some cases they may be considered crude, in so far as the magnitudes are "worst-case", slight overestimates. (In particular instances, tighter bounds can be obtained in a straightforward manner, although the tedium involved might be substantial.) But they are nevertheless useful as a measure of confidence and as guides to implementation parameters. And they will certainly suffice for the writing of good poetry.

Several algorithms discussed in the book are applicable only for arguments within restricted ranges, and small ranges at that. Even in cases, such as with certain Taylor series, where arbitrary ranges are nominally permissible, practical issues—convergence, accuracy, efficiency, and so forth—require that the ranges be restricted. Typical ranges that we shall encounter include $[0, 1]$, $[-1, 1]$, $[-\pi/2, \pi/2]$, $[0, \ln 2)$, $[1/2, 1)$ and $[1, 2)$. *Range reduction* refers to the conversion of an approximation on one interval to an approximation on a smaller interval and is the subject of the second section of the chapter.

The last section of the chapter deals with *rounding*. In contrast with the situation of the basic arithmetic operations and typical algebraic functions,

---

[1] A subtraction is no more than an addition, but division is different: in computer hardware, division is about as hard as the evaluation of the functions we are interested in, and we shall almost always aim to avoid its use.

rounding is not a particularly straightforward matter with transcendental functions.

Our discussions here only scratch the surface, and the reader interested in more substantial discussions is referred to other published literature. Standard texts on numerical computation[2] will have much on errors, and there are numerous good publications on range reduction and rounding, e.g. [3–12].

1.1   Errors

In considering errors, naturally the first issue is of exactly *how* to measure error or *what* to consider a useful measure of error. Given an approximation, $\hat{x}$, to some value, x, the most obvious "how–what" measure is the difference between the two. Accordingly, the *absolute error*[3] is the difference $\varepsilon_x \overset{\triangle}{=} \hat{x} - x$. We shall always be interested in the absolute error, but it must be kept in mind that the significance of an absolute error is also in relation to the exact value. Take, for example, the case where $x = 2.71$ and $\hat{x} = 2.72$. The absolute error is 0.01, which is about 0.4% of the exact value. On the other hand, with $x = 0.0015$, and $\hat{x} = 0.002$, the absolute error is 0.0005, which is smaller than in the preceding case but is 33% of the exact value. Accordingly, another useful measure of error is the *relative error*, which is defined as the absolute error relative to the exact value: $\tilde{\varepsilon}_x \overset{\triangle}{=} \varepsilon_x/x = (\hat{x} - x)/x$, with $x \neq 0$.

The preceding definitions can be problematic. We are, after all, concerned with approximations *in practice*, and analysis on the basis of exact results will sometimes be of limited value, given that exact results might not be available. So, in general, we shall look for bounds, b_x and $\tilde{b}_x$, such that $|\varepsilon_x| \leq b_x$ and $|\tilde{\varepsilon}_x| \leq \tilde{b}_x$. In the case of relative error, we may also approximate ε_x/x with $\varepsilon_x/\hat{x}$, on the basis of a truncated Taylor series:

$$\frac{\varepsilon_x}{\hat{x}} = \frac{\varepsilon_x}{x(1 + \varepsilon_x/x)}$$

---

[2]Our personal preference is for texts aimed at computing types rather than mathematicians, e.g. [1], which our general discussion on errors mirrors. [2] is a good compromise between the two types.

[3]Some authors use the term to refer to the *magnitude* of the error, i.e. $|\hat{x} - x|$.

$$= \frac{\varepsilon_x}{x} \left[1 - \frac{\varepsilon_x}{x} + \left(\frac{\varepsilon_x}{x}\right)^2 - \left(\frac{\varepsilon_x}{x}\right)^3 + \cdots \right]$$

$$\approx \frac{\varepsilon_x}{x}$$

This of course assumes that ε_x/x is small. If that is not so, then the method being analyzed is most likely flawed and probably not worth the bother anyway.

Having considered how or what to measure in error, the next issue is the manner in which errors arise in computations; this may be seen as an identification of the *types* of errors. To describe these, let us take, as an example, the case where $f(x)$ is a function such as e^x, and the approximation is by a polynomial obtained from a Taylor series, $p(x) \triangleq \sum_{k=0}^{n} c_k x^k$, where the c_ks are constants. Given that the infinite polynomial has been truncated at the term of order n, there is obvious error between $f(x)$ and $p(x)$. This is an *approximation error*.[4]

Next, consider the evaluation of the aforementioned polynomial, and, for simplicity, assume that the c_ks have been computed beforehand. We may carry out the evaluation by using the recurrences

$$\begin{aligned} Q_n &= c_n \\ Q_k &= c_k + xQ_{k+1} \qquad k = n-1, n-2, \ldots, 0 \\ p(x) &= Q_0 \end{aligned} \tag{1.1}$$

in which each step involves the machine addition and multiplication of real numbers. (The operands themselves will most likely be approximations, but for the moment let us assume that they are exact.) In general, these arithmetic operations will not be exact and will give rise to errors that we shall call *generated errors*. Further, the errors generated in one step of Equation 1.1 will be carried into the next step and will there become a different type of error—an error that is "passed on" rather than produced at the step in question. We shall accordingly refer to *propagated errors*.

Note that the last definitions apply as well to more complex operations. What we have in Equation 1.1 is merely a case where the function in question is a simple operation (i.e. addition or multiplication), and its approximation is equally simple (i.e. the corresponding machine operation). In other words, any functional operator can generate and propagate error. We shall use the term *arithmetic error* to refer to the special case of generated error where the function is a basic arithmetic operation.

---

[4]Some authors use the term *truncation error* for such a case.

Lastly, because of the limitations of machine representation, there may also be errors in the values of the c_ks and x. We shall refer to these as *representation errors*,[5] and it may sometimes be convenient to consider these too as just generated errors. Evidently, arithmetic errors are closely related to representation errors, in that arithmetic operations generally end with a rounding to some final machine representation. It is therefore frequently convenient to consider the two types of error together: *computation error* is the sum of arithmetic error and representation error.

What the totality of all the preceding errors mean is that instead of computing the intended approximation, $p(x)$, we will, most likely, end up with something different.

The general situation therefore is as follows. We are interested in evaluating some function, f, at a point, x. We start by approximating f with some other function, f_a, of a mathematical formulation that can be implemented easily on a machine. But, because of machine limitations in representation and arithmetic, what we actually end up computing is instead yet another approximation, f_m. The machine limitations also mean that the computation is actually on some value, $\widehat{x}$, that approximates x. So, at the end the total error is

$$f_m(\widehat{x}) - f(x)$$
$$= [f_m(\widehat{x}) - f_a(\widehat{x})] + [f_a(\widehat{x}) - f(\widehat{x})] + [f(\widehat{x}) - f(x)] \qquad (1.2)$$
$$= (computation\ error + approximation\ error) + propagated\ error$$
$$= generated\ error + propagated\ error$$

The combination of the last two main terms in Equation 1.2 may be replaced, whenever convenient, with the equivalent

$$f_a(\widehat{x}) - f(x) = [f_a(\widehat{x}) - f_a(x)] + [f_a(x) - f(x)] \qquad (1.3)$$
$$= propagated\ error + generated\ error$$

As indicated above, both computation error and approximation error are generated errors, and generated error at one point may become propagated error at another point; so the distinguishing line seems imprecise. The general rule of thumb in making the distinction is that when we have a function and its approximation, and both are applied to the same input, then the error is a generated one; and when we have some value and its

---

[5] Where the representation error arises from rounding, it is also frequently referred to as *rounding error*.

approximation, with the same function applied to both, then the error is a propagated one.

We conclude this introduction with the mention of a situation in which the generation (and subsequent propagation) of error can be especially disastrous—that of the subtraction of two numbers that are close in value can result in very large relative errors, with the effects magnified by the limitations of machine representation. Suppose the nominal values to be operated on are x and y, but that the values actually operated on are $\hat{x}$ and $\hat{y}$, with errors ε_x and ε_y. (For simplicity, assume that all values are positive.) Then $\hat{x}$ can be as large as $x + \varepsilon_x$, and $\hat{y}$ can be as small as $y - \varepsilon_y$, and the relative error in subtraction is

$$\frac{(\hat{x} - \hat{y}) - (x - y)}{x - y} = \left| \frac{[(x + \varepsilon_x) - (y - \varepsilon_y)] - (x - y)}{x - y} \right|$$

$$= \frac{|\varepsilon_x + \varepsilon_y|}{|x - y|}$$

$$\leq \frac{|\varepsilon_x| + |\varepsilon_y|}{|x - y|}$$

Evidently, the relative error can be quite large if $x \approx y$; that is, the effects of ε_x and ε_y can be greatly amplified in operators that use the result of the subtraction. For example, suppose $x = 3.14159$, $\varepsilon_x = 0.00001$, $y = 3.14158$, and $\varepsilon_y = 0.00001$; then the relative error can be as much as 200% of the exact result. This example assumes that the arithmetic is exact to the precision given; any loss of significant digits in the result will only make matters worse, and in practice this is where the real problem lies.

In the preceding example, the relative errors in both inputs are quite small. So the basic problem here is that small relative errors in the input can be propagated into very large relative errors. Such errors are known as *subtractive-cancellation* errors or just *cancellation errors*.

1.1.1 *Computation errors*

The essence of representation error and, therefore, of arithmetic error, is the reduction in precision that occurs because the number of digits used to represent some value is limited to that permitted by the machine. If basic machine-arithmetic operations[6] are implemented properly, then the errors

---

[6] Addition, subtraction, multiplication, and division.

generated in the arithmetic approximations are also just representation errors: computations are carried out in a higher precision than that of the final results, and the intermediate results are then rounded to final machine representations. The following is a brief consideration of such errors.

Suppose that an intermediate fixed-point result has been computed to infinite precision[7] and is then to be rounded to a representation with n fractional radix-r digits.[8] (Without loss of generality, we shall assume that the operand is positive.) With *chopping (truncation)*, the worst error occurs when digit n is the radix-r digit m instead of $m + 1$, which constitutes an error of magnitude r^{-n}. *Round to nearest* is equivalent to adding 1 in digit position $n+1$ and then chopping; so the worst error is halved. In summary, the bound on the magnitude of the absolute representation error is

$$b = \begin{cases} r^{-n} \text{ with } \textit{chopping} \\ r^{-n}/2 \text{ with } \textit{round to nearest} \end{cases} \tag{1.4}$$

The rounding modes *round to plus infinity* and *round to minus infinity*, i.e. *round up* and *round down*, give the same bounds as chopping.[9] In considering errors in subsequent chapters, we will be conservative and (unless otherwise specified) assume that a reduction in precison, of intermediate and final results, is through chopping, this being the worst of the possible cases.

Now, consider a floating-point value $x \overset{\triangle}{=} r^e s$, where s is the significand (mantissa), e is the exponent, and r is the radix. Suppose s is rounded to s_n, a significand of n radix-r digits, so that the value now represented is $\hat{x} \overset{\triangle}{=} r^e s_n$. Then the bound on the magnitude of the absolute error is

$$b_x = |r^e(s_n - s)|$$

and that on the magnitude of the relative error is

$$\tilde{b}_x = |(r^e(s_n - s))/(r^e s)| = |s_n - s|/|s|$$

Since the bound on $|s_n - s|$ is r^{-n} or $r^{-n}/2$, according to Equation 1.4, the bound b_x is $|r^{e-n}|$ or $|r^{e-n}/2|$. For the relative error, we need a bound on $|s|$. Let us assume that radix-r significands are normalized to the form

---

[7]In practice, for basic arithmetic operations, a proper implementation can achieve the same effect in finite precision.

[8]The reader should keep in mind that the radix used for representation may differ from that used in the computations.

[9]The reader who is not familiar with these rounding modes will find descriptions in Section 1.3.

$0 \cdot * * * \cdots *$. Then $|s| \geq r^{-1}$, and the number represented is of magnitude at least $|r^e r^{-1}|$. Therefore

$$\widetilde{b}_x = \begin{cases} r^{-n+1} \text{ with } \textit{chopping} \\ r^{-n+1}/2 \text{ with } \textit{round to nearest} \end{cases} \tag{1.5}$$

The same bounds are obtained if the initial operands are unnormalized but a sufficient number of guard digits—i.e. extra digits that are not retained in the final result—are used in the computations and the result is then normalized.

In the IEEE standard on floating-point arithmetic, normalized binary operands have form $1 \cdot * * * \cdots *$. So $\widetilde{b}_x = |2^e 2^{-n}|/|2^e| = 2^{-n}$ or 2^{-n-1}, according to the rounding mode. It should, however, be noted that several of the algorithms discussed in the following chapters assume an argument in the range $[1/2, 1)$, which corresponds to normalized binary fractions. In such a case, the argument for the approximation must satisfy such constraints, regardless of the original values and their representations; this can be achieved by range reduction (Section 1.2).

The value r^{-n} appears often in error analysis at this level, and it has a special name: *ulp*, for **u**nit in the **l**ast **p**lace, because it is the value represented by the last fractional digit. So, for example, if $x = 0.314$ and $\widehat{x} = 0.317$, then $|x - \widehat{x}|$ is three ulps.

1.1.2 *Propagated errors*

We shall now consider bounds on propagated error, starting with the basic arithmetic operations. We shall assume that the exact operands are x and y and that the errors in these are ε_x and ε_y; that is, that the operational values are $\widehat{x} \stackrel{\triangle}{=} x + \varepsilon_x$ and $\widehat{y} \stackrel{\triangle}{=} y + \varepsilon_y$. We then seek to determine how the errors are propagated in the arithmetic operations.

- Addition:

$$\widehat{x} + \widehat{y} \leq x + \varepsilon_x + y + \varepsilon_y$$

$$|(\widehat{x} + \widehat{y}) - (x + y)| \leq |\varepsilon_x| + |\varepsilon_y|$$

- Subtraction:

$$\widehat{x} - \widehat{y} \leq x + \varepsilon_x - (y - \varepsilon_y)$$

$$|(\widehat{x} - \widehat{y}) - (x - y)| \leq |\varepsilon_x| + |\varepsilon_y|$$

- Multiplication:

$$\widehat{xy} \le (x + \varepsilon_x)(y + \varepsilon_y)$$

$$= xy + \varepsilon_x y + \varepsilon_y x + \varepsilon_x \varepsilon_y$$

$$\widehat{xy} - xy \le \varepsilon_x y + \varepsilon_y x + \varepsilon_x \varepsilon_y$$

$$\left| \frac{\widehat{xy} - xy}{xy} \right| \le \left| \frac{\varepsilon_x}{x} + \frac{\varepsilon_y}{y} + \frac{\varepsilon_x \varepsilon_y}{xy} \right|$$

$$\approx \left| \frac{\varepsilon_x}{x} \right| + \left| \frac{\varepsilon_y}{y} \right|$$

- Division (applying a Taylor-series expansion):

$$\widehat{x/y} \le \frac{x + \varepsilon_x}{y - \varepsilon_y}$$

$$= \frac{x + \varepsilon_x}{y} \frac{1}{1 - \varepsilon_y/y}$$

$$= \frac{x}{y} \frac{1}{1 - \varepsilon_y/y} + \frac{\varepsilon_x}{y} \frac{1}{1 - \varepsilon_y/y}$$

$$= \frac{x}{y} \left[1 + \frac{\varepsilon_y}{y} + \left(\frac{\varepsilon_y}{y} \right)^2 + \left(\frac{\varepsilon_y}{y} \right)^3 + \cdots \right] +$$

$$\frac{\varepsilon_x}{y} \left[1 + \frac{\varepsilon_y}{y} + \left(\frac{\varepsilon_y}{y} \right)^2 + \left(\frac{\varepsilon_y}{y} \right)^3 + \cdots \right]$$

$$\widehat{x/y} - x/y \le \frac{x}{y} \frac{\varepsilon_y}{y} + \cdots + \frac{\varepsilon_x}{y} + \cdots$$

$$\left| \frac{\widehat{x/y} - x/y}{x/y} \right| \le \left| \frac{\varepsilon_y}{y} + \cdots \frac{\varepsilon_x}{x} + \cdots \right|$$

$$\approx \left| \frac{\varepsilon_x}{x} \right| + \left| \frac{\varepsilon_y}{y} \right|$$

From these expressions, we conclude that in addition and subtraction, the propagation of errors tends to result in the summation of absolute errors; and in multiplication and division, the propagation tends to result in the summation of relative errors. We next consider the case of operators that are more complex than the basic arithmetic ones.

Hardware approximators are generally constructed from units for the basic arithmetic operations and lookup tables (stored values), and error analysis is best carried out in terms of these. Nevertheless, excluding the possibility that we might be interested in examining error propagation at the level at which one function is used to approximate another, there are instances of (essentially) basic operations where consideration in terms of a "higher-level" function is useful or necessary. A simple example is that the computation of x^3 may be carried out in a specialized unit, in which case the it might not be possible to carry out an analysis in terms of the individual multiplications. In general, a group of basic operators may be taken as a single "complex" operator. Accordingly, we next briefly consider propagation with a more general and arbitrary function, $f(x)$.

Suppose ε_x is the error in x—i.e. the operational value is $\widehat{x}$ is $x + \varepsilon_x$—and that with the application of f we wish to wish to find a bound, b_f, for the magnitude of the absolute propagated error and a bound, $\widetilde{b}_f$, for the magnitude of the relative propagated error.

Consider the Taylor-series expansion of f about x:

$$f(\widehat{x}) = f(x + \varepsilon_x) = f(x) + f'(x)\varepsilon_x + \frac{f''(\mu)}{2}\varepsilon_x^2 \qquad \text{where } x < \mu < \widehat{x}$$

If ε_x is sufficiently small that the magnitude of second term is much smaller than the first—and this is usually so in most reasonable practical situations—then

$$f(\widehat{x}) - f(x) \approx \varepsilon_x f'(x)$$

So we may take

$$b_f \approx |\varepsilon_x|\,|f'(x)|$$

and

$$\widetilde{b}_f \approx \left|\frac{\varepsilon_x}{x}\right|\left|\frac{xf'(x)}{f(x)}\right|$$

In general, we do not have $|\varepsilon_x|$ and $|\varepsilon_x/x|$ but instead have corresponding bounds, b_x and $\widetilde{b}_x$. The above expressions may then be replaced with

$$b_f \approx b_x|f'(x)|$$

$$\widetilde{b}_f \approx \widetilde{b}_x \left|\frac{xf'(x)}{f(x)}\right|$$

And alternative expressions, in terms of $\widehat{x}$, $f(\widehat{x})$, and $f'(\widehat{x})$, can be readily obtained by starting with an expansion of

$$f(x) = f(\widehat{x} - \varepsilon_x)$$

It is straightforward to extend all of the above to to a function of n variables, $f(\mathbf{x}) \stackrel{\triangle}{=} f(x_1, x_2, \ldots, x_n)$, with approximations $\widehat{x}_i \stackrel{\triangle}{=} x_i + \varepsilon_i$: the approximations of the absolute and relative errors are

$$\sum_{i=1}^{n} |\varepsilon_i| \left| \frac{\partial}{\partial x_i} f(\mathbf{x}) \right|$$

and

$$\sum_{i=1}^{n} \left| \frac{\varepsilon_i}{x_i} \right| \frac{\left| \frac{\partial}{\partial x_i} f(\mathbf{x}) \right|}{|f(\mathbf{x})|}$$

1.1.3 *Iterative algorithms*

Several of the algorithms described in this book are iterative. For such algorithms, we shall be concerned with convergence (i.e. whether and how fast an algorithm converges), errors in intermediate results, and total (i.e. final) error.

Let us suppose that we have an iterative process that consists of some steps, $0, 1, 2, 3$, and so on. At the end of step $i + 1$, the total error consists of

$$initial\ errors\ propagated\ through\ to\ step\ i + 1 \tag{1.6}$$

$$+ \sum_{k=1}^{i} errors\ generated\ in\ step\ k\ \ and\ propagated\ through\ to\ step\ i + 1$$

$$+ errors\ generated\ in\ step\ i + 1$$

(It is sometimes convenient to consider the initial errors as just errors that are generated errors in some hypothetical preliminary step.)

What we aim for is to have bounds on all errors, to the extent that we can be confident that the final result is correct to the precision that we desire.

With iterative algorithms, our first concerns are usually convergence and the rate at which it occurs. To determine these, we assume that there are no generated errors and consider only propagated error. For the methods covered in this book, the relationship between such errors, ε, at iterations i and $i + 1$ will have the general form

$$\varepsilon_{i+1} = k\varepsilon_i^m \qquad\qquad k \text{ a constant}$$

In *linearly convergent* methods, such as the CORDIC algorithms of Chapter 3, $m = 1$; and in *quadratically convergent* methods, such as the Newton–Raphson (and related methods) of Chapter 8, $m = 2$. Higher values of m are possible, but the corresponding methods are mostly not well-suited to hardware computation, and we shall therefore not consider them in this book.

If $m = 1$, then for convergence we require $|k| < 1$; and the smaller $|k|$ is, the better. And if $m > 1$, then the algorithm will converge if $|\varepsilon_i| < 1$. In both cases, a sufficient number of iterations must be carried out to obtain a result of the desired accuracy and precision.

Once we have determined the propagated error and the rate of convergence, we must then include generated error, in order to determine the total error per iteration:

$$\varepsilon_{i+1} = k\varepsilon_i^m + \varepsilon_{\text{gen}} \tag{1.7}$$

and for convergence we require $|\varepsilon_{i+1}| < |\varepsilon_i|$, i.e.

$$|k||\varepsilon_i^m| + |\varepsilon_{\text{gen}}| < |\varepsilon_i|$$

So what we should like is that, in iterating, one or more of three conditions hold:

(i) There is no error generated at in any step.
(ii) If errors are generated, then their sum (and effect) over all iterations is well below some target accuracy.
(iii) An error that is generated in some step is, in subsequent steps, "converted" (through propagation) into a much smaller error.

Realizing (i) in practice is generally too costly: for example, it implies that all the bits produced in a multiplication always be retained. (ii) is especially important for linearly convergent methods and in practice can be achieved through the use of guard digits in the arithmetic operations; roughly put, the use of such digits stops the generated errors from "contaminating" what will be the final result. (iii) is the normal case with good implementations of quadratically convergent methods.

1.2   Range reduction

The general situation here is that we have an algorithm for some function, f; that the algorithm has been formulated for an argument, x, in some range, $[a, b]$; but that we wish to apply the algorithm to an argument, $\widetilde{x}$, that is in a larger range, $[c, d]$. The computation of $f(\tilde{x})$ is carried out in three steps:

(1) Fom the given $\tilde{x}$, we obtain a corresponding x in the *reduced range*, $[a, b]$. Ideally, this step should involve no more than a few simple arithmetic operations, and it may also yield additional information that is used in the third step.
(2) The algorithm at hand is applied to obtain $f(x)$.
(3) $f(\tilde{x})$ is computed from $f(x)$, using any additional information from the first step. This last step too should, ideally, involve only a few simple arithmetic operations.

There are several places in the book where we assume specific ranges, i.e. that range reduction will have taken place before the application of some algorithm. For such cases, what follows will suffice. Otherwise, the reader who requires more detailed discussions will find some in [3-9].

Range reduction is most effective if it does not lead to a loss of information, and this depends on the nature of the function at hand. Accordingly, [3] identifies several useful properties, including *periodicity*, *symmetry*, and the satisfaction of *addition theorems*.

For examples of *periodicity* and *symmetry*, we may take the sine function. An approximation on any interval can be converted into an approximation on the interval $[0, 2\pi]$, by making use of the identity

$$\sin(x + 2k\pi) = \sin x \qquad k \text{ an integer}$$

That is, to compute $\sin \tilde{x}$, we first find a k and $x \in [0, 2\pi]$ such that $x = \tilde{x} - 2k\pi$ and then obtain $\sin \tilde{x} = \sin x$. Further reduction, to $[0, \pi]$, can then be achieved by making use of the anti-symmetry around $x = \pi$:

$$\sin(x + \pi) = -\sin x$$

And still more reduction is possible, to $[0, \pi/2]$, by making use of the symmetry around $x = \pi/2$:

$$\sin(x + \pi/2) = \sin(x - \pi/2)$$

For examples of the use of *addition theorems*, we may take the logarithm and exponential functions. For the former,

$$\log mx = \log m + \log x \qquad m \text{ an integer}$$

So, for example, we can reduce an approximation of $\log \tilde{x}$, for any $\tilde{x}$, to an approximation on the interval $[1/2, 1]$, by finding an integer k such that

$$\frac{1}{2} \leq \frac{\tilde{x}}{2^k} \leq 1 \qquad m = 2^k \text{ and } x = \tilde{x}/2^k$$

and then computing

$$\log \widetilde{x} = k \log 2 + \log x$$

And for the exponential function, we have

$$e^{m+x} = e^m e^x \qquad m \text{ an integer}$$

So for any $\widetilde{x}$, we can reduce the computation to one on the interval $[0, \log 2]$, for example, by finding an integer k and an x such that

$$x = \widetilde{x} - k \log 2 \qquad m = \log 2^k \text{ and } 0 \le x \le \log 2$$

and then computing

$$e^{\widetilde{x}} = 2^k e^x$$

From the above examples, we can readily identify two types of range reduction: *additive range reduction*, in which an approximation of $f(\widetilde{x})$ is converted, primarily through an "additive" operation, to an approximation of $f(x)$, with

$$x = \widetilde{x} - mC \qquad \text{for some integer } m \text{ and constant } C \qquad (1.8)$$

and *multiplicative range reduction*, in which an approximation of $f(\widetilde{x})$ is converted, primarily through a "multiplicative" operation, to an approximation of $f(x)$, with

$$x = \widetilde{x}/C^m \qquad \text{for some integer } m \text{ and constant } C \qquad (1.9)$$

(There are functions for which it is possible to use both types of range reduction.)

Since additive range reduction involves subtraction, there is the possibility of cancellation error if $\widetilde{x} \approx mC$. Cody and Waite [6] proposed that this problem be dealt with by finding values C_1 and C_2 that are exactly representable and such that:

- $C \approx C_1 + C_2$
- C_1 is very close to C and is representable in just a few digits; that is, the representation of C_1 consists of just the first few digits of that of C.

(With proper rounding, mC_1 will be exactly representable, if it is not too large, and can be computed exactly.) Then, instead of computing $x - mC$, one computes

$$(x - mC_1) - mC_2$$

The effective range of the Cody–Waite algorithm has been extended by replacing the requirement that mC_1 be exactly representable with the requirement that $x - mC_1$ be exactly representable [8].

We next give four examples of range reductions for particular functions. These examples are directly relevant to particular cases in subsequent chapters, in which the given ranges are explicitly assumed.

• *Exponential*: Suppose we have an algorithm to evaluate e^x, for an argument in the range $(-\ln 2, \ln 2)$. If the original argument, $\widetilde{x}$, is not in that range, then preprocessing range reduction is required, as is postprocessing to obtain the final result. Given that

$$\ln 2 \log_2 e = \log_2 \left(e^{\ln 2} \right)$$
$$= 1$$

we have

$$\widetilde{x} = \widetilde{x} \log_2 e \ln 2$$

If we let

$$I = \lceil \widetilde{x} \log_2 e \rceil$$

$$\lambda = \widetilde{x} \log_2 e - I$$

then, I is an integer, $|\lambda| < 1$, and

$$e^{\widetilde{x}} = e^{(I + \lambda) \ln 2}$$

$$= e^{I \ln 2} e^{\lambda \ln 2}$$

$$= 2^I e^x \qquad\qquad -\ln 2 < x \overset{\triangle}{=} \lambda \ln 2 < \ln 2$$

So the procedure for computing $e^{\widetilde{x}}$ consists of four steps:

(1) Multiply $\widetilde{x}$ by $\log_2 e$, and separate the integer and fractional parts of the result, to obtain $I = \lceil \widetilde{x} \log_2 e \rceil$ and $f = \widetilde{x} \log_2 e - I$.
(2) Multiply λ by $\ln 2$, to obtain x.
(3) Compute e^x.
(4) Shift the result from (ii) left by I bit positions to obtain $e^{\widetilde{x}}$.

Note that $\log_2 e$ and $\ln 2$ are constants that can be computed beforehand and stored.

• *Logarithm*: Suppose we have an algorithm to evaluate $\ln x$ for an argument that is in the range $[1/2, 1)$. If the original argument, $\widetilde{x}$, is not in that range, then we:

(1) Find I and x such that $\tilde{x} = 2^I x$, I is an integer, and $1/2 \le x < 1$.
(2) Compute $I \ln 2$ and $\ln x$.
(3) Add the results from (ii) to obtain $\ln \tilde{x}$.

$\ln 2$ is a constant that can be computed beforehand and stored, and the computation of $I \ln 2$ can be overlapped with that of $\ln x$.

• *Square root*: Suppose we have an algorithm to evaluate $\sqrt{x}$ for an argument that is in the range $[1/4, 1)$. If the original argument, $\tilde{x}$, is not in that range, then on the basis that

$$\tilde{x} = 2^{2I} \frac{\tilde{x}}{2^{2I}} \qquad I \text{ an integer}$$

and, therefore,

$$\sqrt{\tilde{x}} = 2^I \sqrt{\frac{\tilde{x}}{2^{2I}}}$$

we:

(1) Find an integer I and an x such that $x = 2^{-2I}\tilde{x}$ and $1/4 \le x < 1$.
(2) Compute $\sqrt{x}$.
(3) Obtain $\tilde{x}$ from an I-bit left shift of the result from (ii).

• *Sine and cosine*: Suppose we have an algorithm for an argument in the range $[-\pi/4, \pi/4]$. If the original argument, $\tilde{x}$, is not in that range, then, on the basis that $\sin(x) = \cos(\pi/2 - x)$ and $\cos x = \sin(\pi/2 - x)$, we:

(1) Determine k, m, and x such that

$$\tilde{x} = k\pi/2 + x \qquad\qquad x \in [-\pi/4, \pi/4]$$
$$m = k \bmod 4$$

(2) Obtain

$$\sin \tilde{x} = \begin{cases} \sin x & \text{if } m = 0 \\ \cos x & \text{if } m = 1 \\ -\sin x & \text{if } m = 2 \\ -\cos x & \text{if } m = 3 \end{cases}$$

$$\cos \tilde{x} = \begin{cases} \cos x & \text{if } m = 0 \\ -\sin x & \text{if } m = 1 \\ -\cos x & \text{if } m = 2 \\ \sin x & \text{if } m = 3 \end{cases}$$

Effectiveness of range reduction

We briefly mention a result that shows the effectiveness of range reduction [3]. Suppose we have a function, $f(x)$, with $n+1$ continuous derivatives and that we approximate it with a polynomial of given degree, n, on the interval $[-a, a]$. Then the following holds.

THEOREM: *Let d_a be the deviation from $f(x)$ of the best approximation on $[-a, a]$. Then there is a constant K, which depends on only n and $f^{(n+1)}(0)$, such that $|d_a| < Ka^{n+1}$.*

This result says that if, for example, we halve the range of approximation, then the reduction in the error is by a factor of about $2^{-(n+1)}$. The result has particular relevance for the polynomial approximations discussed in Chapter 7, which deals with the replacements of approximations over given intervals with approximations over smaller subintervals (or *segments*).

Floating-point operands

All of the algorithms given in this book are for fixed-point (and mostly fractional) operands. In many cases of actual computation, these will be the significands of floating-point operands. If so, then the range reduction and computation of the final result will be with respect to the floating-point format. A consideration of the preceding examples shows that this can be accommodated easily.

Suppose, for example, that we have a square root algorithm that takes an operand in the range $[1/4, 1)$—the range assumed for square root arguments in this book—and that the original argument, $\widetilde{x}$, is not in that range and is represented in binary floating-point form. We proceed as follows.

Find an integer exponent, E and an X such that

$$\widetilde{x} = 2^{2E} X$$

Then

$$\sqrt{\widetilde{x}} = 2^E \sqrt{X}$$

Next, find an integer e and an x such that

$$X = 2^{2e} x \qquad \text{and } 1/4 \leq x < 1$$

Then

$$\sqrt{X} = 2^e \sqrt{x}$$

and

$$\sqrt{\tilde{x}} = 2^{e+E} \sqrt{x}$$

which result can then be recast in the floating-point format.

So, as is the case with the basic arithmetic operations, when moving from fixed-point operations to floating-point ones, additional hardware (beyond what is apparent from the discussions in this book) will required to accommodate floating-point operations. As explained in the Preface, our primary concern is on hardware-implementable *methods*, and we do not dwell on relatively straightforward details of hardware implementation. Accordingly, we shall leave it to the interested reader to work out such secondary details as are required for floating-point implementations.[10]

Hardware implementation

The preceding discussions on logarithms, exponentials, and square roots show that no particularly special hardware is required for range reduction. Indeed, the functional units required are of a type that would already exist in a basic arithmetic unit, for the computation of other functions, although (for good cost and performance) it might be preferrable to have specialized units. The reader who is familiar with the design of arithmetic units will be able to readily see how hardware for range reduction can be devised. There is, however, one special case that we next mention, because there the task is simpler, and unconventional-arithmetic hardware can be used very effectively.

Consider additive range reduction for trigonometric functions. Let us assume that the argument is in fixed-point representation. If we ignore the radix point, then an instance of Equation 1.8 is just the computation of the remainder from an integer division; but in this case the quotient, m, is not required and so need not be explicitly computed. The problem of computing the remainder in division by a constant is a standard one in *residue arithmetic* (modular arithmetic), in which such *modular reduction* is at the heart of *forward conversion*.[11] Efficient hardware—combinational logic, lookup-tables, or a combination of both—can be devised readily for

---

[10][4] is an excellent resource on such matters.

[11]Conversion from conventional representation to residue representation.

this task, and the interested reader is referred to [13]. The same approach can be taken with floating-point operands, essentially by simply treating the representation of an argument as that of an integer. Of course, in this case care must be taken of hidden significand bits, special values of the exponent, and so forth. Some hardware implementations that use residue number systems for range reduction are described in [14, 15].

1.3   Rounding

The general problem of rounding is that having computed an intermediate result in a precision of m digits, we wish to obtain a final result of n digits, where $n < m$. If the final result is what would be obtained by rounding an *infinitely precise* (i.e. exact) intermediate result, then the rounding is said to be *exact* or *correct*. Exact rounding is problematic for transcendental functions.

The fundamental question in practical computation is this: What is the smallest value of m that will suffice to ensure exact rounding to the target precision of n? The answer is that for transcendental functions, in general, we cannot say. Suppose, for example, that the rounding mode is *round to nearest*, that we have computed 1.2345 as an intermediate result, and that we wish to round to four figures. We have to make a decision on whether to round to 1.235 or 1.234, both of which are the same distance from 1.2345. But it could be that computing more digits would show that the five-digit intermediate result came from $1.234500\cdots0$ or from $1.234499\cdots9$, which lead to two different results in four figures. With a transcedental function, we cannot say how many additional digits would be required to distinguish between these two cases, a problem that is known the *Table-Maker's Dilemma* (TMD) [4, 5, 10]. It is therefore not surprising that the IEEE-754 standard for floating-point arithmetic requires exact rounding for the basic arithmetic operations and square root evaluation—for which proper implementation will ensure correct rounding—but not for transcendental functions. (The other functions of interest to us are reciprocals and inverse square roots. As these too are algebraic, exact rounding is not problematic.)

For normalized intermediate binary results in the IEEE standard on floating-point arithmetic,[12] the problematic patterns are

---

[12]The significands are of the form $1 \cdot * * \cdots *$.

$$\overbrace{1 \cdot \underbrace{bb \cdots b}_{n \text{ bits}} 1000 \cdots 00}^{m \text{ bits}} b' b' b' \cdots$$

$$\overbrace{1 \cdot \underbrace{bb \cdots b}_{n \text{ bits}} 0111 \cdots 11}^{m \text{ bits}} b' b' b' \cdots$$

for *round to nearest even*[13] and

$$\overbrace{1 \cdot \underbrace{bb \cdots b}_{n \text{ bits}} 0000 \cdots 00}^{m \text{ bits}} b' b' b' \cdots$$
,

$$\overbrace{1 \cdot \underbrace{bb \cdots b}_{n \text{ bits}} 0111 \cdots 11}^{m \text{ bits}} b' b' b' \cdots$$

for *round to zero*, *round to plus infinity*, and *round to minus infinity*[14] [10].

It is, however, the case that floating-point numbers are algebraic; after all, only so many numbers can be represented with a given number of bits. This means that for a given floating-point format, there exists an m such that, for all possible arguments, the TMD does not exist. If n is small enough—e.g. up to 32 bits—then we can determine a value for m by a simple exhaustive search for values at which the TMD-patterns occur with smaller values of m. Exhaustive search means taking every possible argument, computing the intermediate result at that argument with increasingly higher precision, and checking for such patterns. For large precision, exhaustive search might be impractical, but results have been obtained for binary double-precision (53-bit) significands in the IEEE standard, and they put m at 120 bits to cover several elementary functions [12].

Additional results of exhaustive searches are given in [11, 12]:

- With $n = 16$: $m = 32$ for square root and reciprocal, $m = 35$ for $\log_2 x$, and $m = 29$ for the 2^x.

---

[13] If the intermediate result is halfway between two representable values, then rounding is to the even one, i.e. with a least significant bit of 0.

[14] The first is simple chopping/truncation, the second rounds up, and the third rounds down.

- With $n = 24$: $m = 48$ for reciproal, square root, and 2^x; and $m = 51$ for $\log_2 x$.

These suggest $m \approx 2n$ as a rough guide. Nevertheless [12] also shows that the m found by exhaustive search is likely to be larger than is strictly necessary in practice.

In hardware implementation, the results obtained from searches of the type described may be used in several ways. One is to implement hardware with a value of m for which the TMD pattern never occurs; but, in light of the mentioned result of [12], this can lead to unnecessary cost. An alternative is to determine the highest *practical* precision, m_0, and build hardware to that. Then for arguments for which the TMD pattern occurs, store in a table the corresponding values of the correctly rounded function results and read out stored values as necessary for correct rounding. The table may be addressed with a hash code of the argument, and it need store only the last bit of the correctly rounded result.

Other methods have been proposed to support exact rounding in hardware, of which a noteworthy one will be found in [11]. There, the functions are approximated using polynomials,[15] and the cofficients of the polynomials are obtained in a "normal" manner but are then adjusted to ensure subsequent exact rounding. The hardware is designed to appropriate precision, which is less than that indicated by exhaustive search.

Additional and extensive discussions of elementary-function rounding will be found in [4] and the references therein. The reader should nevertheless note that many algorithms that have been devised for exact rounding are more appropriate for software implementations than for hardware ones.

---

[15]The Chebyshev polynomials of Chapters 6 and 7.

Chapter 2

Redundant Representations and High-Speed Arithmetic

This chapter is primarily on algorithms for high-speed multiplication and division; it is intended to be an introduction or a review, depending on the reader's background. All such algorithms, as well as those for many of the functions we are interested in, are based on *redundant number-representation systems*, i.e. systems in which a given number has more than one representation. Therefore, an introduction to these systems precedes the two main sections that make up most of the chapter. Some of the discussions on the evaluation of other functions (in Chapters 5 and 8) rely on similarities with division algorithms, and frequent references are made there to particular points in this chapter. So even the reader who has a good knowledge of basic computer arithmetic should at least skim through the chapter. (Additional explanation is given in the remainder of this introduction.) This is not a book on basic arithmetic operations, so there is a great deal that we have left out. The reader who requires additional information should consult standard books on computer arithmetic [1-4].

The basic operations in all of the algorithms in this book are addition/subtraction, multiplication, and table lookup. Multiplication is discussed here mainly as an example of the use of redundant number representation, but there are also special instances that are of interest. The latter includes the computations of squares and cubes, such as are required in the evaluation of polynomials and which can be implemented with greater efficiency than general multiplication. Division, on the other hand, is not used as a basic operation but is especially important; the following briefly explains why.

Many algorithms for the computation of elementary functions are very similar to the division algorithms described here and are derived in similar ways. This is not accidental: many of the former algorithms started life as "pseudo-divsion" methods. Accordingly, a good understanding of division algorithms, although not strictly necessary, can be very helpful in understanding the other algorithms; in subsequent chapters we shall also make frequent and significant references to the discussions here of division algorithms and their implementations. In practical terms, the similarities between the algorithms for division and those for other functions mean that essentially the same hardware can be used for division and several other operations, which is siginficant for cost-effectiveness. For the reader who is not familiar with high-speed division algorithms, perhaps the following brief summary will help clarify the claimed importance.

Consider the division of N by D, and assume that both operands are fixed-point fractions. The divison may be carried out in one of two main ways: by the application of some variation of the standard "paper-and-pencil" algorithm or by the computation $1/D$ and the multiplication of that by N.

A paper-and-pencil method will consist of the computation of two sequences: one sequence consisting of partial remainders, the first of which is the dividend and the last of which is the final remainder, and the other sequence consisting of partial quotients, the first of which is zero and the last of which is the quotient. In the computation of elementary functions, this is generalized under the rubric of "normalization"—the computation of two sequences of which the values of one tend to some constant as those of the other tend to the value sought. Indeed, at a certain level, many other normalization algorithms differ from the division algorithms only in terms of what one views as the "remainder"and the "quotient".

With the second approach to division, $1/D$ can be computed in several ways. One is to compute the root of the function $f(x) = 1/x - D$, another is to use table lookup, a third is by normalization, and a fourth is to use a polynomial approximation. There are several variations with all these methods, and they are applicable to other functions.

The preceding summary of division algorithms captures the essence of all other algorithms in this book: they are all based on normalization, or root finding, or table lookup, or polynomial evaluation; and in many cases the relationship to division is very direct. It is also the case that even a basic arithmetic unit will include division, which as a basic operation, is required in the IEEE standard on floating-point arithmetic. So algorithmic similarities have the beneficial consequence that whatever hardware is provided for division can, with some enhancements, also be used for other functions.

2.1   Redundant number representations

In a *redundant number-representation system*, the set of values that a single digit can assume exceeds the radix in use; so a given number will have more than one representation. There are two redundant-number-representation systems that are commonly used in computer arithmetic: *carry–save* (CS)[1] and *redundant signed digit* (RSD).

A basic implementation of multiplication or division will comprise a sequence of cycles, each of which consists of the addition or subtraction of a multiple of the multiplicand (for multiplication) or the divisor (for division). During these cycles, there might be instances when the multiple in question is zero, and so there need not be an arithmetic operation. In such cases a *recoding*—usually "on the fly"—of the multiplier or the dividend, from conventional representation (e.g. two's complement) into RSD representation can help reduce the number of cycles in which "real" arithmetic operations are required.[2] For want of better terminology, we shall sometimes refer to such usage of RSD as *"outside the arithmetic"*.

Another common use of RSD representation is to facilitate high-radix arithmetic. As a general rule, if a radix-2 operation requires n cycles for n-bit operands, then the corresponding radix-2^k algorithm will require $\lceil n/k \rceil$ cycles.[3] And, typically, in basic radix-r computation, the multiples required of some operand, X—e.g. multiplicand or divisor—are a subset of $0, X, 2X, \cdots, (r-1)X$. Such multiples should be easy to compute, and, ideally, should require no more than simple shifting: $2X$, $4X$, etc. The use of RSD reduces the number of awkward multiples, i.e. $3X$, $5X$, etc. Such usage too is *outside-the-arithmetic* usage.

Regardless of whether or not RSD is used outside the arithmetic, the arithmetic itself may be in conventional or redundant representation. For high-speed computation, the arithmetic will usually be in redundant representation. With conventional representation, the operational time for an

---

[1] There is also a *borrow–save*, but this is rarely used, and it is essentially equivalent to the carry–save. The difference between the two is whether the underlying operation is an addition or a subtraction, and either can be expressed in terms of the other.

[2] This is not often done nowadays, because it leads to operand-dependent operational times, and the benefits will be marginal if the arithmetic to be avoided in each cycle is not sufficiently time-consuming.

[3] For optimal representation in a digital computer and the simplification of the design of arithmetic circuits, radices larger than two will usually be powers of two. This is therefore assumed henceforth. Of course, decimal will become increasingly significant, with its inclusion, in the IEEE's standard on floating-point arithmetic, but even then a distinction must be made between the radix of representation and radix of implementation.

addition or subtraction is largely determined by carry propagation, which is of little or no concern with CS or RSD representation. Either representation may be used for arithmetic, but CS is the preferred form, as RSD arithmetic units tend to be slightly more complex. We shall refer to any such usage, of either representation, as "*in* (or *for*) *the arithmetic*".

2.1.1 Carry–save representation

A basic computer algorithm for multiplication will be no more than a version of the standard paper-and-pencil decimal algorithm. Briefly, in the computer version:

- A *partial product* is initialized to zero and at the end is the final product.
- The multiplier is scanned one digit at a time, starting from the least significant digit.
- For each multiplier-digit, the corresponding multiplicand–multiple is formed.
- each multiplicand–multiple is added to the most significant digits of the partial product, which is then shifted one digit to the right.

So there are two straightforward ways to speed up the multiplication. One is to speed up the additions; and the other is to reduce the number of cycles. CS representation is used for the former, and that is discussed here; RSD is used for the latter, and that is discussed in Section 2.2.

In a "normal" basic addition, the digits are added one at a time, starting from the least significant pair, and any carry produced from the addition of one pair of digits is propagated to the addition of the next pair of digits. This is an inherently slow process that, for n-digit operands, takes a time that is proportional to n in the basic case and to $\log n$ in the best case.[4]

With a sequence of additions, such as occurs in a multiplication, carries need not be propagated with every addition. Instead, the carries from one addition may be "saved" and included in the next addition, with a one-digit relative shift to the left. If that is done, then the ouput from each addition consists of unassimilated sum digits, constituting a *partial sum*, and unassimilated carry digits, constituting a *partial carry*.

---

[4]The simplest case of such a *carry–propagate adder* (CPA) consists of one-digit adders (DAs) that are connected by making the carry output of one DA the carry input to the next DA, thus giving a *carry chain* of length proportional to n. In the best case the carry-chain is replaced with a tree with a worst-case path proportional to $\log n$.

Multiplicand = 00111 (7)   Multiplier = 01111 (15)

Cycle 1   00000   Initial partial sum
                           00000   Initial partial carry
                           00111   Add 1st multiple
                           00111   1st partial sum
                           00000   1st partial carry

Cycle 2   000111   Shift 1st partial sum right
                           00111   Add 2nd multiple
                           00000   Add 1st partial carry
                           001001   2nd partial sum
                           00011   2nd partial carry

Cycle 3   0001001   Shift 2nd partial sum right
                           00111   Add 3rd multiple
                           00011   Add 2nd partial carry
                           0011001   3rd partial sum
                           00011   3rd partial carry

Cycle 4   00011001   Shift 3rd partial sum right
                           00111   Add 4th multiple
                           00011   Add 3rd partial carry
                           00111001   4th partial sum
                           00011   4th partial carry

Cycle 5   000111001   Shift 4th partial sum right
                           0000   Add 5th multiple
                           00011   Add 4th partial carry
                           000001001   5th partial sum
                           00011   5th partial carry

Propagate   0000001001   Shift final partial sum
carries   00011   Add final partial carry
                           001101001   Product (105)

Table 2.1: Multiplication with carry–save addition

The unassimilated pair of sum–bits and carry–bits constitutes a *carry–save representation*, and the corresponding adder is a *carry–save adder*. There will be different ⟨partial-sum, partial-carry⟩ pairs that represent the same number; so the notation is evidently redundant. There is another way to see the redundancy: Take the radix-2 case as an example. In the conventional case, the digit set is $\{0, 1\}$; here the digit set is $\{(0,0), (1,0), (1,0), (1,1)\}$, according to the $\langle$partial-sum, partial-carry$\rangle$ bit pairs. If we consider the sum of each pair, then the middle two are equivalent, and we may view the new digit set as $\{0, 1, 2\}$. The size of the digit set exceeds the radix, whence the redundancy in representation.

Because there is no carry propagation, the operational delay for a single carry–save addition is just the time taken to add a pair of digits.[5] But the saving of carries eventually comes to an end—when there is no "next addition"—and the partial-sum bits and partial-carry bits must be assimilated, by propagating the carries. This assimilation requires a normal *carry–propagate* adder and is a conversion from the redundant representation into conventional representation. Table 2.1 gives an example of a multiplication with CS addition.

Division is the "inverse" of multiplication; so basic division consists of a sequence of subtractions, which are just additions of the negations of the subtrahends; therefore, CS addition can be used in the arithmetic for division as well. Division is, however, more complicated than multiplication, in that the subtrahend (multiple of the divisor) chosen at any step depends on the magnitude result of the preceding subtraction and that magnitude is not readily available with CS representation.

Assuming two's complement representation, subtraction with carry–save representation is carried out in the usual manner of forming the ones' complement of the subtrahend and then adding that with a 1 also added into the least significant bit position.[6] Depending on the particular situation, the addition of the 1 may be a "delicate" affair; examples of useful tricks will be found in the literature, e.g. [20].

2.1.2   *Redundant signed-digit representation*

As indicated above, the essence of redundancy in representation is that the number of values that a digit can assume exceeds the radix.[7] In

---

[5] In contrast with a carry–propage adder, an n-digit *carry–save adder* consists of just n unconnected one-digit adders.

[6] The placement of the apostrophes is not an error: *two's* complement, but *ones'* complement [21].

[7] We here exclude the sort of "trivial" redundancy that exists in ones' complement and sign-and-magnitude notations, in which zero has two representations: one corresponding to -0, and the other corresponding to $+0$.

a conventional (i.e. non-redundant) radix-r number system, each representable number has exactly one representation and the number of values that any digit may take is r, from the set $\{0, 1, \cdots, r - 1\}$. On the other hand, in a radix-r RSD system, the number of values that a digit may take will be between $r + 1$ and $2r - 1$, with each digit, except that for zero, being signed (as positive or negative). The digit set in a radix-r RSD system is $S \triangleq \{-p, -(p - 1), \ldots, -1, 0, 1, \ldots, m - 1, m\}$, where $\lceil (r - 1)/2 \rceil \leq m, p \leq r - 1$, and $|S| > r$. The digit sets of some RSD systems are given in Table 2.2, in which $\bar{x}$ represents $-x$, this being standard notation.

Radix	Digit set
2	$\{\bar{1}, 0, 1\}$
3	$\{\bar{2}, \bar{1}, 0, 1\}$ $\{\bar{1}, 0, 1, 2\}$ $\{\bar{2}, \bar{1}, 0, 1, 2\}$
4	$\{\bar{2}, \bar{1}, 0, 1, 2\}$ $\{\bar{3}, \bar{2}, \bar{1}, 0, 1\}$ $\{\bar{1}, 0, 1, 2, 3\}$ $\{\bar{3}, \bar{2}, \bar{1}, 0, 1, 2\}$ $\{\bar{2}, \bar{1}, 0, 1, 2, 3\}$ $\{\bar{3}, \bar{2}, \bar{1}, 0, 1, 2, 3\}$

Table 2.2: Digit sets for some RSD systems

RSD systems were originally devised to deal with the problem of carry propagation [5], a point we shall return to below. Compared with the use of CS representation, RSDs are now rarely used for that purpose; where carry propagation is an issue, CS will do and is generally easier to implement. Nevertheless, RSD systems have significant applications in other respects, as will be seen in this and other chapters.

Commonly used RSD digit sets are symmetric about 0, i.e. $p = m$, and we shall henceforth assume that to be so when we discuss RSD systems.[8]

---

[8] *Generalized RSD* systems allow $p \neq m$. See [9].

So we shall have one parameter, m, such that

$$\left\lceil \frac{r-1}{2} \right\rceil \leq m \leq r - 1 \qquad (2.1)$$

Such a system is said to have *minimal redundancy* when $m = \lceil (r-1)/2 \rceil$ and *maximal redundancy* when $m = r - 1$; the degree of redundancy can be measured by calculating the *redundancy constant* (or *redundancy factor*), which is defined as $m/(r-1)$. As an example, the first radix-4 set in Table 2.2 is minimally redundant, and the last set is maximally redundant. We shall see that this redundancy factor crops up "naturally" in the formulation of several algorithms, and its value has significant practical implications: there is a delicate trade-off to be made between the theoretical advantages of using a large factor and the practical ones of using a small factor. This point will become clearer in the discussions that follow on division and similar algorithms.

One can readily see that in an RSD system, each representable number will have several possible representations. For example, in the radix-2 RSD system with the digit set $\{\bar{1}, 0, 1\}$, three five-bit representations of the number eleven are 01011 (i.e. $8 + 2 + 1$), $10\bar{1}0\bar{1}$ (i.e. $16 - 4 + 1$), and $0110\bar{1}$ (i.e. $8 + 4 - 1$).

To represent the negation of a number represented in RSD form, the sign of every non-zero digit is inverted. So, for example, the three representations, obtained from the preceding example, of negative eleven are $0\bar{1}0\bar{1}\bar{1}$ (i.e. $-8 - 2 - 1$), $\bar{1}0101$ (i.e. $-16 + 4 + 1$), and $0\bar{1}\bar{1}01$ (i.e $-8 - 4 + 1$).

If $X_{n-1}X_{n-2}\cdots X_0$ is an n-digit RSD representation in a radix-r system, then the value, X, that it represents is computed as in a conventional, weighted number system:

$$X = \sum_{i=0}^{n-1} X_i r^i \qquad (2.2)$$

RSD systems were originally invented to deal with the problem of carry–propagation in conventional addition. It can be shown that if the bounds in Inequations 2.1 are changed to

$$\left\lceil \frac{r+1}{2} \right\rceil \leq m \leq r - 1 \qquad (2.3)$$

then carry–propagation will limited to a single digit position; that is, a carry from digit position i will not go beyond digit position $i + 1$. The new bounds are not satisfied if $r = 2$, a case that we shall deal with separately.

2.1.2.1 *Addition*

Assuming that $r > 2$ and $m \geq \lceil (r + 1)/2 \rceil$, addition in an RSD system consists of two steps. The first step produces carries and partial-sum digits that are assimilated in the second step; there are no carries in the second step.

Let the operands be $A_{n-1}A_{n-2} \cdots A_0$ and $B_{n-1}B_{n-2} \cdots B_0$, where $A_i, B_i \in \{\overline{m}, \overline{m-1}, \cdots, 1, 0, 1, \cdots, m-1, m\}$. Then the addition may be expressed as

$$
\begin{array}{cccccc}
 & A_{n-1} & A_{n-2} & \cdots & A_1 & A_0 \\
+ & B_{n-1} & B_{n-2} & \cdots & B_1 & B_0 \\
\hline
\end{array}
$$

$$
\begin{array}{cccccccl}
C_{n-1} & C_{n-2} & C_{n-3} & \cdots & C_0 & & \text{carries} \\
+ & S^*_{n-1} & S^*_{n-2} & \cdots & S^*_1 & S^*_0 & \text{partial sum} \\
\hline
S_n & S_{n-1} & & \cdots & S_1 & S_0 & \text{sum}
\end{array}
$$

where $S_i \in \{\overline{m}, \overline{m-1}, \cdots, 1, 0, 1, , \cdots m-1, m\}$, $S^*_i \in \{\overline{m-1}, \overline{m-2}, \cdots, \overline{1}, 0, 1, \cdots m-2, m-1\}$, and $C_i \in \{\overline{1}, 0, 1\}$. The range for S^*_i ensures that there are no carries generated in the second step; and S^*_i and

$$
C_i = \begin{cases}
1 & \text{if } A_i + B_i \geq m \\
0 & \text{if } -m < A_i + B_i < m \\
\overline{1} & \text{if } A_i + B_i \leq -m
\end{cases}
$$

$$
S^*_i = A_i + B_i - rC_i
$$

An example addition in the maximally redundant radix-4 system:

$$
\begin{array}{clccccl}
A & & 1 & \overline{3} & \overline{2} & 2 & \text{(10 in decimal)} \\
B & & 0 & \overline{2} & 1 & 3 & \text{(−25 in decimal)} \\
\hline
S^* & & 1 & \overline{1} & \overline{1} & 1 & \\
C & 0 & \overline{1} & 0 & 1 & & \\
\hline
S & & 0 & \overline{1} & 0 & 1 & \text{(−15 decimal)}
\end{array}
$$

We have thus far assumed a non-binary radix, as Inequations 2.3 do not hold for $r = 2$. For radix-2 RSD addition, special rules are required if carry–propagation is to be limited to, at most one, digit position [7]. These rules require that S_i^* and C_i be produced by considering the digits at both positions i and $i-1$. The rules are summarized in Table 2.3; for $i = 0$, it is assumed that $A_{-1} = B_{-1} = 0$. The sum digits are computed as

$$S_i = S_i^* + 2C_i$$

An example radix-2 addition:

i	8	7	6	5	4	3	2	1	0	
A		1	$\bar{1}$	1	0	$\bar{1}$	$\bar{1}$	0	1	(85 in decimal)
B		0	1	0	0	0	$\bar{1}$	$\bar{1}$	1	(59 in decimal)
C	0	0	0	0	0	$\bar{1}$	$\bar{1}$	0	1	
S^*		1	0	1	0	1	0	$\bar{1}$	0	
S		1	0	1	$\bar{1}$	0	0	0	0	(144 in decimal)

$\mathbf{A_i}$	$\mathbf{B_i}$	$\mathbf{A_{i-1}}$	$\mathbf{B_{i-1}}$	$\mathbf{C_i}$	$\mathbf{S_i^*}$
0	0	−	−	0	0
0	1	both not $\bar{1}$		1	$\bar{1}$
		otherwise		0	1
0	$\bar{1}$	both not $\bar{1}$		0	$\bar{1}$
		otherwise		$\bar{1}$	1
1	0	both not $\bar{1}$		1	$\bar{1}$
		otherwise		0	1
1	1	*	*	1	0
1	$\bar{1}$	*	*	0	0
$\bar{1}$	0	both not $\bar{1}$		0	$\bar{1}$
		otherwise		$\bar{1}$	1
$\bar{1}$	1	*	*	0	0
$\bar{1}$	$\bar{1}$	*	*	$\bar{1}$	0

* = *don't care*

Table 2.3: Rules for binary RSD addition

2.1.2.2 *Conversion*

The addition algorithm can also be used for conversion from a conventional radix-r representation to a radix-r RSD representation, by making the second operand zero. An example in the maximally redundant radix-4 system:

$$
\begin{array}{lccccl}
A & & 0 & 1 & 2 & 3 & \text{(27 in decimal)} \\
B & & 0 & 0 & 0 & 0 \\
\hline
S^* & & 0 & 1 & \bar{2} & \bar{1} \\
C & 0 & 0 & 1 & 1 \\
\hline
S & & 0 & 2 & \bar{1} & \bar{1} & \text{(27 in decimal)}
\end{array}
$$

An alternative method for conversion is as follows.

To convert a binary representation, $X_{n-1}X_{n-2}\cdots X_0$, to a binary RSD representation $Y_{n-1}Y_{n-2}\cdots Y_0$, we append a hypothetical bit $X_{-1} = 0$ and then consider bit-pairs according to the rules[9] of Table 2.4. Thus, for example, given 001101 (13 in decimal), we would start with 0011010 and end up with $010\bar{1}1\bar{1}$. This algorithm may be applied from left to right, right to left, or in parallel to all bit-pairs, depending on the availability of the operand-bits. Similar algorithms can be devised easily for non-binary radices that are powers of two and for which the bit-patterns are therefore the same, regardless of the radix, since a radix-2^k digit is represented in exactly k bits. Some conversion tables for radices four and eight are given in Section 2.2.1.

$\mathbf{X_i}$	$\mathbf{X_{i-1}}$	$\mathbf{Y_i}$
0	0	0
0	1	1
1	0	$\bar{1}$
1	1	0

Table 2.4: Conversion rules for binary RSD

[9]For a justification of these rules, see Section 2.2.1.

The process of such a conversion is commonly referred to as *recoding* and is widely used (implicitly) in the design of high-speed multipliers (Section 2.2). It should be noted that because a given number can have several representations in a given RSD system, it follows that one can devise several different algorithms for conversion from conventional representation to RSD representation.

The conversion from a radix-r RSD representation to conventional radix-r representation is easiest done by a radix-r subtraction of the negatively signed digits from the positively signed ones. For example, working backward from the last example, the conversion from $0\,2\,\overline{1}\,\overline{1}$ is

+ve bits:	0	2	0	0	
−ve bits:	0	0	1	1	(subtract)
result:	0	1	2	3	

This straightforward method for conversion implicitly assumes that all the digits to be converted are available at once, in which case a fast carry–propagate adder will suffice, or that they are available serially, from the least significant digit, in which case a one-digit serial adder will suffice. There are, however, cases, in which the digits are available serially but from the most significant end, examples being the quotient in SRT division (Section 2.3.3) and similar outputs from algorithms for several other functions. For such cases, there is an "on-the-fly" conversion algorithm that produces the result from the most significant digit to the least significant digit, thus doing away with the inherent delay [6]. We next briefly describe that algorithm. We shall assume that the representation to be converted is that of a fraction; this entails no loss of generality and directly corresponds to the applicable situations in this book.

Suppose the representation to be converted into conventional form is $0.x_1x_2\cdots x_n$, where x_i ($i = 1, 2, \ldots, n$) is a signed radix-r digit. And suppose the digits are available, one at a time, from the most significant to the least significant. The conversion then consists of the nominal computation of

$$X = \sum_{i=1}^{n} x_i r^{-i}$$

If we define

$$X_j = \sum_{i=1}^{j} x_i r^{-i}$$

then the computation may be expressed as

$$X_0 = 0$$

$$X_{j+1} = X_j + x_{j+1} r^{-(j+1)} \qquad\qquad j = 0, 1, 2, \ldots, n$$

$$X = X_n$$

If $x_{j+1} \geq 0$, then the computation of X_{j+1} is just the concatenation of x_{j+1} to the digits of X_j. Otherwise, it is the subtraction of $|x_{j+1}|$, and that may be expressed as

$$X_{j+1} = X_j + x_{j+1} r^{-(j+1)}$$

$$= X_j - |x_{j+1}| r^{-(j+1)}$$

$$= \left(X_j - r^{-j} \right) + \left(r^{-j} - |x_{j+1}| r^{-(j+1)} \right)$$

$$= \left(X_j - r^{-j} \right) + \left(r - |x_{j+1}| \right) r^{-(j+1)}$$

There are at most r possible values of $(r - |x_{j+1}|)$, and this is a small number that can be built into the control logic; that is, no actual subtraction is necessary. Therefore, if the digits of $X_j - r^{-j}$ are available, then here too the computation of X_{j+1} can be reduced to the concatenation of one digit to an existing string of digits. The algorithm computes the digits of $X_j - r^{-j}$ at the same time as those of X_j.

Let X_j^- denote $X_j - r^{-j}$. These values may be computed as

$$X_{j+1}^- = X_{j+1} - r^{-(j+1)}$$

$$= \begin{cases} X_j + (x_{j+1} - 1) r^{-(j+1)} & \text{if } x_{j+1} > 0 \\ X_j^- + ((r-1) - |x_{j+1}|) r^{-(j+1)} & \text{otherwise} \end{cases}$$

The values of $(r-1) - |x_{j+1}|$ will be sufficiently few that they too can be built into the control logic.

Using $\circ$ to denote concatenation, all of the above computations may be summarized as

$$X_{j+1} = \begin{cases} X_j \circ x_{j+1} & \text{if } x_{j+1} \geq 0 \\ X_j^- \circ (r - |x_{j+1}|) & \text{otherwise} \end{cases}$$

$$X_{j+1}^- = \begin{cases} X_j \circ (x_{j+1} - 1) & \text{if } x_{j+1} > 0 \\ X_j^- \circ ((r-1) - |x_{j+1}|) & \text{otherwise} \end{cases}$$

Little hardware is required to implement this: two shift registers to hold X_j and X_j^-, two multiplexors to effect the choices required to compute these, and a small amount of control logic. Futher details will be found in [1].

As an example, the conversion of the radix-4 representation $0.2\bar{1}1\bar{3}$, which is $113/256$ as a decimal fraction, is given in Table 2.5. The result is 0.1301 in radix-4, which is 01110001 in binary.

j	x_j	X_j	X_j^-
0	*	0	0
1	2	0.2	0.1
2	$\bar{1}$	0.13	0.12
3	1	0.131	0.130
4	$\bar{3}$	0.1301	0.1300

Table 2.5: Example on-the-fly conversion from RSD

2.1.2.3 *Absolute values*

By Equation 2.2, to obtain the representation of the negation of a number that is represented in RSD form, the sign of each non-zero digit in the latter is inverted. Therefore, to obtain an absolute value from a given RSD number representation, the procedure is as follows. The first non-zero digit, starting from the most significant one, is examined. If that digit is positive, then nothing is done, and the result consists of the weighted sum of all digits as they are. Otherwise, the result is obtained by inverting the signs of all the non-zero digits and computing the weighted sum.

The procedure just described is inherently serial, in that digit-by-digit addition is inherently a serial operation; and it will work best in most-significant-digit-first, serial implementatations, generally known as *online-arithmetic* [1, 8] or other similar implementations. Nevertheless, it can be put to good use in non-serial implementations, if several absolute-value computations are to be carried out, the key being the use of pipelining and temporal parellelism. One such case is described in Section 4.4.

2.2   High-speed multiplication

The most common use of redundant representation outside arithmetic is that of redundant signed-digit (RSD) representation in *multiplier recoding*, a standard technique in the implementation of high-speed multipliers. Multiplier recoding is usually, but need not necessarily be, combined with the the use of carry–save (CS) representation for the actual arithmetic.

The first part of this section is on multiplier recoding. The second part is on squaring, which, as a special case of multiplication, can be implemented at lower cost and higher performance than general multiplication. Squaring is important in such cases as polynomial evaluation (Chapters 6 and 7). The types of optimization described for that computation are also equally applicable to the computation of higher powers.

2.2.1   *Multiplier recoding*

The basic multiplication of two n-digit numbers requires n cycles. In each cycle, the next digit (starting from the least significant end) of the multiplier is examined and the corresponding multiple of the multipler (appropriately weighted through shifting) is added to a running product that is initially zero.[10] So there are at least two straightforward ways to speed up multiplication. One is to speed up the arithmetic, and this is almost always done through the use of redundant representation (CS), as described in Section 2.1.1. The other is to reduce the number of cycles or avoid unnecessary additions; this is where RSD representation comes in.

The essential idea that gives rise to RSD representation is that it is possible to skip past a sequence of 0s or a sequence of 1s in the multiplier and thus perform no arithmetic for such sequences. The process by which this is done amounts to an implicit on-the-fly *recoding*, from conventional representation into RSD representation. We explain this next, initially assuming that the radix is two.

The case for shifting over 0s in the multiplier requires little justification. In the ordinary procedure, the multiplicand–multiple that is added for each 0 is just zero, which at the end leaves the partial product shifted by several places but otherwise unchanged; evidently, the addition of zero may be omitted. The justification for shifting over 1s is, perhaps, less obvious. Consider the string $\ldots 0111 \ldots 10 \ldots$ of $j-i+1$ 1s in bit positions j through

---

[10]A careful examination of the steps in standard paper-and-pencil multiplication will clarify the details.

i of the multiplier. Multiplication by the number represented by this string is equivalent to multiplication by the number with value $2^{j-1} + 2^{j-2} + \cdots + 2^{i-1}$, which is equal to $2^j - 2^{i-1}$. So the $j - i + 1$ additions that are required in positions j through i when using the ordinary multiplication procedure may be replaced with two additions: one (of a negative number) in position i and one (of a positive number) in position $j + 1$.

As an example, take the decimal multiplication of decimal 6 (multiplicand) and decimal 226 (multiplier). In binary notation, this is the multiplication of 110 and 011100010, which would require nine additions with the ordinary procedure. By shifting over 0s and 1s only four additions are required. These are at the underlined positions in the string $0\underline{11}\underline{1}000\underline{1}0$. The multiplication is therefore carried out as $110 \times 100000000 - 110 \times 100000 + 110 \times 100 - 110 \times 1$ or $6 \times 2^7 - 6 \times 2^5 + 6 \times 2^2 - 6 \times 2^1$, which is $6 \times (256 - 32 + 4 - 2) = 6 \times 226$.

For implementation, the preceding explanation implies the variable-length shifting of the multiplier and the running product. Assuming non-serial operations, the costs of a barrel shifter are high enough that such an operation is usually not considered worthwhile,[11] and variable, i.e. operand-dependent, operational times are undesirable in many contexts. Nevertheless, the fundamental idea is useful and is employed in all high-speed multipliers—with the restriction that the shift length per cycle is fixed: at one bit at a time (which is radix-2 computation), or two bits at a time (radix-4), or three bits at a time (radix-8), and so forth.

B_i	B_{i-1}	Action
0	0	Shift P one bit
0	1	Add A; shift P one bit
1	0	Subtract A; shift P one bit
1	1	Shift P one bit

Table 2.6: Actions for 1-bit multiplier recoding

The rules for the radix-2 case are given in Table 2.6, in which A denotes the multiplicand, B_i denotes bit i of the multiplier, P denotes the running

---

[11] An obvious exception is in arithmetic for cryptography, in which the operands tend to be of very high precision.

product, and a hypothetical B_{-1} is set to 0 to start the process. The pair 00 corresponds to the middle of a string of 0s, the pair 11 corresponds to the middle of a string of 1s, the pair 01 corresponds to the end of a string of 1s and the start of a string of 0s, and the pair 10 corresponds to the end of a string of 0s and the start of a string of 1s.

$B_{i+1,i}$	B_{i-1}	Action
00	0	Shift P two bits
00	1	Add A; shift P two bits
01	0	Add A; shift P two bits
01	1	Add $2A$; shift P two bits
10	0	Subtract $2A$; shift P two bits
10	1	Subtract A; shift P two bits
11	0	Subtract A; shift P two bits
11	1	Shift P two bits

Table 2.7: Actions for 2-bit multiplier recoding

$B_{i+2,i+1,i}$	B_{i-1}	Action	
000	0	Shift P three bits	
000	1	Add A; shift P three bits	[0, 0, 1]
001	0	Add A; shift P three bits	[0, 2, −1]
001	1	Add $2A$; shift P three bits	[0, 2, 0]
010	0	Add $2A$; shift P three bits	[4, −2, 0]
010	1	Add $3A$; shift P three bits	[4, −2, 1]
011	0	Add $3A$; shift P three bits	[4, 0, −1]
011	1	Add $4A$; shift P three bits	[4, 0, 0]
100	0	Subtract $4A$; shift P three bits	[−4, 0, 0]
100	1	Subtract $3A$; shift P three bits	[−4, 0, 1]
101	0	Subtract $3A$; shift P three bits	[−4, 2, −1]
101	1	Subtract $2A$; shift P three bits	[−4, 2, 0]
110	0	Subtract $2A$; shift P three bits	[0, −2, 0]
110	1	Subtract A; shift P three bits	[0, −2, 1]
111	0	Subtract A; shift P three bits	[0, 0, −1]
111	1	Shift P three bits	

Table 2.8: Actions for 3-bit multiplier recoding

An examination of the example multiplication given above, of 6 and 226, and the rules of Table 2.6 show that if, in the multiplier, addition is mapped to 1, subtraction is mapped to $\overline{1}$, and each of the "no-arithmetic" cases is mapped to 0, then the rules reflect an implicit recoding from the digit set $\{0, 1\}$ to the RSD digit set $\{\overline{1}, 0, 1\}$; whence the term *multiplier recoding*.

As additional examples, Tables 2.7 and 2.8 give the rules for 2-bit (i.e. radix-4) and 3-bit (i.e. radix-8) multiplier recoding. In the radix-4 case, the digit set is the minimally redundant $\{\overline{2}, \overline{1}, 0, 1, 2\}$ and not the maximally redundant $\{\overline{3}, \overline{2}, \overline{1}, 0, 1, 2, 3\}$; the latter requires the relatively hard-to-form multiple of $3A$. The relative difficulty of computing multiples of odd numbers—full carry–propagate additions are required—is why the most commonly-used non-binary digit set is the radix-4 set $\{\overline{2}, \overline{1}, 0, 1, 2\}$. This should be kept in mind for several of the algorithms in this book. Nevertheless, radix-8 and maximally-redundant radix-4 algorithms are not unknown, and there have also been practical radix-16 implementations [15].

Multiplicand $= 5 = 0\ 0\ 0\ 0\ 0\ 1\ 0\ 1$ Multiplier $= 114 = 0\ 1\ 1\ 1\ 0\ 0\ 1\ 0$

$0\ 0\ 0\ 0\ 0\ 0\ 0\ 0$	Initial PP
$\underline{0\ 0\ 0\ 0\ 1\ 0\ 1\ 0}$	Add 2MD
$0\ 0\ 0\ 0\ 1\ 0\ 1\ 0$	
$0\ 0\ 0\ 0\ 0\ 0\ 0\ 1\ 0\ 1\ 0$	Shift PP
$\underline{0\ 0\ 0\ 0\ 1\ 0\ 1\ 0}$	Subtract MD
$1\ 1\ 1\ 1\ 1\ 0\ 1\ 1\ 1\ 0\ 1\ 0$	
$1\ 1\ 1\ 1\ 1\ 1\ 1\ 0\ 1\ 1\ 1\ 0\ 1\ 0$	Shift PP
$\underline{0\ 0\ 0\ 0\ 1\ 0\ 1\ 0}$	Add 2MD
$570 \quad = \quad 0\ 0\ 0\ 0\ 1\ 0\ 0\ 0\ 1\ 1\ 1\ 0\ 1\ 0$	Final product

Table 2.9: Example of multiplication with 3-bit recoding

Tables 2.7 and 2.8 show the advantage of using RSD representation for high-radix computation. In conventional radix-4 computation, the digit set is $\{0, 1, 2, 3\}$, and there is no way to avoid the multiple $3A$, which is not required in the minimally redundant RSD case. Similarly, for the radix-8 case, the conventional system would require three hard-to-form multiples—$3A$, $5A$, and $7A$—whereas in the RSD case only one of those is required. We will leave it to the reader to formulate detailed justfications of Tables 2.7 and 2.8, by application of the type of reasoning used for Table 2.5. The following remarks will help in the case of Table 2.8. (If the number of bits that comprise the multiplier is not a multiple of three, then the multiplier has to be sign extended so that there are enough bits to scan in the last cycle.)

The last column in Table 2.8 shows how the action in each line has been derived. A line in this column is an expression of the form $[x, y, z]$, where x, y, and z correspond to the bit positions, $i + 2, i + 1$, and i of the multiplier. Each of x, y, and z is zero, a positive number, or a negative number. A positive number is for the end of a string of 1s, and a negative number is for the beginning of such a string. Thus $[x, y, z]$ means that the multiplicand–multiple is $(x + y + z)A$. As an example, a multiplication with 3-bit recoding is given in Table 2.9; PP stands for "partial product", and MD stands for "multilplicand". There, the multiplier has been recoded (implicitly) into the radix-4 pattern $2\bar{1}02$, which represents the decimal value $2 \times 4^3 - 1 \times 4^2 + 0 \times 4^1 + 2 \times 4^0 = 114$.

In summary, with multiplier recoding, it is possible to use larger radices than would otherwise be practical; the radix-16 example in [15] shows this.

The sketch of a hardware architecture for a radix-4 recoding multiplier is shown in Figure 2.1. This is for a sequential multiplier, but other arrangements—completely parallel, sequential parallel, etc.—are possible [1–4]. The multiplicand and multiplier are held in two registers, MD and MR, with the latter a shift-register. Two registers, PC and PS, hold the partial-carry and partial-sum from the addition in each cycle and are initialized to 0s. And the final product is held in two registers, FP1 and FP2, with FP2 a shift register. Each cycle consists of the following steps:

- The three least significant bits of the multiplier are used to select a multiplicand–multiple.
- The selected multiple, current product partial-sum, and current product partial-carry are added in a carry–save adder, to produce new partial-sum and partial-carry.

- The two least significant bits of the partial-sum/partial-carry output make up the corresponding bits of the final product. Accordingly they are assimilated in a 2-bit carry–propagate adder (CPA) and inserted into FP2, whose contents are then shifted two bit-places to the right.
- The contents of MR are shifted two bit-places to the right.

At the end of n cycles, the lower n bits of the final product will be in FP2, and the upper n bits are obtained by using a carry–propagate adder to assimilate the final partial-sum and partial-carry bits.

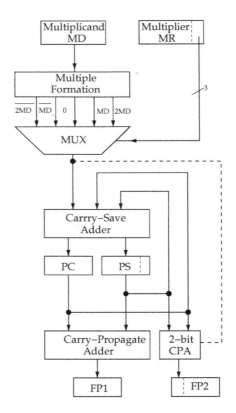

Figure 2.1: Radix-4 sequential multiplier

Subtraction is performed by adding the negation of the subtrahend, which in two's complement representation consists of the ones' complement and the addition of a 1 in the least significant bit position. The Multiple Formation unit forms $2MD$ by a one-bit wired shift and also produces the required complement. The 1 is included in the small CPA, in the free slot created by a right shift. A carry output of the CPA in one cycle is saved, say in a flip-flop, and becomes its carry input in the next cycle; in the last cycle the carry out of the 2-bit CPA becomes a carry in to the CPA used to complete the top half of the product. A detailed description of the timing will be found in [3].

In a high-performance implementation, the multiplicand–multiples would be added in a completely parallel array of carry–save adders. Figure 2.2 shows an an arrangement in which five multiples are to be added.

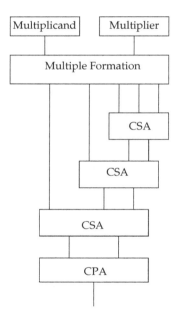

Figure 2.2: Parallel-array multiplier

$$
\begin{array}{ccccc}
A_4A_0 & A_3A_0 & A_2A_0 & A_1A_0 & A_0A_0 \\
A_4A_1 & A_3A_1 & A_2A_1 & A_1A_1 & A_0A_1 \\
A_4A_2 & A_3A_2 & A_2A_2 & A_1A_2 & A_0A_2 \\
A_4A_3 & A_3A_3 & A_2A_3 & A_1A_3 & A_0A_3 \\
A_4A_4 & A_3A_4 & A_2A_4 & A_1A_4 & A_0A_4 \\
\end{array}
$$

(a)

$$
\begin{array}{ccccccccc}
A_3A_4 & A_2A_4 & A_1A_4 & A_0A_4 & A_0A_3 & A_0A_2 & A_0A_1 & 0 & A_0 \\
A_4 & & A_2A_3 & A_1A_3 & A_1A_2 & & A_1 & 0 & \\
& & A_3 & & A_1 & & & & \\
\end{array}
$$

(b)

$$
\begin{array}{ccccccccc}
A_3A_4 & A_3\overline{A_4} & A_2A_4 & A_1A_4 & A_0A_4 & A_0A_3 & A_0A_2 & A_0\overline{A_1} & 0 & A_0 \\
& & A_2A_3 & A_2\overline{A_3} & A_1A_3 & A_1\overline{A_2} & A_1A_0 & A_1 & \\
& & & & A_1A_2 & & & & \\
\end{array}
$$

(c)

Figure 2.3: Partial-product array in squaring

2.2.2 *Squaring*

Squaring—a key operation in some of the algorithms in this book, such as those that involve polynomial approximations—is a special case of multiplication. On that basis it is possible to devise a hardware unit that is both less costly and faster than for general multiplication.

Figure 2.3(a) shows the normal multiplication array for the product of a 5-bit operand, A, and itself. Every other term in the anti-diagonal has the form A_iA_i, which is equivalent to just A_i, since A_i is 0 or 1. There is also a symmetry around the same diagonal, since $A_iA_j = A_jA_i$. So two terms A_iA_j and A_jA_i in the same column may be replaced with their sum, $2A_iA_j$; and since multiplication by two is a 1-bit left shift, this is just A_iA_j moved into the next column to the left. Therefore, the matrix of Figure

2.3(a) can be compressed to the equivalent one in Figure 2.3(b). Lastly, consider the addition of A_i and $A_i A_j$ in the same column:

- If $A_i = 0$, then $A_i + A_i A_j = 0$.
- If $A_i = 1$, and $A_j = 0$, then $A_i + A_i A_j = A_i = A_i \overline{A_j}$.
- If $A_i = 1$ and $A_j = 1$, then $A_i + A_i A_j = 2 = 2 A_i A_j$.

So $A_i + A_i A_j = 2 A_i A_j + A_i \overline{A_j}$, which sum corresponds to $A_i \overline{A_j}$ in the same column and $2 A_i A_j$ moved into the next column to the left. Applying this to Figure 2.3(b) gives the array of Figure 2.3(c), which is a substantial improvement on that of Figure 2.3(a).

For the implementation, the fastest arrangement will be a parallel array of carry–save adders, optimized appropriately, and terminating in a carry–propagate adder. As a comparison, the arrangement of Figure 2.3(a) requires three carry–save adders; on the other hand, that of Figure 2.3(c) requires just one. And in the latter, the carry–save adder consists of just one full adder and four half adders.

Some implementations of methods described in Chapter 7 may require the fast computation of cubes. Such computation too can be optimized as done above for squaring.

2.3 High-speed division

Several algorithms in this book are based on the concept of *normalization*, which is introduced here. In normalization algorithms, the basic idea is that to compute $f(x)$, for some function f and value x, two sequences are produced in such a way that as the values of one are reduced to some known constant (usually one or zero), those of the other tend to $f(x)$. The computations of the values of the sequences are typically by multiplication with a set of predetermined constants, a process known as *multiplicative normalization*, or by the addition of a set of predetermined constants, a process known as *additive normalization*.[12] For the algorithms we are interested in, the additive-normalization target will be zero, and for multiplicative normalization it will be one; the explanation for this choice is given in Section 5.1. In practice, the constants in multiplicative normalization are usually chosen so that any nominal multiplications are realized with just SHIFT and ADD operations.

---

[12] We shall distinguish an algorithm as being of one or the other type according to the operation used on the variable whose values are driven to a constant.

The first part of this section is on multiplicative-normalization algorithms for division; numerous aspects of these algorithms are especially relevant in algorithms for reciprocals, square roots, and inverse square roots. The second part is a brief discussion of additive-normalization algorithms for divison; these algorithms too are closely related to other algorithms covered in the book. Also, one of the objectives in both parts is to show the use of RSD outside the arithmetic.

The third part of the section, and the longest one, is on the SRT division algorithm. On the face of it, this is just a variation of the additive-normalization algorithm of the second part. It is, however, a very significant algorithm, for at least two reasons: one, it shows the use of RSD in and outside the arithmetic; two, it is closely related to several other algorithms in the book—those already indicated above and others (e.g. for the trigonometric functions).

2.3.1 *Multiplicative normalization*

Suppose we wish to compute $Q = N/D$. Without loss of generality, we shall assume that $0 \leq N < 1$ and $1/2 \leq D < 1$. Then multiplicative normalization is used for division in the following way.

If we have a set of non-zero constants $\{c_i\}$ such that

$$D \prod_i c_i \to 1 \text{ as } i \to \infty$$

then, since $\prod_i c_i \to 1/D$, and

$$\frac{N}{D} = \frac{N \prod_i c_i}{D \prod_i c_i} \tag{2.4}$$

we have

$$N \prod_i c_i \to \frac{N}{D} = Q$$

Defining

$$Q_{i+1} = N \prod_{k=0}^{i} c_k \tag{2.5}$$

$$D_{i+1} = D \prod_{k=0}^{i} c_k \tag{2.6}$$

we obtain two recurrences that correspond to the numerator and denominator of the right-hand side of Equation 2.4:

$$D_{i+1} = c_i D_i \qquad D_0 = D$$
$$Q_{i+1} = c_i Q_i \qquad Q_0 = N$$

where $D_i \to 1$ and $Q_i \to N/D = Q$ as $i \to \infty$.

The values of c_i should be chosen to drive D_i to one. A simple rule for that: In a given iteration, if D_i is not "very close" to one, then c_i should be slightly larger than one; otherwise no action should be taken. Evidently the value of c_i should decrease (and tend to one) as i increases and D_i gets closer to one. Accordingly, we choose[13]

$$c_i = 1 + s_i 2^{-i}$$
$$s_i = \begin{cases} 1 & \text{if } D_i \left(1 + s_i 2^{-i}\right) < 1 \\ 0 & \text{otherwise} \end{cases}$$

This choice for c_i also means that the nominal multiplications are reduced to simple shifts and additions.

Putting together all of the preceding, the complete algorithm, which is a multiplicative analogue of the basic (subtractive) non-performing[14] division algorithm, is

$$D_{i+1} = c_i D_i \qquad D_0 = 0$$
$$Q_{i+1} = c_i Q_i \qquad Q_0 = N$$
$$c_i = 1 + s_i 2^{-i}$$
$$s_i = \begin{cases} 1 & \text{if } D_i \left(1 + s_i 2^{-i}\right) < 1 \\ 0 & \text{otherwise} \end{cases}$$

An example computation is given in Table 2.10.

The algorithm will produce the quotient at a rate of one bit per iteration, which is not better than the basic and paper-and-pencil method. But it is nevertheless of interest for two reasons. First, the general form is useful for the derivation of algorithms for other functions. Second, it provides a basis for faster algorithms, especially through the use of different multipliers, c_i, redundant-representation arithmetic, and radices larger than two.

---

[13] A more general discussion on the choice of such constants is given in Section 5.1.
[14] For the reader who does not have a detailed knowledge of basic arithmetic, this is is roughly that the primary arithmetic operation is performed only when it is "safe" to do so.

$$N = 0.56 \qquad D = 0.67$$

i	s_i	c_i	D_i	Q_i
0	0	1.0000000000000000	0.1010101110000101	0.1000111101011100
1	0	1.0000000000000000	0.1010101110000101	0.1000111101011100
2	1	1.0100000000000000	0.1010101110000101	0.1000111101011100
3	1	1.0010000000000000	0.1101011001100110	0.1011001100110011
4	0	1.0000000000000000	0.1111000100110011	0.1100100110011001
5	1	1.0000100000000000	0.1111000100110011	0.1100100110011001
6	1	1.0000010000000000	0.1111100010111100	0.1100111111100110
7	1	1.0000001000000000	0.1111110010011111	0.1101001100100110
8	1	1.0000000100000000	0.1111111010011000	0.1101010011001100
9	0	1.0000000000000000	0.1111111110010111	0.1101010110100001
10	1	1.0000000001000000	0.1111111110010111	0.1101010110100001
11	1	1.0000000000100000	0.1111111111010111	0.1101010111010110
12	0	1.0000000000000000	0.1111111111110111	0.1101010111110001
13	1	1.0000000000001000	0.1111111111110111	0.1101010111110001
14	0	1.0000000000000000	0.1111111111111111	0.1101010111110111
15	0	1.0000000000000000	0.1111111111111111	0.1101010111110111
				$N/D \approx 0.8358$

Table 2.10: Example of multiplicative-normalization division

2.3.1.1   *Goldschmidt normalization*

We next describe essentially the same normalization algorithm as above, but in a slightly different and better-known form; the essence of the difference is in the formulation of the constants, c_i.

The recurrences above will produce a very fast division algorithm, if the normalizing constant multipliers are chosen appropriately: the number of quotient bits will be doubled with each iteration—one, two, four, eight, sixteen, and so forth. The details are as follows.

We have assumed that $1/2 \le D < 1$. So $D = 1 - u$ for some u such that $0 < u \le 1/2$, and the quotient may be expressed as[15]

$$\frac{N}{D} = \frac{N}{1 - u} = N\left(1 + u + u^2 + u^3 + \cdots u^i + \cdots\right)$$

---

[15]See Table 6.2.

Repeatedly factoring:

$$\frac{N}{D} = N\left(1 + u\right)\left(1 + u^2\right)\left(1 + u^4\right)\cdots\left(1 + u^{2^i}\right) + \cdots$$

So for the multipliers we may take $c_i = 1 + u^{2^i}$.

Since $D_0 = 1 - u$ and $c_0 = 1 + u$,

$$c_0 = 2 - D_0$$

and

$$\begin{aligned}
D_1 &= D_0 c_0 \\
&= (1 - u)(1 + u) \\
&= 2 - (1 + u^2) \\
&= 2 - c_1
\end{aligned}$$

So

$$c_1 = 2 - D_1$$

And so on, and so forth. It is straightforward to show, by induction, that

$$c_i = 2 - D_i \qquad \text{for all } i$$

which in binary is just the two's complement[16] of D_i, since $D_i < 1$.

$$N = 0.56 \qquad D = 0.67$$

i	c_i	D_i	Q_i
0	1.0101010001111010	0.1010101110000101	0.1000111101011100
1	1.0001101111100000	0.1110010000011111	0.1011111010101011
2	1.0000001100001001	0.1111110011110110	0.1101001101101110
3	1.0000000000001001	0.1111111111110110	0.1101010111110000
4	1.0000000000000000	0.1111111111111111	0.1101010111111000
5	1.0000000000000000	0.1111111111111111	0.1101010111111000
6	1.0000000000000000	1.0000000000000000	0.1101010111111000
			$N/D \approx 0.8358$

Table 2.11: Example of Goldschmidt-normalization division

---

[16]The result of the two's-complement operation is interpretated as the representation of a positive number.

The complete algorithm:

$$D_0 = D$$
$$Q_0 = N$$
$$c_i = 2 - D_i$$
$$D_{i+1} = c_i D_i$$
$$Q_{i+1} = c_i Q_i$$

It will be observed that, in contrast with the first normalization algorithm, here the multiplications are real ones and are therefore more costly; however, the convergence is much more rapid. We can readily verify the latter by looking at the binary representation of D_i. The number of 1s in the representation doubles in each iteration as D_i is driven to one,[17] and the correct number of quotient bits is produced at the same rate:

$$D_0 = 0 \cdot 1 * * * \cdots$$
$$D_1 = 0 \cdot 11 * * * \cdots$$
$$D_2 = 0 \cdot 1111 * * * \cdots$$
$$D_3 = 0 \cdot 11111111 * * * \cdots$$

An example computation is given in Table 2.11. A comparison with the example of Table 2.10 shows that convergence here is indeed much faster.

2.3.1.2 *Use of RSD representation*

We shall now consider the use of RSD representation with the basic multiplicative-normalization recurrences, in which $c_i = 1 + s_i 2^{-i}$; such usage affects only the choice of s_i. In the algorithms as given, RSD representation is not used in the arithmetic; the primary function of such representation is to help avoid some arithmetic or to facilitate the use of large radices or CS representation in the arithmetic.

We shall start with the radix-2 case, i.e. the digit set $\{\overline{1}, 0, 1\}$, and then proceed to the radix-4 case with the digit set $\{\overline{2}, \overline{1}, 0, 1, 2\}$. In each case, we shall first consider the use of RSD in s_i selection, but with arithmetic in non-redundant representation. We shall then look at ways in which the arithmetic can be speeded up, which ways include the use of CS arithmetic.

The algorithms described are slightly more complex than the corresponding algorithms based on additive normalization, and the latter will

[17]A slightly more detailed and complete justification can be arrived at by considering the Chapter-8 discussions on the computation of reciprocals.

most likely be preferred if it is just division that is to be implemented.[18] The chief merit of the multiplicative-normalization algorithms is that they have the same form as algorithms for several other functions—described in Chapters 5 and 8—and so the same hardware can be used for all.

Radix-2 algorithm: The reasoning behind the choice of c_i here is as for the non-redundant-representation case above. In that case, in each iteration D_i is multiplied by a value that brings the result closer to one. In the redundant-representation case, we have an additional option: if D_i is "nearly" one, then nothing is done in *that* iteration; that is, no arithmetic is required in that iteration. The new selection rule is

$$s_i = \begin{cases} 1 & \text{if } D_i \leq 1 - k \\ 0 & \text{if } 1 - k < D_i < 1 + k \\ \bar{1} & \text{if } D_i \geq 1 + k \end{cases}$$

where k is a suitably small value. Evidently, the value of k needs to be adjusted as D_i approaches one, i.e. when it falls in the middle range, in order to be able to continue applying the selection rules, and it should be easily computable. A good value is $k = \alpha 2^{-i}$ at step i, with α a small constant. The selection rule then becomes

$$s_i = \begin{cases} 1 & \text{if } D_i - 1 \leq -\alpha 2^{-i} \\ 0 & \text{if } -\alpha 2^{-i} < D_i - 1 < \alpha 2^{-i} \\ \bar{1} & \text{if } D_i - 1 \geq \alpha 2^{-i} \end{cases}$$

In implementing the algorithm, it is convenient to keep the values of the comparison variables within a fixed range and so avoid having to adjust the values against which $D_i - 1$ is compared. This can be accomplished by replacing $D_i - 1$ with the auxiliary values $U_i \triangleq 2^i (D_i - 1)$. The replacement also eliminates any difficulty in making a choice when the value of D_i is very close to one: the scaling removes leading 1s in the representation of a positive number and leading 0s in the representation of a negative number, thus ensuring that the significant bits to be examined are always in the same position and at the front.

---

[18]The argument can be extended to the combined implementation of both division and square root evaluation.

$$N = 0.56 \qquad D = 0.67$$

i	s_i	c_i	U_i	Q_i
0	0	1.0000000000000000	-0.0101010001111010	0.1000111101011100
1	1	1.1000000000000000	-0.1010100011110101	0.1000111101011100
2	0	1.0000000000000000	0.0000010100011110	0.1101011100001010
3	0	1.0000000000000000	0.0000101000111101	0.1101011100001010
4	0	1.0000000000000000	0.0001010001111010	0.1101011100001010
5	0	1.0000000000000000	0.0010100011110101	0.1101011100001010
6	0	1.0000000000000000	0.0101000111101011	0.1101011100001010
7	-1	0.1111111000000000	0.1010001111010111	0.1101011100001010
8	1	1.0000000100000000	-0.1011101011100001	0.1101010101011100
9	-1	0.1111111110000000	0.1000100011000111	0.1101011000110001
10	1	1.0000000001000000	-0.1110111011111001	0.1101010111000110
11	0	1.0000000000000000	0.0010000110010101	0.1101010111111011
12	0	1.0000000000000000	0.0100001100101011	0.1101010111111011
13	-1	0.1111111111111000	0.1000011001010110	0.1101010111111011
14	1	1.0000000000000100	-0.1111001101011011	0.1101010111110101
15	0	1.0000000000000000	0.0001100101000010	0.1101010111111000
				$N/D \approx 0.8358$

Table 2.12: Example of redundant multiplicative-normalization division

The complete radix-2 algorithm:

$$U_0 = D_0 - 1$$

$$Q_0 = N$$

$$U_{i+1} = 2\left(U_i + s_i + s_i U_i 2^{-i}\right) \tag{2.7}$$

$$Q_{i+1} = Q_i(1 + s_i 2^{-i})$$

$$= Q_i + s_i Q_i 2^{-i}$$

$$s_i = \begin{cases} 1 & \text{if } U_i < -\alpha \\ 0 & \text{if } -\alpha \le U_i < \alpha \\ \bar{1} & \text{if } U_i \ge \alpha \end{cases}$$

To determine a value for the constant α, we need to first determine the conditions required for convergence and how s_i is to be selected to meet those conditions. For convergence, it is sufficient that $|U_i|$ be bounded by some constant, γ. That is so because

$$D_i = 1 + U_i 2^{-i}$$

and if $|U_i| \leq \gamma$, then

$$D_i \leq 1 + \gamma 2^{-i}$$

Evidently, $D_i \to 1$ as $i \to \infty$, as required, which in turn means that Q_i converges to the quotient.

In the worst case $U_{i+1} = U_i = \gamma$, and $s_i = \bar{1}$. So

$$2\left(\gamma - 1 - \gamma 2^{-i}\right) = \gamma$$

i.e.

$$\gamma = \frac{2}{1 - 2^{-i+1}}$$

This has its smallest value as $i \to \infty$, so we may take $\gamma = 2$ for the bound on $|U_i|$. (On the other side, $s_i = 1$ gives the value -2.)

As $i \to \infty$, Equation 2.7 is effectively

$$U_{i+1} = 2\left(U_i + s_i\right) \qquad (2.8)$$

We may therefore conclude that for sufficiently large i—i.e. provided the "small-i" iterations give values within bounds—the algorithm will converge, if $|U_i| \leq 2$ and at each step s_i is chosen so that

$$-2 \leq 2(U_i + s_i) \leq 2$$

Substituting for each possible value of s_i gives three intervals:

$$s_i = 1: \quad -2 \leq U_i \leq 0$$
$$s_i = 0: \quad -1 \leq U_i \leq 1$$
$$s_i = \bar{1}: \quad 0 \leq U_i \leq 2$$

The intervals overlap in the ranges $[-1, 0]$ and $[0, 1]$, so the basic range in which to choose α is $[0, 1]$. $\alpha = 0$ should obviously be included, as it gives an algorithm that is just the non-redundant one. For other values, we must consider that the preceding analysis was on the assumption that Equations 2.7 and 2.8 are equivalent, which is reasonable for large value values of i, but not for small ones. The implication of that assumption is that care must be taken for small values of i, and the initialization will depend on the choice of comparison constant. This is not a major concern here—it suffices to exclude $\alpha = 1$—but it is with larger radices. We are therefore left with (0, 1) as the range for α, and it is straightforward to show that the algorithm will converge for this range.[19] A good value within that range is $\alpha = 1/2$, as it requires only one bit for representation.[20] Table 2.12 gives an example computation with this choice of α.

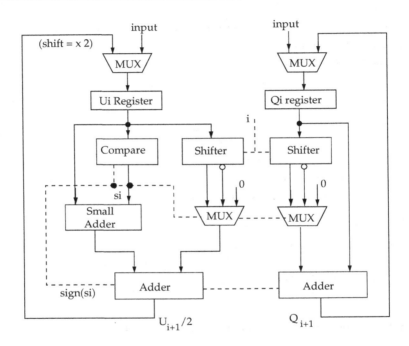

Figure 2.4: Radix-2 multiplicative-normalization divider

The sketch of a hardware architecture for the algorithm is shown in Figure 2.4. The computation of U_{i+1} is done in three parts. In the first part, there is a comparison against U_i, to determine s_i, and at the same time shifted to obtain $U_i 2^{-i}$ and its ones' complement, $\overline{U_i 2^{-i}}$. (For two's comple-

---

[19]By induction, show that if $|U_i| \leq 2$, then for each possible value of s_i, it is the case that $|U_{i+1}| \leq 2$. We have omitted to do so here as the reader can readily follow a similar exercise in the radix-4 case below.

[20]Other values may be chosen, depending on the desired objective. For example, in [1], in order to increase the probability of $s_i = 0$, and, therefore, the cycles in which there need not be any arithmetic, the choice is $\alpha = 3/4$.

ment representation, subtraction is adding the negation of the subtrahend, which negation is formed by taking the ones' complement and adding a 1 in the least significant bit position.) In the second part, a Small Adder adds s_i to the top non-sign bit of U_i, to obtain $U_i + s_i$, and at the same time a multiplexor chooses $U_i 2^{-i}$ or zero, according to the value of $|s_i|$. The last stage consists of the addition or subtraction of $U_i 2^{-i}$ to $U_i + s_i$, according to the sign of s_i; the s_i determines whether or not to include the complementing 1. The result of that addition is then wire-shifted by one bit position (multiplication by two) relative to the multiplexor on that path and thus becomes U_{i+1}. The operation of the Q_i loop is similar, but without the "small addition". (A version of the architecture that assumes carry–save arithmetic is shown in Figure 2.5.)

In the architecture of Figure 2.4, the components in the Q loop are somewhat "replicated" in the U loop: the latter has three components that perform similar functions to three components in the former. Therefore, at the cost of a slight reduction in performance, a unit with a better cost:performance ratio can be obtained by using a single, pipelined structure that is shared for both computations. A two-stage pipeline will suffice: the U_i values are processed in one stage of the pipeline while at the same time the Q_i values are processed in the other stage, and this is then alternated in the next cycle.

The algorithm above produces the result at the rate of one bit per iteration.[21] Therefore, as it stands, it seemingly has little merit over the simplest division algorithm, other than allowing the possibility of no-arithmetic iterations, and that might be undesirable, because it means variable, operand-dependent operational times. But the algorithm is a basis from which faster algorithms can be obtained, through two modifications: the use of low-precisions approximations of U_i and the use of a larger radix—for example, radix-4 for two bits of the result in each iteration. Both these modifications, which we next discuss, are facilitated by the use of redundant signed-digit (RSD) representation for s_i.

The cycle time in an implementation of the architecture of Figure 2.4 can be reduced substantially if carry–save (CS) representation is used for the arithmetic; this would give a lower operational time, even if the result is still produced at the rate of one bit per iteration. If U_i is represented in CS form (and the arithmetic is in that representation), then, of course, its full value is not available for a comparision to determine the values of s_{i+1},

---

[21]This can be verified by proceeding as done for in the radix-4 case below.

as that would require the very type of carry–propagatation that the use of carry–save arithmetic is intended to eliminate. But the redundancy in the s_i digit set means that an approximation of U_i may be used instead. All that is required is that the approximation be good enough to choose one digit or the other in the relevant regions of overlaps—to chosse between $s_i = 0$ and $s_i = 1$ and between $s_i = 0$ and $s_i = \overline{1}$. In such a case, the representation error in each of the carry and sum parts will be 2^{-p}, if each is truncated to p fraction bits. The interval for the selection of the comparison constant, α, is therefore narrowed, to $[2 \times 2^{-p}, 1 - 2 \times 2^{-p}]$. So, with $\alpha = 1/2$, we require $p \geq 3$, and to obtain a suitable approximation, at least five bits of the carry–save U_i must be assimilated for use in the comparison: one sign bit, one integer bits, and three fraction bits.

Figure 2.5 shows the U_i loop of Figure 2.4 "directly" modified for CS arithmetic; the Q_i loop is similarly modified. We assume that the final conversions from carry–save to conventional representation are done using fast carry–propagate adders (CPAs). In changing to CS arithmetic, the primary additions are faster, because CPAs get replaced with carry–save adders (CSAs), but there is only a slight increase in adder-cost. There is, however, a significant increase in overall cost because the shifters have to be replicated—each part (C and S) of a carry–save representation requires its own shifter.

If carry–save arithmetic is not used, then better performance can still be obtained, by overlapping the computations of U_{i+1} and s_{i+1} (which depends on U_{i+1}): during the computation of U in a given iteration, s for the next iteration is also computed. That can be done because the digit set redundancy means that the comparison may be based on just an approximation. A straightforward approximation can be obtained by taking

$$\widehat{U}_{i+1} = 2(U_i + s_i)$$

in place of

$$U_{i+1} = 2\left(U_i + s_i + s_i U_i 2^{-i}\right)$$

Evidently, the computation of $\widehat{U}_{i+1}$ can be overlapped with that of U_{i+1}, but its value will be available much earlier; essentially, the arrangement allows a type of "lookahead", since s_{i+1} and U_{i+1} can be computed within the same period. It is also not strictly necessary to have the full value of $\widehat{U}_{i+1}$: because of the redundancy, a truncation[22] of that and the comparison

---

[22]The "sloppy" language is in aid of brevity; in all such instances, we mean the truncation of the representation.

constants will suffice. With such an approximation, the range for α is now narrowed by the effect of two errors: one is the approximation error from the "missing term", $s_i U_i 2^{-i}$; the other is the representation error in the truncation. If the truncation is to p fraction bits, then we now require

$$\alpha \in \left[s_i U_i 2^{-i} + 2^{-p}, \ 1 - s_i U_i 2^{-i} - 2^{-p} \right]$$

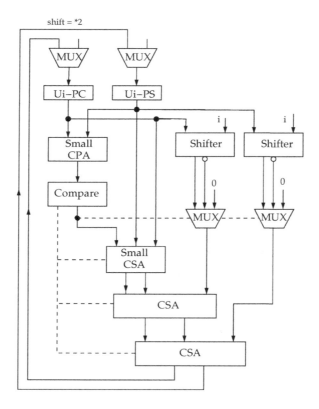

Figure 2.5: Divider U_i loop, CS arithmetic

For $\alpha = 1/2$ (or any other similarly "easy" value), this requires $i \geq 3$ and $p \geq 3$. So, we can obtain a good approximation by adding s_i to the five leading bits of U_i: one sign bit, one integer bits, and three fraction bits. The first three iterations need to be accounted for, and this can be done in one of two ways. The first is to compute the full U_is (i.e. use Equation 2.7) for those iterations; the second is to store values of U_3 (in a table addressed with leading bits of the argument) and use these values to start the iterations. In the latter case, the table will be quite small, since U_3 is accurate to only a few bits.

Both types of U_i approximations—using a simplified recurrence and truncating computed values (in carry–save or conventional representation)—are applicable to all algorithms of this form, and we shall see this in subsequent chapters.

Radix-4 algorithm: The radix-2 algorithm above can be easily extended to a radix-4 one, in which two bits of the quotient are generated in each iteration [11]. The relative difficulty of forming multiples of three makes it inconvenient to use the maximally redundant radix-4 signed-digit set, $\{\bar{3}, \bar{2}, \bar{1}, 0, 1, 2, 3\}$. Therefore, in such algorithms, the minimally redundant $\{\bar{2}, \bar{1}, 0, 1, 2\}$ is used much more frequently, and it is what we consider here. The minimally redundant digit set also has the advantage that, being smaller, fewer clauses are required in the selection rule for s_i. (On the other hand, the maximally redundant digit set permits more convenient comparison values for the determination of s_i.)

We shall proceed as we have done above in the radix-2 case. The rationale for the s_i-selection rule is largely the same. The informal explanation in the radix-2 case is that s_i is selected according to how far some value is from one (D_i) or zero (U_i), so that the corresponding arithmetic operation brings the result closer to one or zero; here, there is a gradation in "far". So for the minimally redundant radix-4 digit set, we start with the recurrences

$$c_i = 1 + s_i 4^{-i}$$
$$D_{i+1} = c_i D_i$$
$$Q_{i+1} = c_i Q_i$$

$$s_i = \begin{cases} 2 & \text{if } D_i \leq 1 - \beta 4^{-i} \\ 1 & \text{if } 1 - \beta 4^{-i} < D_i \leq 1 - \alpha 4^{-i} \\ 0 & \text{if } 1 - \alpha 4^{-i} < D_i < 1 + \alpha 4^{-i} \\ \bar{1} & \text{if } 1 + \alpha 4^{-i} \leq D_i < 1 + \beta 4^{-i} \\ \bar{2} & \text{if } D_i \geq 1 + \beta 4^{-i} \end{cases}$$

and by substituting the auxiliary variable $U_i \triangleq 4^i(D_i - 1)$, we obtain

$$U_{i+1} = 4\left(U_i + s_i + s_i U_i 4^{-i}\right) \tag{2.9}$$

with

$$Q_{i+1} = Q_i(1 + s_i 4^{-i})$$

and

$$s_i = \begin{cases} 2 & \text{if } U_i \leq -\beta \\ 1 & \text{if } -\beta < U_i \leq -\alpha \\ 0 & \text{if } -\alpha < U_i < \alpha \\ \overline{1} & \text{if } \alpha \leq U_i < \beta \\ \overline{2} & \text{if } U_i \geq \beta \end{cases}$$

To determine the constants α and β, we first determine a value γ such that $|U_i| \leq \gamma$ and then determine how to select each possible value of s_i. Here, the worst possible case $(U_{i+1} = U_i = \gamma)$ is with $s_i = \overline{2}$, which gives

$$4\left(\gamma - 2 - \gamma 4^{-i}\right) = \gamma$$

i.e.

$$\gamma = \frac{8}{3 - 8 \times 2^i}$$

So we may take $\gamma = 8/3$, i.e. the value as $i \to \infty$. (On the other side, $s_i = 2$ gives $-8/3$.)

As $i \to \infty$, Equation 2.9 is effectively

$$U_{i+1} = 4(U_i + s_i) \tag{2.10}$$

and, provided the initial iterations—i.e. those of "small" i—are taken care of, the algorithm should converge, if $|U_i| \leq 8/3$ and at each step s_i is chosen so that

$$-\frac{8}{3} \leq 4(U_i + s_i) \leq \frac{8}{3}$$

i.e.

$$-\frac{2}{3} - s_i \leq U_i \leq \frac{2}{3} - s_i$$

If we now define

$$U_i^{\min} = -s_i - 2/3$$

$$U_i^{\max} = -s_i + 2/3$$

and substitute in turn each of the possible values of s_i, then we get Table 2.13 as a summary of the selection bounds. The effect of the redundancy in the digit set is reflected in the overlapping of the intervals—in the ranges

$[1/3, 2/3]$ and $[4/3, 5/3]$—and similar ranges on the negative side. Within a region of overlap, either of the corresponding s-values may be chosen as the next quotient digit.

The preceding analysis has been carried out for "large" i. The bounds so obtained will work for "small" i, but sufficient care is necessary in the initialization to cover those values. The chosen comparison constants too can affect the initialization.

The most convenient values[23] for α and β in the intervals $[1/2, 2/3]$ and $[4/3, 5/3]$ are $\alpha = 1/2$ and $\beta = 3/2$. With these values, the iterations converge only from $i = 3$, and a relatively complex initialization procedure is required to cover U_0, U_1, and U_2. The next convenient values are $\alpha = 5/8$ and $\beta = 13/8$, for which the iterations will converge from $i = 1$, provided $|U_1| < 13/8$. (This is shown below.) With these constants, the initialization is

$$U_1 = 4(c_0 D - 1)$$
$$Q_1 = c_0 Q_0 = c_0 N$$
$$c_0 = \begin{cases} 2 & \text{if } 1/2 \leq D < 5/8 \\ 1 & \text{if } 5/8 \leq D < 1 \end{cases}$$

(This is explained below.)

U_i^{min}	U_i^{max}	s_i
$-8/3$	$-4/3$	2
$-5/3$	$-1/3$	1
$-2/3$	$2/3$	0
$1/3$	$5/3$	$\bar{1}$
$4/3$	$8/3$	$\bar{2}$

Table 2.13: Radix-4 digit-selection parameters

We shall now look at convergence and errors, and, in so doing, justify the preceding remarks. For convergence, we assume that $|U_i| \leq 8/3$, take in turn each possible value of s_i and the corresponding interval, and then look at the value of $|U_{i+1}|$ to determine the conditions required to ensure that it too does not exceed $8/3$.

[23]The advantage of a maximally redundant digit set is that the regions of such overlap are larger, and, therefore, there is greater freedom in making choices. The end result would be more relaxed precision requirements and nominally faster operation.

- $s_i = 0$: $-5/2 \leq U_{i+1} < 5/2$; so $|U_{i+1}| \leq 8/3$
- $s_i = \overline{1}$: $5/8 \leq U_i < 13/8$.

  At the lower extreme, we want

  $$4\left(\frac{5}{8} - 1 - \frac{5}{8} \cdot 4^{-i}\right) \geq -\frac{8}{3}$$

  i.e. that $4^{-i} \leq 7/15$, which is the case for $i \geq 1$.
  And at the upper extreme, we want

  $$4\left(\frac{13}{8} - 1 - \frac{13}{8} \cdot 4^{-i}\right) \leq \frac{8}{3}$$

  i.e. that $4^{-i} \geq -1/39$, which is the case for all i.
- $s_i = \overline{2}$: $13/8 \leq U_i < 8/3$.

  At the lower extreme, we want

  $$4\left(\frac{13}{8} - 2 - 2 \cdot \frac{13}{8} \cdot 4^{-i}\right) \geq -\frac{8}{3}$$

  i.e. that $4^{-i} \leq 7/78$, which is the case for $i \geq 2$.
  At the upper extreme, we want

  $$4\left(\frac{8}{3} - 2 - 2 \cdot \frac{8}{3} \cdot 4^{-i}\right) \leq \frac{8}{3}$$

  i.e. that $-4^{-i} \leq 0$, which is the case for all i.

Noting that U_i and s_i are always of opposite sign, symmetry implies similar bounds for $s_i = 1$ and $s_i = 2$. We may therefore conclude that the algorithm will converge for $i \geq 2$ and with $|U_i| \leq 8/3$ for all i. A straightforward way to ensure convergence from $i = 1$ is to arrange matters so as to preclude the choice of $s_1 = 2$ or $s_1 = \overline{2}$. That is easily accomplished by an initialization that makes $|U_1| < 13/8$, and the one above does that.

We now turn to errors. We shall assume that there are no errors generated (and subsequently propagated) in the process—a sufficient number of guard digits in the datapath will take care of such errors[24]—and therefore consider only the approximation error.

After K iterations

$$|U_K| = \left|4^K(D_K - 1)\right| \leq \frac{8}{3}$$

i.e.

$$|D_K - 1| \leq \frac{8}{3}4^{-K}$$

---

[24]See Section 3.5 for how to determine the required number of guard digits; about $\log_2 n + 3$ digits will do.

and the magnitude of the absolute error is

$$\varepsilon = \left| Q_K - \frac{N}{D} \right| = \left| N \prod_{i=0}^{K-1} c_i - \frac{N}{D} \right| \qquad \text{by Equation 2.5}$$

$$= \left| \frac{N}{D} \left(D \prod_{i=0}^{K-1} c_i - 1 \right) \right|$$

$$= \frac{N}{D} |D_K - 1| \qquad \text{by Equation 2.6}$$

Since $0 \le N < 1$ and $1/2 \le D \le 1$

$$\varepsilon < 2|D_K - 1|$$

Therefore

$$\varepsilon < 2|D_K - 1| \le 2 \times \frac{8}{3} 4^{-K}$$

$$< 2 \times 4^{-K}$$

$$= 2^{-(2K-1)}$$

which shows that $n/2 + 1$ iterations will suffice to produce a result accurate to n bits—effectively, a rate of two bits per iteration.

In the implementation, low-precision approximations of U_i can be used in the same manner as described above for the radix-2 case.

If carry–save arithmetic is used and truncation is to p fractional bits, then the intervals for the comparison constants change to

$$\alpha \in \left[\frac{1}{3} + 2 \times 2^{-p}, \; \frac{2}{3} - 2 \times 2^{-p} \right]$$

and

$$\beta \in \left[\frac{4}{3} + 2 \times 2^{-p}, \; \frac{5}{3} - 2 \times 2^{-p} \right]$$

$p = 4$ will suffice.

If carry–save arithmetic is not used, then the computations of U_{i+1} and s_{i+1} can be overlapped:

$$\widehat{U}_{i+1} = 4(U_i + s_i)$$

is taken as an approximation for

$$U_{i+1} = 4 \left(U_i + s_i + s_i U_i 4^{-i} \right)$$

The representations of that approximation and the comparison constants are then truncated to p fraction bits each and the result used to determine s_{i+1}. In this case, the intervals for the comparison constants change to

$$\alpha \in \left[\frac{1}{3} + s_i U_i 4^{-i} + 2^{-p}, \ \frac{2}{3} - s_i U_i 4^{-i} - 2^{-p} \right]$$

and

$$\beta \in \left[\frac{4}{3} + s_i U_i 4^{-i} + 2^{-p}, \ \frac{5}{3} - s_i U_i 4^{-i} + 2^{-p} \right]$$

The smallest values that will work are $i = 4$ and $p = 5$, with the initial iterations handled as in the radix-2 case.

For implementation, straightforward architectures will be similar to those of Figures 2.4 and 2.5, except in the changes (e.g. in shifting) required for the change of radix from two to four. Relative to Figure 2.4: the Small Adder now adds s_i to the two top non-sign bits of U_i; the U_i-multiplexor now has two more inputs, for $s_i = 2$ and $s_i = \bar{2}$, with the nominal multiplications easily accomplished by wired shifts; and the situation is similar for the Q_i path. Figure 2.5 can be similarly modified in a straightforward manner.

If it is just division that is to be implemented (or division and square root evaluation), then the RSD multiplicative-normalization algorithms are not the best:

- In variants of the paper-and-pencil division algorithms, the multiples of the divisor that are added or subtracted are known beforehand. On the other hand, with the multiplicative normalization algorithms, there are values ($s_i r^{-i}$, where r is the radix) that change in every cycle.
- Computing the aforementioned "problematic" terms requires relatively costly shifters, and the cost is replicated if carry–save arithmetic is implemented.

The additive-normalization algorithms that we look at next more closely resemble paper-and-pencil algorithms and so do not give rise to such problems. Nevertheless, it is possible to formulate for several functions—Chapters 3, 4, 5, and 8—algorithms that have similar structures to those of the multiplicative-normalization division algorithms, which means that very cost-effective sharing of hardware is possible [11]. In such a case, the "problematic" division algorithms have obvious merits.

2.3.2 *Additive normalization*

As in multiplicative-normalization algorithms, we shall assume that $0 \leq N < 1$ and $1/2 \leq D < 1$. Additive normalization is used for the division of N by D in the following way. If we express $Q \triangleq N/D$ as

$$Q = \frac{N}{D} = \frac{N}{D} - \sum_i c_i + \sum_i c_i \qquad c_i \text{ constants}$$

and multiply through by D, then we have

$$QD = (N - D\sum_i c_i) + D\sum_i c_i \qquad (2.11)$$

If we then choose the c_i so that

$$N - D\sum_i c_i \to 0 \qquad \text{as } i \to \infty$$

then

$$D\sum_i c_i \to DQ$$

$$\sum_i c_i \to Q$$

By defining

$$Q_{i+1} = \sum_{k=0}^{i} c_k$$

$$D_{i+1} = N - D\sum_{k=0}^{i} c_k$$

we obtain two recurrences from the right hand side of Equation 2.11:

$$D_{i+1} = D_i - c_i D \qquad\qquad D_0 = N$$
$$Q_{i+1} = Q_i + c_i \qquad\qquad Q_0 = c_0$$

where $D_i \to 0$ and $Q_i \to Q$ as $i \to \infty$.

To apply RSD notation, we proceed in the same manner as in the multiplicative-normalization case above. In this case, the normalization is towards zero; so the constants, c_i, are chosen to have the form $s_i 2^{-i}$ in the binary case. This choice of constants means that the algorithm can be implemented in such a way that there is very little actual arithmetic involved: the nominal addition to form Q_{i+1} can be reduced to just appending the next bit of the quotient to the bits already obtained; and if s_i is chosen appropriately, then, as we shall see, there will be no real multiplication in the computation of $c_i D$. (The subtraction to form D_{i+1} remains a real operation.) For binary computation, if $s_i \in \{\bar{1}, 1\}$, we then have what the reader who is familiar with basic division algorithms will recognize as an ordinary non-restoring algorithm (an example of which is given at the start of Section 2.3.3). Our main interest, however, is in the use of RSD, which in the binary case means $s_i \in \{\bar{1}, 0, 1\}$. So, the radix-2 algorithm is

$$D_0 = N$$
$$Q_0 = 0$$
$$c_i = s_i 2^{-i} \qquad\qquad i = 0, 1, 2, \ldots$$
$$D_{i+1} = D_i - c_i D$$
$$Q_{i+1} = Q_i + c_i$$

$$s_i = \begin{cases} 1 & \text{if } D_i \geq \alpha 2^{-i} \\ 0 & \text{if } -\alpha 2^{-i} < D_i < \alpha 2^{-i} \\ \bar{1} & \text{if } D_i \leq -\alpha 2^{-i} \end{cases}$$

where α is a small constant. The rationale for the s_i-selection rule is similar to that given for the radix-2 multiplicative-normalization algorithm (Section 2.3.1.2), except that here D_i is driven to zero.

In order to keep the comparison variable within a fixed range, D_i is replaced with the scaled variable $U_i \overset{\triangle}{=} 2^i D_i$, thereby obtaining (after also replacing c_i) the recurrences

$$U_0 = N$$

$$Q_0 = 0$$

$$U_{i+1} = 2(U_i - s_i D) \qquad\qquad i = 0, 1, 2, \ldots \qquad\qquad (2.12)$$

$$Q_{i+1} = Q_i + s_i 2^{-i}$$

$$s_i = \begin{cases} 1 & \text{if } U_i \geq \alpha \\ 0 & \text{if } -\alpha < U_i < \alpha \\ \bar{1} & \text{if } U_i \leq -\alpha \end{cases}$$

Equation 2.12 is the same as Equation 2.8, except in the multiplicative factor of $-D$. So the type of analysis carried out for Equation 2.8 will yield similar bounds, but with a multiplicative factor of $-D$. Therefore, comparing the s_i selection rule for Equation 2.8 and that for Equation 2.12, we have the overlaps $[-D, 0]$ and $[0, D]$ and so may take $\alpha = D/2$. But the fact that one end of each of these intervals is zero indicates that the comparison value may be independent of D; accordingly, $\alpha = 1/2$ will suffice.

$$N = 0.78 \qquad D = 0.87$$

i	s_i	c_i	U_i	Q_i
0	1	00.0000000000000000	00.1101111010111000	00.0000000000000000
1	0	00.0000000000000000	00.1101111010111000	01.0000000000000000
2	0	00.0000000000000000	00.1101111010111000	01.0000000000000000
3	-1	00.0000000000000000	00.1101111010111000	01.0000000000000000
4	0	00.0000000000000000	00.1101111010111000	00.1110000000000000
5	1	00.0000000000000000	00.1101111010111000	00.1110000000000000
6	-1	00.0000000000000000	00.1101111010111000	00.1110100000000000
7	1	00.0000000000000000	00.1101111010111000	00.1110010000000000
8	0	00.0000000000000000	00.1101111010111000	00.1110011000000000
9	-1	00.0000000000000000	00.1101111010111000	00.1110011000000000
10	0	00.0000000000000000	00.1101111010111000	00.1110010110000000
11	0	00.0000000000000000	00.1101111010111000	00.1110010110000000
12	0	00.0000000000000000	00.1101111010111000	00.1110010110000000
13	0	00.0000000000000000	00.1101111010111000	00.1110010110000000
14	1	00.0000000000000000	00.1101111010111000	00.1110010110000000
15	0	00.0000000000000000	00.1101111010111000	00.1110010110000100

$$N/D \approx 0.8965$$

Table 2.14: Example of redundant additive-normalization division

The recurrence for the quotient, i.e.

$$Q_{i+1} = Q_i + s_i 2^{-i}$$

can be implemented in one of two ways. In the first, the quotient is generated in conventional representation, and the addition is therefore a real one (consider $s_i = \bar{1}$); this is shown in the example computation of Table 2.14. (The computation of 2^{-i} does not require a shifter as it can be done iteratively in a shift register, with a one bit-place shift in each iteration.)

The other way is to generate the quotient in the redundant representation of s_i, in which case the nominal addition is no more than appending s_i to the end of the quotient digits formed thus far; a relevant example is given in Table 2.16. In the latter case the quotient must finally be converted into conventional representation; this can be done on the fly, as the result digits are produced.

There is an additional point worth noting about the first case, in which the quotient is generated in conventional form. Consider that at the start, the representation of Q_0 consists of all 0s, and reason inductively as follows. If $s_i \neq \bar{1}$, then the addition consists of just replacing the 0 at position i with s_i. It is only when $s_i = \bar{1}$ that an arithmetic operation (a subtraction) is required, and it will be an i-bit subtraction. Both aspects may be used to speed up an implementation, if variable operational times are acceptable.

Extending the above to radix 4, with the minimally redundant digit set, is straightforward [15]. The starting recurrences are

$$U_{i+1} = 4(U_i - s_i D) \qquad (2.13)$$
$$Q_{i+1} = Q_i + s_i 4^{-i}$$

$$s_i = \begin{cases} 2 & \text{if } U_i \geq \beta \\ 1 & \text{if } \alpha \leq U_i < \beta \\ 0 & \text{if } -\alpha \leq U_i < \alpha \\ \bar{1} & \text{if } -\beta \leq U_i < -\alpha \\ \bar{2} & \text{if } U_i < -\beta \end{cases}$$

As in the radix-2 case, there is a similarity here between the multiplicative-normalization equation analyzed above and the additive-normalization one here—i.e. Equations 2.10 and 2.13—the only difference being in the multiplicative factor of $-D$. Therefore, from Table 2.13 we directly obtain Table 2.15. And because of the symmetry in the intervals shown in the table, it suffices for what follows to consider just the overlaps on the positive side, i.e. $[D/3, 2D/3]$ and $[4D/3, 5D/3]$.

The most convenient values in the regions of overlap are $\alpha = D/2$ and $\beta = 3D/2$. These values imply full-length comparison, but because of the redundancy in the digit set, whose effect can be seen in the overlaps between the intervals of Table 2.15, it is possible to devise comparisons that require only low-precision values. The redundancy in s_i also makes it easy to use redundant representation for the arithmetic.

For performance, the comparisons may be low-precision ones based on an approximation, $\hat{U}_i$, of U_i. The following discussion on this covers both the radix-2 and radix-4 cases.

One way to obtain $\widehat{U}_i$ is to take a few bits of each of U_i and the comparison values and then use a small adder to obtain $\widehat{U}_i$ from the truncated operands. This leads to a faster determination of s_i, because the computation of $\widehat{U}_i$ can be overlapped with that of U_i but will be completed much earlier. (See also the explanation in Section 2.3.1.2 of similar approximations.) If $\widehat{U}_i$ and the comparison values are each of p bits, then the difference between $\widehat{U}_i$ and U_i will be bounded by 2^{-p}, as will be the error in truncating a comparison value. For the radix-2 computation, the comparison value $\alpha \overset{\triangle}{=} D/2$ is chosen from the range $[0, D]$; so the total error permissible is $D/2$, which in the worst case is $1/4$ (given the range of D). We therefore require $2 \times 2^{-p} \leq 1/4$, which is satisfied with $p = 3$. So the aforemnetioned small adder needs to be of five-bit precision: three fraction bits, one integer bit, and one sign bit.

$U_i^{\min}$	$U_i^{\max}$	s_i
$4D/3$	$8D/3$	2
$D/3$	$5D/3$	1
$-2D/3$	$2D/3$	0
$-5D/3$	$-D/3$	$\overline{1}$
$-8D/3$	$-4D/3$	$\overline{2}$

Table 2.15: s_i-selection parameters for radix-4 additive normalization

In the radix-4 case, the chosen values of α and β within the regions of overlap show that the magnitude of the errors in using the approximations must not exceed $D/6$, i.e. $1/12$, since $D \in [1/2, 1)$. This bound will be satisfied if the magnitude of error in each of $\widehat{U}_i$ and the comparison operands does not exceed $1/24$; for this, five fraction bits in each are sufficient. Two integer bits are required for values that can be as large as $8/3$, and one bit is required for the sign. So a total of eight bits will suffice for an approximation.

If carry–save arithmetic is used, then the approximation $\widehat{U}_i$ is obtained by truncating each of the carry and sum parts of U_i to p bits and assimilating those in a small adder. The total error in such a case is bounded by 2×2^{-p} (2^{-p} for each part of U_i), and each comparison-value interval is reduced by that amount at either end. Therefore, one more fraction bit is required when compared with the preceding cases.

The remarks made in the radix-2 discussion above on the implementation of the recurrence for Q_{i+1} are equally applicable here. That is, the arithmetic may be real, if the result is generated in conventional form, or consist of just appending a bit to an already-formed string of bits, if the result is in RSD form.

One useful aspect of this type of algorithm is that it can be readily modified to compute the more general function of multiply–divide: $Q \triangleq N \times Z/D$. From

$$Q_{i+1} = Z \sum_{k=0}^{i} s_k 4^{-k}$$

we get the new recurrence for a multiply–divide:

$$Q_{i+1} = Q_i + s_i Z 4^{-i}$$

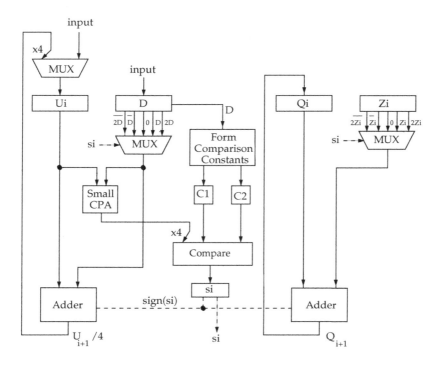

Figure 2.6: Radix-4 additive-normalization multiply–divider

The sketch of a straightforward (i.e. not necessarily optimal) hardware architecture for the radix-4 multiply-divide algorithm is shown in Figure 2.6 in which we have not assumed the use of carry–save arithmetic. The value of Z is loaded into a shift-register whose contents are shifted to the right, by two bit positions, in each cycle; this computes $Z_i \stackrel{\triangle}{=} 4^{-i}Z$. The dividend is initially in the register U. The divisor in the register D and is used to produce the two comparison constants; this can be done by a shift (for $D/2$) and a low-precision addition (for $3D/2 = D + D/2$) or by a table lookup. (We assume that the negations of the constants are taken care of the Compare unit.) The quotient is formed in the register Q, whose contents are initially zero. The inititialization also includes the computation of s_0, which is done by comparing $\widehat{U}_i$ with the comparison constants and storing the result in the register si. Multiplications by two and four are accomplished by wired shifts, shown as slanted lines in Figure 2.6. Each of the remaining iterations is as follows.

On the U-path, the partial remainder is diminished by adding or subtracting D, $2d$, or zero, according to the sign of s_i. On the Q-path, the quotient is improved by adding or subtracting $|s_i|4^{-i}Z$; that is, by subtracting zero, $4^{-i}Z$, or $2 \times 4^{-i}Z$. At the same time as all these operations, the value of s_{i+1} is determined and stored in the register for $s+i$ at the end of the cycle; this determination consists of using the Small CPA to form an eight-bit approximation $(\widehat{U}_{i+1})$ of U_{i+1}, from the top eight bits of U_i and the divisor-multiple, and then comparing the result against the constants.[25]

The design of Figure 2.6 can be modified in a straightforward way for carry–save arithmetic: each of the Adders is replaced with a carry–save adder whose inputs are a partial sum, a partial carry, and a third operand (s_iD or $s_i4^{-i}Z$); each of Q_i and U_i is replaced with the corresponding partial-sum/partial-carry pair; and carry–propagate adders are required, outside the loop, for conversion, into conventional form, of the result and partial remainder. The consequence of such replacement is that the arithmetic is now much faster and using a $\widehat{U}$ approximation of the type above is neither necessary nor beneficial; therefore, there is also no advantage in computing s_{i+1} values in advance. In the modified architecture, a diferent type of approximation, $\widehat{U}_i$, of U_i, is obtained by assimilating the appropriate number of top bits of the partial carry and partial sum parts of U_i; that approximation is then used in the comparisons. The initialization also

---

[25]Note that such a technique would not be useful with the multiplicative-normalization diviider of Figure 2.4 because the shifter time would be dominant.

changes as it is no longer necessary to produce s_0 in advance.

The preceding discussion is an introduction to the technique of additive normalization, which, in subsequent chapters is used for the evaluation of several other functions. With respect to just division, the discussion is also included for completeness, as the reader will find such algorithms in the literature; for example, a radix-4 version is described in [15]. Additive-normalization division is most often implemented in the form of the SRT algorithm, which we describe next. The main difference between the two formulations is that in the description above, the comparison values are directly dependent on D, which implies slightly more complex computation, whereas in the latter the dependence is indirect: in the latter, what would be lines such as D and $3D/2$ in plots against the divisor are replaced with stepwise approximations consisting of horizontal lines (constants), such approximation being possible because the redundancy in s_i allows some imprecision. (This point will become clearer in what follows.)

Both the SRT form and the form above are also used in similar algorithms for square root evaluation; and there too, the former is used more often than the latter.

2.3.3 SRT

The SRT[26] division algorithm is one of the best-known and most-used high-speed division algorithms. Its best implementations exemplify the use of redundant number representations both in the arithmetic and outside the arithmetic: arithmetic is carried out in carry–save (CS) representation,[27] but the quotient digits are selected using RSD representation and generated in that form.[28]

Redundant signed-digit (RSD) representation is useful in such algorithms in three main ways. First, the redundancy makes it possible to have iterations in which there are no arithmetic operations, in a manner similar to skipping over a string of 0s or a string of 1s in multiplier recoding.[29] Second, because of the redundancy, there is some flexibility in the choice of quotient digit in any given step; this facilitates the easy use of CS representation for the main arithmetic operations. And third, the

---

[26]The algorithm was invented by **S**weeney, **R**obertson, and **T**ocher.

[27]Redundant signed-digit representation may be used, but that is rare.

[28]In the basic (original) SRT algorithm, redundant representation was used only outside the arithmetic—to determine the arithmetic operation to be performed next, because the main motivation was to reduce the number of cycles with arithmetic operations.

[29]In practice, this is rarely done nowadays.

representation makes it easy to use radices larger than two.

Skipping over 0s (in a positive partial remainder) or 1s (in a negative partial remainder) without performing an arithmetic operation was the original motivation in the formulation of the basic SRT algorithm, which may be viewed as the result of modifying the basic non-restoring division algorithm with digit set $\{\overline{1}, 1\}$ to an algorithm with the digit set $\{\overline{1}, 0, 1\}$. But the number of such "skips" is operand-dependent and leads to variable operational time, which may be considered undesirable. Nevertheless, the algorithm has several merits beyond the "skipping". The flexibility in the choice of quotient digit—i.e. that for some values of the partial remainder, one or another digit may be selected—means that the determination of a quotient digit does not require the full value of the partial remainder. The decision can be made, quite quickly, on the basis of a few leading bits, and it is this that allows the use of redundant representation in the arithmetic.

For the following discussions, we shall assume, without loss of generality, that the dividend (N) and the divisor (D) are such that $0 \leq N < 1$, $1/2 \leq D < 1$, and $N < D$. So the quotient, Q, too will be a positive fraction:

$$Q \triangleq 0.s_1 s_2 \cdots s_n$$

As indicated above (Section 2.3.2), the quotient may be generated in conventional representation, with real arithmetic involved for the Q-recurrence (as in the example of Table 2.14), or it may be generated in RSD representation, with no real arithmetic involved. In what follows, we shall assume the latter, which is the norm for SRT algorithms.

The discussions follow the manner in which SRT algorithms are usually presented and so differ from the preceding presentations of other normalization algorithms.

2.3.3.1 *Radix-2 algorithm*

We shall start with a brief discusssion of basic division algorithms and then show how SRT are extensions and improvements of those.

The typical paper-and-pencil "long division" of an $(n+m)$-digit dividend (N) and an m-digit divisor (D) starts with the initialization of a *partial remainder* to the dividend, followed by n repetitions of two main steps ($i = 0, 1, 2, \ldots, n-1$):

1) The next quotient digit, s_{i+1}, is determined and entered in the quotient formed so far.

2) A multiple, $s_{i+1}D$, of the divisor is shifted by i places to the right, relative to the partial remainder and subtracted from the partial remainder.

The value of the partial remainder at the end of the iterations is the final remainder.

The most straightforward computer version of the paper-and-pencil algorithm differs from the preceding description in two ways. First, instead of shifting the divisor-multiple by i places to the right, the required relative positioning is more easily achieved by shifting the partial remainder one digit to the left in each iteration; similar considerations apply to the formation of the quotient. Second, in the paper-and-pencil version, the divisor–multiple to be subtracted in a given step will be determined through a computation "on the side", and that is not easy in a computer. It is, for example, easier to subtract and restore—by an addition—the remainder if the subtraction should not have taken place (i.e. if the partial remainder is negative). On these bases, the radix-2 *restoring* algorithm is

$$Q_0 = 0$$

$$U_0 = N$$

$$\tilde{U}_{i+1} = 2U_i - D \tag{2.14}$$

$$s_{i+1} = \begin{cases} 1 & \text{if } \tilde{U}_{i+1} \geq 0 \\ 0 & \text{otherwise} \end{cases} \quad i = 0, 1, \ldots, n-1 \tag{2.15}$$

$$Q_{i+1} = 2Q_i + s_{i+1} \tag{2.16}$$

$$U_{i+1} = \begin{cases} \tilde{U}_{i+1} & \text{if } \tilde{U}_{i+1} \geq 0 \\ \tilde{U}_{i+1} + D & \text{otherwise} \end{cases} \tag{2.17}$$

$$U = U_n$$

where $\tilde{U}_i$ is the i-th tentative partial remainder, U_i is the corresponding partial remainder after any necessary correction, Q_i is the i-th partial quotient, s_{i+1} is the next bit of the quotient, and U is the final remainder. The nominal multiplications by two are just one-bit left shifts; and, in forming Q_{i+1}, the nominal addition is just the "insertion" of a bit into the "empty slot" that is created when Q_i is shifted to the left.

A better algorithm is obtained if any required corrections of the partial remainder are done without "restorations". That is possible if in each iteration the partial remainder can be reduced by a subtraction or an addition. In such a case, a negative partial remainder gets "corrected" by an addition in the *next cycle*. If the partial remainder is negative at the end of the iterations, then there is no "next cycle", and a special addition is necessary to obtain the correct final remainder.

The resulting *non-restoring* algorithm:

$$Q_0 = 0$$

$$U_0 = N$$

$$s_{i+1} = \begin{cases} 1 & \text{if } 2U_i \geq D \\ 0 & \text{if } 2U_i < D \end{cases}$$

$$U_{i+1} = 2U_i - s_{i+1}D$$

$$Q_{i+1} = 2Q_i + s_{i+1} \qquad\qquad i = 0, 1, 2, \ldots, n-1$$

$$U = \begin{cases} U_n & \text{if } U_n \geq 0 \\ U_n + D & \text{otherwise} \end{cases}$$

It will be noted that the only real arithmetic in the above is subtractions. The computation of $2U_i$ is just a one-bit left shift of U_i; the nominal multiplication $s_{i+1}D$ is just the selection of $-D$, 0, or D; and the addition in the computation of Q_{i+1} is just the insertion of s_{i+1} in the "space" created by the left-shift of U_i.

With a reformulation,[30] the digit set for the non-restoring radix-2 division algorithm may be taken to be $\{\bar{1}, 1\}$, where $\bar{1}$ corresponds to a subtraction in the formulation of the partial remainder, and 1 corresponds to an addition. The s_i-selection rule is then changed to

$$s_{i+1} = \begin{cases} 1 & \text{if } 0 \leq 2U_i < 2D \\ \bar{1} & \text{if } -2D < 2U_i < 0 \end{cases}$$

We may then introduce 0 into the digit set, for "no operation", by splitting the two intervals into three, with the core of the algorithm then changed to

$$s_{i+1} = \begin{cases} 1 & \text{if } 0 \leq 2U_i < 2D \\ 0 & \text{if } -D \leq 2U_i < D \\ \bar{1} & \text{if } -2D < 2U_i \leq 0 \end{cases} \qquad (2.18)$$

$$U_{i+1} = 2U_i - s_{i+1}D$$

---

[30] See standard texts on computer arithmetic [1–4].

(Note that the nominal comparisons against $2D$ and $-2D$ need not be realized in practice, because it is guaranteed that $|2U_i| < 2D$.) That the algorithm is just a version of the additive-normalization one above is shown in Section 2.3.3.2.

We have seen above that multiplication can be speeded up by shifting over 0s and 1s in the multiplier. A similar effect is possible in SRT division. The following explanation, concluding with the example of Table 2.16, shows how.

In studying division algorithms of this type, it is helpful and the norm, especially for non-binary radices, to use a *Roberston diagram*, which is a plot of U_{i+1} against rU_i, where r is the radix in use. The Roberston diagram for the radix-2 algorithm is shown in Figure 2.7. The overlaps on either side of the middle—i.e. the regions covered by $\langle s_i = \bar{1}, s_i = 0 \rangle$ and $\langle s_i = 0, s_i = 1 \rangle$—show the effect of redundancy. Within such a region, either value may be chosen for s_i. The significance of this is that the exact value of the partial remainder need not be known in order to choose one digit or the other: it suffices to know that the partial remainder is within the region of overlap. The redundancy therefore allows a choice in the values against which the partial remainders are compared: we may choose any values in the ranges $[-D, 0]$ and $[0, D]$. As we shall see, the "fuzziness" means that full-precision comparisons are not strictly necessary; fast, low-precision ones can be used instead.

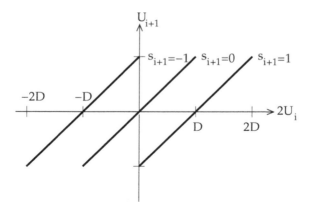

Figure 2.7: Robertson diagram for radix-2 SRT division

The selection rule in Inequations 2.18 implies full comparisons against the divisor and its negation. It would obviously be better—and it is possible—to have comparisons against constants. To determine such constants, it is conventional to use a *P–D diagram*, which consists of plots of the shifted partial remainder, $P \triangleq rU_i$ (for radix r), against the divisor.

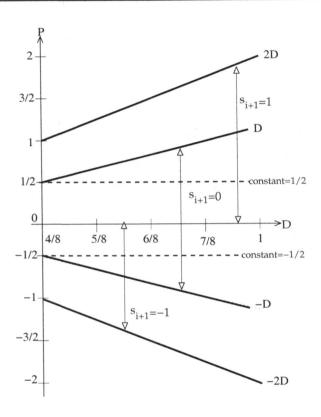

Figure 2.8: P–D diagram for radix-2 SRT division

Since we have assumed that $D \geq 1/2$, the radix-2 P–D diagram is as shown in Figure 2.8. To formulate a rule for choosing between $s_i = 0$ and $s_i = 1$ and between $s_i = 0$ and $s_i = \bar{1}$, one or more separating lines are required in each region of overlap in the figure. The constant line $2U_i = 1/2$ gives such a separation, and, by symmetry, so does $2U_i = -1/2$ on the other side. Therefore, we may take the comparison constants to be $-1/2$ and $1/2$, and the selection rule is then

$$s_{i+1} = \begin{cases} 1 & \text{if } 2U_i \geq 1/2 \\ 0 & \text{if } -1/2 \leq 2U_i < 1/2 \\ \bar{1} & \text{if } 2U_i < -1/2 \end{cases} \qquad (2.19)$$

The corresponding Roberston diagram is shown in Figure 2.9. The comparison is independent of D and requires only three bits of $2U_i$: one sign bit, one integer bit, and one fraction bit.

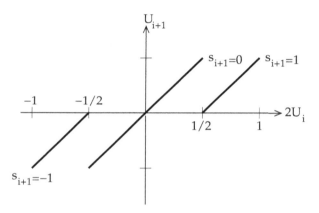

Figure 2.9: Modified radix-2 Robertson diagram

Figures 2.7 and 2.8 show that other comparison constants are possible. For example, instead of $-1/2$ and $1/2$, we could have $-1/4$ and $1/4$, although this requires one more fraction bit for representation. Also, there need not be symmetry in the use of the selected comparison constants. We could, for example, have

$$s_{i+1} = \begin{cases} 1 & \text{if } 2U_i \geq 0 \\ 0 & \text{if } -1/2 \leq 2U_i < 0 \\ \bar{1} & \text{if } 2U_i < -1/2 \end{cases}$$

As we shall see below, such asymmetry is "natural" when two's complement, carry–save representation is used for the arithmetic.

The type of simplification above in the choice of comparison values— i.e. the replacement of comparisons against D $(-D)$ with comparisons against $1/2$ $(-1/2)$—is not always possible. For radices larger than two, the intrinsic dependency of the comparison values on the divisor is unavoidable, and it is not possible to find for each region of overlap a single P–D line that works as in the case of the radix-2 algorithm. We shall see below that for larger radices, several lines (which correspond to several constants) are required, according to the value of the divisor.

Dividend = 0.000110 = 3/32   Divisor = 0.1101 = 13/16

i	U_i	q_i	Q_i	Action
0	0.000110	0	*.*********0	Shift
1	0.001100	0	*.********00	Shift
2	0.011000	0	*.*******000	Shift
3	0.110000	1	*.******0001	Subtract
	1.0011			(*Add -D*)
	1.111100			Shift
4	1.111000	0	*.*****00010	Shift
5	1.110000	0	*.****000100	Shift
6	1.100000	0	*.***0001000	Shift
7	1.000000	$\overline{1}$	*.**0001000$\overline{1}$	Add
	0.1101			(*Add D*)
	1.110100			Shift
8	1.101000	0	*.*000100$\overline{1}$0	Shift
9	1.010000	$\overline{1}$	*·000100$\overline{1}$0$\overline{1}$	Add
	0.1101			(*Add D*)
10	0.00100		0·00100$\overline{1}$0$\overline{1}$0	Shift

Quotient $= \frac{1}{8} - \frac{1}{128} - \frac{1}{512} \approx \frac{3}{26}$

Table 2.16: Example of SRT division

An example of binary SRT division is given in Table 2.16. The quotient is now produced in RSD form and at the end of the iterations must be converted into conventional form.[31] It is assumed in the table that negative

---

[31]The conversion can be done on the fly as the quotient digits are produced [6]; so the implied delay need not occur. See Section 2.1.2.2.

numbers are represented in two's complement notation and that subtraction is by the addition of the negation of the subtrahend. In each of the first three cycles, $0 < 2U_i \leq 1/2$; so 0s are entered in the quotient, and shifting without any arithmetic takes place. In the fourth cycle, $2U_i > 1/2$; so a 1 is entered in the quotient, and a shift and subtraction take place. In each of the next three cycles, $-1/2 \leq 2U_i < 0$; so 0s are entered in the quotient, and shifting without arithmetic again takes place. In the eighth, cycle $2U_i < -1/2$, and a $\bar{1}$ is entered in the quotient, followed by an addition and a shift. And so on, and so forth. If it is desirable to have a predictable operational time, then "no arithmetic" should be replaced with "add zero"/"subtract zero". As in multiplier recoding, such a change would mean no speed advantage (over basic non-restoring division) if arithmetic is in non-redundant form.

We have thus far assumed the use of a (relatively) slow carry–propagate adder (CPA) for the reductions of the partial remainder. But the redundancy in the RSD notation allows some flexibility in choosing the next quotient digit. The practical implication of that is that only an approximation, consisting of a few leading bits, is needed of the partial remainder in order to select the next quotient digit. So a carry–save adder (CSA) may be used in place of the CPA and an approximation of the remainder then obtained by assimilating[32] a few bits of the CSA's output. The remainder will now be in carry–save (CS) form and at the end of the iterating must be converted into conventional form.

Let $\widehat{U}_i$ denote the approximation that is obtained by truncating the CS representation of $2U_i$ and then assimilating the sum and carry parts. If the truncation is to p fraction bits, then the error in the partial-carry part is bounded by 2^{-p}, and the error in the partial-sum part is similarly bounded—a total of 2^{-p+1}. Now, Figures 2.9 and 2.10 show that at $D = 1/2$, $P = D$; so there is no margin for error with the selection rule of Equation 2.18. Replacing $1/2$ and $-1/2$ with $1/4$ and $-1/4$ would provide such a margin and will work with $p \geq 3$. An alternative, which gives a smaller value of p, is to make use of the asymmetry in the effect of truncating two's complement CS representations: truncating a two's complement representaton reduces the number represented; if the number is positive, then its magnitude is decreased; otherwise, its magnitude is increased. This has the following effect.

In Figure 2.8, the separation between $s_i = 0$ and $s_i = 1$ has to be made between the lines $P = 0$ and $P = D$. If $2U_i$ is positive, then $\widehat{U}_i \geq 0$; so

---

[32]This can be done in a small CPA or by using a lookup table.

this gives an error tolerance of at most $1/2$ (at $D = 1/2$). Therefore, if we take $p = 2$, then we may take $P = 0$ as the separating line. On the negative side, the truncation can only increase the magnitude, so its effect is that where before the separating line had to be found in $[0, -D]$, now the range is $[0, -D - 2^{-p}]$. Evidently $P = -1/2$ will still do, with $p = 2$. We therefore have the selection rule

$$s_{i+1} = \begin{cases} 1 & \text{if } \widehat{U}_i \geq 0 \\ 0 & \text{if } -1/2 \leq \widehat{U}_i < 0 \\ \bar{1} & \text{if } \widehat{U}_i < -1/2 \end{cases}$$

With the values $-1/2$ and $1/2$, only one fraction bit of $\widehat{U}_i$ is needed to make the selection. And with one fraction bit, the only representable number in the range $[-1/2, 0)$ is $1/2$. Therefore, the rule may be modified to

$$s_{i+1} = \begin{cases} 1 & \text{if } \widehat{U}_i \geq 0 \\ 0 & \text{if } \widehat{U}_i = -1/2 \\ \bar{1} & \text{if } \widehat{U}_i < -1/2 \end{cases}$$

A quick examination of Figure 2.8 will confirm that the constants 0 and $-1/2$ will indeed work and with an error tolerance of $1/2$.

We can also arrive at a slightly different rule on the basis that the truncation results in a reduction by $1/2$; so we may modify the original rule, i.e.

$$s_{i+1} = \begin{cases} 1 & \text{if } 2U_i \geq 0 \\ 0 & \text{if } -1/2 \leq 2U_i < 0 \\ \bar{1} & \text{if } 2U_i < -1/2 \end{cases}$$

by subtracting $1/2$ from the ends of the intervals, to get

$$s_{i+1} = \begin{cases} 1 & \text{if } \widehat{U}_i \geq 0 \\ 0 & \text{if } 1 \leq \widehat{U}_i < 0 \\ \bar{1} & \text{if } \widehat{U}_i < -1 \end{cases}$$

In either case, since $|2U_i| < 2$, we have $-5/2 \leq \widehat{U}_i \leq 3/2$, which requires one sign bit and two integer bits for representation. So, in summary, with CS representation, $\widehat{U}_i$ will be formed by assimilating five bits of the representation of U_i—one sign bit, two integer bits, and two fraction bits—and then using four of those (one fraction bit less) to make the s_i selection.

2.3.3.2 *High-radix algorithms*

An extension to a radix-r SRT algorithm with the digit set $\{\overline{m}, \overline{m-1}, \ldots, \overline{1}, 0, 1, \ldots, m-1, m\}$ is made by changing the core of the basic algorithm to

$$s_{i+1} = \begin{cases} m & \text{if } \alpha_m D \le rU_i < \beta_m D & \alpha_i \text{ and } \beta_i \text{ constants} \\ m-1 & \text{if } \alpha_{m-1} D \le rU_i < \beta_{m-1} D \\ \vdots & \qquad\qquad \vdots \\ 2 & \text{if } \alpha_2 D \le rU_i < \beta_2 D \\ 1 & \text{if } \alpha_1 D \le rU_i < \beta_1 D \\ 0 & \text{if } -\alpha_0 D \le rU_i < \alpha_0 D \\ \overline{1} & \text{if } -\beta_1 D \le rU_i < -\alpha_1 D \\ \overline{2} & \text{if } -\beta_2 D \le rU_i < -\alpha_2 D \\ \vdots & \qquad\qquad \vdots \\ \overline{m-1} & \text{if } -\beta_{m-1} D \le rU_i < -\alpha_{m-1} D \\ \overline{m} & \text{if } -\beta_m D \le rU_i < -\alpha_m D \end{cases}$$

$$Q_{i+1} = rQ_i + s_{i+1} \qquad i = 0, 1, 2, 3, \ldots$$

$$U_{i+1} = rU_i - s_{i+1} D \tag{2.20}$$

It is not apparent from what is given, but we shall see below that the various intervals overlap. $Q_0 = 0$, and the initialization U_0 is discussed below.

The general SRT algorithm is easily seen to be an additive-normalization algorithm, of a slightly different formulation from that given in Section 2.3.2. There, the initial equation for diminishing the partial remainder is

$$D_{i+1} = c_i D$$

$$= D_i - s_i r^{-i} D$$

and using the scaled variable $U_i \triangleq r^i D_i$ gives

$$U_{i+1} = r(U_i - s_i D)$$

If, instead, the scaled variable was $U_i = r^{i-1} D_i$, then (ignoring the slight difference in s-indices) we would have the SRT form:

$$U_{i+1} = rU_i - s_i D$$

Informally, the difference is in how one considers that the operands are aligned at the start of the process: one may diminish the partial remainder and then shift, or shift and then diminish the partial remainder.

Similarly, and again taking into account the different indexing, from slightly different starting points, the recurrences for the quotient, i.e.

$$Q_{i+1} = Q_i + s_i r^{-i}$$

and

$$Q_{i+1} = rQ_i + s_i$$

are easily seen to be equivalent. In iteration $i+1$, the next quotient digit, s_i is to be appended to the quotient formed so far, i.e. Q_i. This can be done by holding Q_i in place and shifting s_i to the right, all the way to the end, and then adding it to its right position (the first equation). Alternatively, it can be done by shifting Q_i one place to the left and then "adding" s_i in the "empty position" at the right (the second equation).

Returning to the general SRT equations: For convergence, we want $|U_i|$ to be bounded and $|U_{i+1}| \leq |U_i|$, for all i. At the positive extreme, $s_i = m$; so we want

$$rU_i - mD \leq U_i$$

i.e.

$$U_i \leq \frac{m}{r-1} D$$

and at the negative extreme, $s_i = \overline{m}$; so we want

$$rU_i + mD \geq U_i$$

i.e.

$$U_i \geq -\frac{m}{r-1} D$$

We should therefore have

$$|U_i| \leq \frac{m}{r-1} D$$

$$\stackrel{\triangle}{=} \rho D$$

where ρ is the redundancy factor.[33] $|U_i|$ will be so bounded if the values of s_i are chosen appropriately, and we next look at how to ensure that. The last expression also indicates that the initialization U_0 will depend on ρ.

---

[33] See Section 2.1.2.

The intervals determined by the constants α_i and β_i (and values for the constants) are obtained as follows. From Equation 2.20, we have

$$rU_i = U_{i+1} + s_{i+1}D$$

And from the bound on $|U_{i+1}|$, we see that U_i has its largest value when $U_{i+1} = \rho D$ and its smallest value when $U_{i+1} = -\rho D$. If, for the upper and lower bounds for rU_i, we define

$$U_i{}^{\max} = (s_{i+1} + \rho)D \qquad (2.21)$$

$$U_i{}^{\min} = (s_{i+1} - \rho)D \qquad (2.22)$$

then the interval bounds for the choice of $s_{i+1} = k$ are determined by considering this pair of equations, with k ranging in units of one, from $-m$ to m. In each instance, the selection of s_i should ensure that

$$U_i{}^{\min} \leq rU_i \leq U_i{}^{\max}$$

The preceding is as general as we shall get. Although there is some satisfaction to be had in mathematical generalities, it is nevertheless the case that in *practical and direct* implementations of SRT algorithms, the radix rarely exceeds four.[34] Moreover, in almost all such cases, the digit set will be the minimally redundant one. Therefore, the rest of what follows is accordingly restricted; the reader who requires generalities will find them done quite well in [1, 17].

For the minimally redundant radix-4 (i.e. $r = 4$, $m = 2$, and $\rho = 2/3$), the starting selection rule is

$$s_{i+1} = \begin{cases} 2 & \text{if } \alpha_2 D \leq 4U_i < \beta_2 D \\ 1 & \text{if } \alpha_1 D \leq 4U_i < \beta_1 D \\ 0 & \text{if } -\alpha_0 D \leq 4U_i < \alpha_0 D \\ \overline{1} & \text{if } -\beta_1 D \leq 4U_i < -\alpha_1 D \\ \overline{2} & \text{if } -\beta_2 D \leq 4U_i < -\alpha_2 D \end{cases}$$

So according to the value of U_i, $s_{i+1} = k$ is chosen so that

$$\left(k - \frac{2}{3}\right) D \leq 4U_i \leq \left(k + \frac{2}{3}\right) D \qquad k = \overline{2}, \overline{1}, 0, 1, 2 \qquad (2.23)$$

---

[34] We shall, in this chapter and Chapter 8, look at *indirect high-radix* implementations in which radices larger than four are effected through the use of multiple units of radix-2 and radix-4 units.

This gives the pair of equations

$$U_i{}^{\max} = \left(k + \frac{2}{3}\right) D \qquad k = \overline{2}, \overline{1}, 0, 1, 2 \qquad (2.24)$$

$$U_i{}^{\min} = \left(k - \frac{2}{3}\right) D \qquad\qquad\qquad (2.25)$$

which yield $\alpha_0 = 2/3, \alpha_1 = 1/3, \beta_1 = 5/3, \alpha_2 = 4/3$, and $\beta_2 = 8/3$. A summary is given in Table 2.17. Figure 2.10 shows one half of the corresponding Robertson diagram; the negative-side half is similar, by symmetry. Figure 2.11 shows the corresponding P–D diagram. The initialization must be such that $|U_0| \leq 2D/3$. This can be achieved by setting $U_0 = N/4$, where N is the divisor, and correspondingly scaling the quotient at the end of the iterations.

s_{i+1}	$U_i{}^{\min}$	$U_i{}^{\max}$
2	4D/3	8D/3
1	D/3	5D/3
0	−2D/3	2D/3
$\overline{1}$	−5D/3	−D/3
$\overline{2}$	−8D/3	−4D/3

Table 2.17: Digit-selection parameters for radix-4 SRT

To formulate a practical s_i-selection rule, it is necessary to have clear demarcating lines in the regions of overlap (Figures 2.10 and 2.11). These can be determined as follows.

The top region of overlap in Figure 2.11 is bounded by $P = 4D/3$ and $P = 5D/3$, and a convenient demarcating line, in choosing between $s_i = 2$ and $s_i = 1$, is that of $P = 3D/2$. Similarly, for the overlap determined by $P = D/3$ and $P = 2D/3$, a convenient line is that of $P = D/2$. And because of the symmetry below the axis we may take $P = -3D/2$ and $P = -D/2$. The selection rule then becomes

$$
s_i = \begin{cases}
2 & \text{if } 4U_i \geq 3D/2 \\
1 & \text{if } D/2 \leq 4U_i < 3D/2 \\
0 & \text{if } -D/2 \leq 4U_i < D/2 \\
\bar{1} & \text{if } -3D/2 \leq 4U_i < -D/2 \\
\bar{2} & \text{if } 4U_i < -3D/2
\end{cases}
$$

As given, this implies full-length comparisons. But the comparison values are exactly those of Section 2.3.2, and we have shown there that low-precision comparisons are possible, although the comparison values are dependent on D and must be computed as such [15]. There is, however, another way to find demarcations in the regions of overlap, and in what follows we shall describe a standard alternative, in which, essentially, the lines $D/2$ and $3D/2$ (and, similarly, those on the negative side) are replaced with stepwise approximations made up of several constants that form a staircase around each line. This arrangement allows low-precision comparisons and works because the only requirement is that there be some demarcation within a region of overlap; that the demarcation might not be very refined is a secondary matter.

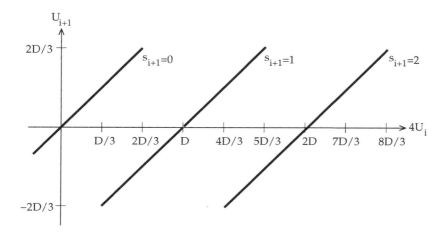

Figure 2.10: Radix-4 Roberston diagram

Consider the positive half of the P–D diagram (Figure 2.11). At $P = 1/2$, we have $4D/3 = 4/6$ and $5D/3 = 5/6$. The difference is $1/6$, and so we require a granularity of at least three fraction bits in P to locate a point in that interval. We may therefore start by assuming that three bits suffice. (At the end of the exercise it will be clear that this is good enough for all cases.) Accordingly, we shall look at the P scale at intervals of size 2^{-3}.

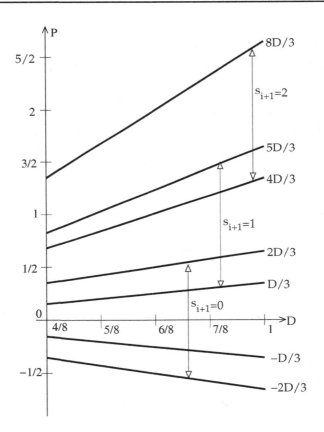

Figure 2.11: Radix-4 P–D diagram

At the specified P granularity, the only point on the $D = 1/2$ line that is within the region of overlap is at $P = 3/4$. This value of P corresponds to $D = 9/16$ on the $P = 4D/3$ line and at a point that can be identified with the three-bit fraction granularity in P, but which requires at least four fraction bits in D. At this stage, we have identified $P = 3/4$ as a suitable constant for the interval $[1/2, 9/16)$. We have also determined that at least four fraction bits are required of D. We shall assume exactly four fraction bits, and the remainder of the construction will show that this is in fact sufficient for all cases.

Next, we carry out a similar process, starting at the $D = 9/16$ line, to find that $7/8$ is a suitable constant for the interval $[9/16, 10/16)$. And we continue in this manner until the entire range of D is covered. The region of overlap between $P = D/3$ and $P = 2D/3$ is dealt with in the same way.

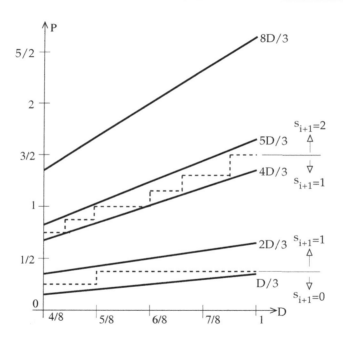

Figure 2.12: Constants selection in radix-4 SRT

The results are summarized in Figure 2.12 and Table 2.18, for the positive range of P, and symmetry gives us the constants for the negative side of the range: they are just the negations of the corresponding positive values. In contrast with the radix-2 case, in which single horizontal lines suffice, here the separation in the regions of overlap requires several horizontal lines—"staircases" that are determined by the constants of Table 2.18. (It should be noted that other staircases and constants are possible.) In implementation, the constants may be stored in a lookup table or hardwired in.

We shall continue with our discussion of the minimally redundant radix-4 case, but first a brief side-note on the maximally redundant case: With the latter, the regions of overlap will be larger, and "staircases" that involve fewer and more convenient constants can be constructed, but the relatively difficult-to-form multiple $3D$ is required in the computation of the partial remainder.[35]

Overlap	D-Interval	Constant
$[D/3, 2D/3]$	$[8/16, 10/16)$	$2/8$
	$[10/16, 16/16)$	$3/8$
$[4D/3, 5D/3]$	$[8/16, 9/16)$	$6/8$
	$[9/16, 10/16)$	$7/8$
	$[10/16, 12/16)$	$8/8$
	$[12/16, 13/16)$	$9/8$
	$[13/16, 15/16)$	$10/8$
	$[15/16, 16/16)$	$12/8$

Table 2.18: Radix-4 SRT constants

We have thus far assumed that the full partial remainder is available and that this is then truncated for the decision making. Faster arithmetic can be realized by using carry–save (CS) representation, and the considerations here are as above for the radix-2 case. Truncating a CS representation to p fraction bits introduces an error of magnitude at most 2^{-p+1}, and the precise effect of this error depends on whether the represented number is positive or negative. In what follows, we shall not make the latter distinction but will comment on it. We shall also consider only the positive side

---

[35] If the arithmetic is in non-redundant representation, then forming $3D$ is just one of several carry–propagate additions and so may be acceptable. But if the arithmetic is in carry–save form, then the time to form $3D$ is relatively excessive.

of the P–D diagram and assume symmetry for the negative side.

We may take it that the effect of the truncation is to change the region of overlaps to

$$\left[D + 2^{-p+1}, \ 2D/3 - 2^{-p+1}\right]$$

and

$$\left[4D/3 + 2^{-p+1}, \ 5D/3 - 2^{-p+1}\right]$$

This is simple but conservative. It does not take into account the difference between truncating the representation of a positive number and that of a negative number, but not making that distinction gives a nice symmetry in the comparison constants. (If the distinction is made, then the minimum value of p will be reduced by one bit, but some of the constants on the negative side will not have counterparts on the positive side; this means that more constants must be stored.)

Overlap	D-Interval	Constant
$[D/3, 2D/3]$	$[8/16, 10/16)$	$4/16$
	$[10/16, 12/16)$	$5/16$
	$[12/16, 16/16)$	$7/16$
$[4D/3, 5D/3]$	$[8/16, 9/16)$	$13/16$
	$[9/16, 10/16)$	$14/16$
	$[10/16, 11/16)$	$16/16$
	$[11/16, 12/16)$	$17/16$
	$[12/16, 13/16)$	$18/16$
	$[13/16, 14/16)$	$20/16$
	$[14/16, 15/16)$	$22/16$
	$[15/16, 16/16)$	$24/16$

Table 2.19: Radix-4 SRT constants (CS arithmetic)

The rightmost interval, $[8/16, 9/16]$, is determinative: a quick paper-and-pencil computation will show that the best choice of constant for that interval is $13/16$, with $p = 6$; a grind through the other intervals will show that $p = 5$ will suffice in each of those cases. Assuming $p = 6$, a summary of the constants is given in Table 2.19, and, by symmetry, the negations of these work for the negative side. In summary, $\widehat{U}_i$ is to be formed by assimilating nine bits of the partial-sum and partial-carry components of U_i: one sign bit, two integer bits, and six fraction bits.

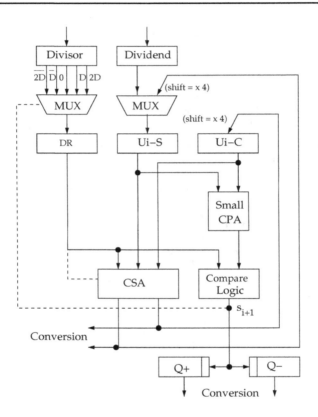

Figure 2.13: Radix-4 SRT divider

A sketch of hardware architecture for a radix-4 SRT divider is shown in Figure 2.13. We assume two's complement representation; so subtraction is done by adding the negation of the subtrahend, which negation consists of a ones' complement and the addition of a 1 in the least siginificant bit position. Forming the divisor-multiples therefore consists of complementing the divisor or twice the divisor, the with the latter formed by a one-bit-place wired shift. The Small CPA (carry–propagate adder) adds a few bits of each of the partial carry and partial sum that make up the partial remainder, and the output of that goes to the Compare Logic, which also takes a few bits of the divisor and does the comparisons required to determine the next quotient digit. (The Compare Logic may be implemented as combinational logic or as a lookup table.) The carry–save adder (CSA) reduces the partial remainder by the selected divisor-multiple; the output of this is multiplied by four, which is effected by a two-bit-place wired shift (indicated as slanted lines in the figure). A digit of the quotient is entered in either the register $Q+$ or the register $Q-$, according to whether it is positive or negative; the conversion of the quotient to conventional representation is as described in Section 2.1.2.2. The final remainder will be in carry–save form and is converted, using a CPA.

The radix-4 SRT divider is one of the most implemented types of high-performance dividers, and numerous detailed descriptions of practical implementationsand realizations will be found in the literature (e.g. [16, 18]).

We now pick up a thread that we started in the discussion on multiplicative-normalization division—the possibility of overlapping s_i-selection with the main arithmetic. A consideration of Figure 2.13 shows that with the arithmetic so fast, the s_i-selection time is now the dominant element in the critical path, and it could be worth it to overlap that phase with the arithmetic phase and other actions. If the increased cost in logic is acceptable, that can be done by computing all five possible partial remainders at the same time as s_{i+1} and then immediately selecting the correct one. A recent version of such a divider is described in [16]. Such replication can also be used to effect high-radix computation, by overlapping low-radix ones [12]. Additional discussions in this regard will be found in Section 8.3.7.

2.3.4 *Very high radix*

In subtractive division as described above, radices larger than four immediately raise the problem of hard-to-form multiples of the divisor, and that is the main reason for the lack of such dividers. Even with radix 4, the minimally redundant digit set is preferred (over the maximally redundant one) for the same reason. There have been implementations of dividers with nominally larger radices, but such implementations basically use multiple low-radix units—for example, radix-16 division may be implemented by overlapping two radix-4 units [12]—and so there is the cost of a substantial replication in logic.[36] The general approach is of dubious worth with radices larger than sixteen and certainly not very practical for truly large radices.

On the other hand, one conclusion that may be drawn from a consideration of the Goldschmidt division algorithm (Section 2.3.1.1) is that a relatively costly operation (multiplication) may be acceptable if the entire quotient can be produced in a small number of cycles. This leads to the idea that hard-to-form multiples may be acceptable in nominally subtractive division if the radix used is so large that the reduction in the number of cycles makes up for the time taken to generate such multiples—provided, of course, that the cycle time per iteration does not increase too much.

A very large radix in subtractive-division algorithms of the type above also implies a similarly very large number of intervals and constants for the selection of quotient digits as well as numerous hard-to-form multiples of the divisor. A more practical arrangement is required, and we next describe one.

Quotient-digit selection by rounding is a method for the selection of quotient digits that deals with what would be the problem (in algorithms of the type discussed above) of numerous hard-to-form multiples of the divisor and the requirement for a large number of constants [13]. The method has been devised for use with large radices and in a manner that does not require comparisons of the SRT type. Originally proposed for division, selection-by-rounding has since been applied to other algorithms, such as the CORDIC algorithms (Chapter 3 and 4), algorithms for the logarithm and exponential functions (Chapter 5), and algorithms for reciprocals, square roots, and inverse square roots (Chapter 8). The basic idea is quite straightforward: the next quotient digit is obtained by truncating the shifted partial remainder and then rounding to the nearest integer. The details are as follows.

Without loss of generality, it is assumed that the dividend, N, and the divisor, D, are such that $1/2 \leq N < 1, 1/2 \leq D < 1$, and $N < D$. It is also necessary that the divisor be close to one; if that is not the case to start with, then appropriate prescaling is required of both the divisor and the dividend. The algorithm is therefore applied to a scaled divisior, D_*:

$$D_* = \mu D \qquad \text{where } \mu \approx 1/D$$

(The divisor is similarly scaled.)

μ may be obtained by a variety of methods, such as table lookup and polynomial approximation (as described in Chapters 7 and 8).

---

[36]Such algorithms are described in Section 8.3.5.

The specific condition that D_* must satisfy for radix-r division is

$$1 - \frac{r-2}{4r(r-1)} < D_* < 1 + \frac{r-2}{4r(r-1)}$$

The core of the division algorithm consists of the recurrences

$$U_{i+1} = rU_i - s_{i+1}D_*$$

$$s_{i+1} = \left\lfloor \widehat{U}_i + 1/2 \right\rfloor$$

where U_i is the partial remainder and $\widehat{U}_i$ is the result of truncating[37] rU_i. The value of s_iD_* is computed by a direct multiplication; [14] shows how the basic method can be modified so as to keep the width of the multiplier(s) small.

As an example, a radix-512 (nine bits at a time) algorithm is proposed in [13], with the digit set $\{\overline{511}, \ldots, \overline{1}, 0, 1, \ldots, 511\}$. The value μ is obtained by truncating to 13 fraction bits the result of a linear approximation:

$$\mu = c_0 - c_1 \lfloor D \rfloor_{15}$$

$$c_0 = \frac{2\lfloor D \rfloor_6 + 2^{-6}}{\lfloor D \rfloor_6 + \lfloor D \rfloor_6 2^{-6} + 2^{-15}}$$

$$c_1 = \frac{1}{\lfloor D \rfloor_6 + \lfloor D \rfloor_6 2^{-6} + 2^{-15}}$$

where $\lfloor D \rfloor_6$ and $\lfloor D \rfloor_{15}$ are the results of truncating D to six and fifteen fraction bits, respectively. c_0 and c_1 are also truncated to thirteen fraction bits each, and $\widehat{U}_i$ is obtained by truncating rU_i to two fraction bits. The sets of constants c_0 and c_1 are stored in two small tables, one pair for each subrange of D.

---

[37]Strictly, here and below, we mean truncating the representation.

Chapter 3

CORDIC

The CORDIC algorithms have long been studied for the evaluation of elementary functions. Their origins lie in a special-purpose computer, the **Co**ordinate **R**otational **Di**gital **C**omputer, that was designed for the evaluation of some trigonometric functions [1, 2]. Subsequently, the algorithms were extended to other elementary functions [3, 4], and new variants continue to appear [5]. As implied by the name, the underlying idea is that of a rotation in a geometric space. The CORDIC algorithms can also be derived through the concept of *normalization*, a more "algebraic" process that is discussed in Chapter 5.

There are numerous variations on the CORDIC theme, and our discussion is in two main parts. The first part, which is this chapter, covers the basics that are relevant to all CORDIC algorithms. Chapter 4 makes up the second part and deals with several high-performance variants of the basic algorithms and implementations of those variants.

The first section of this chapter is on the trigonometric functions, and the second covers the inverse trigonometric functions; these two categories form the *circular* functions, for which the algorithms were originally invented. The CORDIC algorithms can also be used to compute several other functions: the *hyperbolic* functions, which are discussed in the third section, and the *linear* functions (multiplication and division), which are discussed in the fourth section. Several other functions—including logarithms, exponentials, and square roots—can be computed indirectly[1] from the algorithms for the preceding functions and are mentioned in the corresponding "direct" context. The fifth section of the chapter deals with errors and the

---

[1] As will become apparent, this is not particularly efficient, and, unless it is desirable to make use of already exisiting hardware, there are much better ways to compute these functions.

sixth with basic implementation. Given the signficance of CORDIC, we we have in this chapter a rarity in this book—a detailed mathematical proof, in the form of a complete convergence proof. That, and several aspects of the discussions in this chapter, are (with appropriate modifications) applicable to other roughly-similar algorithms discussed elsewhere in the book. Accordingly, we shall later make frequent "back-references".

There are two *modes* of operation in CORDIC: *rotation mode*, in which a vector is rotated by a known angle,[2] and *vectoring mode*, in which a vector is rotated so as to determine a previously unknown and sought angle. Different functions can be evaluated in one or the other mode, by using different initializations in, essentially, the same algorithms.

3.1   Trigonometric functions

The evaluation of the sine and cosine best exemplify CORDIC. We shall therefore start with a discussion of these two and then proceed to other functions. The former discussions will also be more detailed than the latter: because of the similarities between different classes of CORDIC, it will suffice to give a detailed treatment for one class of functions; extensions to other functions are mostly straightforward.

The computations for sine and cosine are done in *rotation mode*, by rotating a (nominally) unit-length vector through the given angle. Suppose we wish to compute $\sin\theta$ and $\cos\theta$, for some angle[3], θ. If we take the vector $(X_0, Y_0) \triangleq (1, 0)$, rotate it on the circle $X^2 + Y^2 = 1$, through a series of positive angles, $\theta_0, \theta_1, \ldots, \theta_n$ such that $\theta_0 + \theta_1 + \cdots, \theta_n = \theta$, and end up with the vector (X_{n+1}, Y_{n+1}), then $X_{n+1} = \cos\theta$ and $Y_{n+1} = \sin\theta$. We next look at the details of the rotation process.

Figure 3.1 shows the rotation, by an angle θ_i, of the unit-length vector with coordinates (X_i, Y_i) at an angle ϕ from the x axis. The coordinates, (X_{i+1}^*, Y_{i+1}^*), of the new vector are

$$
\begin{aligned}
X_{i+1}^* &= \cos(\theta_i + \phi) \\
&= \cos\phi\cos\theta_i - \sin\phi\sin\theta_i \\
&= X_i\cos\theta_i - Y_i\sin\theta_i \\
&= (X_i - Y_i\tan\theta_i)\cos\theta_i
\end{aligned}
\tag{3.1}
$$

---

[2]In some cases, the term "angle" will be used somewhat loosely.
[3]We shall assume that all angles are given in radians.

$$Y_{i+1}^* = \sin(\theta_i + \phi)$$
$$= \sin\phi\cos\theta_i + \cos\phi\sin\theta_i$$
$$= Y_i\cos\theta_i + X_i\sin\theta_i$$
$$= (Y_i + X_i\tan\theta_i)\cos\theta_i \qquad (3.2)$$

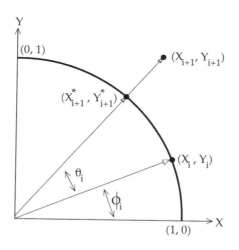

Figure 3.1: CORDIC rotation mode ($\sin\theta$ and $\cos\theta$)

In CORDIC, the rotation of (X_i, Y_i) to (X_{i+1}^*, Y_{i+1}^*), as shown in Figure 3.1, is replaced by a *pseudo-rotation*—that is, a true rotation with an elongation of the vector—to (X_{i+1}, Y_{i+1}), where

$$X_{i+1} = X_i - Y_i\tan\theta_i \qquad (3.3)$$
$$Y_{i+1} = Y_i + X_i\tan\theta_i \qquad (3.4)$$

As we shall see below, the use of a pseudo-rotation, instead of a true rotation, simplifies both the algorithm and the design of the corresponding hardware implementation.

A comparison of Equations 3.1–3.2 and Equations 3.3–3.4 shows that the vector (X_{i+1}, Y_{i+1}) is longer than the vector (X_{i+1}^*, Y_{i+1}^*), by a factor of $1/\cos\theta_i$. Therefore, in order to get $\sin\theta$ and $\cos\theta$ at the end of the rotations, it is necessary to scale each X_i and Y_i by this factor. If the total number of rotations and the magnitudes of the rotation angles are constant, regardless of the given angle, θ—and this will be the case with the recurrences above if the θ_is are appropriately chosen—then the product of the scaling factors is also constant. So instead of scaling by $1/\cos\theta_i$ at each step, i, for $n+1$ iterations, it is sufficient to just scale the final result by the factor

$$K = \prod_{i=0}^{n} \frac{1}{\cos\theta_i}$$

$$= \prod_{i=0}^{n} \sqrt{1 + \tan^2\theta_i}$$

In practice, a final operation involving K is easily avoided by setting X_0 to $1/K$. This initial scaling in X subsequently introduces a similar scaling in Y.

The equations for the rotations indicate multiplications (by $\tan\theta_i$) and additions, but the multiplications can be replaced with just SHIFT operations, if the rotation angles are chosen appropriately. If we choose $\theta_i = \tan^{-1} 2^{-i}$, then

$$X_{i+1} = X_i - 2^{-i}Yi$$

$$Y_{i+1} = Y_i + 2^{-i}X_i$$

in which the term 2^{-i} represents a simple shift to the right, by i bits, and

$$K = \prod_{i=0}^{n} \sqrt{1 + 2^{-2i}} \tag{3.5}$$

The final issue in this introduction is convergence. We shall get into the details of that below, but we make some preliminary remarks here in order to complete the description of the algorithm.

In the preceding discussion, there is an implicit requirement that any given angle, θ, must be expressible (at least to a good approximation) in terms of the finite number of predetermined θ_is. That is possible only if two conditions hold. The first condition is that given the limitation of the sum of θ_is, the range of θ be must be restricted; $[-\pi/2, \pi/2]$ is sufficient,[4] and other values can be accommodated through range reduction (Section 1.2). The second condition arises from the observation that if we wish to express

---

[4]The actual range for convergence is slightly larger, as shown below. It is approximately $[-1.74, 1.74]$ for sufficiently large n.

(or approximate) a given number in terms of smaller numbers, then the best expression (or approximation) is obtained if we can add or subtract each of the smaller numbers. (For example, given $\{1, 1/2, 1/3, 1/4\}$, it is possible to express $5/12$ exactly if subtractions are allowed—as $1 - (1/3) - (1/4)$— but not otherwise.) So it should be possible to rotate in either direction; that is, to add or subtract each θ_i, according to how close the sum of the rotation angles in a given step is to θ. So, in general, we will have $\theta \approx \theta_0 \pm \theta_2 \pm \theta_2 \pm \cdots \pm \theta_n$. We therefore introduce a new parameter, s_i, to indicate the direction of rotation: $+1$ for forward and -1 for backward.

To determine whether to add or subtract in each iteration, the total rotation angle so far is subtracted from θ. If the difference is negative, then an addition takes place; and if it is positive, then a subtraction takes place. Intuitively, taking the "sign" for the action to be the "inverse" of that of the angle residual is a correction for a rotation made too far in one or the other direction. If the last rotation was too far forward (backward), then the next one should be backward (forward). In the algorithm, the difference is computed incrementally—as $\theta_0 \pm \theta_1$, $\theta_0 \pm \theta_1 \pm \theta_2$, $\theta_0 \pm \theta_1 \pm \theta_2 \pm \theta_3$, etc.—and the preceding actions therefore correspond to making adjustments according to "how much farther we have to go". The angle residual is computed in a third variable, Z_i.

To summarize then, the recurrences for the computation of sine and cosine are

$$X_0 = 1/K \qquad\qquad K = \prod_{i=0}^{n} \sqrt{1 + 2^{-2i}}$$

$$Y_0 = 0$$

$$Z_0 = \theta$$

$$\theta_i = \tan^{-1} 2^{-i} \qquad\qquad i = 0, 1, 2 \ldots, n$$

$$X_{i+1} = X_i - s_i 2^{-i} Y_i$$

$$Y_{i+1} = Y_i + s_i 2^{-i} X_i$$

$$Z_{i+1} = Z_i - s_i \theta_i$$

$$s_i = \begin{cases} 1 \text{ if } Z_i \geq 0 \\ -1 \text{ otherwise} \end{cases}$$

We will show below that each iteration produces one correct bit of the result in each of X_i and Y_i.

At the end of the $n + 1$ iterations with these recurrences, since $\theta \approx \sum_{i=0}^{n} s_i \theta_i$, we will have

$$Z_{n+1} \approx 0$$
$$X_{n+1} \approx \cos\theta$$
$$Y_{n+1} \approx \sin\theta$$

This can be seen from the informal explanation at the start of this section[5] and is justified more fully below. An example of CORDIC computation is given in Table 3.1.

From the values of $\sin\theta$ and $\cos\theta$, the values of $\tan\theta$ and $\cot\theta$ may be computed by division. This division too can be done with CORDIC rotations (Section 3.4).

$\theta = 0.375$ radians $\sin\theta = 0.366273\cdots$ $\cos\theta = 0.930508\cdots$

i	X_i	Y_i	Z_i	s_i
0	0.1001101101110100	0.0000000000000000	0.0110000000000000	1
1	0.1001101101110100	0.1001101101110100	-0.0110100100001111	-1
2	0.1110100100101111	0.0100110110111010	0.0000110110100001	1
3	0.1101010111000000	0.1000100000000110	-0.0011000100010101	-1
4	0.1110011011000001	0.0110110101001110	-0.0001000100111111	-1
5	0.1110110110010110	0.0101111011100010	-0.0000000101000100	-1
6	0.1111000010001101	0.0101011101110101	0.0000011010111010	1
7	0.1110111100101111	0.0101101100110111	0.0000001010111010	1
8	0.1110111001111001	0.0101110100010101	0.0000000010111010	1
9	0.1110111000011100	0.0101111000000100	-0.0000000001000101	-1
10	0.1110111001001011	0.0101110110001101	0.0000000000111010	1
11	0.1110111000110011	0.0101110111001000	-0.0000000000000101	-1
12	0.1110111000111111	0.0101110110101011	0.0000000000011010	1
13	0.1110111000111001	0.0101110110111010	0.0000000000001010	1
14	0.1110111000110110	0.0101110111000001	0.0000000000000010	1
15	0.1110111000110101	0.0101110111000101	-0.0000000000000001	-1
	$\cos\theta \approx 0.9305$	$\sin\theta \approx 0.3662$		

Table 3.1: Examples of CORDIC $\sin\theta$ and $\cos\theta$ computations

[5] Page 94, second paragraph in Section 3.1.

The recurrences above—specifically, the initializations—represent just one "instance" of the algorithm. In general, for given values of X_0, Y_0 and Z_0, the algorithm computes

$$X_{n+1} \approx K(X_0 \cos Z_0 - Y_0 \sin Z_0)$$
$$Y_{n+1} \approx K(X_0 \sin Z_0 + Y_0 \cos Z_0)$$
$$Z_{n+1} \approx 0$$

This may be confirmed as follows.

For brevity, we shall use ϕ_i to denote $s_i \theta_i$. Then

$$Z_0 = \theta \approx \sum_{i=0}^{n} \phi_i$$

and the recurrences are[6]

$$X_{i+1} = X_i - Y_i \tan \phi_i$$
$$Y_{i+1} = Y_i + X_i \tan \phi_i$$
$$Z_{i+1} = Z_i - \phi_i$$

Considering the rotation by the angle ϕ_k, and applying standard trigonometric identities:

$$X_{k+1} = X_k - Y_k \tan \phi_k$$

$$= (X_{k-1} - Y_{k-1} \tan \phi_{k-1}) - (Y_{k-1} + X_{k-1} \tan \phi_{k-1}) \tan \phi_k$$

$$= X_{k-1} (1 - \tan \phi_{k-1} \tan \phi_k) - Y_{k-1} (\tan \phi_{k-1} + \tan \phi_k)$$

$$= X_{k-1} (1 - \tan \phi_{k-1} \tan \phi_k) - Y_{k-1} \tan(\phi_{k-1} + \phi_k)(1 - \tan \phi_{k-1} \tan \phi_k)$$

$$= 1 - \frac{\sin \phi_{k-1} \sin \phi_k}{\cos \phi_{k-1} \cos \phi_k} \left[X_{k-1} - Y_{k-1} \frac{\sin(\phi_{k-1} + \phi_k)}{\cos(\phi_{k-1} + \cos \phi_k)} \right]$$

$$= \frac{1}{\cos \phi_{k-1} \cos \phi_k} [X_{k-1} \cos(\phi_{k-1} + \phi_k) - Y_{k-1} \sin(\phi_{k-1} + \phi_k)]$$

Unwinding this, we end up with

$$X_{k+1} = \frac{1}{\prod_{i=0}^{k} \cos \phi_i} \left[X_0 \cos \left(\sum_{i=0}^{k} \phi_i \right) - Y_0 \sin \left(\sum_{i=0}^{k} \phi_i \right) \right]$$

---

[6]The recurrences above are expressed in terms of $s_i \tan^{-1} \theta_i$. As explained in Section 4.6, the "more correct" form is $\tan^{-1}(s_i \theta_i)$, which arises "naturally" and is the more general form. Here, it will suffice to note that if $s_i = \pm 1$, then $s_i \tan^{-1} \theta_i = \tan^{-1}(s_i \theta_i)$.

whence

$$X_{n+1} \approx K(X_0 \cos Z_0 - Y_0 \sin Z_0)$$

where

$$K = \frac{1}{\prod_{i=0}^{n} \cos \phi_i}$$

$$= \prod_{i=0}^{n} \sqrt{1 + \tan^2(s_i \theta)}$$

$$= \prod_{i=0}^{n} \sqrt{1 + 2^{-2i}} \qquad \text{if } s_i = \pm 1 \text{ and } \theta = \tan^{-1} 2^{-i}$$

Similarly, from

$$Y_{i+1} = Y_i + X_i \tan \phi_i$$

we obtain

$$Y_{n+1} \approx K(X_0 \sin Z_0 + Y_0 \cos Z_0)$$

Lastly, $Z_0 = \theta \approx \sum_{i=0}^{n} \phi_i$; so unwinding the recurrence for Z:

$$Z_{n+1} = Z_0 - \sum_{i=0}^{n} \phi_i \approx 0$$

Convergence

In general, it is not possible to express an arbitrary angle, θ, exactly in terms of a given set of rotation angles, each of which is used just once, even if the range of θ is restricted; any expression will be an approximation, with some error. So, convergence here means that each rotation must bring the cumulative rotation angle closer to θ—i.e. the residual, Z_i, closer to zero—and the last rotation should leave both "sufficiently close" to θ and zero, respectively. Given that the smallest (and last) rotation angle is θ_n, that may reasonably be taken as a measure of "sufficiently close".

If we can prove that

$$|Z_i| \leq \theta_n + \sum_{j=i}^{n} \theta_j \qquad 0 \leq i \leq n \qquad (3.6)$$

then it follows that

$$|Z_{n+1}| \leq \theta_n$$

and we also obtain the argument range required for convergence:

$$|Z_0| \leq \theta_n + \sum_{j=0}^{n} \theta_j \qquad (3.7)$$

The proof of Inequation 3.6 is via the *Decomposition Theorem*, which is given next. The following proof was first sketched out in [3], with most details subsequently given in [6]. The essence of the proof is equally applicable, with appropriate modifications, to the other cases of CORDIC discussed below; so we shall not consider in detail the convergence of those other algorithms.

The initial conditions in the statement of the theorem reflect the requirements that (a) after any iteration, i, the remaining iterations must be sufficient to bring the residual angle to within θ_n of zero, and (b) that it should be possible to decompose (approximately) the angle θ in terms of the rotation angles, θ_i.

DECOMPOSITION THEOREM: *Suppose σ is a real number and $\sigma_0 \geq \sigma_1 \geq \sigma_1 \geq \cdots \geq \sigma_n > 0$ is a finite sequence of real numbers such that*

$$\sigma_i \leq \sigma_n + \sum_{j=i+1}^{n} \sigma_j \qquad\qquad 0 \leq j \leq n \qquad (3.8)$$

and

$$|\sigma| \leq \sum_{j=0}^{n} \sigma_j \qquad (3.9)$$

If

$$U_0 = 0$$
$$U_{i+1} = U_i + s_i\sigma_i , \qquad\qquad i = 0, 1, \ldots, n \qquad (3.10)$$

where

$$s_i = \begin{cases} 1 \text{ if } \sigma - U_i \geq 0 \\ -1 \text{ otherwise} \end{cases}$$

then

$$|\sigma - U_i| \leq \sigma_n + \sum_{j=i}^{n} \sigma_j \qquad\qquad 0 \leq i \leq n \qquad (3.11)$$

and in particular

$$|\sigma - U_{n+1}| \le \sigma_n \qquad (3.12)$$

$\square$

The proof is by induction on i.

For $i = 0$

$$|\sigma - U_0| = |\sigma| \le \sum_{j=0}^{n} \sigma_j \qquad \text{by Inequation 3.9}$$

$$\le \sigma_n + \sum_{j=0}^{n} \sigma_j$$

For the inductive step, assume that the theorem holds for i. We then need to show that

$$|\sigma - U_{i+1}| \le \sigma_n + \sum_{j=i+1}^{n} \sigma_j$$

By hypothesis

$$|\sigma - U_i| \le \sigma_n + \sum_{j=i}^{n} \sigma_j$$

and so

$$|\sigma - U_i| - \sigma_i \le \sigma_n - \sigma_i + \sum_{j=i}^{n} \sigma_j$$

and

$$|\sigma - U_i| - \sigma_i \le \left(\sigma_n + \sum_{j=i+1}^{n} \sigma_j \right) \qquad (3.13)$$

From Inequation 3.8:

$$- \left(\sigma_n + \sum_{j=i+1}^{n} \sigma_j \right) \le -\sigma_i \qquad (3.14)$$

whence

$$- \left(\sigma_n + \sum_{j=i+1}^{n} \sigma_j \right) \le |\sigma - U_i| - \sigma_i \qquad (3.15)$$

Combining Inequations 3.13 and 3.15:

$$-\left(\sigma_n + \sum_{j=i+1}^{n} \sigma_j\right) \le |\sigma - U_i| - \sigma_i \le \left(\sigma_n + \sum_{j=i+1}^{n} \sigma_j\right)$$

so

$$\left|\, |\sigma - U_i| - \sigma_i \right| \le \sigma_n + \sum_{j=i+1}^{n} \sigma_j \tag{3.16}$$

For $\sigma - U_{i+1}$, we have

$$|\sigma - U_{i+1}| = |\sigma - U_i - s_i\sigma_i| \qquad \text{by Equation 3.10}$$

If $\sigma - U_i \ge 0$, then $s_i = 1$; so

$$|\sigma - U_i - s_i\sigma_i| = |\sigma - U_i - \sigma_i|$$

$$= \left|\, |\sigma - U_i| - \sigma_i \right|$$

and if $\sigma - U_i < 0$, then $s_i = -1$; so

$$|\sigma - U_i + s_i\sigma_i| = |U_i - \sigma - \sigma_i|$$

$$= \left|\, |\sigma - U_i| - \sigma_i \right|$$

In either case

$$|\sigma - U_{i+1}| = \left|\, |\sigma - U_i| - \sigma_i \right|$$

Combining this with Inequation 3.16, we have

$$|\sigma - U_{i+1}| \le \sigma_n + \sum_{j=i+1}^{n} \sigma_j$$

which is what we had to show, and, therefore,

$$|\sigma - U_{i+1}| \le \sigma_n$$

We next proceed to apply the theorem to CORDIC. We start by showing that the choice $\sigma_i = \theta_i = \tan^{-1} 2^{-i}$ satisfies Inequation 3.8. First, a standard result from analysis:

MEAN VALUE THEOREM: *If the function $f(x)$ is defined and continuous on the interval $[a, b]$ and differentiable on the interval (a, b), then there is at least one c in (a, b) such that*

$$f'(c) = \frac{f(b) - f(a)}{b - a}$$

$\square$

Applying this theorem to $f(x) = \tan^{-1}(x)$ gives

$$\frac{1}{1 + c^2} = \frac{\tan^{-1}(b) - \tan^{-1}(a)}{b - a} \qquad a < c < b$$

and

$$\tan^{-1}(b) - \tan^{-1}(a) = \frac{b - a}{1 + c^2} \qquad (3.17)$$

Substituting $a = 2^{-(j+1)}$ and $b = 2^{-j}$ in Equation 3.17, i.e. $\theta_j = \tan^{-1}(b)$ and $\theta_{j+1} = \tan^{-1}(a)$

$$\theta_j - \theta_{j+1} = \frac{2^{-j} - 2^{-(j+1)}}{1 + c^2}$$

$$< \frac{2^{-(j+1)}}{1 + a^2}$$

$$= \frac{2^{j+1}}{1 + 2^{2j+2}} \qquad (3.18)$$

And substituting $a = 0$ and $b = 2^{-j}$ in Equation 3.17

$$\theta_j = \frac{2^{-j}}{1 + c^2}$$

$$\geq \frac{2^{-j}}{1 + b^2}$$

$$= \frac{2^j}{1 + 2^{2j}} \qquad (3.19)$$

So

$$\theta_i - \theta_n = \sum_{j=i}^{n-1} (\theta_j - \theta_{j+1})$$

$$\leq \sum_{j=i}^{n-1} \frac{2^{j+1}}{1 + 2^{2j+2}} \qquad \text{by Inequation 3.18}$$

$$= \sum_{j=i+1}^{n} \frac{2^j}{1 + 2^{2j}}$$

$$\leq \sum_{j=i+1}^{n} \theta_j \qquad \text{by Inequation 3.19}$$

from which we conclude Inequation 3.8:

$$\theta_i \le \theta_n + \sum_{j=i+1}^{n} \theta_j \qquad\qquad 0 \le i < n \qquad\qquad (3.20)$$

Next, we need to show that Inequation 3.9 too is satisfied, with $\sigma = \theta$ and $\sigma_i = \theta_i$. Now,

$$\frac{\pi}{2} < \sum_{j=0}^{3} \theta_j = \sum_{j=0}^{3} \tan^{-1} 2^j < \sum_{j=0}^{n} \theta_j$$

So Inequation 3.9 is satisfied if $|\theta| \le \pi/2$, which establishes $[-\pi/2, \pi/2]$ as an argument range that will ensure convergence. Strictly, the range that will guarantee convergence is larger: the theorem tells us that the algorithm will converge for any angle θ that can be expressed as

$$\theta = \sum_{i=0}^{n} s_i \theta_i \qquad\qquad s_i \in \{-1, 1\} \text{ and } \theta_i = \tan^{-1} 2^{-i}$$

with an error of at most 2^{-n} (which[7] is $\tan^{-1} 2^{-n}$, for large n), provided

$$|\theta| < \theta_n + \sum_{i=0}^{n} \theta_i$$

With $\theta_i = \tan^{-1} 2^{-i}$, this gives the range for Z_0, the argument, as approximately $[-1.74, 1.74]$, for large n.

To complete the proof and obtain Inequation 3.6 and its consequences, we make the substitution, in Inequations 3.11 and 3.12, of

$$\sigma = \theta$$
$$U_i = \theta - Z_i$$

($U_0 = 0$, and $U_i = \sum_{k=0}^{i-1} s_k \theta_k$ is the cumulative rotation angle up to iteration i.) That substitution gives

$$|Z_i| \le \theta_n + \sum_{j=i}^{n} \theta_j \qquad\qquad 0 \le i \le n$$

$$|Z_{n+1}| \le \theta_n$$

For later reference, we note also that in the limit, as $n \to \infty$, $\theta_n \to 0$; so

$$|Z_i| \le \sum_{j=i}^{\infty} \theta_j \qquad\qquad\qquad (3.21)$$

---

[7]See Table 6.4.

Having shown that the process will converge, we conclude with an examination of the rate of convergence. For that, it suffices to consider just the specific case with $X_0 = 1/K$ and $Y_0 = 0$, which means that $X_{n+1} = \cos U_{n+1}$ and $Y_{n+1} = \sin U_{n+1}$.

By the Mean Value Theorem, with $f(x) = \cos x$, there exists a number c such that $U_{n+1} < c < \theta$ and

$$- \sin c = \frac{\cos \theta - \cos U_{n+1}}{\theta - U_{n+1}}$$

So

$$
\begin{aligned}
|\cos \theta - X_{n+1}| &= |\cos \theta - \cos U_{n+1}| \\
&= |-\sin c|\,|\theta - U_{n+1}| \\
&\le |\theta - U_{n+1}| \\
&\le 2^{-n} \qquad \text{by Inequation 3.12, with } \sigma = \theta \text{ and} \\
&\qquad\qquad\quad \sigma_n = \theta_n = \tan^{-1} 2^{-n} < 2^{-n}
\end{aligned}
$$

And, similarly,

$$|\sin \theta - Y_{n+1}| = |\sin \theta - \sin U_{n+1}| \le 2^{-n}$$

We may therefore conclude that provided there are no other errors—or that such errors are properly taken care of—the CORDIC recurrences will produce the correct bits of $\sin \theta$ and $\cos \theta$ at a rate of one bit per iteration, for each of the two functions. Errors are discussed further in Section 3.5.

3.2   Inverse trigonometric functions

The recurrences used above for the computation of sine and cosine can also be used to evaluate the arctangent function. This is done by reversing the process depicted in Figure 3.1. There, we started with a vector on the x axis and rotated through a known angle, θ. Here, we start with a vector at an unknown angle, θ, and rotate to the x axis to determine θ. This is the *vectoring mode* in CORDIC.

Suppose we start with a vector (X_0, Y_0), at some unknown angle, θ, from the x axis and rotate (backwards and forwards, as necessary) through a series of known angles, $\theta_0, \theta_1, \ldots, \theta_n$, so that we end up with a vector on the x axis; that is, with $(X_{n+1}, Y_{n+1}) = (X_{n+1}, 0)$ and a total rotation angle of $\sum_{i=0}^{n} s_i \theta_i$, where $s_i = \pm 1$. If the length of the initial vector is l, then $X_0 = l\cos\theta$ and $Y_0 = l\sin\theta$. So $\tan\theta = (Y_0/l)/(X_0/l) = Y_0/X_0$, and $\theta = \tan^{-1}(Y_0/X_0)$. Therefore, the accumulation of the rotation angles, with directions taken into account, amounts to a computation of an arctangent: if we start with $Z_0 = 0$ and accumulate the rotation angles in Z_i, then at the end we shall have $Z_{n+1} \approx \theta$.

To determine when the total rotation has been completed, the distance from the x axis of the vector being rotated is monitored. This corresponds to determining how close Y_i is to zero; so the direction of rotation is chosen as

$$s_i = \begin{cases} -1 \text{ if } Y_i \geq 0 \\ 1 \text{ if } Y_i < 0 \end{cases}$$

and the recurrences for the complete algorithm are

$$X_0 = x$$

$$Y_0 = y$$

$$Z_0 = 0$$

$$\theta_i = \tan^{-1} 2^{-i} \qquad i = 0, 1, 2, \ldots, n$$

$$X_{i+1} = X_i - s_i 2^{-i} Y_i$$

$$Y_{i+1} = Y_i + s_i 2^{-i} X_i$$

$$Z_{i+1} = Z_i - s_i \theta_i$$

$$s_i = \begin{cases} -1 \text{ if } Y_i \geq 0 \\ 1 \text{ otherwise} \end{cases}$$

The initial length of the vector being rotated is $l = \sqrt{X_0^2 + Y_0^2}$, and each iteration extends the length by a factor of $1/\cos\theta_i$. So at the end of $n+1$ iterations, we will have

$$X_{n+1} \approx K\sqrt{x^2 + y^2} \qquad K = \prod_{i=0}^{n} \sqrt{1 + 2^{-2i}}$$

$$Y_{n+1} \approx 0$$

$$Z_{n+1} \approx \tan^{-1}(y/x)$$

with a convergence range that is the same as that for rotation mode: for sufficiently large n—most practical values—the range for $\tan^{-1}(Y_0/X_0)$ is determined as for sine/cosine and is approximately $[-1.74, 1.74]$.

An example computation is given in Table 3.2. In general, the algorithm will compute

$$Z_{n+1} \approx Z_0 + \tan^{-1}(Y_0/X_0)$$

and $\tan^{-1}(y)$ is obtained by setting $Y_0 = y, X_0 = 1$, and $Z_0 = 0$.

$$x = 0.5 \qquad y = 0.25 \qquad \tan^{-1}(y/x) = 0.463648 \cdots$$

i	X_i	Y_i	Z_i	s_i
0	0.1000000000000000	0.0100000000000000	0.0000000000000000	-1
1	0.1100000000000000	-0.0100000000000000	0.1100100100001111	1
2	0.1110000000000000	0.0010000000000000	0.0101001001011110	-1
3	0.1110100000000000	-0.0001100000000000	0.1001000100010101	1
4	0.1110101100000000	0.0000010100000000	0.0111000100111111	-1
5	0.1110101101010000	-0.0000100110110000	0.1000000100111010	1
6	0.1110101110011101	-0.0000001001010101	0.0111100100111010	1
7	0.1110101110100110	0.0000000101011000	0.0111010100111010	-1
8	0.1110101110101001	-0.0000000001111110	0.0111011100111010	1
9	0.1110101110101010	0.0000000001101101	0.0111011000111010	-1
10	0.1110101110101010	-0.0000000000001000	0.0111011010111010	1
11	0.1110101110101010	0.0000000000110010	0.0111011001111010	-1
12	0.1110101110101010	0.0000000000010100	0.0111011010011010	-1
13	0.1110101110101010	0.0000000000000110	0.0111011010101010	-1
14	0.1110101110101010	-0.0000000000000001	0.0111011010110010	1
15	0.1110101110101010	0.0000000000000010	0.0111011010101110	-1
			$\tan^{-1}(y/x) \approx 0.4636$	

Table 3.2: Example of CORDIC $\tan^{-1} x$ computation

The $\sin^{-1} x$ and $\cos^{-1} x$ functions too can be computed by using the CORDIC recurrences—this time in rotation mode—but, as we next show, the process here is not as straightforward as for the sine, cosine, and arctangent.

Suppose we are given x and wish to compute $\cos^{-1} x$. (One can envisage a similar algorithm for $\sin^{-1} x$, by using Y_i to determine the direction of rotation.) In this case, a seemingly straightforward method would be to start with the unit-length vector, $(1, 0)$, and rotate to (X_n, Y_n), so that

$X_n = x$. If the angle accumulated during the rotation is θ, then we should have $\theta = \cos^{-1} x$. So it *appears* that the basic recurrences should change only in the comparsion step—the direction of rotation now being determined by a comparison of X_i with x—and therefore that the recurrences *should* be

$$X_0 = 1$$

$$Y_0 = 0$$

$$Z_0 = 0$$

$$\theta_i = \tan^{-1} 2^{-i}$$

$$X_{i+1} = X_i - s_i 2^{-i} Y_i$$

$$Y_{i+1} = Y_i + s_i 2^{-i} X_i$$

$$Z_{i+1} = Z_i + s_i \theta_i$$

$$s_i = \begin{cases} 1 & \text{if } X_i \geq x \\ -1 & \text{otherwise} \end{cases}$$

These "obvious" recurrences will not work, specifically in the determination of s_i: in each iteration i, X_i will be in excess by a factor of K_i, where

$$K_i = \prod_{k=0}^{i-1} \frac{1}{\cos \theta_k}$$

$$= \prod_{k=0}^{i-1} \sqrt{1 + 2^{-2k}}$$

and that needs to be taken into account.

An attempt to solve the problem by scaling the initial values, as is done above in the sine/cosine algorithm, will not work in a general solution: if $X_0 = 1/K$, then the algorithm will work only for $x \in [0, 1/K] \approx [0, 0.607]$. Unless that range is satisfactory, that leaves a substantial gap in the range, and a different solution is required. The remainder of this section discusses such solutions.

Given the extension factor in X_i, a better solution is to have the comparisons be between X_i and xK_i:

$$s_i = \begin{cases} 1 & \text{if } X_i \geq x_i \\ -1 & \text{otherwise} \end{cases} \qquad \text{where } x_i = xK_i$$

It is, however, not practical to compute x_i in each iteration. A direct way to do so would be to compute it cumulatively, by making use of the recurrence for x_{i+1} in terms of x_i:

$$x_{i+1} = \frac{x_i}{\cos \theta_i}$$

$$= x_i \sqrt{1 + 2^{-2i}}$$

but this would require a real multiplication instead of just SHIFT–ADD, (assuming the individual constants $1/\cos \theta_i$ are computed beforehand and stored). One way to eliminate the need for a real multiplication is to use double rotations instead of single ones [7]. That is, instead of a rotation by θ_i in each iteration, have two rotations, each by θ_i. The multiplicative factor per iteration is then $1/\cos^2 \theta_i$, and the comparisons are against xK_i^2:

$$s_i = \begin{cases} 1 \text{ if } X_i \geq x_i \\ -1 \text{ otherwise} \end{cases} \qquad \text{where } x_i = xK_i^2$$

We then have

$$x_{i+1} = x_i \left(\sqrt{1 + 2^{-2i}} \right)^2$$

$$= x_i + x_i 2^{-2i}$$

This is simpler than the first x_i recurrence above, but it still requires additional hardware in the implementation.

The complete set of recurrences for the computation of arccosine is then

$$X_0 = 1$$

$$Y_0 = 0$$

$$Z_0 = 0$$

$$x_0 = x$$

$$\theta_i = \tan^{-1} 2^{-i} \qquad\qquad i = 0, 1, 2, \ldots, n$$

$$x_{i+1} = x_i + x_i 2^{-2i}$$

$$X_{i+1}^* = X_i - s_i 2^{-i} Y_i$$

$$Y_{i+1}^* = Y_i + s_i 2^{-i} X_i$$

$$X_{i+1} = X_{i+1}^* - s_i 2^{-i} Y_{i+1}^*$$

$$Y_{i+1} = Y_{i+1}^* + s_i 2^{-i} X_{i+1}^*$$

$$Z_{i+1} = Z_i + 2 s_i \theta_i$$

$$s_i = \begin{cases} 1 \text{ if } X_i \geq x_i \\ -1 \text{ otherwise} \end{cases}$$

After $n + 1$ iterations, $Z_{n+1} \approx \cos^{-1} x$, and, considering the final length of the rotated vector, $Y_{n+1} = K^2 \sqrt{1 - x^2}$, where $K^2 = \prod_{i=0}^{n} \left(1 + 2^{-2i}\right)$. An example of the application of these recurrences is given in Table 3.3.

An algorithm for the computation of arcsine can be derived similarly, by considering Y_i instead of X_i and replacing x_i with y_i:

$$X_0 = 1$$

$$Y_0 = 0$$

$$Z_0 = 0$$

$$y_0 = x$$

$$\theta_i = \tan^{-1} 2^{-i} \qquad i = 1, 2, 3, \ldots$$

$$y_{i+1} = y_i + y_i 2^{-2i}$$

$$X_{i+1}^* = X_i - s_i 2^{-i} Y_i$$

$$Y_{i+1}^* = Y_i + s_i 2^{-i} X_i$$

$$X_{i+1} = X_{i+1}^* - s_i 2^{-i} Y_{i+1}^*$$

$$Y_{i+1} = Y_{i+1}^* + s_i 2^{-i} X_{i+1}^*$$

$$Z_{i+1} = Z_i + 2 s_i \theta_i$$

$$s_i = \begin{cases} 1 \text{ if } Y_i \leq y_i \\ -1 \text{ otherwise} \end{cases}$$

After $n + 1$ iterations, $Z_{n+1} \approx \sin^{-1} x$.

The obvious issue with the type of algorithm just presented is in the modifications required of the basic CORDIC algorithm and in the implementation. In implementation, the hardware that constitutes the inner loop of the basic CORDIC must be extended to allow for the double rotations (with attendant increases in cost or time per cycle), or, if the basic

CORDIC hardware is retained, twice as many cycles will be required. Additionally, extra hardware will be required for the computation of x_i; that computation is also on the critical path and so will increase the cycle time. We next sketch the basics of a different approach, for just the $\cos^{-1}$ case; the reader will find additional details in [8].

Consider the first proposal above for an algorithm for $\cos^{-1} x$. If X_0 is set to $1/K$, where $K = \prod_{i=0}^{n} \sqrt{1 + 2^{-2i}}$, then in iteration i, X_i will be in excess by K_i/K, where $K_i = \prod_{k=0}^{i-1} \sqrt{1 + 2^{-2k}}$. The proposal in [8] is to determine s_i on the basis of a comparison between X_i and xK_i/K; this is on the grounds that it is easier to obtain and use good approximations of K_i/K than of K_i. An approximation will suffice, provided it is easy to compute and ensures convergence, and one can be obtained by taking the first few terms in the Taylor-series expansion[8] corresponding to K_i/K:

$x = 0.5$ $\qquad\qquad$ $\cos^{-1} x = 1.047198\cdots$

i	X_i	Y_i	Z_i	s_i
0	01.0000000000000000	00.0000000000000000	00.0000000000000000	1
1	00.0000000000000000	10.0000000000000000	01.1001001000011111	-1
2	10.0000000000000000	01.1000000000000000	00.1010010010111100	1
3	01.0010000000000000	10.0110100000000000	01.0010001000101010	-1
4	01.1011010110000000	10.0001011001100000	00.1110001001111110	1
5	01.0111000011111110	10.0100101011111001	01.0000001001110100	1
6	01.0100101111110010	10.0110000101110110	01.0001001001110010	-1
7	01.0101111011101001	10.0101011011110001	01.0000101001110011	1
8	01.0101010110001000	10.0101110001100011	01.0000111001110011	-1
9	01.0101101000111111	10.0101100110110101	01.0000110001110011	-1
10	01.0101110010011001	10.0101100001011011	01.0000101101110011	1
11	01.0101101101101100	10.0101100100001001	01.0000101111110011	1
12	01.0101101011010110	10.0101100101100000	01.0000110000110011	-1
13	01.0101101100100001	10.0101100100110100	01.0000110000010011	1
14	01.0101101011111100	10.0101100101001010	01.0000110000100011	-1
15	01.0101101100001111	10.0101100100111111	01.0000110000011011	-1
			$\cos^{-1}(x) \approx 1.047$	

Table 3.3: Example of CORDIC $\cos^{-1} x$ computation

[8]See Table 6.2.

$$\frac{K_i}{K} = \prod_{k=i}^{n} \sqrt{1 + 2^{-2k}}$$

$$\approx \prod_{k=i}^{n} \left(1 - \frac{1}{2}2^{-2k} + \frac{3}{8}2^{-4k}\right)$$

$$\approx 1 - \frac{1}{2}2^{-2i} \sum_{k=0}^{n-i} 2^{-2k} + \frac{3}{8}2^{-4i} \sum_{k=0}^{n-i} 2^{-4k}$$

If n is large enough, then $\sum_{j=0}^{n-1-k} 2^{-4j} \approx 1$; so the last expression is approximately

$$1 - \frac{1}{2}2^{-2i} \left[\sum_{k=0}^{n-i} 2^{-2k} + \frac{3}{4}2^{-2i}\right]$$

A good approximation should have as few terms as possible but still be good enough to ensure convergence. The first term alone is clearly insufficient, and it can be shown that the first two terms together are also insufficient. A simple approximation that that doesn't completely neglect the third term is obtained by observing that the signs of the first two terms are different and also taking into account the relative weights of the terms. One then arrives at

$$1 - \frac{1}{2}2^{-2i} \sum_{k=0}^{\min(i-1,n/2)} 2^{-2k}$$

For the implementation, a formulation is used such that the values of xK_i/K can be computed recursively using only additions and shifts.

Compared with the double-rotation algorithm, the algorithm here also allows for the easy computation of $\sqrt{1 - x^2}$ without the final scaling by K^2 that is required in the former: here, $Y_{n+1} \approx \sqrt{1 - x^2}$. On the other hand, the precisions required of the operands and in the datapath are higher, and the implementation is less straightforward in the details.

3.3   Hyperbolic functions and inverses

Recurrences similar to those for sine and cosine (and their inverses) can be derived for the evaluation of sinh and cosh (and their inverses). The rotation here is on the hyperbola $X^2 - Y^2 = 1$, as shown in Figure 3.2.

The parametric equations for the hyperbola are

$$X = \cosh u$$
$$Y = \sinh u$$

where u is the nominal rotation angle. Proceeding as above for sine and cosine, suppose we start here with (X_i, Y_i) at an angle ϕ, and rotate by θ_i. Then

$$\begin{aligned}
X^*_{i+1} &= \cosh(\theta_i + \phi) \\
&= \cosh\theta_i \cosh\phi + \sinh\theta_i \sinh\phi \\
&= X_i \cosh\theta_i + Y_i \sinh\theta_i
\end{aligned}$$

$$\begin{aligned}
Y^*_{i+1} &= \sinh(\theta_i + \phi) \\
&= \sinh\theta_i \cosh\phi + \cosh\theta_i \sinh\phi \\
&= X_i \sinh\theta_i + Y_i \cosh\theta_i
\end{aligned}$$

Setting $X_{i+1} = X^*_{i+1}/\cosh\theta_i$ and $Y_{i+1} = Y^*_{i+1}/\cosh\theta_i$, we obtain

$$X_{i+1} = X_i + Y_i \tanh\theta_i$$
$$Y_{i+1} = Y_i + Y_i \tanh\theta_i$$

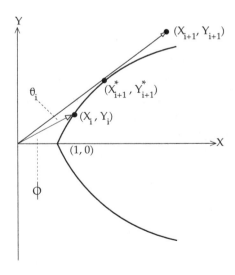

Figure 3.2: CORDIC rotation mode ($\sinh x$ and $\cosh x$)

In a manner similar to the case of the sine–cosine algorithm, we eliminate the nominal multiplications by taking the constants θ_i to be $\tanh^{-1} 2^{-i}$. With this choice, the rotations must now start at $i = 1$ because $\tanh^{-1} 2^0 = \infty$. Therefore, the rotation-mode recurrences for the computation of $\sinh x$ and $\cosh x$ are

$$X_1 = 1/K_*$$

$$Y_1 = 0$$

$$Z_1 = x$$

$$\theta_i = \tanh^{-1} 2^{-i} \qquad\qquad i = 1, 2, 3, \ldots, n$$

$$X_{i+1} = X_i + s_i 2^{-i} Y_i$$

$$Y_{i+1} = Y_i + s_i 2^{-i} X_i$$

$$Z_{i+1} = Z_i - s_i \theta_i$$

$$s_i = \begin{cases} 1 \text{ if } Z_i \geq 0 \\ -1 \text{ otherwise} \end{cases}$$

(The value of the scaling constant, K_*, depends on how convergence is ensured; this is discussed below.)

At the end of n iterations

$$Z_{n+1} \approx 0$$

$$X_{n+1} \approx \cosh x$$

$$Y_{n+1} \approx \sinh x$$

An example computation is given in Table 3.4; the repetitions there of iterations 4 and 13 are explained below. With $\theta_i = \tanh^{-1} 2^{-i}$, the application of Inequation 3.21 gives the range for Z_1 (the argument) as about $[-1.12, 1.12]$ for large n.

In general, the recurrences will compute

$$X_{n+1} \approx K_*(X_1 \cosh Z_1 + Y_1 \sinh Z_1)$$

$$Y_{n+1} \approx K_*(Y_1 \cosh Z_1 + X_1 \sinh Z_1)$$

and from the values of $\sinh x$ and $\cosh x$, exponentials are readily available:

$$e^x = \sinh x + \cosh x$$

Convergence here is not achieved as easily as in the sine–cosine algorithm, because the choice $\theta_i = \tanh^{-1} 2^{-i}$ does not satisfy Inequation 3.8 of the Decomposition Theorem. This can be seen by, for example, considering the case $i = n - 1$:

$$\theta_{n-1} > \theta_n + \theta_n = 2\theta_n$$

contrary to what Inequation 3.8 requires. On the other hand

$$\theta_{n-1} \leq \theta_n + 2\theta_n = 3\theta_n$$

which shows that Inequation 3.8 would be satisfied if iteration n were repeated.

$x = 1$ $\quad$ $\cosh x = 1.543081 \cdots$ $\quad\quad$ $\sinh x = 1.175201 \cdots\cdots$

i	X_i	Y_i	Z_i	s_i
1	1.0011010100011110	0.0000000000000000	1.0000000000000000	1
2	1.0011010100011110	0.1001101010001111	0.0111001101100000	1
3	1.0101101111000010	0.1110011111010110	0.0011000111111101	1
4	1.0111100010111101	1.0001001101001111	0.0001000111010010	1
4	1.1000100111110010	1.0010101011011011	0.0000000111001101	1
5	1.1001110010011111	1.0100001101111010	-0.0000111000110111	-1
6	1.1001001010000100	1.0011011010010101	-0.0000011000110111	-1
7	1.1000110110101001	1.0011000001001011	-0.0000001000110111	-1
8	1.1000101101001001	1.0010110100101111	-0.0000000000110111	-1
9	1.1000101000011011	1.0010101110100100	0.0000000011001000	1
10	1.1000101010110001	1.0010110001101001	0.0000000001001000	1
11	1.1000101011111100	1.0010110011001100	0.0000000000001000	1
12	1.1000101100100010	1.0010110011111101	-0.0000000000010111	-1
13	1.1000101100001111	1.0010110011100100	-0.0000000000000111	-1
13	1.1000101100000110	1.0010110011011000	0.0000000000000000	-1
14	1.1000101011111100	1.0010110011001100	0.0000000000001000	1
15	1.1000101100000001	1.0010110011010010	0.0000000000000100	1
16	1.1000101100000011	1.0010110011010101	0.0000000000000010	1
	$\cosh x \approx 1.543$	$\sinh x \approx 1.175$		

Table 3.4: Examples of CORDIC $\sinh x$ and $\cosh x$ computations

---

It is straightforward to show that in all cases Inequation 3.8 will be satisfied if, say, every iteration is repeated, or if every other iteration is repeated, or if every third iteration is repeated, and so forth. But, fortunately, far fewer iterations must be repeated: it is sufficient to repeat iterations $4, 13, 40, \ldots, i, 3i + 1, \ldots$; that is, iterations $g(k) = (3^{k+1} - 1)/2, k = 1, 2, 3, \ldots$. So the iteration numbers will now be 1, 2, 3, 4, 4, 5, 6, 7, 8, 9, 10, 11, 12, 13, 13, 14, and so forth. For practical computations, the precisions are such that the number of repeated iterations is unlikely to exceed four (which is sufficient for 120-bit results).

The value of the scaling constant, K_*, evidently depends on which iterations are repeated. If the repeated iterations are $g(1), g(1), \ldots, g(m)$ then

$$K_* = \prod_{i=1}^{n} \frac{1}{\cosh \theta_i} \prod_{k=1}^{m} \frac{1}{\cosh \theta_{g(k)}}$$

$$= \prod_{i=1}^{n} \sqrt{1 - 2^{-2i}} \prod_{k=1}^{m} \sqrt{1 - 2^{-2g(k)}}$$

Inverses

The algorithm for $\tan^{-1} x$ was obtained by "reversing" the mode of computation used in the algorithm for $\sin x$ and $\cos x$, i.e. by changing from rotation mode to vectoring mode. An algorithm for $\tanh^{-1} x$ can be similarly obtained by using the recurrences for $\sinh x$ and $\cosh x$ in vectoring mode:

$$X_1 = x$$

$$Y_1 = y$$

$$Z_1 = 0$$

$$\theta_i = \tanh^{-1} 2^{-i} \qquad\qquad i = 1, 2, 3, \ldots$$

$$X_{i+1} = X_i + s_i 2^{-i} Y_i$$

$$Y_{i+1} = Y_i + s_i 2^{-i} X_i$$

$$Z_{i+1} = Z_i - s_i \theta_i$$

$$s_i = \begin{cases} -1 \text{ if } Y_i \geq 0 \\ 1 \text{ otherwise} \end{cases}$$

At the end of n iterations, the length of the rotated vector is $K_* \sqrt{X_0^2 - Y_0^2}$; so we have

$$X_{n+1} \approx K_* \sqrt{x^2 - y^2}$$

$$Y_{n+1} \approx 0$$

$$Z_{n+1} \approx \tanh^{-1}\left(\frac{y}{x}\right)$$

with a convergence range that is the same as that for rotation mode: for large n, the range for $\tanh^{-1}(Y_0/X_0)$ is approximately $[-1.12, 1.12]$. An example computation is given in Table 3.5.

In general, the algorithm will compute $Z_1 + \tanh^{-1}(Y_1/X_1)$. So $\tanh^{-1}(y)$ is obtained by setting $Y_1 = y, X_1 = 1$, and $Z_1 = 0$.

$$x = 0.03 \qquad y = 0.02 \qquad \tanh^{-1}(2/3) = 0.804719\cdots$$

i	X_i	Y_i	Z_i	s_i
1	0.0000011110101110	0.0000010100011110	0.0000000000000000	-1
2	0.0000010100011110	0.0000000101000111	0.1000110010011111	-1
3	0.0000010011001100	0.0000000000000000	0.1100111000000010	-1
4	0.0000010011001100	-0.0000000010011001	0.1110111000101101	1
4	0.0000010011000011	-0.0000000001001100	0.1101111000100111	1
5	0.0000010010111110	-0.0000000000000000	0.1100111000100010	1
6	0.0000010010111110	0.0000000000100101	0.1100011000100001	-1
7	0.0000010010111101	0.0000000000010010	0.1100101000100001	-1
8	0.0000010010111101	0.0000000000001000	0.1100110000100001	-1
9	0.0000010010111101	0.0000000000000100	0.1100110100100001	-1
10	0.0000010010111101	0.0000000000000001	0.1100110110100001	-1
11	0.0000010010111101	0.0000000000000000	0.1100110111100001	-1
12	0.0000010010111101	0.0000000000000000	0.1100111000000001	-1
13	0.0000010010111101	-0.0000000000000000	0.1100111000010001	1
13	0.0000010010111101	-0.0000000000000000	0.1100111000001001	1
14	0.0000010010111101	0.0000000000000000	0.1100111000000001	-1
15	0.0000010010111101	-0.0000000000000000	0.1100111000000101	1
16	0.0000010010111101	-0.0000000000000000	0.1100111000000011	1
			$\tanh^{-1}(y/x) \approx 0.8047$	

Table 3.5: Example of CORDIC $\tanh^{-1} x$ computation

Once we are able to compute $\tanh^{-1}(Y_1/X_1)$, we can also compute natural logarithms (and, therefore, logarithms to any base), by applying the identity

$$\ln u = 2\tanh^{-1}\frac{u+1}{u-1}$$

$\ln u \approx 2Z_{n+1}$ if we set $X_1 = u + 1$ and $Y_1 = u - 1$.

The square root function too can be computed indirectly through the same reccurrences: at the end of the iterations, $X_{n+1} = K_*\sqrt{X_1^2 - Y_1^2}$; so setting $X_1 = (u + 1/4)/K_*^2$ and $Y_1 = (u - 1/4)/K_*^2$ gives $X_{n+1} \approx \sqrt{u}$.

The same approach used, in Section 3.2, to derive double-rotation algorithms for $\sin^{-1} x$ and $\cos^{-1} x$ can be used here to derive algorithms for $\sinh^{-1}$ and $\cosh^{-1}$. (It is understood that all rotations including the "special" ones—i.e. 4, 13, 40, etc.—are repeated.) For $\cosh^{-1}$, the recurrences are

$$X_1 = 1/K_*{}^2$$

$$Y_1 = 0$$

$$Z_1 = 0$$

$$x_1 = x$$

$$\theta_i = \tanh^{-1}(2^{-i}) \qquad\qquad i = 1, 2, 3, \ldots, n$$

$$x_{i+1} = x_i + x_i 2^{-2i}$$

$$X_{i+1}^* = X_i + s_i 2^{-i} Y_i$$

$$Y_{i+1}^* = Y_i + s_i 2^{-i} X_i$$

$$X_{i+1} = X_{i+1}^* + s_i 2^{-i} Y_{i+1}^*$$

$$Y_{i+1} = Y_{i+1}^* + s_i 2^{-i} X_{i+1}^*$$

$$Z_{i+1} = Z_i + 2 s_i \theta_i$$

$$s_i = \begin{cases} 1 \text{ if } X_i \geq x_i \\ -1 \text{ otherwise} \end{cases}$$

After n iterations, $Z_{n+1} \approx \cosh^{-1} x$, and, considering the length of the rotated vector, $Y_{n+1} = \sqrt{1 + x^2}$.

And for $\sinh^{-1} x$, the recurrences are

$$X_1 = 1/K_*^2$$

$$Y_1 = 0$$

$$Z_1 = 0$$

$$y_1 = x$$

$$\theta_i = \tanh^{-1}(2^{-i}) \qquad\qquad i = 1, 2, 3, \ldots$$

$$y_{i+1} = y_i + y_i 2^{-2i}$$

$$X_{i+1}^* = X_i + s_i 2^{-i} Y_i$$

$$Y_{i+1}^* = Y_i + s_i 2^{-i} X_i$$

$$X_{i+1} = X_{i+1}^* + s_i 2^{-i} Y_{i+1}^*$$

$$Y_{i+1} = Y_{i+1}^* + s_i 2^{-i} X_{i+1}^*$$

$$Z_{i+1} = Z_i + 2 s_i \theta_i$$

$$s_i = \begin{cases} 1 \text{ if } Y_i \leq y_i \\ -1 \text{ otherwise} \end{cases}$$

After n iterations, $Z_{n+1} \approx \sinh^{-1} x$.

3.4 Linear functions

The CORDIC recurrences can also be used for several other functions, such as multiplication and division. This, however, is not a particularly efficient way to do things. It is rarely done, and should probably not be done, unless it is critical to amortize cost (assuming the hardware is already there to compute the functions for which CORDIC is well suited).[9] The nominal rotations here are on a line parallel to the y axis, as shown in Figure 3.3.

When used in rotation mode, i.e.

$$s_i = \begin{cases} 1 \text{ if } Z_i \geq 0 \\ -1 \text{ otherwise} \end{cases}$$

---

[9]This remark applies as well to all "indirect" uses of CORDIC to compute other functions.

$n + 1$ iterations of the corresponding recurrences

$$X_0 = x$$

$$Y_0 = y$$

$$Z_0 = z$$

$$\theta_i = 2^{-i} \qquad i = 0, 1, 2, 3, \ldots$$

$$X_{i+1} = X_i$$

$$Y_{i+1} = Y_i + s_i 2^{-i} X_i \qquad (3.22)$$

$$Z_{i+1} = Z_i - s_i \theta_i \qquad (3.23)$$

will, as we next show, compute the multiply–add function

$$Y_{n+1} \approx Y_0 + X_0 \times Z_0$$

$$Z_{n+1} \approx 0$$

of which plain multiplication is just the special case with $Y_0 = 0$.

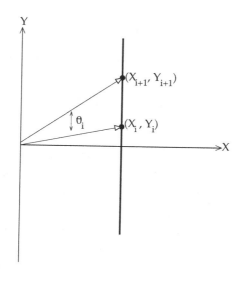

Figure 3.3: CORDIC rotation for multiplication and division

The values $\theta_i = 2^{-i}$ evidently satisfy the conditions in the Decomposition Theorem; so the iterations will converge. And from Equations 3.22 and 3.23:

$$Y_{n+1} = Y_0 + \sum_{i=0}^{n} s_i 2^{-i} X_i$$

$$= Y_0 + X_0 \sum_{i=0}^{n} s_i 2^{-i}$$

$$Z_{n+1} = Z_0 - \sum_{i=0}^{n} s_i 2^{-i} X_i$$

Since $Z_{n+1} \approx 0$, we have $Z_0 \approx \sum_{i=0}^{n} s_i 2^{-i}$. Therefore, $Y_{n+1} \approx Y_0 + X_0 \times Z_0$.

With $\theta_i = 2^{-i}$, the application of Equation 3.21 gives the range $|Z_0| \leq 2$. And the bound on the magnitude of error is 2^{-n}.

$$x = 0.37 \qquad z = 0.48 \qquad x \times z = 0.1776$$

i	X_i	Y_i	Z_i	s_i
0	0.0101111010111000	0.0000000000000000	0.0111101011100001	1
1	0.0101111010111000	0.0101111010111000	-0.1000010100011110	-1
2	0.0101111010111000	0.0010111101011100	-0.0000010100011110	-1
3	0.0101111010111000	0.0001011110101110	0.0011101011100001	1
4	0.0101111010111000	0.0010001110000101	0.0001101011100001	1
5	0.0101111010111000	0.0010100101110000	0.0000101011100001	1
6	0.0101111010111000	0.0010110001100110	0.0000001011100001	1
7	0.0101111010111000	0.0010110111100001	-0.0000000100011110	-1
8	0.0101111010111000	0.0010110100100011	0.0000000011100001	1
9	0.0101111010111000	0.0010110110000010	-0.0000000000011110	-1
10	0.0101111010111000	0.0010110101010011	0.0000000001100001	1
11	0.0101111010111000	0.0010110101101010	0.0000000000100001	1
12	0.0101111010111000	0.0010110101110110	0.0000000000000001	1
13	0.0101111010111000	0.0010110101111100	-0.0000000000001110	-1
14	0.0101111010111000	0.0010110101111001	-0.0000000000000110	-1
15	0.0101111010111000	0.0010110101111000	-0.0000000000000010	-1
		$x \times z \approx 0.1776$		

Table 3.6: Example of CORDIC multiplication

$$x = 0.37 \qquad y = 0.48 \qquad y/x = 1.297297\cdots$$

i	X_i	Y_i	Z_i	s_i
0	0.0101111010111000	0.0111101011100001	0.0000000000000000	-1
1	0.0101111010111000	0.0001110000101000	1.0000000000000000	-1
2	0.0101111010111000	-0.0001001100110011	1.1000000000000000	1
3	0.0101111010111000	0.0000010001111010	1.0100000000000000	-1
4	0.0101111010111000	-0.0000011101011100	1.0110000000000000	1
5	0.0101111010111000	-0.0000000101110000	1.0101000000000000	1
6	0.0101111010111000	0.0000000110000101	1.0100100000000000	-1
7	0.0101111010111000	0.0000000000001010	1.0100110000000000	-1
8	0.0101111010111000	-0.0000000010110011	1.0100111000000000	1
9	0.0101111010111000	-0.0000000001010100	1.0100110100000000	1
10	0.0101111010111000	-0.0000000000100101	1.0100110010000000	1
11	0.0101111010111000	-0.0000000000001101	1.0100110001000000	1
12	0.0101111010111000	-0.0000000000000001	1.0100110000100000	1
13	0.0101111010111000	0.0000000000000100	1.0100110000010000	-1
14	0.0101111010111000	0.0000000000000001	1.0100110000011000	-1
15	0.0101111010111000	-0.0000000000000000	1.0100110000011100	1
			$y/x \approx 1.2973$	

Table 3.7: Example of CORDIC division

An example of CORDIC multiplication is given in Tables 3.6. In vectoring mode, i.e. with

$$s_i = \begin{cases} -1 \text{ if } Y_i \geq 0 \\ 1 \text{ otherwise} \end{cases}$$

$n + 1$ iterations of the same recurrences will compute the divide–add function:

$$Z_{n+1} \approx Z_0 + Y_0/X_0$$
$$Y_{n+1} \approx 0$$

of which plain division is just the special case with $Z_0 = 0$. And for the convergence range, Equation 3.21, with $\theta_i = 2^{-i}$ gives $|Y_0/X_0| \leq 2$, with the magnitude of error at most 2^{-n}. In this case, $Y_{n+1} \approx 0$; so, from Equations 3.22 and 3.23:

$$Y_0 + X_0 \sum_{i=0}^{n} s_i 2^{-i} X_i \approx 0$$

$$\sum_{i=0}^{n} s_i 2^{-i} X_i = -\frac{Y_0}{X_0}$$

and

$$Z_{n+1} = Z_0 - \sum_{i=0}^{n} s_i 2^{-i} X_i$$

Therefore, $Z_{n+1} \approx Z_0 + Y_0/X_0$.

An example of CORDIC division ($Z_0 = 0$) is given in Tables 3.7.

3.5   Errors and datapath precision

We now take another look at errors. The objective here is to determine the datapath precisions that are required in the implementation, as well as the precisions required for the rotation angles, θ_i. We shall consider only the computations for sine and cosine, the others being largely similar.[10] The error analysis is not very refined, but it is adequate as a guide for implementation parameters. More detailed discussions on errors will be found in [9, 11]; the primary results are similar to those given here.

In CORDIC, approximation error occurs because what is essentially an infinite process gets truncated to a finite number of iterations. As we have noted above, after $n + 1$ iterations, this error is at most 2^{-n}. In order to achieve this accuracy in a practical implementation, it is necessary to take care of the errors that are generated in each iteration and propagated through subsequent ones.

Consider the recurrences for X_i and Y_i. In each iteration, the new values computed involve values from the preceding iteration but shifted right by i bits. If we wish to completely eliminate the effect (on final results) of generated errors, then, in principle, the datapath must be of sufficient precision to retain all bits after the shifting. Now, the total shift

---

[10]Depending on the function and the range of arguments, additional integer bits may be required—to accommodate $1/K_*$ for the hyperbolic functions, the argument range for the linear functions, and the magnitudes of the variables in the inverse-trigonometric computations (such as that of Table 3.3), etc.

length is $\sum_{i=0}^{n} i = (n+1)(n+2)/2 \approx n^2/2$, and it would not be practical to realize that much additional precision in the datapath. So in practice, the results of each iteration must be rounded to an acceptable precision, say, m. We seek to determine a reasonable value for m. Specifically, we seek to determine how many additional bits, beyond n, are required to "absorb" all generated errors before they can "contaminate" the n bits of the result proper.

Assume that the aforementioned rounding is through simple chopping[11] and that the arithmetic includes the use of g guard bits at the low-order end of each of representation. Then the error, in each of the X and Y variables, after each iteration is at most $2^{-(n+g)}$. So after $n+1$ iterations, the total error is bounded by

$$(n+1)2^{-(n+g)}$$

and we want this to be less than 2^{-n}:

$$(n+1)2^{-(n+g)} < 2^{-n}$$

which implies that

$$g > \lceil \log_2(n+1) \rceil$$

An additional bit is required for the sign; so we should have

$$m > n + \lceil \log_2(n+1) \rceil + 1$$

For the computation of Z_i, there is no shifting involved. Therefore, there are no generated errors, provided the datapath precision is sufficiently high.[12] The propagated errors are just the representation errors in the angles θ_i; these do add up, and limiting them determines the precisions for the datapath and the angles. If we assume that each angle is represented with p fractional bits, and we want the error after $n+1$ iterations to be less than 2^n, then we must have

$$(n+1)2^{-p} < 2^{-n}$$

i.e.

$$p > n + \lceil \log_2(n+1) \rceil$$

To this is to be added two integer bits: one bit to accommodate the range of Z_0 and one bit for the sign. Therefore, the required precision is

$$n + \lceil \log_2(n+1) \rceil + 3$$

---

[11] With round to nearest, one bit less is required. See Section 1.1.
[12] A close examination will show that it costs little to ensure exact arithmetic.

3.6   Implementation

Excluding the variations that have been discussed above, which variations the reader can readily accommodate by refining what follows, the CORDIC recurrences may be summarized as

$$X_{i+1} = X_i - \mu s_i 2^{-i} Y_i$$
$$Y_{i+1} = Y_i + s_i 2^{-i} X_i$$
$$Z_{i+1} = Z_i - s_i \theta_i$$

where:

- For *circular* rotations, $\mu = 1$ and $\theta_i = \tan^{-1} 2^{-i}$.
- For *linear* rotations, $\mu = 0$ and $\theta_i = 2^{-i}$.
- For *hyperbolic* rotations, $\mu = -1$ and $\theta_i = \tanh^{-1} 2^{-i}$.

In rotation mode, Z_i is forced towards zero by choosing

$$s_i = \begin{cases} 1 \text{ if } Z_i \geq 0 \\ -1 \text{ otherwise} \end{cases}$$

and in vectoring mode, Y_i is forced towards zero by choosing

$$s_i = \begin{cases} -1 \text{ if } Y_i \geq 0 \\ 1 \text{ otherwise} \end{cases}$$

On the basis of the preceding summary, the organization of a generic and basic hardware unit for the CORDIC computations is as shown in Figure 3.4. The arrangement consists of three loops: one for the computation of X_i, one for the computation of Y_i, and one for the computation of Z_i. The operational details are largely self-explanatory. There are nevertheless two aspects, one minor and one major, that are worth noting.

The minor point is that for large enough i, $\tan^{-1} 2^{-i} = 2^{-i}$ to within machine precision; so fewer constants need be stored than at first appears to be the case. That is so because[13]

$$\tan^{-1} 2^{-i} = 2^{-i} - \frac{2^{-3i}}{3} + \frac{2^{-5i}}{5} - \frac{2^{-7i}}{7} + \cdots$$

and for n-bit precision, if $i > n/3$, then all of the terms after the first are negligible.

The major point is that all the adders in Figure 3.4 are carry–propagate adders; and if performance is important, then these should be replaced

---
[13]See the Taylor series in Table 6.4.

with carry–save adders or signed-digit adders. The changes required to facilitate such replacement include fundamental changes in the nature of the algorithms and are discussed in Chapter 4.

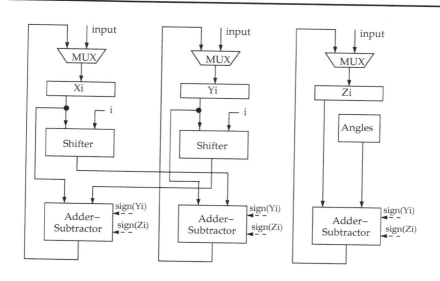

Figure 3.4: Basic hardware organization for CORDIC

The basic architecture of Figure 3.4 can be enhanced in several straightforward ways. One is to "unroll" the hardware loop—i.e. replicate the core of Figure 3.4, once for each iteration—in order to exploit more parallelism and pipelining [10]. This is appropriately known as *unrolled* (or *unfolded*) CORDIC and is depicted in Figure 3.5. It will be observed that the hardware costs do not increase in proportion to the degree of unrolling. In particular, in contrast with the architecture of Figure 3.4, the relatively costly barrel shifters are no longer required, as each shift is now hardwired through the inter-stage connections. The lookup table too is no longer required, as the constants may be hardwired, but this does not necessarily result in any useful reduction in cost. Lastly, some of the control logic can be simplified. Between architectures of Figures 3.4 and 3.5, different degrees of partial unrolling and pipelining are possible, the degrees being determined by the desired trade-off between increased cost and increased performance (latency or throughput).

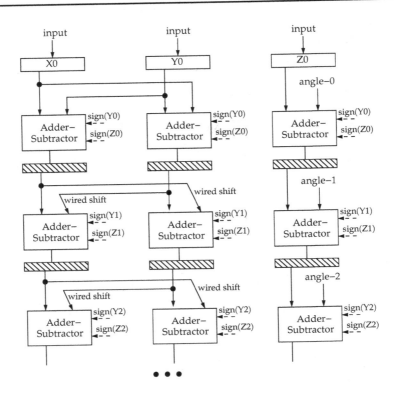

Figure 3.5: Hardware organization for unrolled CORDIC

If, on the other hand, one seeks to reduce cost (relative to the architecture of Figure 3.4), then hardware may be shared. The X_i and Y_i recurrences are largely similar, as are the corresponding hardware components. So the same hardware components can be shared, by using a pipelined structure in which the X_i and Y_i computations for a given iteration proceed concurrently, but in different stages of the pipeline. (One could also include the Z computations in the same pipeline and share the adder.) Figure 3.6 is indicative of how such an arrangement might work. The pipeline consists of two stages and operates in two cycles per iteration. In the first cycle, the Y_i (X_i) gets shifted in the first stage while at the same time the addition to compute X_{i+1} (Y_{i+1}) takes place in the second stage. In the second cycle, the value of $2^{-i}Y_i$ ($2^{-i}X_i$) from the first cycle is used to compute X_{i+1} (Y_{i+1}) while the result of the last second cycle is returned for a new iteration. The price to be paid for such sharing is a small penalty in the operational time, but the reduction in hardware cost is substantial.

And at the extreme end of low-cost design is of totally bit-serial, shared hardware components. Considering such a design and the fully unrolled hardware, we see that there is a wide range in designs, according to the cost:performance ratio desired.

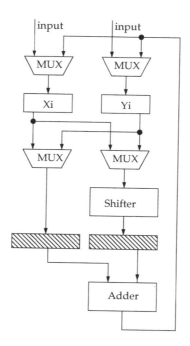

Figure 3.6: Shared X-Y pipeline for CORDIC

Chapter 4

High-Performance CORDIC

This chapter covers extensions of the CORDIC algorithms of Chapter 3. The main basis of the variants discussed here is the use of redundant number representations to achieve high performance—by allowing the elimination of arithmetic operations in some cyles, facilitating faster arithmetic, and making it easy to use radices larger than two.

The starting point in speeding up the algorithms of Chapter 3 is the observation that in implementations (Figures 3.4–3.6) of those algorithms, carry–propagate adders lie on the critical paths. So there are two basic ways in which computations can be speeded up. One way is to reduce the number of iterations in which arithmetic operations are carried out; this is done by using redundant number representation in the selection process for the arithmetic operation to be performed and is the subject of the first section of the chapter. The other way, covered in the second through fifth sections, is to eliminate the carry propagation, by implementing the arithmetic operations in redundant representations; this requires that results ultimately be converted into conventional form. And the two may be combined in a single implementation. Redundant number representations also facilitate the use of radices larger than two; this aspect is covered in the last section of the chapter. All these techniques are also standard in the implementation of high-speed multipliers and dividers (Chapter 2).

We shall not give much by way of convergence proofs or error analysis. For the most part, the discussions of Chapter 3 can readily be extended to cover the new instances; the reader who insists on satisfaction on these points should have a go at modifying the approaches taken in that chapter. We shall also consider only the sine and cosine functions, extensions to the other CORDIC functions being largely straightforward. For the implementations, it is assumed that in all cases the stored values, computed values, and datapaths include the requisite number of guard digits ($\lceil \log_r K \rceil + 1$ for K iterations in radix r), as discussed in Section 3.5.

The CORDIC industry has been active for over fifty years, and its products are numerous. The algorithms discussed in this book are only a few notable ones that have been selected to demonstrate particular points. The reader will find many more variants in the published literature, but is also likely to find that the variations are mostly of a minor nature relative to the algorithms included here.

4.1   De Lugish CORDIC

This algorithm might be viewed as "largely historical", but it is nevertheless included for two main reasons. First, as we shall see below, some of the essential ideas in its formulation will be found in "modern" algorithms. Second, its formulation highlights the primary difficulties that arise when one considers the use of redundant number representation in CORDIC. Also, as we explain below, the algorithm might still be useful even now.

One of the earliest proposals for the use of redundant representations is in [1], the motivation there being the possibility of avoiding arithmetic operations, as well as shifting, in some iterations. The introduction of 0 into the digit set for s_i facilitates this: no actions are required when $s_i = 0$. So in the binary case, the digit set changes from $\{\bar{1}, 1\}$ to $\{\bar{1}, 0, 1\}$.

The basic algorithm for the modification is that for the binary computation of sine and cosine (Section 3.1):

$$X_0 = \frac{1}{K} \qquad\qquad K = \prod_{i=0}^{n} \sqrt{1 + 2^{-2i}}$$

$$Y_0 = 0$$

$$Z_0 = \theta$$

$$\theta_i = \tan^{-1}(2^{-i}) \qquad\qquad i = 0, 1, 2, \ldots$$

$$s_i = \begin{cases} 1 & \text{if } Z_i \geq 0 \\ \bar{1} & \text{otherwise} \end{cases}$$

$$X_{i+1} = X_i - s_i 2^{-i} Y_i$$

$$Y_{i+1} = Y_i + s_i 2^{-i} X_i$$

$$Z_{i+1} = Z_i - s_i \theta_i$$

The obvious difficulty that arises if the digit set is changed to $\{\overline{1}, 0, 1\}$ is in the computation of the scaling factor, K. In the basic algorithm, scaling by K is required in order to correct the vector-length extension, by a factor of $\sqrt{1 + 2^{-2i}}$, that occurs in each iteration, i, because of the use of pseudo-rotations rather than true rotations. The general expression for the per-iteration extension factor is $\sqrt{1 + s_i^2 2^{-2i}}$. If the digit set is $\{\overline{1}, 1\}$, then $s_i^2 = 1$ in all cases, and the extension factor is $\sqrt{1 + 2^{-2i}}$. As there is a rotation in every iteration, the total scaling required over a given number of iterations can be computed beforehand; and, by appropripate scaling in the initialization of X_i, per-iteration scaling by $\sqrt{1 + s_i^2 2^{-2i}}$, or final scaling by K, is thus avoided. In general, computing K beforehand and then scaling in the initialization is obviously problematic when the digit set for s_i is $\{\overline{1}, 0, 1\}$: no scaling is required when $s_i = 0$, but these instances are operand-dependent. On the other hand, per-iteration scaling is not practical, unless performance is to be ignored. And, for the same reason, scaling by division at the end of the iterations should be avoided, if possible, given that division is about as difficult as the main task.

In the De Lugish algorithm, the solution to the scaling problem is to run the first few iterations with the non-redundant digit set, $\{\overline{1}, 1\}$, and then run the remainder with the redundant one, $\{\overline{1}, 0, 1\}$. The fundamental idea is that after a sufficiently large number of iterations, the per-iteration scaling factors don't change (to within the given machine precision) because 2^{-2i} is extremely small: for large enough i, it is the case that $\sqrt{1 + s_i^2 2^{-2i}} \approx 1$. So from that point, on redundant representation may be used for s_i without any awkward issues about scaling. Before that point, either non-redundant representation is used, with an appropriate scaling factor computed beforehand (for all the corresponding iterations), or redundant representation is used (with appropriate corrections). The details are as follows.

The Taylor-series expansion of the per-iteration scaling factor is[1]

$$\frac{1}{\sqrt{1 + s_i^2 2^{-2i}}} = 1 - \frac{1}{2} s_i^2 2^{-2i} + \frac{3}{8} \left(s_i^2 2^{-2i} \right)^2 - \frac{5}{16} \left(s_i^2 2^{-2i} \right)^3 + \cdots \quad (4.1)$$

and at the end of the iterations, for an n-bit result, we should like the result to be correct to within 2^{-n}, this being a reasonable expectation given the machine limitations. Now, at some point during the iterations, say after iteration $i = j$, 2^{-2i} will be sufficiently small that

$$\frac{3}{8} \left(2^{-2i} \right)^2 < 2^{-n} \qquad i > j \qquad (4.2)$$

---

[1] See Table 6.2.

at which point, to machine precision (i.e. after rounding), Equation 4.1 may be viewed as

$$\frac{1}{\sqrt{1 + s_i^2 2^{-2i}}} \approx 1 - \frac{1}{2} \left(s_i^2 2^{-2i} \right) \tag{4.3}$$

And at some point after that, say after iteration $i = m$, it will be the case that

$$\frac{1}{2} s_i^2 2^{-2i} < 2^{-n}$$

and therefore

$$\frac{1}{\sqrt{1 + s_i^2 2^{-2i}}} \approx 1 \qquad\qquad i > m \tag{4.4}$$

with error not exceeding 2^{-n}. So in iterations $m+1, m+2, \ldots, n$, no scaling is required.

The nominal values for j and m are $\lceil (n-2)/4 \rceil + 1$ and $\lceil (n-1)/2 \rceil$; but for practical implementation, g guard digits would mostly likely be used (Section 3.5) and are taken into account replacing n with $n + g$ in these expressions.

Equations 4.2–4.4 are applied as follows. The digit set $\{\bar{1}, 1\}$ is used until iteration j, and up to that point, s_i is determined, as usual, by comparing Z_i with zero:

$$s_i = \begin{cases} 1 & \text{if } Z_i \geq 0 \\ \bar{1} & \text{otherwise} \end{cases} \qquad\qquad i = 0, 1, \ldots, j$$

The scaling factor to which X_0 is set is $1/K_j$, where

$$K_j = \prod_{i=0}^{j} \sqrt{1 + 2^{-2i}}$$

From iteration $j+1$ to m, the digit set $\{\bar{1}, 0, 1\}$ is used, and s_i is determined by comparing the magnitude of Z_i with a suitable, small constant, k:

$$s_i = \begin{cases} 1 & \text{if } Z_i > k \\ 0 & \text{if } -k \leq Z_i \leq k \\ \bar{1} & \text{if } Z_i < -k \end{cases} \qquad\qquad i = j+1, j+2, \ldots, m$$

For iterations $j+1$ to m, it is also necessary to include the correction implied by Equation 4.3. So the effective X and Y recurrences are

$$X_{i+1} = \kappa \left(X_i - s_i 2^{-i} Y_i \right) \qquad \kappa = 1 - s_i^2 2^{-(2i+1)}$$

$$Y_{i+1} = \kappa \left(Y_i + s_i 2^{-i} X_i \right)$$

The correction is easily realized by shifting and subtracting. Such corrections can be avoided if more iterations—say half the total number—are carried out with the non-redundant digit set. We shall see this in the algorithms of Section 4.6.

For the remaining iterations, i.e. $m + 1$ to n, the digit set is $\{\bar{1}, 0, 1\}$, and s_i is determined as in the preceding case. But, as a consequence of Equation 4.4, no additional actions are necessary.

The value of k in the the s_i-selection rule is determined by two factors. First, in order to continue iterating when the value of Z_i falls into the middle range, k should change with i; second, k should be easily computable. A good choice is to take $k = \alpha 2^i$, for some constant α. It is easy to show that the algorithm will converge if $\alpha = 1/2$. If the objective is to reduce the number of iterations with no arithmetic, then other choices of α will be better.[2] For an example of the latter, including a detailed convergence proof, the interested reader is referred to [1], in which $\alpha = 3/4$.

The comparison in the the s_i-selection rule can be made against a constant value, by scaling Z_i by 2^i: if $U_i \triangleq 2^i Z_i$, then the equations for s_i and Z_i are replaced with

$$s_i = \begin{cases} 1 & \text{if } U_i > 1/2 \\ 0 & \text{if } -1/2 \leq U_i \leq 1/2 \\ \bar{1} & \text{if } U_i < -1/2 \end{cases}$$

$$U_{i+1} = 2(U_i - s_i 2^i \theta_i)$$

Such replacement of variables is standard practice with algorithms of this type, and several instances will be found elsewhere in this book (Chapters 2, 5 and 8). The scaling removes leading non-significant bits, thus ensuring that the bits to be examined are always in the same positions at the front.

Although redundant representation is used in the algorithm, it is outside the arithmetic. As given, the arithmetic will still be in conventional representation, and any performance gains (over the basic alogorithm of

---

[2] Briefly: the use here of redundant signed-digit (RSD) representation is similar to such use in certain multiplication algorithms, in which an on-the-fly recoding takes place from conventional notation into RSD notation (Chapter 2). The value of α determines how close to optimal the recoding is.

Chapter 3) would have to come from avoiding shifting and arithmetic operations in those instances when $s_i = 0$. Such computation means variable, i.e. operand-dependent, operational times, which in some cases is undesirable. Nevertheless, as we shall see in Section 4.6 and elsewhere in this book, the use of redundancy in the manner indicated does facilitate the employment of radices larger than two; in that, the essential idea above— i.e. running some iterations with one digit set, until the scaling factor is effectively a constant, and then switching to another digit set—is very useful. It might also be the case that one has to work with whatever arithmetic functional units are available and that doing so precludes the option of implementing redundant-representation arithmetic. In such a case, the present algorithm, even though not "state of the art", can still be useful.

If one starts with the intention of using redundant representation— carry–save (CS) or redundant signed-digit (RSD)—for the arithmetic, then one is also more naturally led to the use of RSD for s_i. The explanation for this is as follows.

In the basic CORDIC algorithms, $s_i \in \{\bar{1}, 1\}$ is chosen on the basis of the *sign* of the current value of some variable, and this requires the examination of just one bit. Moreover, it can be done exactly. With CS and RSD representations for the arithmetic, the exact sign cannot be determined without performing a conversion to conventional notation. But such a conversion would require the equivalent of a relatively slow, full-length carry–propagate operation, which is exactly what the use of redundant representation is supposed to eliminate. So in practice, the decision will be made on the basis of an "approximate sign" that is obtained from just a few bits of the relevant CS or RSD operand. That poses a difficulty, given that the decision is based on an approximation that might be incorrect. A direct way to deal with the uncertainty is to allow a third possibility in the decision: $s_i = 0$. We then have three possibilities in rotation: the direction is definitely known to be forward ($+1$), or definitely known to be backward (-1), or not known with certainty (0, i.e. no rotation). Therefore, in radix 2, the non-redundant digit set $\{\bar{1}, 1\}$ is replaced with the redundant digit set $\{\bar{1}, 0, 1\}$. This approach, when used with radices larger than two, is the "high-end extreme" of the CORDIC algorithms and is discussed in Section 4.6.

It is, however, possible to handle the aforementioned uncertainty in ways that do not require the explicit choice of $s_i = 0$, although the overall effect will be similar; this alternative might be desirable in order to avoid complications in the calculation of the scaling factor, K. We next discuss such algorithms. In these, wherever RSD is used for the arithmetic, it is equally possible to use CS instead. The latter is generally to be preferred for the relative simplicity of the basic arithmetic units; but in several algorithms that have been devised specifically for RSD, a change to CS is likely to complicate the detailed algorithm. We leave it to the reader to work out the relevant details in each case.

4.2   Correcting-Rotations CORDIC

In the *Correcting-Rotations CORDIC* [3], the arithmetic is in RSD representation, which means that, as indicated above, there will sometimes be some uncertainty when determining the arithmetic operations. This is dealt with in a manner that does not require $s_i = 0$ (i.e. the use of a redundant digit set) in the operation selection. The details are as follows.

In the algorithm, most iterations are "normal" ones, but in every m-th iteration a "correction" is made that covers the preceding $m - 1$ rotations. For every iteration j, where $j \bmod m \neq 0$, the applicable recurrences are exactly the standard ones:

$$X_{i+1} = X_i - s_i 2^{-i} Y_i$$
$$Y_{i+1} = Y_i + s_i 2^{-i} X_i$$
$$Z_{i+1} = Z_i - s_i \theta_i$$

but for each of the other iterations, there is a "correction" that consists of an extra rotation:

$$\widetilde{X}_{i+1} = X_i - s_i 2^{-i} Y_i$$
$$\widetilde{Y}_{i+1} = Y_i + s_i 2^{-i} X_i$$
$$\widetilde{Z}_{i+1} = Z_i - s_i \theta_i$$

$$X_{i+1} = \widetilde{X}_{i+1} - \widetilde{s}_i 2^{-i} \widetilde{Y}_{i+1}$$
$$Y_{i+1} = \widetilde{Y}_{i+1} + \widetilde{s}_i 2^{-i} \widetilde{X}_{i+1}$$
$$Z_{i+1} = \widetilde{Z}_{i+1} - \widetilde{s}_i \theta_i$$

The values of all these variables are represented in RSD notation,[3] and Z_i and $\widetilde{Z}_i$ are binary fractions whose most significant bits are at positions i after the binary point. (Further details on this point are given below.) At the end of the iterations, the values of X_i and Y_i are converted from RSD representation into conventional representation.

---

[3]CS representation would be equally applicable.

In the "no-correction" case, s_i is determined on the basis of the leading $m - k + 3$ signficant bits of Z_i, where $k = j \bmod m$:

$$s_i = \begin{cases} 1 & \text{if } \left[Z_i^i Z_i^{i+1} \cdots Z_i^{i+m-k+2} \right] \geq 0 \\ \bar{1} & \text{otherwise} \end{cases}$$

where the representation of Z_i is taken to be $Z_i^0 . Z_i^1 \cdots Z_i^n$, and $[***]$ denotes the value represented by the $***$.

In the "correction" case, s_i is chosen according to the leading three significant bits of Z_i, and $\tilde{s}_i$ is chosen according to the leading $m+2$ significant bits of $\widetilde{Z}_i$:

$$s_i = \begin{cases} 1 & \text{if } \left[Z_i^i Z_i^{i+1} Z_i^{i+2} \right] \geq 0 \\ \bar{1} & \text{otherwise} \end{cases}$$

$$\tilde{s}_i = \begin{cases} 1 & \text{if } \left[\widetilde{Z}_{i+1}^{i+1} \widetilde{Z}_{i+1}^{i+2} \cdots \widetilde{Z}_{i+1}^{i+m+2} \right] \geq 0 \\ \bar{1} & \text{otherwise} \end{cases}$$

The total scaling factor is constant and is a combination of the per-iteration scaling factors over all iterations and the scaling factors for the repeated iterations (whose number is known beforehand):

$$K_* = \prod_{i=0}^{n} \sqrt{1 + 2^{-2i}} \prod_{i=0}^{\lfloor (n+1)/m \rfloor} \sqrt{1 + 2^{-2im}}$$

So the complete algorithm is as shown in Table 4.1.

In the arithmetic, some care is needed to ensure that the most significant digit of Z_i is at position i, and this is done as follows. An addition or subtraction is performed, to yield a result whose most signficant digit is at position $i - 1$. The $i + m - k + 3$ most significant digits of Z_i are evaluated, and digit $i + 1$ of Z_{i+1} is set to that value, which will be $\bar{1}$, or 0, or 1. This works because it can be shown, by straightforward induction over i, that

$$-\tan^{-1} 2^{-i} - 2^{-i-m+k-1} < Z_i < \tan^{-1} 2^{-i}$$

and, since $\tan^{-1} 2^{-(i+1)} < 2^{-(i+1)}$, it follows that

$$-2^{-i} - 2^{-i-m+k-1} < Z_i < 2^{-i}$$

Therefore, Z_i can be represented by a fraction whose most significant digit is at position i. (Note also the restriction on the range of θ: it is always fractional.)

An example computation is shown in Table 4.2. Evidently, the choice of m involves a trade-off: a large value means fewer corrections, but also an increase in the latency of a single iteration, because of the required conversion[4] of the $m - k + 3$ bits of Z_i.

Relative to plain CORDIC, the cost of implementing the Correcting-Rotations CORDIC is an increase in the operational latency from the extra rotations, and the control logic will also be slightly more complex.

---

i = 0, 1, 2, 3, ...

$X_0 = 1/K_*$
$Y_0 = 0$

$Z_0 = \theta \qquad 0 \leq \theta \leq \pi/4$

$\theta_i = \tan^{-1}(2^{-i})$

$k = i \bmod m$
if $k \neq 0$

$s_i = \begin{cases} 1 \text{ if } \left[Z_i^i \cdots Z_i^{i+m-k+2}\right] \geq 0 \\ \bar{1} \text{ otherwise} \end{cases}$

$X_{i+1} = X_i - s_i 2^{-i} Y_i$
$Y_{i+1} = Y_i + s_i 2^{-i} X_i$
$Z_{i+1} = Z_i - s_i \theta_i$
}

else
{

$s_i = \begin{cases} 1 \text{ if } \left[Z_i^i \cdots Z_i^{i+2}\right] \geq 0 \\ \bar{1} \text{ otherwise} \end{cases}$

$\widetilde{s}_i = \begin{cases} 1 \text{ if } \left[\widetilde{Z}_{i+1}^{i+1} \cdots \widetilde{Z}_{i+1}^{i+m+2}\right] \geq 0 \\ \bar{1} \text{ otherwise} \end{cases}$

$\widetilde{X}_{i+1} = X_i - s_i 2^{-i} Y_i$
$\widetilde{Y}_{i+1} = Y_i + s_i 2^{-i} X_i$

$X_{i+1} = \widetilde{X}_{i+1} - \widetilde{s}_i 2^{-i} \widetilde{Y}_{i+1}$
$Y_{i+1} = \widetilde{Y}_{i+1} + \widetilde{s}_i 2^{-i} \widetilde{X}_{i+1}$
$Z_{i+1} = \widetilde{Z}_i - \widetilde{s}_i \theta_i$
}

Table 4.1: Double-Rotations CORDIC algorithm

4.3 Branching CORDIC

As we have noted above, when redundant-representation arithmetic is used, there may be some uncertainty in the selection of s_i (between $\bar{1}$ and 1) and that one way to deal with this is to allow the choice of $s_i = 0$; but that complicates the computation of the scaling factor, K. In *Branching*

---

[4]The conversion is to conventional form, for the comparisons, and is equivalent to a carry–propagate addition over those bits.

CORDIC, the uncertainly is handled by running two parallel computations of the standard CORDIC algorithm (Section 3.1)—one for $s_i = \bar{1}$ and one for $s_i = 1$—until the correct path can be determined [4, 5]. The details are as follows.

$\theta = \pi/6$ $\sin\theta = 0.500000\cdots$ $\cos\theta = 0.866025\cdots$

i	s_i	Z_i	X_i	Y_i
0	1	0.10000110000	0.11011011011	0.00000000000
1	1	0.0001000$\bar{1}$1$\bar{1}$0	0.11011011011	0.11001101101
2	$\bar{1}$	0.0$\bar{1}$1$\bar{1}$0000100	1.00000000000	0.1010010010$\bar{1}$
3	$\bar{1}$	0.000$\bar{1}$0001$\bar{1}$0$\bar{1}$	1.0$\bar{1}$111$\bar{1}$101$\bar{1}$00	1.$\bar{1}$0010$\bar{1}$01$\bar{1}$01
$\tilde{4}$	1	0.00000001$\bar{1}$0$\bar{1}$	1.0$\bar{1}$100$\bar{1}$1$\bar{1}$1$\bar{1}$0	1.$\bar{1}$0000001011
4	$\bar{1}$	0.000$\bar{1}$0001$\bar{1}$0$\bar{1}$	1.0$\bar{1}$1$\bar{1}$1$\bar{1}$1$\bar{1}$1$\bar{1}$0	1.$\bar{1}$01$\bar{1}$01$\bar{1}$1$\bar{1}$000
5	$\bar{1}$	0.0000$\bar{1}$001$\bar{1}$0$\bar{1}$	1.0$\bar{1}$101010$\bar{1}$1$\bar{1}$1	1.$\bar{1}$00010$\bar{1}$010$\bar{1}$
6	$\bar{1}$	0.00000$\bar{1}$01$\bar{1}$0$\bar{1}$	1.00$\bar{1}$01100$\bar{1}$10	1.$\bar{1}$00001$\bar{1}$1000
7	$\bar{1}$	0.000000$\bar{1}$1$\bar{1}$0$\bar{1}$	1.00$\bar{1}$00$\bar{1}$010$\bar{1}$0	1.$\bar{1}$0000011$\bar{1}$1$\bar{1}$0
$\tilde{8}$	$\bar{1}$	0.00000000$\bar{1}$0$\bar{1}$	1.00$\bar{1}$00$\bar{1}$1$\bar{1}$1$\bar{1}$0	1.$\bar{1}$000000010$\bar{1}$
8	1	0.00000001$\bar{1}$0$\bar{1}$	1.00$\bar{1}$00$\bar{1}$100$\bar{1}$0	1.$\bar{1}$0000000$\bar{1}$00
9	1	0.0000000000$\bar{1}$	1.00$\bar{1}$000$\bar{1}$1100	1.$\bar{1}$0000000000
			↓	↓
			CONVERSION	CONVERSION
			↓	↓
			0.11011101100	0.10000000000
			≈ 0.865	≈ 0.500

Table 4.2: Example computation in Correcting-Rotations CORDIC

The value represented by a few leading digits of Z_i is examined. If that value indicates clearly that $s_i = \bar{1}$ or $s_i = 1$ is the correct choice, then that choice is made, and the X_{i+1}, Y_{i+1}, and Z_{i+1} computations are carried out accordingly. If, however, there is some uncertainty, then two parallel computations are initiated, one corresponding to $s_i = \bar{1}$ and the other to $s_i = 1$. This is the "branching".

Using "+" for the $s_i = 1$ path and "−" for the $s_i = \bar{1}$ path, we now have two sets of recurrences:

$$X_{i+1}^{+} = X_i^{+} - s_i 2^{-i} Y_i^{+}$$
$$Y_{i+1}^{+} = Y_i^{+} + s_i 2^{-i} X_i^{+}$$
$$Z_{i+1}^{+} = Z_i^{+} - s_i \theta_i$$

$$X_{i+1}^- = X_i^- - s_i 2^{-i} Y_i^-$$
$$Y_{i+1}^- = Y_i^- + s_i 2^{-i} X_i^-$$
$$Z_{i+1}^- = Z_i^- - s_i \theta_i$$

Arithmetic is in RSD representation, but CS representation would be equally applicable. Only three digits of Z_i have to be examined in order to choose a path, and additional branching after the first is not possible.[5] The X and Y computations are straightforward, as indicated above. On the other hand, the computation of Z_i and the determination of s_i are more complicated and are according to the algorithm of Table 4.3.

The function eval returns some information on the approximate sign of Z_i, on the basis of the leading three digits of Z_i: it returns a value in $\{-1, 0, 1\}$ such that:

- If eval$(Z_i) \neq 0$, then it is the correct sign of Z_i.
- Otherwise, i.e. if there is some uncertainty, $|Z_i| \leq 2^{-(i+1)}$.

(The significance of the "otherwise" clause will become clear below.)

Let m be the value represented by the leading three digits of Z_i. Then

$$\text{eval}(Z_i) = \begin{cases} 1 & \text{if } m \bmod 8 \text{ is } 1, 2, \text{ or } 3 \\ -1 & \text{if } m \bmod 8 \text{ is } 5, 6, \text{ or } 7 \\ 0 & \text{if } m \bmod 8 \text{ is } 0 \\ * & \text{if } m \bmod 8 \text{ is } 4 \end{cases}$$

It can be shown that another branching cannot occur within any branching. That a branching occurs shows that the value of Z_i is sufficiently small to ensure the convergence of the two subcomputations, i.e. that Z_i is tending to zero, and therefore one of those subcomputations may in fact be stopped. (See the value returned by eval above.) Also, if there is no further branching, then both computations will produce correct results; so the issue of knowing which of the two is the correct one does not arise.

Although Branching CORDIC will, if implemented properly, be faster than the CORDIC algorithms that require repeated iterations, an implementation will not be twice as fast. Therefore, the doubling of logic required means a relatively poor cost:performance ratio. An alternative to the architecture of Figure 4.3 is one of an on-line, most-siginificant-digit-first version of the algorithm. Such a version is described in [4] and should give a better cost:performance figure.

---

[5]The proof of this will be found in [4].

procedure updateZ(i)
begin update
  do parallel
    $Z_i^+ := Z_i^+ - s_i^+ \theta_i;$
    $Z_i^- := Z_i^- - s_{i,}\theta_i$
  end do parallel;
  do parallel
    $s^+ := \text{eval}(Z_{i+1});$
    $s^- := \text{eval}(Z_{i+1});$
  end do parallel;
end update ;
begin main
  $i := 0;$
  $Z_0^+ := \theta;$
  $Z_0^- := \theta;$
  $s^+ := \text{eval}(Z_0^+);$
  $s^- := \text{eval}(Z_0^-)$
1: **while** $(s^+ \neq 0$
     and $s_- \neq 0)$ **do**
    // no branching //
    begin
      $s_i^+ := s_+;$
      $s_i^- := s_-;$
      updateZ(i);
      $i := i + 1;$
    end while;
2: // branching //
  $s_i^+ := 1;$
  $s_i^- := -1;$
  updateZ(i);
  $i := i + 1$
  goto 1;
  // branching ended //

3: **while** $(s^+ = -1$ **and** $s^- = 1)$ **do**
    // while branching //
    begin
      $s_i^+ := s^+$
      $s_i^- := s^-;$
      updateZ(i);
      $i := i + 1$
  end while;
  // new branching or
    end of branching //
  if $s^+ = 0$ **then**
  // "+" module performed
   the correct computation//
  begin
    $Z_i^+ := Z_i^-;$
    goto 2; // branching //
  end if
  else if $s^+ = 1$ **then**
  // "+ module performed
   the correct computation //
  begin
    $Z_i^- := Z_i^+;$
    $s^- := s^+;$
    goto 1; // branching ended //
  end elseif
  else if $s^- = 0$ **then**
  // "-" module correct //
  begin
    $Z_i^+ := Z_i^-;$
    goto 2; //branching //
  end elseif;
  else if $s^- = -1$ **then**
  // "-" module correct //
  begin
    $Z_i^+ := Z_i^-;$
    $s^+ := s^-;$
    goto 1;
  end elseif;
end main

Table 4.3: Z_i computation in Branching CORDIC

Double-Step Branching CORDIC [6] is a modification of Branching CORDIC, devised so that in each iteration two bits of the result are produced. A key difference between the two types of CORDIC is that whereas in the latter algorithm the two modules perform different computations on branching and otherwise perform identical computations, in the former the two modules always perform different computations at each step. The implementation of the modified algorithm requires additional hardware, but that would compensated for by the gain in performance [7]. Nevertheless, when the cost:performance ratio is considered, it is unlikely that the overall gain will be substantial.

4.4   Differential CORDIC

Differential CORDIC [8] uses binary redundant signed-digit (RSD) representation in the arithmetic, which in implementation means better performance than with basic CORDIC, but it does so in a way that does not require RSD for the arithmetic-operation selection. Therefore, the scaling factor is constant.

Unlike other algorithms discussed in this chapter, the Differential CORDIC is closely coupled to a particular type of architecture—the Unrolled CORDIC of Section 3.6 (Figure 3.5)—for the implementation. Whereas the other algorithms can be implemented reasonably without "unrolling", here the unrolling is essential; without it, the resulting implementation would have an excessively high operational time. This, of, course means that the cost of any reasonable—with respect to performance— implementation of Differential CORDIC must be high, relative to that of typical implementations of other types of CORDIC algorithms.

The basic idea in the Differential CORDIC is this: In the rotation mode of basic CORDIC, the rotations are determined so as to drive the values of $|Z_{i+1}| = ||Z_i| - \theta_i|$ to zero; therefore, the standard Z recurrence may be replaced with one based on absolute values. This is then extended to vectoring mode.

With RSD used for the arithmetic, computing an absolute value is inherently a slow, serial process.[6] But the essence of pipelining is that where the same type of operation is repeated in different instances, hardware can be arranged so that the operational latency shows up for only the first instance. That can be done here too, and it explains why an unrolled/pipelined im-

---

[6]See Section 2.1.2.

plementation is essential for Differential CORDIC. (Additional remarks are made below on this point.)

The starting point for Differential CORDIC is the standard Z-recurrence:

$$Z_{i+1} = Z_i - s_i\theta_i \tag{4.5}$$

$$s_i = \begin{cases} 1 & \text{if } Z_i \geq 0 \\ \overline{1} & \text{otherwise} \end{cases}$$

In terms of absolute values

$$|Z_i| = s_i Z_i \tag{4.6}$$

If we define

$$\widetilde{Z}_{i+1} = s_i Z_{i+1}$$

$$\widetilde{s}_i = \begin{cases} 1 & \text{if } \widetilde{Z}_i \geq 0 \\ \overline{1} & \text{otherwise} \end{cases}$$

then

$$|\widetilde{Z}_{i+1}| = |Z_{i+1}| \tag{4.7}$$

And by considering the different combinations of values of s_i and Z_{i+1}, we see that

$$\widetilde{s}_{i+1} = s_i s_{i+1}$$

so

$$s_{i+1} = \frac{1}{s_i}\widetilde{s}_{i+1}$$

$$= \widetilde{s}_{i+1} s_i \tag{4.8}$$

We also have

$$\widetilde{Z}_{i+1} = s_i Z_{i+1}$$
$$= s_i Z_i - s_i^2 \theta_i$$
$$= |Z_i| - \theta_i \qquad \text{by Equation 4.6 and } s_i = \pm 1$$
$$= |\widetilde{Z}_i| - \theta_i \qquad \text{by Equation 4.7}$$

So the use of Equation 4.5 may be replaced with that of

$$\widetilde{Z}_{i+1} = |\widetilde{Z}_i| - \theta_i$$

The X and Y recurrences are unchanged from the standard CORDIC; in particular, they require the values of s_i, which depend on those of Z_i.

We no longer have the values of Z_i, but, starting with s_0, the values of s_i can be computed recursively, by applications of Equation 4.8.

Putting together all of the above, we obtain the set of recurrences for the rotation mode in Differential CORDIC:

$$X_0 = \frac{1}{K} \qquad\qquad K = \prod_{i=0}^{n} \sqrt{1 + 2^{-2i}}$$

$$Y_0 = 0$$

$$\widetilde{Z}_0 = |Z_0| = |\theta|$$

$$s_0 = \begin{cases} 1 & \text{if } Z_0 \geq 0 \\ -1 & \text{otherwise} \end{cases}$$

$$\theta_i = \tan^{-1}(2^{-i}) \qquad\qquad i = 0, 1, 2, \ldots, n$$

$$X_{i+1} = X_i - s_i 2^{-i} Y_i$$

$$Y_{i+1} = Y_i + s_i 2^{-i} X_i$$

$$\widetilde{Z}_{i+1} = \left| \widetilde{Z}_i \right| - \theta_i$$

$$\widetilde{s}_{i+1} = \begin{cases} 1 & \text{if } \widetilde{Z}_{i+1} \geq 0 \\ -1 & \text{otherwise} \end{cases}$$

$$s_{i+1} = \widetilde{s}_{i+1} s_i$$

An example computation is given in Table 4.4.

For vectoring mode, the recurrences are simplified by assuming that $x > 0$; the negative values can be taken care of through the use of standard algebraic identities.

The vectoring-mode recurrences:

$$\widetilde{X}_0 = x$$

$$\widetilde{Y}_0 = |Y_0| = |y|$$

$$Z_0 = 0$$

$$s_0 = \begin{cases} 1 & \text{if } Y_0 \geq 0 \\ -1 & \text{otherwise} \end{cases}$$

$$\theta_i = \tan^{-1}(2^{-i}) \qquad\qquad i = 0, 1, 2, \ldots, n$$

$$\widetilde{X}_{i+1} = \widetilde{X}_i + 2^{-i}\left|\widetilde{Y}_i\right|$$

$$\widetilde{Y}_{i+1} = \left|\widetilde{Y}_i\right| - 2^{-i}\widetilde{X}_i$$

$$Z_{i+1} = Z_i + s_i\theta_i$$

$$\widetilde{s}_{i+1} = \begin{cases} 1 & \text{if } \widetilde{Y}_{i+1} \ge 0 \\ -1 & \text{otherwise} \end{cases}$$

$$s_{i+1} = \widetilde{s}_{i+1}s_i$$

$\theta = 0.75$ radians

i	X_i	Y_i	Z_i	s_i	$\widetilde{s}_i$
0	$1.\bar1010\bar110\bar1100\bar11\bar10$	0.000000000000000	$1.0\bar10000000000000$	1	*
1	$1.\bar1010\bar110\bar1100\bar11\bar10$	$1.\bar1010\bar110\bar1100\bar11\bar10$	$0.000\bar110\bar11000\bar1001$	-1	-1
2	$1.00\bar11\bar101\bar101\bar1100\bar1$	$0.1\bar1010\bar110\bar1100\bar11\bar1$	$0.\bar101\bar101\bar101\bar110000$	1	-1
3	$1.0\bar1\bar1\bar1\bar1100\bar100000$	$1.\bar1001\bar1000000010\bar1$	$0.01\bar1100\bar1100\bar11\bar11\bar1$	1	1
4	$1.0\bar1001\bar101\bar1100001\bar1$	$1.\bar11001\bar1\bar1\bar1100001\bar1$	$0.0001000\bar1001\bar11\bar10$	1	1
5	$1.\bar1100\bar1\bar1\bar1\bar101\bar11\bar10$	$1.\bar1\bar11000\bar10001\bar11\bar1$	$0.0000000\bar10010\bar110$	-1	-1
6	$1.0\bar10000000001\bar010$	$1.\bar1\bar1\bar1\bar101\bar1010\bar11\bar10$	$0.0000\bar100100\bar10100$	1	-1
7	$1.\bar11000\bar1\bar1\bar110\bar10101$	$1.\bar1\bar1\bar110\bar1000101\bar11\bar10$	$0.0000010\bar10010\bar100$	1	1
8	$1.\bar11000\bar100000100\bar1$	$1.\bar1\bar1\bar110\bar110\bar110\bar1000$	$0.0000001\bar10010\bar100$	1	1
9	$1.\bar1100\bar110\bar110\bar10000$	$1.\bar1\bar1\bar1100\bar1010\bar11010$	$0.000000000010\bar100$	1	1
10	$1.\bar1100\bar110\bar10001\bar1\bar1\bar1$	$1.\bar1\bar1\bar1100\bar110\bar101\bar11\bar1$	$0.00000000\bar1010\bar101$	-1	-1
11	$1.\bar1100\bar110\bar1010\bar11\bar10$	$1.\bar1\bar1\bar1100\bar1\bar1\bar1010\bar11\bar1$	$0.000000000\bar1\bar1010\bar1$	-1	1
12	$1.\bar1100\bar110\bar1\bar1\bar101\bar1\bar1\bar1$	$1.\bar1\bar1\bar1100\bar1\bar1\bar10001\bar10$	$0.00000000000010\bar1$	-1	1
13	$1.\bar1100\bar110\bar1\bar1\bar1\bar1\bar110\bar1$	$1.\bar1\bar1\bar1100\bar101000\bar100$	$0.000000000000\bar1100$	1	-1
14	$1.\bar1100\bar110\bar1\bar1\bar1\bar11000$	$1.\bar1\bar1\bar1100\bar101000001\bar1$	0.000000000000000	1	1
15	$1.\bar1100\bar110\bar1\bar110100\bar1$	$1.\bar1\bar1\bar1100\bar1\bar1\bar1000000$	$0.00000000000000\bar1\bar11$	-1	-1
	$(\cos\theta \approx 0.7317)$	$(\sin\theta \approx 0.6816)$			

Table 4.4: Example of Differential CORDIC computation

The Differential CORDIC was devised for RSD-representation arithmetic, but can be readily modified for CS representation. Absolute RSD values are determined according to a serial version (most significant digit first) of the algorithm described in Section 2.1.2.3, which means that an absolute value cannot be determined correctly until the least significant digits of the representation have been processed. In a non-unrolled implementation, this would cause a substantial delay, and the algorithm would be of dubious worth.[7] But that is not so in the unrolled, pipelined implementation because digit-level parallelism can be exploited. (For that reason the architecture proposed is essentially that of Figure 3.5 but with RSD adders.) If the operand precision is N digits, then computing the first absolute value will take $N+1$ cycles; but thereafter one absolute value (and its sign) will be determined in every cycle. The effect on the computation of s_i of the long latencies in computing absolute values therefore shows up only once. The timing diagram of Figure 4.1 shows the production of the digits of the absolute values; $|Z_i|_j$ denotes digit j of $|Z_i|$.

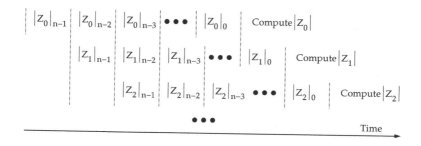

Figure 4.1: Timing of computation of absolute values

4.5 Double-Rotations CORDIC

Probably the earliest proposal for the use of redundant representation in both operation selection and arithmetic is that in [2]. There, the computations of X_i, Y_i, and Z_i are carried out in redundant signed-digit (RSD) representation, and the scaling problem is dealt with by accumulating the

---

[7]Assuming the implementation is not a digit-serial one, for which the effective situation would not be as bad.

scale factor in parallel with the rotations and then carrying out a division at the end of the iterations. This approach is probably acceptable for only a low-cost, low-performance implementation, and indeed the design in [2] is intended for serial hardware.

A different approach in the use of redundant representation in both arithmetic and operation selection is proposed in [3]. In this case too, the values of X_i, Y_i, and Z_i are all computed in RSD form, although carry–save representation would be equally applicable. The scaling problem is solved by always having two rotations in each iteration, thus ensuring a constant scaling factor that can computed beforehand. The basic idea is to replace the "standard" rotation angles, $\theta_i \stackrel{\triangle}{=} \tan^{-1} 2^{-i}$, with smaller angles, $\theta_i \stackrel{\triangle}{=} \tan^{-1} 2^{-(i+1)}$ and then have a rotation in every iteration: where there previously would have been a single backward rotation, there are now two backward rotations; where there previously would have been a single forward rotation, there are now two forward rotations; and instead of no rotation, there are now a backward rotation and a forward rotation. (With RSD explicitly used for s_i, these would correspond to choosing $s_i = \bar{1}, s_i = 1$, and $s_i = 0$ in the algorithms above.) We shall refer to the algorithm as the *Double-Rotations CORDIC*.

With the two rotations per iteration, the scaling factor is constant, K_{**}, which is a key objective in the formulation of the algorithm:

$$K_{**} = \prod_{i=0}^{n} \sqrt{1 + 2^{-2(i+1)}} \ \sqrt{1 + 2^{-2(i+1)}}$$

$$= \prod_{i=0}^{n} \left[1 + 2^{-2(i+1)} \right]$$

True double rotations would double the operational time, relative to that for basic CORDIC. To get around this, the recurrences for the double rotations are combined into single but slightly more complex recurrences, and the selections of the corresponding arithmetic operations are done concurrently.

If $s_i^* \in \{\bar{1}, 1\}$ denotes the direction of the first rotation in iteration i and $\tilde{s}_i^* \in \{\bar{1}, 1\}$ denotes the direction of the second rotation, then the iteration may be expressed as

$$\widetilde{X}_{i+1} = X_i - s_i^* 2^{-(i+1)} Y_i$$
$$\widetilde{Y}_{i+1} = Y_i + s_i^* 2^{-(i+1)} X_i$$
$$\widetilde{Z}_{i+1} = Z_i - s_i^* \theta_i$$

and

$$X_{i+1} = \widetilde{X}_{i+1} - \widetilde{s}_i^* 2^{-(i+1)} \widetilde{Y}_{i+1}$$
$$Y_{i+1} = \widetilde{Y}_{i+1} + \widetilde{s}_i^* 2^{-(i+1)} \widetilde{X}_{i+1}$$
$$Z_{i+1} = \widetilde{Z}_{i+1} - \widetilde{s}_i^* \theta_i$$

By substitution

$$X_{i+1} = \left(X_i - s_i^* 2^{-(i+1)} Y_i \right) - \widetilde{s}_i^* 2^{-(i+1)} \left(Y_i + s_i^* 2^{-(i+1)} X_i \right)$$
$$= X_i - (s_i^* + \widetilde{s}_i^*) 2^{-(i+1)} Y_i - s_i^* \widetilde{s}_i^* 2^{-2(i+1)} X_i$$

Now, $(s_i^* + \widetilde{s}_i^*) \in \{\overline{2}, 0, 2\}$, so we may replace the sum with $2s_i$, where $s_i \in \{\overline{1}, 0, 1\}$; and $s_i^* \widetilde{s}_i^* \in \{\overline{1}, 1\}$, so we may replace the product with $\widetilde{s}_i \in \{\overline{1}, 1\}$. We then end up with

$$X_{i+1} = X_i - s_i 2^{-i} Y_i - \widetilde{s}_i 2^{-2(i+1)} X_i$$

Similarly, the Y recurrence becomes

$$Y_{i+1} = Y_i + s_i 2^{-i} X_i - \widetilde{s}_i 2^{-2(i+1)} Y_i$$

The critical aspect of the algorithm is that s_i and $\widetilde{s}_i$ can be determined concurrently from Z_i.

Taking the $(n+1)$-digit representation of Z_i to be $Z_i^0 . Z_i^1 Z_i^2 \cdots Z_i^n$, the complete algorithm is

$$X_0 = 1/K_{**} \qquad\qquad K_{**} = \prod_{i=0}^{n} \left[1 + 2^{-2(i+1)} \right]$$

$$Y_0 = 0$$

$$Z_0 = \theta \qquad\qquad 0 \le \theta \le \pi/4$$

$$\theta_i = \tan^{-1} 2^{-(i+1)} \qquad\qquad i = 0, 1, 2, \ldots, n$$

$$X_{i+1} = X_i - s_i 2^{-i} Y_i - \widetilde{s}_i 2^{-2(i+1)} X_i$$

$$Y_{i+1} = Y_i + s_i 2^{-i} X_i - \widetilde{s}_i 2^{-2(i+1)} Y_i$$

$$Z_{i+1} = Z_i - 2 s_i \theta_i$$

$$(s_i, \widetilde{s}_i) = \begin{cases} (1, 1) & \text{if } \left[Z_i^i Z_i^{i+1} Z_i^{i+1} \right] > 0 \\ (0, \overline{1}) & \text{if } \left[Z_i^i Z_i^{i+1} Z_i^{i+2} \right] = 0 \\ (\overline{1}, 1) & \text{if } \left[Z_i^i Z_i^{i+1} Z_i^{i+2} \right] < 0 \end{cases}$$

where $[\ast\ast\ast]$ is the value represented by the digits $\ast\ast\ast$, these being the most signficant digits of Z_i. In the arithmetic, some care is needed to ensure that the most significant digit of Z_i is at position i: an addition or subtraction is performed, to yield a result whose most siginficant digit is at position $i-1$; the three most significant digits are evaluated; and digit $i+1$ of Z_{i+1} is set to that value, which will be -1, or 0, or 1. It can be shown, by straightforward induction over i, that

$$-2\tan^{-1}2^{-(i+1)} < Z_i < 2\tan^{-1}2^{-(i+1)}$$

And, since $\tan^{-1}2^{-(i+1)} < 2^{-(i+1)}$, that

$$-2^{-i} < Z_i < 2^{-i}$$

Therefore Z_i can be represented by a fraction whose most significant digit is at position i. (Note also that the restriction on the range of θ facilitates such representation.)

$\theta = \pi/6 \qquad \sin\theta = 0.500000\cdots \qquad \cos\theta = 0.866025\cdots$

i	$(s_i, \widetilde{s}_i)$	Z_i	X_i	Y_i
0	$(1,1)$	0.10000110000	0.11101100000	0.00000000000
1	$(0,\bar{1})$	0.00001001$\bar{1}$00	1.00$\bar{1}$000$\bar{1}\bar{1}\bar{1}$0	0.01110110000
2	$(0,\bar{1})$	0.00001001$\bar{1}$00	1.00$\bar{1}$000010$\bar{1}$0	0.100$\bar{1}$1000010
3	$(1,1)$	0.00001001$\bar{1}$00	1.00$\bar{1}$00010$\bar{1}\bar{1}\bar{1}$	1.$\bar{1}$000$\bar{1}$0001$\bar{1}$0
4	$(\bar{1},0)$	0.000$\bar{1}$1001$\bar{1}$00	1.00$\bar{1}$0$\bar{1}\bar{1}$000$\bar{1}$	1.$\bar{1}$001$\bar{1}$0$\bar{1}$01$\bar{1}$0
5	$(0,0)$	0.00000001$\bar{1}$00	1.00$\bar{1}$000$\bar{1}$001$\bar{1}$	1.$\bar{1}$0000000$\bar{1}$0$\bar{1}$
6	$(1,0)$	0.00000001$\bar{1}$00	1.008000$\bar{1}$0011$\bar{1}$	1.$\bar{1}$0000000$\bar{1}$0$\bar{1}$
7	$(\bar{1},0)$	0.000000$\bar{1}\bar{1}$100	1.00$\bar{1}$00$\bar{1}\bar{1}$101$\bar{1}$	1.$\bar{1}$00001$\bar{1}\bar{1}$011
8		0.00000000$\bar{1}$00	1.00$\bar{1}$001101$\bar{1}\bar{1}$	1.$\bar{1}$0000000010
			$\downarrow$	$\downarrow$
			CONVERSION	CONVERSION
			$\downarrow$	$\downarrow$
			0.11011101101	0.100000000010
			≈ 0.866	≈ 0.500

Table 4.5: Example computation in Double-Rotation CORDIC

The algorithm can be reformulated to use a single operation-selection variable (with the digit set $\{\bar{1}, 0, 1\}$)—instead of the two variables, s_i and

$\widetilde{s}_i$—and so better resemble other algorithms in such use of RSD. Nevertheless, the use here of RSD is still "indirect". In "direct" uses of RSD in operation selection—e.g. in the De Lugish algorithm and some of those that follow—the choice of $s_i = 0$ means that there need not be an arithmetic operation in the computation of X_i and Y_i. Here, there is always an arithmetic operation in every iteration.

The computations of the algorithm can be speeded up by observing that for n-bit results and $i \geq n/2$:

- The value of the third term in the X and Y recurrences is effectively zero, because $2^{-2(i+1)}$ is negligibly small; so that term need not be included in the additions.
- $\theta_i \stackrel{\triangle}{=} \tan^{-1} 2^{-(i+1)}$ is effectively $2^{-(i+1)}$; so the Z computation too can be simplified.

An example computation is given in Table 4.5, with the aforementioned optimization shown as $\widetilde{s}_i = 0$ for the iterations in the second half. In implementation, the "second-half" optimization of the preceding paragraph is easiest accommodated in an unrolled pipeline or in a design for serial computation. For other arrangements, care needs to be taken to ensure that the delay arising from the arrangement used to avoid the addition of the third term is usefully less than the delay that would be incurred in adding that term.

4.6 High-radix CORDIC

One of the advantages of redundant signed-digit representation is that it facilitates high-radix computation. Indeed, the best known applications of such representations have been in the implementations of high-performance multipliers and dividers (Chapter 2). By "high" in "high-radix", we mean larger than two, and this section covers radix-4 versions of CORDIC. There have been proposals for the use of much larger radices—see Section 4.7—and, in principle, these ought to result in hardware of much higher performance than is possible with radices two and four. But the designs are so complex that whether the nominal gains can actually be achieved in practice is unclear.[8]

---

[8] And of dubious worth, if one considers the cost:performance ratios. Indeed, it would not be unreasonable to suggest that, as things stand, the CORDIC world becomes rather shaky right after the most straightforward radix-4 algorithm.

In seeking to extend CORDIC to radices larger than two, the problem of scaling-factor compensation is amplified. Almost all solutions start with the basic idea—from the radix-2 De Lugish algorithm of Section 4.1—of running some iterations with a non-redundant digit set and then changing to a redundant one. So for radix 4, the initial iterations may be with a non-redundant radix-2 digit set and a change then made to a redundant radix-4 digit set. After [1], this idea was first put to use in [9, 10, 11], and it has since appeared elsewhere [12, 13]. In what follows we shall focus on the sine and cosine functions, as these are sufficient to demonstrate the points to be made; extensions to other functions are are mostly straightforward, by interpreting "angle" appropriately and altering recurrences according to the base recurrences for each class of functions.

To generalize from the radix 2 to radix r, for the angles we shall take[9]

$$\theta_i = \tan^{-1} \left(s_i r^{-i} \right)$$

so the Z recurrence will be

$$Z_{i+1} = Z_i - \theta_i$$

In iteration i in the computation of sine and cosine we should nominally scale the "normal" X_i and Y_i CORDIC values, by multiplying each by $1/\sqrt{1 + s_i^2 r^{-2i}}$. Now, consider the Taylor-series expansion[10] of the scaling factor

$$\frac{1}{\sqrt{1 + s_i^2 r^{-2i}}} = 1 - \frac{1}{2} s_i^2 r^{-2i} + \frac{3}{8} \left(s_i^2 r^{-2i} \right)^2 - \frac{15}{36} \left(s_i^2 r^{-2i} \right)^3 + \cdots \quad (4.9)$$

And suppose that we wish to compute this to a precision of n fraction bits.[11] If the magnitude of the second term is less than 2^{-n}, then $1/\sqrt{1 + s_i^2 r^{-2i}} \approx 1$. With $s_i \in \{\overline{m}, \overline{m-1}, \ldots, \overline{1}, 0, 1, \ldots, m-1, m\}$, this means that

$$\frac{m^2}{2} r^{-2i} < 2^{-n}$$

---

[9]Recall that in Chapter 3, for radix 2 computations, the angles $\theta_i \overset{\triangle}{=} \tan^{-1} 2^{-i}$ were chosen in order to replace multiplication with shifting, and s_i was then introduced to indicate direction. We then ended up with $Z_{i+1} = Z_i - s_i \theta_i$. If we consider radix-$r$ computation, then we should have $\theta_i = \tan^{-1}(s_i r^{-i})$ in order to get the "operation-replacement". So the "more correct" form for the radix-2 angles is $\tan^{-1}(s_i 2^{-i})$; however, the form we have used throughout works because $\tan^{-1}(s_i 2^{-i}) = s_i \tan^{-1} 2^{-i}$, if $s_i \in \{-1, 1\}$.

[10]See Table 6.2.

[11]In the datapath, it is most likely that g guard digits will be used to take care of generated error; so the n bits will be the result of rounding from $n + g$ bits. (See Section 3.5.) If so, then in what follows n should be replaced with $n + g$.

If $r = 2^j$, then

$$\frac{m^2}{2} 2^{-2ij} < 2^{-n}$$

$$i > \frac{2 \log_2 m + n - 1}{2j} \tag{4.10}$$

So for $i > (2 \log_2 m + n - 1)/2j$, it may be assumed that $\left(1 + s_i^2 r^{-2i}\right)^{-1/2} = 1$, and the redundant digit set can then be used with no concerns about the scaling factor. For the *equivalent*[12] $i \leq (2 \log_2 m + n - 1)/2j$ iterations, the non-redundant radix-2 algorithm is used; accordingly, X_0 is set to the product of the per-iteration scaling factors for those iterations. Therefore, for radix-4 computation, i.e. $j = 2$, whereas, ideally, only $n/2$ iterations should suffice to produce an n-bit result, Inequation 4.10 shows that only the last $n/4$ iterations (approximately) can be carried out as radix-4 ones; the other $n/4$ nominally radix-4 iterations are carried out as $n/2$ radix-2 iterations. So a total of $3n/4$ iterations are required to produce an n-bit result.

It is convenient, for the implementations of the comparisons used in the s_i selections, to replace Z_i with a scaled variable that brings the most significant digits to the fore and then correspondingly modify the Z_i recurrence:

$$U_i = r^i Z_i$$

$$U_{i+1} = r \left(U_i - r^i \theta_i\right) \tag{4.11}$$

This is a generalization of the replacement mentioned for the radix-2 algorithm of Section 4.1, and the justification is the same in both cases. So the modified basic recurrences for circular functions are

$$\theta_i = \tan^{-1}\left(s_i r^{-i}\right) \tag{4.12}$$

$$X_{i+1} = X_i - s_i r^{-i} Y_i \tag{4.13}$$

$$Y_{i+1} = Y_i + s_i r^{-i} X_i \tag{4.14}$$

$$U_{i+1} = r \left(U_i - r^i \theta_i\right) \tag{4.15}$$

For the arctangent function, the variable on which the comparisons are based is Y_i; so it is that which is to be scaled. Defining $U_i = 4^i Y_i$, the main recurrences are

$$\theta_i = \tan^{-1}\left(s_i r^{-i}\right)$$

$$X_{i+1} = X_i - s_i r^{-i} Y_i$$

$$U_{i+1} = r(U_i + s_i X_i)$$

$$Z_{i+1} = Z_i - \theta_i$$

---

[12] "Equivalent" because each radix-r iteration corresponds to $\log_2 r$, radix-2 iterations.

Similar changes are straightforward for the hyperbolic and linear functions.

For what follows, the reader might find it helpful to review the division algorithms of Section 2.3.

Algorithm A: Equation 4.11 has the same form as Equations 2.8 and 2.10 (for multiplicative-normalization division) and, if analyzed in a similar manner, will yield similar intervals and bounds for the comparison constants. Accordingly, in [9] the same comparison constants are used for both the radix-4 division algorithm and the sine–cosine algorithm. The latter is a mixed radix-2/radix-4 algorithm of the form described above: a radix-2 algorithm with a non-redundant digit set is used for $n/2$ iterations, thus ensuring a constant scaling factor, and a redundant radix-4 digit set is used for the remaining iterations.

The algorithm for sine and cosine:

$$K = \frac{1}{\prod_{i=1}^{n/2} \sqrt{1 + 2^{-2i}}}$$

$$X_1 = 1/K$$

$$Y_1 = 0$$

$$U_1 = 4\theta \qquad\qquad 0 \leq \theta < \pi/4$$

$$\theta_i = \tan^{-1}\left(s_i r^{-i}\right) \qquad r = 2 \text{ if } i \leq n/2;\ r = 4 \text{ otherwise.}$$

$$X_{i+1} = X_i - s_i r^{-i} Y_i$$

$$Y_{i+1} = Y_i + s_i r^{-i} X_i$$

$$U_{i+1} = r\left(U_i - r^i \theta_i\right)$$

$$s_i = \begin{cases} 1 & \text{if } U_i \geq 0 \\ \bar{1} & \text{if } U_i < 0 \end{cases} \qquad i = 1, 2, \ldots, n/2$$

$$s_i = \begin{cases} 2 & \text{if } 13/8 \leq U_i < 21/8 \\ 1 & \text{if } 5/8 \leq U_i < 13/8 \\ 0 & \text{if } -5/8 \leq U_i < 5/8 \\ \bar{1} & \text{if } -13/8 \leq U_i < -5/8 \\ \bar{2} & \text{if } -21/8 \leq U_i < -13/8 \end{cases} \qquad i = n/2+1, n/2+2, \ldots, 3n/4$$

Convergence is easily shown by an inductive proof that is similar to that for the corresponding division algorithm[13]—that is, by showing that if $|U_i| \leq 21/8$, then $|U_{i+1}| \leq 21/8$.

In this algorithm the comparison constants have, for convenience, been chosen to be the same as those used in the radix-4 division algorithm (of Section 2.3.1.2). That need not be so, and other constants are possible, the most convenient being $1/2$ and $3/2$ (instead of $5/8$ and $13/8$, respectively), but care must be taken in the initialization. Algorithm D below uses such constants.

The corresponding algorithm for arctangent is obtained by changing the initialization and replacing the main recurrences with those given above for the function; the general changes are as for the basic CORDIC algorithms of Section 3.2. The same comparison constants may be used.

For the implementation, a straightforward starting point is the architecture of Figure 3.4. The main modifications required for the radix-4 computation of sine and cosine are that:

- The two multiplexors have three inputs each: one for the basic value, one for multiplication by two, and one for multiplication by four.
- To eliminate the need to use a variable shifter on the U_i-path (which replaces the Z_i path, the angle memory stores the constants $2^i \tan^{-1}\left(s_i 2^{-i}\right)$ and $4^i \tan^{-1}\left(s_i 4^{-i}\right)$.

(In computing U_{i+1}, the nominal multiplication by r is accomplished by a wired shift of $\log_2 r$ bit positions.)

As in the basic algorithm, the identity $\tan(-x) = -\tan x$ may be used to halve the number of constants stored, and advantageous use can be made of the fact that for sufficiently large i, $\tan^{-1}\left(s_i r^{-i}\right) = s_i r^{-i}$ to within the machine precision used.[14]

If a high-performance implementation is required, then the most logical extension to the algorithm would be the use of redundant representation in the arithmetic, but that is not without its complications. Such an extension is straightforward for just the radix-4 iterations, because the scaling factor is not affected in those iterations: the situation is similar to that of radix-4 division with redundant-representation arithmetic, in which a few bits of the U_i representation are taken to form an approximation, $\widehat{U}_i$, and a new selection rule formulated in terms of $\widehat{U}_i$. (Examples of such a rule are

---

[13]See the general approach for the radix-4 algorithm in Section 2.3.1.2.
[14]See the Taylor expansion in Table 6.4, and, for n-bit precision, consider the value of i for which the second term is effectively zero.

given below, in Algorithms C and D.) But a problem exists with the radix-2 iterations, because of the scaling-factor computation; and that implies the need for a solution of the types described in the preceding algorithms (Sections 4.1 to 4.5). Assuming a non-unrolled implementation, the viable candidates are correcting rotations and double rotations, of which the latter is easily the better of the two.

Algorithm B: A radix-2/radix-4 algorithm that differs from Algorithm A is given in [13]. The radix-2 iterations are with a non-redundant digit set, $\{\bar{1}, 1\}$ (or, equivalently, $\{0, 1\}$), but the arithmetic is in redundant representation, which means that each s_i selection is based on a possibly-incorrect estimate. That difficulty is resolved using correcting rotations (as in the algorithm of Section 4.2).

For the radix-4 iterations, the novel aspect of the algorithm is in not using radix-4 angles. All the rotation angles, including those for the radix-4 iterations, are radix-2 ones, on the basis that for iterations $i > n/2$, two radix-2 angles are equivalent to a radix-4 angle. The formulation is as follows.

For $i > n/2$, it is the case that $\tan^{-1} 2^{-i} = 2^{-i}$ to within the limitations of n-bit machine precision. Therefore, two successive rotations by the angles $\theta_i = \tan^{-1} 2^{-i}$ and $\theta_{i+1} = \tan^{-1} 2^{-(i+1)}$ are equivalent to a single rotation by

$$\theta_i + \theta_{i+1} = s_i 2^{-i} + s_{i+1} 2^{-(i+1)}$$

$$= (2s_i + s_{i+1}) 2^{-(i+1)}$$

If the digit set is $\{\bar{1}, 1\}$), then the set of values represented by $2s_i + s_{i+1}$ is $\{\pm 3, \pm 2, \pm 1, 0\}$; and if the digit set is $\{0, 1\}$, then the set of values is $\{3, 2, 1, 0\}$. In either case, this raises the problem that generally arises when one considers the use of a maximally redundant radix-4 digit set—that of multiplications by three.[15] The proposed solution is to recode from either of the former digit sets into the digit set $\{\pm 2, \pm 1, 0\}$.

Algorithm C: Algorithm A above can be improved upon by using the digit set $\{\bar{1}, 0, 1\}$ for some of the radix-2 iterations; this allows both faster decision making (in the choice of s_i) and faster arithmetic. Accordingly, in [14], Algorithm A is enhanced in three ways, two of which combined have similarities with the De Lugish algorithm of Section 4.1. The first of

---

[15] Whence the preference for the minimally redundant digit set in almost all radix-4 algorithms.

the three is that instead of some non-redundant radix-2 iterations followed by redundant radix-4 iterations, now redundant radix-2 iterations are interposed between the two sets: up to iteration $n/4 - 1$ (where n is the precision of the final result) the digit set used is $\{\bar{1}, 1\}$; after that, and up to iteration $n/2+1$, the digit set used is $\{\bar{1}, 0, 1\}$; thereafter, the digit set used is $\{\bar{2}, \bar{1}, 0, 1, 2\}$. The second enhancement in is the use of redundant-representation (carry–save) arithmetic. And the third is the inclusion, in a uniform way, of the hyperbolic functions.

We have seen (at the end of Section 4.1) that redundant-representation arithmetic leads "naturally" to the use of RSD in the digit set for s_i and that special actions are required if arithmetic is in redundant representation but with a non-redundant digit set for s_i. That is the case here too, for the first $n/4 - 1$ iterations, in which the digit set is $\{\bar{1}, 1\}$. The "special action" is the use of some correcting rotations, as is done in the Correcting-Rotations CORDIC algorithm (Section 4.2); this ensures that a constant scaling factor can be computed for these iterations.

The scaling-factor problem still exists with the iterations that use the digit set $\{\bar{1}, 0, 1\}$. (Recall that scaling is not an issue only for iterations $i > n/2$.) The solution is as in the De Lugish algorithm and consists of multiplication by a corrective factor that corresponds to the first two terms of Equation 4.9, i.e. $1 - s_i^2 r^{-(2i+1)}$. Here, a similar solution is extended to the other classes of functions computed in CORDIC: the multiplicative factor is $1 + m2^{-(2i+1)}$, where $m = -1$ for circular functions, 0 for linear functions, and 1 for hyperbolic functions.[16] In the implementation, the correction is carried out in additional *scaling stages*.

The arithmetic is in carry-save form, and, with the hyerbolic and linear functions included, the number of bits of Z_i that must be assimilated are ten for the non-redundant radix-2 stages, seven for the redundant radix-2 stages, and six for the radix-4 stages.

Algorithm D: In the algorithms above, the main goal in the radix-4 computations is to reduce (relative to the radix-2 computations) the number of required iterations. But the scaling-factor problem leads to a compromise in which most of the iterations are still radix-2 ones: for n-bit results, instead of n/2 radix-4 iterations, as we would wish, we have $n/2$ radix-2 iterations and $n/4$ radix-4 iterations. So we may expect that with a "pure" radix-4 algorithm the total number of iterations will be reduced but that the scaling-factor compensation will be more complicated and that this

---

[16]The expression and values for m are evident from the per-iteration scaling factors.

will be reflected in the implementation. That is indeed the case, and it is confirmed in the only such algorithm that we are aware of at the time of writing; moreover, it will become apparent that the underlying complications are not an accident of that algorithm but are fundamental in any such algorithm.[17] We next give a brief description of that algorithm; omitted details will be found in [15]. There are some questions as to the practicality of the algorithm, in relation to others, but it is an instructive example, and perhaps some of its aspects could be put to good use elsewhere. Nor should the possibility of future refinements be ruled out.

As in Algorithm A, direct use is made here of the similarity between the computation of the residual angle in CORDIC and the computation of the partial remainder in division: the type of analysis carried out for the relevant division recurrence will yield similar results here. Accordingly, for the minimally redundant radix-4 CORDIC algorithm, from Equation 4.11, let

$$w_i[s_i] = 4^i \tan^{-1}\left(s_i 4^{-i}\right)$$

$$U_{i+1} = 4(U_i - w_i[s_i])$$

And corresponding to Equations 2.21 and 2.22, for the choice $s_i = k$ ($\rho = 2/3$ for the minimally redundant radix-4 digit set):

$$U_i^{\min}[k] = w_i[k] - (2/3)w_i[1] \qquad k \in \{\overline{2}, \overline{1}, 0, 1, 2\}$$

$$U_i^{\max}[k] = w_i[k] + (2/3)w_i[1]$$

The algorithm will then converge if $s_i = k$ is chosen such that

$$U_i^{\min}[k] \le U_i \le U_i^{\max}[k] \tag{4.16}$$

Asssuming that $|Z_0| \le \pi/2$, it is straightforward to show, by induction, that if Inequations 4.16 are satisfied, then

$$|U_i| \le w_i[2] + (2/3)w_i[1] \tag{4.17}$$

which confirms the convergence.

s_i selection on the basis of Equation 4.16 is dependent on i. But for $i > 0$, the selection can be made independent of i, if it is done on the basis of the constraint

$$U_*[k] \le U_i \le U^*[k]$$

---

[17]See also the very-high-radix algorithm of Section 4.7.

where $U_*[k]$ is the largest possible value of $U_i^{\min}[s_i]$ and $U^*[k]$ is the smallest possible value of $U_i^{\max}[s_i]$. The case of $i = 0$ is taken care of through appropriate initialization, as given below.

Carry–save representation is proposed for the arithmetic, which means that the comparisons to determine the values of s_i are based on approximations, $\widehat{U}_i$, of U_i, with the approximations obtained by assimilating a few leading bits of the carry–save U_i. Suppose the approximation is obtained by assimilating q integer bits (including a sign bit) and p fraction bits of U_i. Then, as the error in each of the partial-sum and partial-carry parts is 2^{-p}:

$$\widehat{U}_i \le U_i < \widehat{U}_i + 2^{-p+1} \tag{4.18}$$

The value of p must be sufficient to distinguish between the extremes of two overlapping s_i-selection intervals, and that of q (including the sign bit) must be sufficient to cover the range of U_i. These conditions are met with $p = q = 3$.

The ranges for the comparison constants and the specific values are determined as follows. Define $\widehat{U}_i^{\max}[k]$ as the maximum value of $\widehat{U}_i$ for which the choice is $s_i = k$; and, similarly, define $\widehat{U}_i^{\min}[k+1]$ as the minimum value for which the choice is $s_i = k + 1$. Then, given that in a region of overlap the choice is between k and $k + 1$, the selection must be such that

$$\widehat{U}_i^{\max}[k] \le U^*[k] - 2^{-p+1}$$

$$\widehat{U}_i^{\min}[k+1] = \widehat{U}_i^{\max}[k] + 2^{-p}$$

$$\widehat{U}_i^{\min}[k+1] \ge U_*[k+1]$$

from which we get

$$U_*^{\min}[k+1] - 2^{-p} \le \widehat{U}_*^{\max}[k] \le U_*^{\max}[s] - 2^{-p+1} \tag{4.19}$$

By considering these conditions for each possible value for s_i, the ranges and values for the most convenient comparison constants within those ranges are obtained. The final selection rules are[18]

---

[18]These rules remain valid for non-redundant arithmetic, in which case $\widehat{U}_i$ is replaced with U_i.

$$s_0 = \begin{cases} 2 & \text{if } \widehat{U}_0 \geq 5/8 \\ 1 & \text{if } 3/8 \leq \widehat{U}_0 < 5/8 \\ 0 & \text{if } -1/2 \leq \widehat{U}_0 < 3/8 \\ \overline{1} & \text{if } -7/8 \leq \widehat{U}_0 < -1/2 \\ \overline{2} & \text{if } \widehat{U}_0 < -7/8 \end{cases}$$

$$s_i = \begin{cases} 2 & \text{if } \widehat{U}_i \geq 3/2 \qquad\qquad i > 0 \\ 1 & \text{if } 1/2 \leq \widehat{U}_i < 3/2 \\ 0 & \text{if } -1/2 \leq \widehat{U}_i < 1/2 \\ \overline{1} & \text{if } -3/2 \leq \widehat{U}_i < -1/2 \\ \overline{2} & \text{if } \widehat{U}_i < -3/2 \end{cases}$$

With these rules, straightforward induction will suffice to show[19] that

$$|U_{i+1}| < 2 + (4/3)4^{-2i}$$

and therefore

$$|Z_{n/2-1}| < 2^{-n+1} + (4/3)2^{-3n+4} \approx \tan^{-1} 2^{-n+1}$$

which shows that $n/2$ radix-4 iterations will produce a result of n-bit precision.

One difficulty that is immediately apparent with this algorithm is in the scaling-factor compensation. With one exception, in each of the CORDIC algorithms described earlier in this section (and many others in the literature), matters are arranged so that the scaling factor is constant; it is therefore computed beforehand, and the scaling is carried out through appropriate initialization. If the scaling factor cannot be computed beforehand, as will be the case with unconstrained choices of $s_i = 0$, then a direct solution to the scaling problem is to:

- Compute the scaling factor iteratively, and in parallel with the primary computations, by forming a running product, $1/K$, of the per-iteration scaling factors, $1/K_i \triangleq 1/\sqrt{1 + s_i^2 4^{-2i}}$.
- At the end of the iterations, multiply each of X_{n+1} and Y_{n+1} by $1/K$.

---

[19]See the general approach for the radix-4 algorithm of Section 2.3.1.2.

That is the essence of what is proposed in [15]. But there are few circumstances in which it would be practical to actually carry out the nominal multiplications in a direct manner; therefore, what is proposed is, essentially, that all possible scaling factors be stored in a lookup table and read out as necessary. For radix-4 computations, Equations 4.9 and 4.10 show that only the first $n/4 + 1$ iterations affect K; so, with three possible values for s_i, the nominal table size is $n \times 3^{n/4+1}$. The actual table size can, however, be made much smaller, on the basis of Equation 4.9. For $n/8 < i \leq n/12$, $1/K_i$ may be approximated by the first two terms of that equation, and for $n/12 < i \leq n/4 + 1$, the first three terms will suffice. The table therefore stores the first $n/12 + 1$ scaling factors and is of size $n \times 3^{n/12+1}$. For the other iterations, i.e. $i \geq n/12 + 1$, the scaling factors are obtained through additional operations (SHIFT and ADD) on scaling factors already stored in the table.

Once the $n/2$ primary iterations have been completed, the values of X_{n+1} and Y_{n+1} must be scaled, through multiplication by $1/K$. This is the really problematic aspect of the design. What is proposed is the use of the same CORDIC hardware but in linear mode, via the recurrences

$$X_{i+1} = X_i + s_i 4^{-i} X_c \qquad X_0 = 0$$
$$Y_{i+1} = Y_i + s_i 4^{-i} Y_s \qquad Y_0 = 0$$
$$U_{i+1} = 4(U_i - s_i) \qquad U_0 = 1/K$$

where X_c and Y_s are the final values computed in the circular rotations.

The scaling therefore nominally requires another $n/2$ iterations, which renders questionable the expected benefits in the use of radix 4. To reduce the total number of iterations, a *zero-skipping* technique, similar to that used in some division algorithms, is proposed for iterations in which $s_i = 0$. Zero skipping, which goes back to the original motivation in the De Lugish algorithm of Section 4.1 (and similar algorithms) does, however, result in an operand-dependent operational time, which might be undesirable. The final number of iterations is $4n/5$ on average. This is rather high, but it should be noted that all of the arithmetic is in redundant representation and therefore quite fast.

The algorithm is certainly an improvement on those in which some or all of the arithmetic is in non-redundant representation, but the average number of iterations is not very inspiring. And to the extent that it might be deemed better than mixed radix-2/radix-4 algorithms that use redundant-representation arithmetic, there is the additional cost in hardware. So it is not immediately clear that a direct implementation of this algorithm would offer a great deal beyond that of a well-implemented mixed-radix algorithm. An exception would be in applications for which final scaling is, for whatever reason, not necessary. One can also imagine a situation in which the CORDIC unit is part of a comprehensive arithmetic unit; in such a case, a fast multiplier would most likely be already available and could be put to good use in the scaling. As with any interesting hardware algorithm, future refinements are probable, and this one is worth a careful look on that basis (as well as for its "instructive" element).

4.7   Very-high-radix CORDIC

The discussions of the preceding sections show that there are considerable difficulties in extending CORDIC algorithms beyond the minimally-redundant radix 4. Nevertheless, there have been proposals for extensions to very large radices, and in this section we look at one of these [17].

The most problematic aspect of all large-radix CORDIC algorithms is in the scaling-factor compensation: dealing with this invariably leads to arrangements whose practicality at present is questionable, and, to some extent, that is the case here too. Still, we consider that it is not unreasonable to discuss such algorithms and to include them, for "for completeness", as it were: the reader should at least be aware of the application of an interesting idea, and it is possible that future developments will produce better algorithms along the same lines.

The following covers only the circular functions, as this is sufficient for our "demonstrative" purposes; however, the proposal includes hyperbolic functions, and the reader is referred to [17] for additional information. It is assumed that the arithmetic is in carry–save representation and in radix r, with the digit set $\{\overline{r-1}, \ldots, 0, \ldots, r-1\}$.

The basic recurrences are unchanged (Equations 4.12–4.15), but instead of s_i selection "by intervals", as in all of the preceding algorithms, here it is "by rounding", as in very-high-radix division (Section 2.3.4). That is, s_i is determined by rounding to the nearest integer a truncation of U_i:

$$s_i = \left\lfloor \widehat{U}_i + 1/2 \right\rfloor \tag{4.20}$$

From Equation 4.11

$$U_{i+1} = r\left(U_i - r^i\theta_i\right) \qquad\qquad \theta_i = \tan^{-1}\left(s_i r^{-i}\right)$$

$$= r\left[\left(U_i - s_i\right) + \left(s_i - r^i\theta_i\right)\right]$$

and from Equation 4.20:

$$-\frac{1}{2} \leq U_i - s_i < \frac{1}{2} + 2^{-p}$$

if $\widehat{U}_i$ is represented with p fraction bits.

So, if s_i is selected by rounding as indicated, then U_{i+1} is bounded as

$$r\left(-\frac{1}{2} + s_i - r^i\theta_i\right) \leq U_{i+1} < r\left(\frac{1}{2} + 2^{-p} + s_i - r^i\theta_i\right) \qquad (4.21)$$

For convergence we require (Inequation 3.21)

$$|Z_{i+1}| \leq \sum_{j=i+1}^{\infty} \theta_j$$

which, since $U_i = r^i Z_i$, is equivalent to

$$|U_{i+1}| \leq r^{i+1} \sum_{j=i+1}^{\infty} \theta_j \qquad (4.22)$$

If we define

$$S_{i+1} = r^{i+1} \sum_{j=i+1}^{\infty} \theta_j \qquad \text{with } s_j = r - 1$$

then Inequation 4.21 is

$$-S_{i+1} \leq U_{i+1} \leq S_{i+1} \qquad (4.23)$$

We also must have $|s_{i+1}| \leq r - 1$, which means

$$-r + \frac{1}{2} < \widehat{U}_i < r - \frac{1}{2}$$

and, therefore

$$-r + \frac{1}{2} + 2^{-p} \leq U_{i+1} < r - \frac{1}{2} \qquad (4.24)$$

The combination of Inequations 4.23 and 4.24 gives

$$\max\left\{-S_{i+1}, \ -r + \frac{1}{2} + 2^{-p}\right\} \leq U_{i+1} < \min\left\{S_{i+1}, \ r - \frac{1}{2}\right\} \qquad (4.25)$$

The Taylor expansion[20] of $r^i\theta_i$ is

---

[20]See Table 6.3.

$$r^i \tan^{-1}\left(s_i r^{-i}\right) = r^i \left[\left(s_i r^{-i}\right) - \frac{\left(s_i r^{-i}\right)^3}{3} + \frac{\left(s_i r^{-i}\right)^5}{5} - \cdots\right]$$

$$= s_i - \frac{s_i^3 r^{-2i}}{3} + \cdots$$

and, therefore

$$\left|s_i - r^i \theta_i\right| < \frac{s_i^r r^{-2i}}{3}$$

and since $-(r-1) \le s_i \le r-1$, we have

$$-\frac{(r-1)^3 r^{-2i}}{3} < s_i - r^i \theta_i < \frac{(r-1)^3 r^{-2i}}{3} \qquad (4.26)$$

Substituting from Inequations 4.26 into Inequations 4.21:

$$-r\left[\frac{1}{2} + \frac{(r-1)^3 r^{-2i}}{3}\right] < U_{i+1} < r\left[\frac{1}{2} + 2^{-p} + \frac{(r-1)^3 r^{-2i}}{3}\right] \qquad (4.27)$$

On the other hand, the application of the Taylor expansion for S_{i+1} (i.e. of $\theta_j = \tan^{-1}\left(s_i r^{-i}\right)$), with $i \ge 1$, to Inequation 4.25 gives

$$1 - \frac{1}{2r} < 1 - \frac{1}{(r-1)^2} < \frac{S_{i+1}}{r} < 1$$

which confirms that Inequation 4.24 is satisfactory.

Combining Inequations 4.24 and 4.27:

$$\frac{1}{2} + 2^{-p} + \frac{(r-1)^3 r^{-2i}}{3} < 1 - \frac{1}{2r}$$

and

$$-\frac{1}{2} - \frac{(r-1)^3 r^{-2i}}{3} > -1 + \frac{1}{2r} + \frac{2^{-p}}{r}$$

For the worst case, Inequation 4.27 gives

$$r^{-2i} < \frac{3\left[1/2 - 1/(2r) - 2^{-p}\right]}{(r-1)^3}$$

i.e.

$$i \ge \frac{1}{2} \log_r \left[\frac{(r-1)^3}{3\left(1/2 - 2^{-p} - 1/(2r)\right)}\right] \qquad (4.28)$$

With $r \geq 4$ and $p \geq 2$:

$$r^2 < \frac{(r-1)^3}{3\left[1/2 - 2^{-p} - 1/(2r)\right]} < r^4$$

So Inequation 4.28 is satisfied if $i \geq 2$ and $p \geq 2$; that is, selection-by-rounding cannot be used at $i = 1$.

The selection for the first iteration is done by table lookup. In order to ensure that the size of the table is not too large, the selection is combined with the use of a modified recurrence, in a radix, $\tilde{r}$, that is smaller than r. So $U_1 = \tilde{r}\theta$, where θ is the argument whose sine or cosine is to be computed. Then, for that iteration, the recurrences are appropriately modified, to

$$X_{i+1} = X_i - s_i r^{-I} Y_i$$
$$Y_{i+1} = Y_i + s_i r^{-I} X_i$$
$$U_{i+1} = r(U_i - r^i \theta_i)$$

where

$$r^{-I} = \tilde{r}^{-1} r^{-(i-1)}$$
$$\theta_i = r^I \tan^{-1}\left(s_i r^{-I}\right)$$

To determine the bounds for $\tilde{r}$, Inequation 4.28 is now

$$\frac{1}{2} + 2^{-p} + \frac{(r-1)^3 r^{-2i}}{3} r^{-2I} < 1 - \frac{1}{2r}$$

and the worst case is at $i = 2$:

$$\frac{1}{2} + 2^{-p} + \frac{(r-1)^3 r^{-2i}}{3(rR)^2} < 1 - \frac{1}{2r}$$

which gives

$$\tilde{r} > \sqrt{\frac{2(r-1)^3}{3r^2\left[1 - 1/r - 2^{-(p-1)}\right]}}$$

This, for $r = 2^b$, is satisfied with:

- $\tilde{r} \geq 2^{\lceil (b+1)/2 \rceil}$, for $p = 2$ and $r \geq 8$.
- $\tilde{r} \geq 2^{\lceil b/2 \rceil}$, for $p \geq 3$ and $r \geq 16$.

That is, $\tilde{r} \approx \sqrt{r}$.

If $\tilde{r} = 2^{\tilde{b}}$ and $r = 2^b$, then the algorithm will produce an n-bit result in $\lceil (n - \tilde{b})/b \rceil + 1$ iterations.

As would be expected, the scaling-factor compensation is problematic. In principle, it can be done by

- Computing the scaling factor, $1/K$, iteratively, and in parallel with the primary computations, as the product of the per-iteration scaling factors, $1/K_i \stackrel{\triangle}{=} 1/\sqrt{1 + s_i^2 r^{-2i}}$.
- At the end of the iterations, multiplying each of X_{n+1} and Y_{n+1} by $1/K$.

Per-iteration multiplication would be too costly in practice, and in Algorithm D of Section 4.6 it is avoided by instead storing most of the possible scaling factors and using shift–add operations (on the stored ones) to obtain the others. Here too, the scaling closely mirrors the preceding "in-principle" two steps, but the operations are additions (of logarithms) and exponentiations instead of multiplications and divisions (multiplications by reciprocals):

- The values $\ln(1/K_i)$ are stored in a table.
- Entries are read from the table, as necessary, and added up, to obtain $v \stackrel{\triangle}{=} \ln(1/K)$.
- The scaling is done by computing $X_{n+1}e^v$ and $Y_{n+1}e^v$.

The computations in the last step can be done concurrently and in hardware that has some similarities with CORDIC hardware and with about the same operational times.[21]

One conclusion that may be drawn from the last remarks is that the scaling-factor compensation is likely to cost (in hardware and time) about as much as the primary, CORDIC, computations. Whether or not such a cost is worthwhile will depend on the actual realization—the number of cycles, the time per cycle, the storage costs, etc.

Additional details on the preceding, including the computation of hyperbolic functions, will be found in [17].

---

[21] Algorithms and hardware for the computation of the function ye^x are described in Sections 5.2 and 5.6.

Chapter 5

Normalization Algorithms

The concept of *normalization* was briefly introduced in Section 2.3 and several such algorithms given there for division. For the reader who has arrived here directly, or who simply needs a reminder, the "definition" is repeated just below. Nevertheless, such a reader should note that some aspects of the material covered in Chapter 2 are very relevant here (and in Chapter 8), and it is helpful to be familiar with the redundant number representations of Section 2.1 and the division algorithms of Section 2.3.

In *normalization* algorithms, the basic idea is that to compute $f(x)$, for some function f and value x, two sequences are produced in such a way that as the values of one are driven (*normalized*) to some known constant, those of the other converge to $f(x)$. The computations of the values of the sequences are typically by multiplication with a set of predetermined constants, a process known as *multiplicative normalization*, or by the addition of a set of predetermined constants, a process known as *additive normalization*.[1] For the algorithms we are interested in, the additive-normalization target will be zero, and for multiplicative normalization it will be one. In practice, the constants in multiplicative normalization are often, but not always, chosen so that the nominal multiplications are realized with just a pair of SHIFT and ADD operations.

The procedure just described is also exactly what happens in the CORDIC algorithms of Chapters 3 and 4, and, as we shall see below, some of the algorithms obtained via normalization are exactly the CORDIC algorithms. Nevertheless, the more "algebraic" approach of normalization allows us to obtain algorithms for other functions that are evaluated only indirectly in CORDIC—exponentials, logarithms, and square roots and their

---

[1] We shall distinguish an algorithm as being of one or the other type according to the operation used on the variable whose values are driven to the constant.

inverses. This "uniformity" leads to very similar algorithms for a wide range of functions (including division) and means that essentially the same hardware can be used for all; this is confirmed in [7], a source of several algorithms in this book.

The first section of the chapter consists of a brief commentary on the choices of normalization constants. The three sections after that give the basics of normalization, with algorithms for exponentials, natural logarithms, trigonometric functions, inverse trigonometric functions, and square roots and their inverses. Much of the foundational work here is due to Meggitt and Specker [1, 2], with subsequent work by others [3–10].

The last section of the chapter deals with high-performance versions of the algorithms given earlier for the exponential and logarithm functions; the emphasis is on redundant number representations and high-radix extensions of those algorithms. Similar algorithms for division are given in Chapter 2, those for the trigonometric functions are in Chapter 4, and those for square root and inverse square root are in Chapter 8.

We have not included much discussion on convergence and errors, but enough is given to assure the reader that all is well. With one exception, the algorithms dicsussed here all have forms that are similar to those of the basic CORDIC algorithms of Chapter 3, and the reader who requires the details should either apply here the general approaches given in that chapter or consult the published literature. In particular, in the brief discussions here, we do not consider in detail generated errors and various representation errors. Such errors are easily taken care of through the inclusion of a sufficient number of guard digits in the arithmetic: by reasoning similar to that of Section 3.5, if the radix of computation is r and K iterations are required to obtain an n-digit result, then $\lceil \log_r K \rceil + 1$ radix-r guard digits will suffice to ensure that the magnitude of the sum of these errors is less than r^{-n}.

Because of the similarities with the CORDIC algorithms, hardware architectures for the other functions will largely be similar to those described in Section 3.6—sequential, unrolled, serial, shared-pipeline, and so forth (Figures 3.4–3.6). Therefore, for each function we shall give the sketch of just one hardware architecture and leave it to the reader to imagine others.

Specific ranges are given for the algorithms, and range reduction is assumed for arguments that are not in those ranges (Section 1.2).

5.1 Normalization constants

The forms of the normalization constants are determined by the normalizing operations, how the results are accumulated, and the mathematical formulation of the algorithms. The simplest possible constants are those of the form r^{-i}, where r is the radix used and i is an integer. Such a constant need not be stored, as it can be obtained on the fly, by just an i-place, radix-r shift.

A generalization of the preceding is to constants of the form $s_i r^{-i}$, where s_i is in a digit set determined by r. Depending on the digit set, the computation of $s_i r^{-i}$ too need not involve more than shifting (and perhaps negation), although in some cases addition may also be required. For example, with $r = 4$ and $s_i \in \{\bar{2}, \bar{1}, 0, 1, 2\}$, we have the former case. On the other hand, with $s_i \in \{\bar{3}, \bar{2}, \bar{1}, 0, 1, 2, 3\}$ we have the latter: for a given X, a multiple $3X$ is obtained by shifting (to obtain $2X$) and then adding (X).

Constants of the form $s_i r^{-i}$ arise "directly" or "indirectly", depending on the algorithm at hand. For example, in basic subtractive division and square root algorithms, a result is obtained one digit at a time. So if Y_{i-1} consists of the first $i-1$ digits of the result, then Y_i is obtained by appending the next digit, s_i, to Y_{i-1}:

$$Y_i = Y_{i-1} + s_i r^{-i}$$

and we can see that $s_i r^{-i}$ arises "naturally" and "directly". On the other hand, consider the sine–cosine CORDIC algorithm of Chapter 3. The algorithm nominally requires multiplication by constants of the form $\tan \phi_i$. But such multiplication is reduced to shifting, by choosing $\phi_i = \tan^{-1}\left(s_i r^{-i}\right)$. This is an example of an "indirect" occurrence of $s_i r^{-i}$.

Let us now consider the normalizing operation. For multiplicative-normalization algorithms of the type we are interested in, the operation will be of the form

$$X_{i+1} = k_i X_i \qquad k_i \text{ a normalizing constant}$$

If the algorithm converges, then for sufficiently large i, $X_{i+1} \approx X_i$; so we require that $k_i \to 1$ as $i \to \infty$. Therefore, k_i may not be of the form $s_i r^{-i}$, but it may be of the form $1 + s_i r^{-i}$, which (with a good digit set) is only slightly harder to compute than $s_i r^{-i}$. Indeed, this choice of k_i reduces the nominal normalizing multiplication to SHIFT-AND-ADD:

$$X_{i+1} = X_i + s_i r^{-i} X_i$$

With additive-normalization algorithms of the type we are interested in, the normalization operation will be of the form

$$X_{i+1} = X_i + k_i$$

If the algorithm converges, then for sufficiently large i, $X_{i+1} \approx X_i$; so we require that $k_i \to 0$ as $i \to \infty$. On the face of it, k_i of the form $s_i r^{-i}$ ought to do, and indeed in some cases it will. But there are exceptions, of which the algorithm for exponentials (Section 5.2) is a good example. The mathematical formulation of the algorithm leads to k_i of the form $\ln c_i$, with c_i constant. Evidently, c_i cannot be of the form $s_i r^{-i}$, since s_i can be 0 or negative, but $1 + s_i r^{-i}$ will do. Even if it were not for the normalizing operation, the manner in which the result is accumulated in the algorithm precludes k_i of the form $s_i r^{-i}$:

$$Y_{i+1} = c_i Y_i$$

and, clearly, c_i may not be of the form $s_i r^{-i}$, but again $1 + s_i r^{-i}$ will do.

What we may conclude from the above is that constants of the form $s_i r^{-i}$ and $1 + s_i r^{-i}$ are very handy; and, not surprisingly, we shall encounter them all over the place. Further, for the functions that we are interested in, the normalization algorithms that use constants of these forms differ primarily only in how s_i is selected; the general forms of the algorithms are the same, which facilitates the use of shared hardware.

We have noted that there is a difference between "direct" (and perhaps "essential") and "indirect" usage of some forms of constants, with convenience being the key in the latter. This brings us to the last point in this section: It is clear that in additive normalization the choices for constants are limited, because the only arithmetic operation to work with is addition. On the other hand, with multiplicative normalization, although it is certainly "nice" to be able to replace a multiplication with a SHIFT-AND-ADD operation, there is another arithmetic operation to work with—real multiplication. This raises an obvious question: are there other types of constant that would work well? The answer is YES. The Goldschmidt division algorithm of Section 2.3 exemplifies this, and in Chapter 8 we shall encounter the same general form of multiplicative-normalization algorithms given here for reciprocal and square root, but with different types of constants. The reward for giving up "nice" is that we get much faster algorithms.

5.2   Reciprocals

The division algorithms of Section 2.3.1 compute N/D by multiplying N and increasingly better approximations of $1/D$. Evidently, if $N = 1$, then those same algorithms will compute reciprocals. The reciprocal function is, however, of interest on its own. For that reason, the following highlights the essential aspects of those algorithms, but without repeating much from Section 2.3.1.

Suppose that for some sequence of constants, c_i, it is the case that

$$x \prod_i c_i \to 1$$

as $i \to \infty$. Then

$$\prod_i c_i \to 1/x$$

If we define

$$X_i = x \prod_{k=0}^{i-1} c_k$$

$$Y_i = \prod_{k=0}^{i-1} c_k$$

then we obtain normalization recurrences for the computation of reciprocals:

$$X_{i+1} = c_i X_i$$
$$Y_{i+1} = c_i Y_i$$

where $X_i \to 1$ and $Y_i \to 1/x$.

If $X_0 = x$ and $Y_0 = 1$, then after n iterations, we shall have $X_n \approx 1$ and $Y_n \approx 1/x$. In general, setting $Y_0 = y$ and $X_0 = x$ will produce $Y_n \approx y/x$.

The normalization is to $x \prod_i c_i \approx 1$, so the argument range for convergence is limited to

$$\min \frac{1}{\prod_i c_i} \le x \le \max \frac{1}{\prod_i c_i} \tag{5.1}$$

For the reasons given in Section 5.1, for binary computation we shall here take $c_i = 1 + s_i 2^{-i}$. The values X_i are driven to one; so the values of s_i are determined on the basis of a corresponding comparison. If the argument, $X_0 = x$, is positive, then a simple rule is this: In each iteration, there should be a normalization operation on X_i if it is "too far" from one (for that iteration); otherwise, nothing should be done (for that iteration). The complete algorithm for $1/x$:

$$X_0 = x \qquad\qquad 1/2 \le x < 1 \qquad (5.2)$$

$$Y_0 = 1 \qquad\qquad (5.3)$$

$$s_i = \begin{cases} 1 & \text{if } X_i\left(1 + 2^{-i}\right) < 1 \\ 0 & \text{otherwise} \end{cases} \qquad i = 0, 1, 2, , \ldots \qquad (5.4)$$

$$c_i = 1 + s_i 2^{-i} \qquad (5.5)$$

$$\begin{aligned} X_{i+1} &= c_i X_i & (5.6) \\ &= X_i + s_i 2^{-i} X_i & (5.7) \end{aligned}$$

$$\begin{aligned} Y_{i+1} &= c_i Y_i & (5.8) \\ &= Y_i + s_i 2^{-i} Y_i \end{aligned}$$

An example computation is given in Table 5.1.

<table>
<tr><td colspan="5" align="center">$x = 0.65 \qquad 1/x = 1.5384615\cdots$</td></tr>
<tr><th>i</th><th>s_i</th><th>c_i</th><th>X_i</th><th>Y_i</th></tr>
<tr><td>0</td><td>0</td><td>1.0000000000000000</td><td>0.1010011001100110</td><td>1.0000000000000000</td></tr>
<tr><td>1</td><td>1</td><td>1.1000000000000000</td><td>0.1010011001100110</td><td>1.0000000000000000</td></tr>
<tr><td>2</td><td>0</td><td>1.0000000000000000</td><td>0.1111100110011001</td><td>1.1000000000000000</td></tr>
<tr><td>3</td><td>0</td><td>1.0000000000000000</td><td>0.1111100110011001</td><td>1.1000000000000000</td></tr>
<tr><td>4</td><td>0</td><td>1.0000000000000000</td><td>0.1111100110011001</td><td>1.1000000000000000</td></tr>
<tr><td>5</td><td>0</td><td>1.0000000000000000</td><td>0.1111100110011001</td><td>1.1000000000000000</td></tr>
<tr><td>6</td><td>1</td><td>1.0000010000000000</td><td>0.1111100110011001</td><td>1.1000000000000000</td></tr>
<tr><td>7</td><td>1</td><td>1.0000001000000000</td><td>0.1111110110000000</td><td>1.1000011000000000</td></tr>
<tr><td>8</td><td>0</td><td>1.0000000000000000</td><td>0.1111111101111011</td><td>1.1000100100001100</td></tr>
<tr><td>9</td><td>1</td><td>1.0000000010000000</td><td>0.1111111101111011</td><td>1.1000100100001100</td></tr>
<tr><td>10</td><td>0</td><td>1.0000000000000000</td><td>0.1111111111111010</td><td>1.1000100111010000</td></tr>
<tr><td>11</td><td>0</td><td>1.0000000000000000</td><td>0.1111111111111010</td><td>1.1000100111010000</td></tr>
<tr><td>12</td><td>0</td><td>1.0000000000000000</td><td>0.1111111111111010</td><td>1.1000100111010000</td></tr>
<tr><td>13</td><td>0</td><td>1.0000000000000000</td><td>0.1111111111111010</td><td>1.1000100111010000</td></tr>
<tr><td>14</td><td>1</td><td>1.0000000000000100</td><td>0.1111111111111010</td><td>1.1000100111010000</td></tr>
<tr><td>15</td><td>0</td><td>1.0000000000000000</td><td>0.1111111111111110</td><td>1.1000100111010110</td></tr>
<tr><td colspan="5" align="right">$1/x \approx 1.5384$</td></tr>
</table>

Table 5.1: Normalization computation of $1/x$, $s_i \in \{0, 1\}$

In the algorithm above, $X_i \left(1 + 2^{-i} \right)$ must be computed, even if there is no normalization operation in that iteration. An obvious improvement can be made by changing the s_i digit set to $\{\bar{1}, 0, 1\}$, in the same manner, and on the same basis, as in Section 2.3.1.2, with the primary effect being that no arithmetic operation is necessary when $s_i = 0$. So to drive X_i to one, the actions are as follows. If X_i is "much larger" than one, then it is multiplied by a value that is smaller than one; if it is "much smaller" than one, then it is multiplied by a value that is larger than one; and if it is "close" to one, then nothing is done in that iteration. The algorithm is then

$$X_0 = x \tag{5.9}$$

$$Y_0 = 1 \tag{5.10}$$

$$s_i = \begin{cases} 1 & \text{if } X_i < 1 - 2^{-i}\alpha \\ 0 & \text{if } 1 - 2^{-i}\alpha \le X_i \le 1 + 2^{-i}\alpha \\ \bar{1} & \text{if } X_i > 1 + 2^{-i}\alpha \end{cases} \tag{5.11}$$

$$c_i = 1 + s_i 2^{-i} \tag{5.12}$$

$$X_{i+1} = c_i X_i \tag{5.13}$$

$$Y_{i+1} = c_i Y_i \tag{5.14}$$

The algorithm will converge with $\alpha = 1/2$, and an example computation with that choice is given in Table 5.2. To have comparisons against fixed values, the X_i values may be replaced with the scaled values $U_i \stackrel{\triangle}{=} 2^i(X_i - 1)$ and the X_i recurrence replaced with a U_i recurrence:

$$U_0 = x - 1 \qquad\qquad 1/2 \le x < 1 \tag{5.15}$$
$$Y_0 = 1 \tag{5.16}$$

$$s_i = \begin{cases} 1 & \text{if } U_i < \alpha \\ 0 & \text{if } -\alpha \le U_i \le \alpha \qquad\qquad i = 0, 1, 2, \ldots \\ \bar{1} & \text{if } U_i > \alpha \end{cases} \tag{5.17}$$

$$c_i = 1 + s_i 2^{-i} \tag{5.18}$$

$$U_{i+1} = 2 \left(U_i + s_i + s_i 2^{-i} U_i \right) \tag{5.19}$$

$$Y_{i+1} = c_i Y_i \tag{5.20}$$

The algorithm can be extended to radix-4 computation, as done in Section 2.3.1.2 for division, and can be implemented to use fast, low-precision arithmetic operation. For the details, the reader should simply review Section 2.3.1.2 but take the dividend $N = 1$.

Faster multiplicative-normalization algorithms for the reciprocal function can be obtained by using different normalizing multipliers. Such algorithms are discussed in Section 8.2.2.

$$x = 0.65 \qquad 1/x = 1.5384615\cdots$$

i	s_i	c_i	X_i	Y_i
0	0	1.0000000000000000	0.1010011001100110	1.0000000000000000
1	1	1.1000000000000000	0.1010011001100110	1.0000000000000000
2	0	1.0000000000000000	0.1111100110011001	1.1000000000000000
3	0	1.0000000000000000	0.1111100110011001	1.1000000000000000
4	0	1.0000000000000000	0.1111100110011001	1.1000000000000000
5	1	1.0000100000000000	0.1111100110011001	1.1000000000000000
6	0	1.0000000000000000	1.0000000101100110	1.1000110000000000
7	-1	0.1111111000000000	1.0000000101100110	1.1000110000000000
8	1	1.0000000100000000	0.1111111101100011	1.1000100011101000
9	-1	0.1111111110000000	1.0000000001100010	1.1000101001110000
10	0	1.0000000000000000	0.1111111111100010	1.1000100110101011
11	1	1.0000000000100000	0.1111111111100010	1.1000100110101011
12	0	1.0000000000000000	1.0000000000000010	1.1000100111011100
13	0	1.0000000000000000	1.0000000000000010	1.1000100111011100
14	-1	0.1111111111111100	1.0000000000000010	1.1000100111011100
15	1	1.0000000000000010	0.1111111111111110	1.1000100111010110

$$1/x \approx 1.5384$$

Table 5.2: Normalization computation of $1/x$, $s_i \in \{\overline{1}, 0, 1\}$

5.3 Exponential and logarithm functions

We shall give algorithms for e^x and $\ln x$. But will be apparent that—with different initializations—the same algorithms can be used to compute ye^x and $y + \ln x$. Indeed, with a simple change of some constants, the same algorithms can be used to compute the even more general functions of ya^x and $y + \log_b x$.

5.3.1 *Exponential*

The algorithm for the exponential function is an additive-normalization algorithm one. To compute e^x, suppose we have a set of constants $\{c_i\}$ such that

$$x - \ln \prod c_i \to 0 \quad \text{as } i \to \infty$$

Then

$$\ln \prod_i c_i \to x$$

and

$$\prod_i c_i \to e^x$$

If we define

$$X_i = x - \ln \prod_{k=1}^{i-1} c_k$$

$$= x - \sum_{k=1}^{i-1} \ln c_k$$

and

$$Y_i = \prod_{k=1}^{i-1} c_k$$

then the recurrences for the computation of e^x are

$$X_{i+1} = X_i - \ln c_i$$
$$Y_{i+1} = c_i Y_i$$

If $X_1 = x$ and $Y_1 = 1$, then after n iterations, we shall have $X_{n+1} \approx 0$ and $Y_{n+1} \approx e^x$. In general, setting $Y_1 = y$ and $X_1 = x$ will produce $Y_{n+1} \approx y e^x$.

The normalization is to $x - \sum_i \ln c_i \approx 0$, so that the argument range is limited to

$$\min \sum_i \ln c_i \leq x \leq \max \sum_i \ln c_i \tag{5.21}$$

For the reasons given in Section 5.1, for binary computation we shall here take $c_i = 1 + s_i 2^{-i}$. The values X_i are driven towards zero through reductions by the values $\ln c_i$; so the values of s_i are determined on the basis of a corresponding comparison. If the argument, $X_1 = x$, is positive, then a simple rule is this: in each iteration, X_i should be reduced if it is "too far" from zero (for that iteration); otherwise, nothing should be done (for that iteration).

$$x = 0.5 \qquad e^x = 1.648721\cdots$$

i	s_i	c_i	X_i	Y_i
1	1	1.1000000000000000	0.1000000000000000	1.0000000000000000
2	0	1.0000000000000000	0.0001100000110011	1.1000000000000000
3	0	1.0000000000000000	0.0001100000110011	1.1000000000000000
4	1	1.0001000000000000	0.0001100000110011	1.1000000000000000
5	1	1.0000100000000000	0.0000100010101110	1.1001100000000000
6	0	1.0000000000000000	0.0000000011001101	1.1010010011000000
7	0	1.0000000000000000	0.0000000011001101	1.1010010011000000
8	0	1.0000000000000000	0.0000000011001101	1.1010010011000000
9	1	1.0000000010000000	0.0000000011001101	1.1010010011000000
10	1	1.0000000001000000	0.0000000001001101	1.1010010110010010
11	0	1.0000000000000000	0.0000000000001101	1.1010010111111011
12	0	1.0000000000000000	0.0000000000001101	1.1010010111111011
13	1	1.0000000000001000	0.0000000000001101	1.1010010111111011
14	1	1.0000000000000100	0.0000000000000101	1.1010011000001000
15	0	1.0000000000000000	0.0000000000000001	1.1010011000001111
16	1	1.0000000000000001	0.0000000000000001	1.1010011000001111

$$e^x \approx 1.6487$$

Table 5.3: Normalization computation of e^x

The argument range for the algorithm is $[0, \ln 2)$. Other ranges require range reduction, for which the specific steps are given in Section 1.2.

The complete algorithm for e^x:

$$X_1 = x \qquad\qquad\qquad\qquad 0 \le x < \ln 2 \qquad (5.22)$$

$$Y_1 = 1 \qquad\qquad\qquad\qquad\qquad\qquad\qquad\qquad\quad (5.23)$$

$$s_i = \begin{cases} 1 & \text{if } X_i - \ln\left(1 + 2^{-i}\right) \geq 0 \\ 0 & \text{otherwise} \end{cases} \qquad i = 1, 2, 3, \ldots \quad (5.24)$$

$$c_i = 1 + s_i 2^{-i} \qquad (5.25)$$

$$X_{i+1} = X_i - \ln c_i \qquad (5.26)$$

$$Y_{i+1} = c_i Y_i \qquad (5.27)$$

$$= Y_i + s_i 2^{-i} Y_i$$

In the algorithm, $X_i - \ln\left(+2^{-i}\right)$ must be computed, even if there is no normalization operation in that iteration. We shall see, in Section 5.6.1, that this can be avoided without making any fundamental changes in the algorithm.

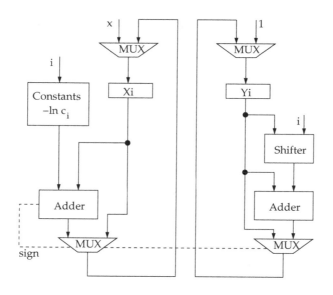

Figure 5.1: Hardware organization for computation of e^x

An example computation is given in Table 5.3. A sketch of hardware architecture for the algorithm is shown in Figure 5.1 and is largely self-explanatory. The only additional remark we make is that not all the constants, $\ln(1 + 2^{-i})$, need be stored. That is because the Taylor expanson for $\ln(1 + x)$ is[2]

$$\ln(1 + x) = x - \frac{x^2}{2} + \frac{x^3}{3} - \frac{x^4}{4} + \cdots \tag{5.28}$$

and with $x = 2^{-i}$, it is the case that within the limitations of n-bit machine precision

$$\ln(1 + 2^{-i}) = 2^{-i} \qquad \text{if } i \geq n/2$$

So constants must be stored for only the first half of the iterations; for the second half, the constants are readily obtained on the fly, by shifting. It is left to the reader to modify Figure 5.1 to accommodate this optimization.

Equation 5.28 also gives us a bit more information on the normalization process: the "small value" that is subtracted from X_i is approximately 2^{-i}, which is the weight of the ith bit in the representation of X_i. So we see that X_i is forced to zero by converting each 1 into a 0, one iteration at a time. We shall return to this point in Section 5.6.1, which includes a discussion on how to speed up this algorithm.

We now look at approximation error and convergence. After K iterations, the magnitude of the absolute approximation error is $|e^x - Y_{K+1}|$. At that point

$$X_{K+1} = x - \sum_{i=1}^{K} \ln c_i$$

$$\stackrel{\triangle}{=} \delta x$$

and

$$Y_{K+1} = \prod_{i=1}^{K} c_i$$

$$= e^{x - \left(x - \sum_{i=1}^{K} \ln c_i\right)}$$

$$= e^{x - \delta x}$$

Now, consider the ratio

$$\left| \frac{e^x - Y_{K+1}}{X_{K+1}} \right|$$

---

[2]See Table 6.3.

For the worst case, we may take the limit as $\delta x \to 0$:

$$\lim_{\delta x \to 0} \left| \frac{e^x - e^{x - \delta x}}{\delta x} \right| = e^x$$

We have assumed that $x \in [0, \ln 2)$; so $e^x < 2$, and, therefore,

$$\frac{|e^x - Y_{K+1}|}{|X_{K+1}|} < 2$$

So

$$|e^x - Y_{K+1}| < 2 |X_{K+1}| \tag{5.29}$$

To progress further, we will show that

$$|X_i| < 2^{-i+1} \qquad\qquad i \geq 1 \tag{5.30}$$

and, therefore, that $|X_{K+1}| < 2^{-K}$. We do that by showing, inductively, that

$$0 \leq X_i < \ln(1 + 2^{-i+1}) \tag{5.31}$$

From this and Equation 5.28 (with $x = 2^{-i+1}$), we may immediately deduce Inequation 5.30.

The normalizing operation on X_i is carried out only if it will leave $X_{i+1} \geq 0$. Since $X_1 \geq 0$, it follows that $X_i \geq 0$ for all i. To show the other side of Inequations 5.31, for the base case in the induction, the range restriction ensures that $X_1 < \ln 2 = \ln(1 + 2^0)$. Now, assume that Inequation 5.31 holds. There are two cases to consider, according to the s_i-selection:

- If $X_i \geq \ln(1 + 2^{-i})$, then

$$\ln(1 + 2^{-i}) \leq X_i < \ln(1 + 2^{-i+1})$$

and so

$$0 \leq X_i - \ln(1 + 2^{-i}) < \ln(1 + 2^{-i+1}) - \ln(1 + 2^{-i})$$

Since $X_{i+1} = X_i - \ln(1 + 2^{-i})$, and expansions on the basis of Equation 5.28 show that $\ln(1 + 2^{-i+1}) - \ln(1 + 2^{-i}) < \ln(1 + 2^{-i})$:

$$0 \leq X_{i+1} < \ln(1 + 2^{-i}) < 2^{-i}$$

- On the other hand, if $X_i < \ln(1 + 2^{-i})$, then $X_{i+1} = X_i$, and Equation 5.28 implies that $X_{i+1} < 2^{-i}$.

Finally, combining Inequations 5.29 and 5.30, we conclude that the magnitude of the absolute approximation error after $n+1$ iterations will be less than 2^{-n}, i.e. convergence at the rate of about one bit per iteration.

The total error includes representation errors in the constants, computation errors during the arithmetic, and the propagation of all these. As indicated in the chapter's introduction, $\lceil \log_2(n+2) \rceil + 1$ guard bits will suffice to ensure that the totality of such errors does not exceed 2^{-n}. With the addition of the approximation error, we may conclude that $n+1$ iterations are sufficient to produce a result that is accurate to n bits. A different confirmation of the rate of convergence is given in Section 5.6, where faster variants of the algorithm are also discussed.

5.3.2 *Logarithm*

The algorithm for the computation of natural logarithms and its derivation are, in many ways, the "inverses" of those for the exponential function. The basis is multiplicative normalization.

Let $\{c_i\}$ be a set of constants, and consider the equation

$$\ln x = \ln\left(x \prod_i c_i \right) - \ln \prod_i c_i$$

If the constants are chosen so that

$$\ln\left(x \prod_i c_i \right) \to 0 \text{ as } i \to \infty$$

then

$$x \prod_i c_i \to 1$$

and

$$-\ln \prod_i c_i \to \ln x$$

Now, define

$$X_i = x \prod_{k=1}^{i-1} c_k$$

$$Y_i = -\ln \prod_{k=1}^{i-1} c_k$$

$$= -\sum_{k=1}^{i-1} \ln c_k$$

Then the recurrences for the computation of $\ln x$ are

$$X_{i+1} = c_i X_i$$

$$Y_{i+1} = Y_i - \ln c_i$$

If $X_1 = x$ and $Y_1 = 0$, then after n iterations $X_{n+1} \approx 1$ and $Y_{n+1} \approx \ln x$, with convergence at the rate of about one bit per iteration. With $X_1 = x$ and $Y_1 = y$, we get $Y_n \approx y + \ln x$. As in the case of the exponential function, and for the similar reasons, we take $c_i = 1 + s_i 2^{-i}$.

The normalization is to $x \prod_i c_i \approx 1$, so the argument range for convergence is limited to

$$\min \frac{1}{\prod_i c_i} \leq x \leq \max \frac{1}{\prod_i c_i} \qquad (5.32)$$

A simple algorithm for $\ln x$:

$$X_1 = x \qquad\qquad\qquad 1/2 \leq x < 1 \quad (5.33)$$

$$Y_1 = 0 \qquad\qquad\qquad\qquad\qquad\qquad (5.34)$$

$$s_i = \begin{cases} 1 & \text{if } X_i\left(1 + 2^{-i}\right) < 1 \\ 0 & \text{otherwise} \end{cases} \qquad i = 1, 2, 3, \ldots \quad (5.35)$$

$$c_i = 1 + s_i 2^{-i} \qquad\qquad\qquad\qquad\qquad (5.36)$$

$$X_{i+1} = c_i X_i$$

$$= X_i + s_i 2^{-i} X_i \qquad\qquad\qquad (5.37)$$

$$Y_{i+1} = Y_i - \ln c_i \qquad\qquad\qquad\qquad (5.38)$$

The justification for the s_i-selection rule is similar to that for the exponential-algorithm, except that here the normalizing operation is a multiplication, and the target is one.

An example computation is given in Table 5.4, and a sketch of the corresponding hardware architecture is shown in Figure 5.2. The constants here are the same as those in the algorithm for exponentials, and, as shown above, not all need be stored. A comparison of Figures 5.1 and 5.2 also shows that it is possible to easily devise an arrangement in which the evaluation of e^x and $\ln x$ are carried out on the same hardware.

$$x = 0.55 \qquad\qquad \ln x = -0.597837\cdots$$

i	s_i	c_i	X_i	Y_i
1	1	1.1000000000000000	0.1000110011001100	0.0000000000000000
2	0	1.0000000000000000	0.1101001100110011	- 0.0110011111001100
3	1	1.0010000000000000	0.1101001100110011	- 0.0110011111001100
4	1	1.0001000000000000	0.1110110110011001	- 0.1000010111110011
5	0	1.0000000000000000	0.1111110001110011	- 0.1001010101111000
6	0	1.0000000000000000	0.1111110001110011	- 0.1001010101111000
7	1	1.0000001000000000	0.1111110001110011	- 0.1001010101111000
8	1	1.0000000100000000	0.1111111001101100	- 0.1001011101110110
9	1	1.0000000010000000	0.1111111101101010	- 0.1001100001110110
10	0	1.0000000000000000	0.1111111111101010	- 0.1001100011110110
11	0	1.0000000000000000	0.1111111111101010	- 0.1001100011110110
12	1	1.0000000000010000	0.1111111111101010	- 0.1001100011110110
13	0	1.0000000000000000	0.1111111111111010	- 0.1001100100000110
14	1	1.0000000000000100	0.1111111111111010	- 0.1001100100000110
15	0	1.0000000000000000	0.1111111111111110	- 0.1001100100001010
16	1	1.0000000000000001	0.1111111111111110	- 0.1001100100001010
				$\ln 0.55 \approx -0.5978$

Table 5.4: Normalization computation of $\ln x$

We next look at convergence and errors. The example of Table 5.4 clearly indicates that the convergence is linear: at each step, bit i of X_i is changed to 1, if it is not already 1, thus driving X_i to one. This suggested linear convergence is confirmed in what follows.

The magnitude of absolute approximation error after K iterations is

$$|\ln x - Y_{K+1}| = \left|\ln x + \ln \prod_{i=1}^{K} c_i\right|$$

$$= \left| \ln\left(x \prod_{i=1}^{K} c_i \right) \right|$$

$$= | \ln X_{K+1} |$$

and from the Taylor expansion[3]

$$\ln(X_{K+1}) = (X_{K+1} - 1) - \frac{(X_{K+1} - 1)^2}{2} + \frac{(X_{K+1} - 1)^3}{3}$$
$$- \frac{(X_{K+1} - 1)^4}{4} + \cdots$$

we may conclude that the magnitude of the absolute error is bounded by $|X_{K+1} - 1|$.

To progress we note that

$$X_i \geq 1 - 2^{-i+1} \qquad \text{for all } i \qquad (5.39)$$

In particular, that:

- If $s_i = 1$, then $X_i \geq 2^{-i+1}$.
- If $s_i = 0$, then $X_i \geq 2^{-i}$.

and, therefore, we have

$$|X_i - 1| < 2^{-i+1}$$

The latter is immediately apparent from the fact that $X_i(1 + 2^{-i}) \geq 1$; so

$$X_{i+1} \geq \frac{1}{1 + 2^{-i}} = 1 - 2^{-i} + 2^{-2i} - 2^{-3i} + \cdots$$

The former is a bit trickier to see, and, given the space required to show it, we leave it as an exercise for the reader.[4]

We may therefore conclude that after $n+1$ iterations the approximation error is at most 2^{-n}. And $\lceil \log_2(n+1) \rceil + 1$ guard bits in the arithmetic will be suffient to control the generated errors. So, $n+1$ iterations are sufficient to produce a result that is accurate to n bits. A different confirmation of the rate of convergence is given in Section 5.6.1, where faster variants of the algorithm are also discussed.

---

[3]See Table 6.3.
[4]Use the fact that $\prod_{i=j}^{k}(1 + 2^{-i}) \geq 1 + 2^{-j+1} - 2^{-k}$, for $j \geq 1$.

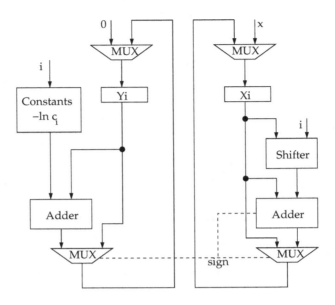

Figure 5.2: Hardware architecture for computation of $\ln x$

5.4   Trigonometric functions and inverses

The application of normalization techniques to the derivation of algorithms
for the trigonometric functions produces exactly the CORDIC algorithms
of Chapter 3. This section is therefore included for "completeness" only.

Let θ be the argument and $\{c_i\}$ a set of complex constants: $c_i = |c_i|e^{j\theta_i}$,
where $j = \sqrt{-1}$ and θ_i is some angle. Now, consider the complex exponential

$$e^{j\theta} = \frac{e^{j\theta} \prod_i c_i}{\prod_i c_i}$$

$$= \frac{e^{j\theta} \prod_i c_i}{e^{j \sum_i \theta_i} \prod_i |c_i|}$$

$$= e^{j(\theta - \sum_i \theta_i)} \frac{\prod_i c_i}{\prod_i |c_i|}$$

If $(\theta - \sum_i \theta_i) \to 0$, then

$$\frac{\prod_i c_i}{\prod_i |c_i|} \to e^{j\theta}$$

Let us suppose that we have achieved such convergence, so that

$$e^{j\theta} = \frac{\prod_i c_i}{\prod_i |c_i|}$$

Applying Euler's formula[5]

$$\cos\theta + j\sin\theta = \frac{\prod_i c_i}{\prod_i |c_i|}$$

and letting X be the real part of $\prod_i c_i$ and Y be the imaginary part, we have

$$\cos\theta + j\sin\theta = \frac{X}{\prod_i |c_i|} + j\frac{Y}{\prod_i |c_i|}$$

whence

$$\cos\theta = \frac{X}{\prod_i |c_i|} \quad \text{and} \quad \sin\theta = \frac{Y}{\prod_i |c_i|}$$

The algorithm to compute X and Y is then obtained as follows. Define

$$Z_i = x - \sum_{k=0}^{i-1} \theta_k$$

$$W_i = \prod_{k=0}^{i-1} c_k$$

Then

$$Z_{i+1} = Z_i - \theta_i$$

$$W_{i+1} = W_i c_i$$
$$= (X_i + jY_i)\, c_i$$

where X_i and Y_i and the real and imaginary parts of W_i.

If for the constants and angles we take $c_i = 1 + js_i 2^{-i}$ and $\theta_i = \tan^{-1} 2^{-i}$, where $s_i \in \{-1, 1\}$, then we get

$$Z_{i+1} = Z_i - \tan^{-1}(s_i 2^{-i})$$
$$= Z_i - s_i \tan^{-1} 2^{-i} \qquad \text{since } s_i \in \{-1, 1\}$$

$$W_{i+1} = (X_i + jY_i)\left(1 + js_i 2^{-i}\right)$$
$$= \left(X_i - s_i 2^{-i}Y_i\right) + j\left(Y_i + s_i 2^{-i}X_i\right)$$

---

[5] This is $e^{j\theta} = \cos\theta + j\sin\theta$.

Separating the real and imaginary parts of W_{i+1} gives us the recurrences for the computation of X and Y:

$$X_{i+1} = X_i - s_i 2^{-i} Y_i$$

$$Y_{i+1} = Y_i + s_i 2^{-i} X_i$$

The reader will observe that these X_i, Y_i, and Z_i recurrences are exactly the sine–cosine CORDIC recurrences of Chapter 3.

For convergence, $Z_i = \theta - \sum_i \theta_i$ is driven to zero; so s_i is chosen as

$$s_i = \begin{cases} 1 & \text{if } Z_i \geq 0 \\ -1 & \text{otherwise} \end{cases}$$

Lastly, note that $\cos\theta = X / \prod_i |c_i|$ and $\sin\theta = Y / \prod_i |c_i|$, and from with the choice of c_i:

$$\prod_i |c_i| = \prod_i \sqrt{1 + s_i^2 2^{-i}}$$

$$= \prod_i \sqrt{1 + 2^{-2i}} \qquad \text{since } s_i \in \{-1, 1\}$$

which is just the scaling constant, K, in the sine–cosine CORDIC recurrences.

A similar exercise in deriving a normalization algorithm for the arctangent function will produce the same recurrences but with Y_i driven to zero and the result accumulated in X_i, as we next show.

Suppose that the complex number $1 + jx$ is repeatedly multiplied by a set of constants, $\{c_i\}$, so that

$$(1 + jx) \prod_i c_i \to R \qquad \text{for some real } R$$

Assume that such convergence has been achieved, so that

$$1 + jx = \frac{R}{\prod_i c_i}$$

If we take $c_i = 1 + j s_i 2^{-i}$, with $s_i \in \{-1, 1\}$, then in polar coordinates[6] the last equation is

$$\sqrt{1 + x^2}\, e^{j \tan^{-1} x} = \frac{R}{\prod_i \sqrt{1 + s_i^2 2^{-2i}}} e^{-j \sum_i \tan^{-1}(s_i 2^{-i})}$$

---

[6]This is $a + jb = \sqrt{a^2 + b^2}\, e^{j\phi}$, where $\phi = \tan^{-1}(b/a)$.

Taking the natural logarithms of both sides and equating the imaginary parts, we get

$$\tan^{-1} x = -\sum_i \tan^{-1}\left(s_i 2^{-i}\right)$$

Now, define

$$W_i = (1 + jx) \prod_{k=0}^{i-1} c_k$$

$$Z_i = -\sum_{k=0}^{i-1} c_k$$

Then

$$W_{i+1} = W_i c_i$$

$$Z_{i+1} = Z_i - \tan^{-1}(s_i 2^{-i})$$

$$= Z_i - s_i \tan^{-1} 2^{-i} \qquad \text{since } s_i \in \{-1, 1\}$$

where $W_i \to R$ and $Z_i \to \tan^{-1} x$.

If we separate the real and imaginary parts of W_{i+1}, as done above for sine and cosine, then we get the same recurrences:

$$X_{i+1} = X_i - s_i Y_i 2^{-i}$$

$$Y_{i+1} = Y_i + s_i X_i 2^{-i}$$

where X_i corresponds to the real part, and Y_i corresponds to the imaginary part. In this case, however, we accumulate an angle in Z_i and drive W_i to a real number. The latter means driving Y_i to zero, which is just the vectoring mode in CORDIC.

5.5 Square root and inverse

Algorithms for these functions are discussed in detail in Chapter 8; so the following is a brief introduction that omits numerous details. The algorithms given are both multiplicative-normalization and additive-normalization ones.

Both the square root function and its inverse can be evaluated through the same multiplicative-normalization algorithm. The algorithm is closely related to a well-known multiplicative-normalization algorithm for division

(Section 2.3.1.1.), in which N/D is computed by repeatedly multiplying N by increasingly better approximations to $1/D$. Here, x replaces N, and $\sqrt{x}$ replaces D; in essence, $1/\sqrt{x}$ is computed iteratively, and at the same time, running multiplications by x iteratively produce $\sqrt{x}$. The details are as follows.

Let $\{c_i\}$ be a set of constants such that

$$x \prod_i c_i^2 \to 1 \text{ as } i \to \infty$$

Then

$$\prod_i c_i^2 \to \frac{1}{x}$$

$$\prod_i c_i \to \frac{1}{\sqrt{x}}$$

$$x \prod_i c_i \to \sqrt{x}$$

Now, define

$$X_i = x \prod_{k=1}^{i-1} c_k^2$$

$$Y_i = x \prod_{k=1}^{i-1} c_k$$

$$Z_i = \prod_{k=1}^{i-1} c_i$$

Then

$$X_{i+1} = c_i^2 X_i$$
$$Y_{i+1} = c_i Y_i$$
$$Z_{i+1} = c_i Z_i$$

where $X_i \to 1, Y_i \to \sqrt{x}$, and $Z_i \to 1/\sqrt{x}$.

The normalization is to $x \prod_i c_i^2 \approx 1$, so the argument range for convergence is

$$\min \frac{1}{\prod_i c_i^2} \le x \le \max \frac{1}{\prod_i c_i^2} \tag{5.40}$$

For the reasons given in Section 5.1, we will take $c_i = 1 + s_i 2^{-i}$, with s_i is chosen to drive the values of X_i to 1, on a basis that is similar to that for the other algorithms above.

The complete set of recurrences for an algorithm for the computation of $\sqrt{x}$ and $1/\sqrt{x}$:

$$X_1 = x \qquad\qquad 1/4 \leq x < 1 \qquad (5.41)$$

$$Y_1 = x \qquad\qquad (5.42)$$

$$Z_1 = 1 \qquad\qquad (5.43)$$

$$s_i = \begin{cases} 1 & \text{if } X_i \left(1 + 2^{-i}\right)^2 < 1 \qquad i = 1, 2, 3, \dots \\ 0 & \text{otherwise} \end{cases} \qquad (5.44)$$

$$c_i = 1 + s_i 2^{-i} \qquad\qquad (5.45)$$

$$X_{i+1} = X_i c_i^2 \qquad\qquad (5.46)$$

$$Y_{i+1} = Y_i c_i \qquad\qquad (5.47)$$

$$Z_{i+1} = Z_i c_i \qquad\qquad (5.48)$$

At the end of n iterations, $X_{n+1} \approx 1$, $Y_{n+1} \approx \sqrt{x}$, and $Z_{n+1} \approx 1/\sqrt{x}$. In general, if $Y_1 = y$, then the algorithm will compute $Y_n \approx y/\sqrt{x}$. The rate of convergence is about one bit per iteration, and this can be shown by considering the bounds on $|X_i - 1|$, in the manner done above for the computation of logarithms. An example computation is given in Table 5.5.

Square root evaluation is covered in detail in Chapter 8; so we leave it to the reader to imagine hardware organizations for the algorithm here, noting that the nominal multiplications by c_i and c_i^2 can be implemented as shifts and additions. In Chapter 8 we shall also see another, much faster, multiplicative-normalization algorithm for square root that has many similarities with the one just given, but which uses multipliers of a very different form. That later algorithm mirrors the Goldschmidt division algorithm of Section 2.3.1.1.

There is also for square root an additive-normalization algorithm that is very similar to subtractive algorithms for division, which means that with judicious choices, the same hardware can be used for both square root evaluation and division. The reader who is familiar with paper-and-pencil algorithms for square root computation will readily recognise the following algorithm as a version of the *"completing-the-square"* algorithm.

$$x = 0.65 \qquad \sqrt{x} = 0.8062257\cdots \qquad 1/\sqrt{x} = 1.240347\cdots$$

i	s_i	$\mathbf{X_i}$	$\mathbf{Y_i}$	$\mathbf{Z_i}$
1	0	0.1010011001100110	0.1010011001100110	1.0000000000000000
2	0	0.1010011001100110	0.1010011001100110	1.0000000000000000
3	1	0.1010011001100110	0.1010011001100110	1.0000000000000000
4	1	0.1101001010011001	0.1011101100110011	1.0010000000000000
5	1	0.1110110110111111	0.1100011011100110	1.0011001000000000
6	0	0.1111110011010110	0.1100110100011101	1.0011101110010000
7	0	0.1111110011010110	0.1100110100011101	1.0011101110010000
8	1	0.1111110011010110	0.1100110100011101	1.0011101110010000
9	1	0.1111111011010001	0.1100110111101010	1.0011110011001011
10	0	0.1111111111010000	0.1100111001010001	1.0011110101101001
11	0	0.1111111111010000	0.1100111001010001	1.0011110101101001
12	1	0.1111111111010000	0.1100111001010001	1.0011110101101001
13	0	0.1111111111110000	0.1100111001011110	1.0011110101111101
14	1	0.1111111111110000	0.1100111001011110	1.0011110101111101
15	1	0.1111111111111000	0.1100111001100001	1.0011110110000010
16	1	0.1111111111111100	0.1100111001100011	1.0011110110000101
			$\sqrt{x} = 0.8062$	$1/\sqrt{x} = 1.2403$

Table 5.5: Normalization computation of $\sqrt{x}$ and $1/\sqrt{x}$

Suppose that for some constants, $\{c_i\}$, we have

$$x - \left(\sum_i c_i\right)^2 \to 0 \text{ as } i \to \infty$$

then

$$\left(\sum_i c_i\right)^2 \to x$$

and

$$\sum_i c_i \to \sqrt{x}$$

If we define

$$X_i = x - Y_i^2$$

$$Y_i = \sum_{k=0}^{i-1} c_k$$

Then $Y_i \to \sqrt{x}$, provided $X_i \to 0$.

So, the recurrences for X_i and Y_i are

$$X_{i+1} = x - (Y_i + c_i)^2$$

$$= (x - Y_i^2) - 2c_{i+1}Y_i - c_i^2$$

$$= X_i - 2c_iY_i - c_i^2$$

$$Y_{i+1} = Y_i + c_i$$

with c_i chosen to ensure that the values of X_i converge to zero.

Recalling the remarks in Section 5.1, a good choice here for c_i is $s_i 2^{-i}$, and an s_i-selection rule may be formulated that is similar to that for the other algorithms above.

The algorithm:

$$X_0 = x \qquad\qquad 1/4 \leq x < 1 \qquad (5.49)$$

$$Y_0 = 0 \qquad\qquad (5.50)$$

$$c_i = s_i 2^{-i} \qquad\qquad i = 0, 1, 2, \ldots \qquad (5.51)$$

$$X_{i+1} = X_i - 2c_iY_i - c_i^2 \qquad\qquad (5.52)$$

$$= X_i - s_i 2^{-i} \left(2Y_i + s_i 2^{-i} \right) \qquad\qquad (5.53)$$

$$Y_{i+1} = Y_i + c_i \qquad\qquad (5.54)$$

$$= Y_i + s_i 2^{-i} \qquad\qquad (5.55)$$

$$s_i = \begin{cases} 1 & \text{if } X_i - 2^{-i} \left(2Y_i + 2^{-i} \right) \geq 0 \\ 0 & \text{otherwise} \end{cases} \qquad (5.56)$$

The essence of the s_i-selection rule is that the next bit of the square root is determined according to the difference between the original argument and the "square of the square root-formed-so-far", whence the term "completing the square": X_i is driven to zero as the square is completed. At the end of n iterations, $X_n \approx 0$ and $Y_n \approx \sqrt{x}$.

It will be observed that there is no real arithmetic in the computation of Y_{i+1}: s_i is the next bit of the square root and is simply appended to the bits computed before that; more precisely, since Y_0 is represented in all 0s, at each step, s_i replaces the 0 at bit position i of Y_i. Therefore, there is no computation error, and no guard bits will be required in the implementation. It is also apparent that the algorithm computes one bit of the result in iteration; so the approximation error is at most 2^{-n} after n iterations. We leave it to the reader to verify this, by considering the values $|X_i|$, as done above for exponentials.

An example computation is given in Table 5.6. As with the multiplicative-normalization algorithm given just above, the algorithm here too is subsumed in the discussions of Chapter 8, and we leave it to the reader to consider a hardware organization for the present case.

$$x = 0.65 \qquad\qquad \sqrt{x} = 0.8062257\cdots$$

i	s_i	X_i	Y_i
0	0	0.101001100110011	0.000000000000000
1	1	0.101001100110011	0.000000000000000
2	1	0.011001100110011	0.100000000000000
3	0	0.000101100110011	0.110000000000000
4	0	0.000101100110011	0.110000000000000
5	1	0.000101100110011	0.110000000000000
6	1	0.000010100010011	0.110010000000000
7	1	0.000000111101011	0.110011000000000
8	0	0.000000001010001	0.110011100000000
9	0	0.000000001010001	0.110011100000000
10	1	0.000000001010001	0.110011100000000
11	1	0.000000000011101	0.110011100100000
12	0	0.000000000000011	0.110011100110000
13	0	0.000000000000011	0.110011100110000
14	1	0.000000000000011	0.110011100110000
15	0	0.000000000000000	0.110011100110010

$$\sqrt{0.65} \approx 0.0.8062$$

Table 5.6: Additive-normalization computation of $\sqrt{x}$, $s_i \in \{0, 1\}$

$$x = 0.65 \qquad \sqrt{x} = 0.8062257\cdots$$

i	s_i	X_i	Y_i
0	1	00.1010011001100110	00.0000000000000000
1	1	00.0110011001100110	00.1000000000000000
2	1	00.0001011001100110	00.1100000000000000
3	-1	-00.0001110110011001	00.1110000000000000
4	-1	-00.0000001010011001	00.1101000000000000
5	1	00.0000101000100110	00.1100100000000000
6	1	00.0000001111010110	00.1100110000000000
7	1	00.0000000010100010	00.1100111000000000
8	-1	-00.0000000011111010	00.1100111100000000
9	-1	-00.0000000000101011	00.1100111010000000
10	1	00.0000000000111011	00.1100111001000000
11	1	00.0000000000000111	00.1100111001100000
12	-1	-00.0000000000010010	00.1100111001110000
13	-1	-00.0000000000000101	00.1100111001101000
14	1	00.0000000000000001	00.1100111001100100
15	-1	-00.0000000000000001	00.1100111001100110

$$(\sqrt{0.65} \approx 0.0.8062)$$

Table 5.7: Additive-normalization computation of $\sqrt{x}$, $s_i \in \{\bar{1}, 1\}$

A slightly different algorithm can be obtained by choosing an s_i-selection rule that is similar to that of non-restoring division:

$$X_0 = x \qquad\qquad 1/4 \le x < 1 \tag{5.57}$$

$$Y_0 = 0 \tag{5.58}$$

$$s_i = \begin{cases} 1 & \text{if } X_i \ge 0 \\ -1 & \text{otherwise} \end{cases} \qquad i = 0, 1, 2, \ldots \tag{5.59}$$

$$c_i = s_i 2^{-i} \tag{5.60}$$

$$X_{i+1} = X_i - 2c_i Y_i - c_i^2 \tag{5.61}$$

$$= X_i - s_i 2^{-i} \left(2Y_i + s_i 2^{-i} \right) \tag{5.62}$$

$$Y_{i+1} = Y_i + c_i \qquad (5.63)$$

$$= Y_i + s_i 2^{-i} \qquad (5.64)$$

An example computation is given in Table 5.7. Here, the computation of Y_i requires real arithmetic, either in every iteration or at the end of the iterating. The former is the case if the Y_i is generated in conventional form, which implies a carry–propagate addition in every iteration. On the other hand, if Y_i is produced with the digit set $\{\bar{1}, 1\}$, then the computation of Y_{i+1} is again just the appending of s_i to the digits formed thus far of the result. In this case, there must be a final conversion to the digit set $\{0, 1\}$. That conversion can be done by a single carry–propagate subtraction of the negative digits from the positive ones, once the iterating is completed, or on the fly (Section 2.1.2).

Further discussions on the computation of $\sqrt{x}$ and $1/\sqrt{x}$ will be found in Chapter 8. Those discussions include convergence and errors, and, as the algorithms considered are extensions of those given here, we have here omitted the details of such matters.

5.6   High-performance exponential and logarithm

We next describe faster versions of the basic algorithms for the computation of exponentials and logarithms. The discussion is in three parts of "progressive improvement". In the first part we shall show that, with certain restrictions, the algorithms of Section 5.2 can be converted into algorithms in which there need not be any arithmetic operations in some iterations and that the iterating can be stopped early, with half of the original iterations replaced with a single multiplication (for exponentials) or subtraction (for logarithms) [5]. The second and third parts, which comprise most of the section, deal with the use of large radices and redundant representations.

5.6.1   *Early termination and zero skipping*

Consider the algorithm of Equations 5.22–5.27 for the computation of exponentials:

$$X_1 = x \qquad\qquad\qquad 0 \le x < \ln 2$$

$$Y_1 = 1$$

$$s_i = \begin{cases} 1 & \text{if } X_i - \ln(1 + 2^{-i}) \ge 0 \\ 0 & \text{otherwise} \end{cases} \qquad i = 1, 2, 3, \ldots$$

$$c_i = 1 + s_i 2^{-i}$$

$$X_{i+1} = X_i - \ln c_i$$

$$Y_{i+1} = c_i Y_i$$

The normalization is to drive X_i to zero, a process that we may view as one of changing each 1 in the representation of[7] X_i into a 0. Note that the value of $X_i - \ln(1 + 2^{-i})$ is computed in every iteration, even if there is no normalizing operation. We will show that this need not be so.

Let k be the position, after the binary point, of the leading 1 in X_i. Then

$$X_i = 2^{-k} + u_i$$

where

$$0 \le u_i < 2^{-k}$$

That is, u_i is represented by the bits of X_i after the kth one, and 2^{-k} is the weight of the leading 1 in X_i.

Now, the Taylor expansion

$$\ln(1 + x) = x - \frac{x^2}{2} + \frac{x^3}{3} - \frac{x^4}{4} + \cdots \tag{5.65}$$

shows that if the normalizing constant is taken to be $\ln(1 + 2^{-k})$, then the normalizing operation

$$X_{i+1} = X_i - \ln(1 + 2^{-k}) \tag{5.66}$$

will change bit k of X_i, from 1 to 0. We can therefore turn all 1s in X_i into 0s, one at a time, by choosing

$$s_i = \begin{cases} 1 & \text{if bit } i \text{ of } X_i \text{ is } 1 \\ 0 & \text{otherwise} \end{cases} \qquad i = 1, 2, 3, \ldots$$

---

[7]For brevity, in what follows we frequently omit the "the representation of" where, strictly, we should have it.

The example of Table 5.8 shows this, in the underlined bits from $i = 1$ to $i = 8$.

$$x = 0.5 \qquad e^x = 1.648712\cdots$$

i	s_i	c_i	X_i	Y_i
1	1	1.1000000000000000	0.1000000000000000	1.0000000000000000
2	0	1.0000000000000000	0.0001100000110011	1.1000000000000000
3	0	1.0000000000000000	0.0001100000110011	1.1000000000000000
4	1	1.0001000000000000	0.0001100000110011	1.1000000000000000
5	1	1.0000100000000000	0.0000100010101110	1.1001100000000000
6	0	1.0000000000000000	0.0000000011001101	1.1010010011000000
7	0	1.0000000000000000	0.0000000011001101	1.1010010011000000
8	0	1.0000000000000000	0.0000000011001101	1.1010010011000000
9	1	1.0000000010000000	0.0000000011001101	1.1010010011000000
10	1	1.0000000001000000	0.0000000001001101	1.1010010110010010
11	0	1.0000000000000000	0.0000000000001101	1.1010010111111011
12	0	1.0000000000000000	0.0000000000001101	1.1010010111111011
13	1	1.0000000000001000	0.0000000000001101	1.1010010111111011
14	1	1.0000000000000100	0.0000000000000101	1.1010011000001000
15	0	1.0000000000000000	0.0000000000000001	1.1010011000001111
16	1	1.0000000000000001	0.0000000000000001	1.1010011000001111
				$e^{0.5} \approx 1.6487$

Table 5.8: Normalization computation of e^x

If $k \geq n/2$ in Equation 5.66, then by Equation 5.65, $\ln(1 + 2^{-i}) = 2^{-i}$ to within n-bit machine precision; so the normalizing operation

$$X_{i+1} = X_i - 2^{-k}$$

will change bit k from 1 to 0 and also leave all other bits unchanged; that is, X_i and X_{i+1} will differ only in the changed bit. Therefore, at the start of iteration $i = n/2 + 1$, all the subsequent values of s_i are known. The example of Table 5.8 shows this: the underlined bits of X_8 at $i = 9$ are exactly the s_i values from that that point on. Given that all those values of s_i are known at that point, we may immediately stop the process of driving X_i to zero, by performing the nominal subtraction

$$X_{n+1} = X_i - X_i \qquad i = n/2 + 1$$

and then use those s_i-values to compute Y_{n+1}, as follows.

Let $X_{i,j}$ denote bit j of X_i. On termination, for $i \geq n/2$, we choose $s_i = X_{n/2, i}$, and

$$Y_{n+1} = \prod_{i=k}^{n} c_i$$

$$= Y_k \prod_{i=k}^{n} \left(1 + s_i 2^{-i}\right) \qquad\qquad k = n/2$$

$$= Y_k \left[1 + s_k 2^{-k} + s_{k+1} 2^{-(k+1)} + \cdots + s_n 2^{-n}\right]$$

where smaller powers have been omitted, because they are zero to within n-bit machine precison. And on the basis on which the s_i values have been determined and given that $X_{k, i}=0$, for all $i < n/2$,

$$Y_{n+1} = Y_k \left[1 + 2^{-k} X_{k, k} + 2^{-(k+1)} X_{k, k+1} + \cdots + s_n 2^{-n} X_{k, n}\right]$$

$$= Y_k(1 + X_k)$$

In the example of Table 5.8, $Y_8 \approx 1.6436$, $X_8, \approx 0.0031$, and the computed terminating value is $Y_{17} \approx 1.6487$.

We may therefore conclude that the effect of what would have been the last $n/2$ iterations can be achieved with a single multiplication. (There is no real addition in $1 + X_k$: since $X_k < 1$, the $+1$ is by insertion.) Further optimizations in a similar vein, of both algorithm and hardware, are described in [6, 12].

It should be noted that the multiplier used in the termination need not be particularly fast. Even a good sequential multiplier will do, for the following reason. In the architecture of Figure 5.1, all the additions are carried in carry propagate adders. But a multiplication can be accomplished with a sequence of fast carry–save additions and a single (relatively slow) carry–propagate addition (see Section 2.2). Therefore $n/2$ carry–propagate additions can be replaced with the much faster combination of $n/2$ carry–save additions and one carry–propagate addition.

Early termination also has another important effect: the computation error over $n/2$ operations (additions) is replaced with computation error over one operation (a multiplication), with one consequence being a reduction in the number of guard bits required.

The discussion above also shows that the computations up to $i = n/2$ can also be speeded up, if there is a way to count[8] the number of leading 0s (i.e. determine the position, k, of the leading 1) in X_i. Given that the effect of the normalizing operations is to change 1s in X_i into 0s, and that there is no effect for a bit that is already 0, the choice of s_i as bit i of X_i makes it possible skip past a string of 0s without performing any arithmetic operation, whence the "*zero-skipping*". (Thus in the example of Table 5.8, it is possible to skip five of the first eight iterations.) Of course, this has implications that must be considered carefully: the extra cost in hardware, an increase in the complexity of the control logic, and a change in the critical path, with an attendant slight increase in cycle time.

Putting together all of the preceding, we see that the number of iterations required for an n-bit result can be reduced to an average of about $n/4$, assuming that, on average, the number of 1s to be eliminated is n/2 and that half of these are in the first $n/2$ iterations. This, of course, assumes that both the increased hardware costs and variable, operand-dependent operational times are acceptabe.

The speed-up techniques just described are possible with the basic algorithm (Equations 5.33–5.38) for the computation of logarithms too, as we next show. For the following discussion, the reader might find it helpful to refer to the example computation given in Table 5.9. Also note that the normalization drives X_i to one, i.e. $1 - X_i$ to zero, and this may be taken as changing all 1s in $1 - X_i$ into 0s.

Let k be the position (after the binary point) of the leading 1 in $1 - X_i$. Then

$$1 - X_i = 2^{-k} + u_i \tag{5.67}$$

where

$$0 \le u_i < 2^{-k}$$

So 2^{-k} is the weight of the leading 1 in $1 - X_i$, and u_i is represented by the bits of $1 - X_i$ after bit k.

If the normalizing multiplier is taken to be $1 + 2^{-k}$, then the normalizing operation is the computation of

$$X_{i+1} = X_i \left(1 + 2^{-k}\right)$$
$$= \left(1 - 2^{-k} - u_i\right)\left(1 + 2^{-k}\right)$$
$$= 1 - u_i \left(1 + 2^{-k}\right) - 2^{-2k}$$

---

[8]Such an operation is standard in floating-point arithmetic, and efficient and fast hardware has been developed for the task.

and

$$1 - X_{i+1} = u_i + u_i 2^{-k} + 2^{-2k} \qquad (5.68)$$

i	s_i	c_i	$x = 0.56$ $\mathbf{X}_i$	$\ln x = -0.579818\cdots$ $\mathbf{Y}_i$
1	1	1.1000000000000000	0.1000111101011100 *0.0111000010100011*	0.0000000000000000
2	0	1.0000000000000000	0.1101011100001010 *0.0010100011110101*	-0.0110011111001100
3	1	1.0010000000000000	0.1101011100001010 *0.0010100011110101*	-0.0110011111001100
4	0	1.0000000000000000	0.1111000111101011 *0.0000111000010100*	-0.1000010111110011
5	1	1.0000100000000000	0.1111000111101011 *0.0000111000010100*	-0.1000010111110011
6	1	1.0000010000000000	0.1111100101111010 *0.0000011010000101*	-0.1000110111010100
7	1	1.0000001000000000	0.1111110101100000 *0.0000001010011111*	-0.1001000111001100
8	0	1.0000000000000000	0.1111111101011011 *0.0000000010100100*	-0.1001001111001010
9	1	1.0000000010000000	0.1111111101011011 *0.0000000010100100*	-0.1001001111001010
10	0	1.0000000000000000	0.1111111111011011 *0.0000000000100100*	-0.1001010001001010
11	1	1.0000000000100000	0.1111111111011011 *0.0000000000100100*	-0.1001010001001010
12	0	1.0000000000000000	0.1111111111111011 *0.0000000000000100*	-0.1001010001101010
13	0	1.0000000000000000	0.1111111111111011 *0.0000000000000100*	-0.1001010001101010
14	1	1.0000000000000100	0.1111111111111011 *0.0000000000000100*	-0.1001010001101010
15	0	1.0000000000000000	0.1111111111111111 *0.0000000000000000*	-0.1001010001101110
16	0	1.0000000000000000	0.1111111111111111 *0.0000000000000000*	-0.1001010001101110
				$\ln 0.56 \approx -0.5798$

($1 - X_i$, to precision, in italics underneath the corresponding X_i values)

Table 5.9: Normalization computation of $\ln x$, $s_i \in \{0, 1\}$

Comparing Equations 5.67 and 5.68, we see that in computing X_{i+1}, the leading 1 in $1 - X_i$ has been changed to a 0. Also, if $k \geq n/2$, then the last two terms in Equation 5.68 are zero to within n-bit machine precision; therefore, in such a case, the bits of X_i and X_{i+1} differ only in the changed bit. So for $i \geq n/2$ we may choose s_i to be bit i of $1 - X_i$. (The example of Table 5.9 shows this: the bits of $1 - X_i$ underlined at $i = 9$ are exactly the values of s_i from that iteration on.)

Given that all the values of s_i are known at $i = n/2 + 1$, the normalization process may be terminated, and Y_{n+1} computed as

$$Y_{n+1} = Y_k - \sum_{i=k}^{n} \ln\big(1 + s_i 2^{-i}\big) \qquad k = n/2$$

From Equation 5.65, to n-bit machine precision

$$\ln\big(1 + s_i 2^{-i}\big) = s_i 2^{-i} \qquad i \geq n/2$$

so

$$Y_{n+1} = Y_k - \sum_{i=k}^{n} s_i 2^{-i}$$

For $i \geq n/2$, we choose s_i as bit i of $1 - X_i$. And the leading $n/2$ bits of $1 - X_i$ are all 0s. Therefore, $\sum_{i=k}^{n} s_i 2^{-i} = 1 - X_k$, and so

$$Y_{n+1} = Y_k - (1 - X_k)$$

In the example of Table 5.9, $Y_8 \approx 0.5773$, $X_8, \approx 0.9975$, and the computed terminating value is $Y_{17} \approx 0.5789$.

5.6.2 *Redundant representation and high radix*

The use of redundant representation allows faster operation in three ways. One is that in an iterative process, such representation makes it possible to have iterations in which there need not be any arithmetic operation.[9] Another is that with such representation, a given number has multiple representations, and so in a given step there is some flexibility in choosing a digit and the corresponding arithmetic operation; this means that decisions can be made without complete information and therefore made faster than would otherwise be the case. And the third, which follows from the second, is that fast arithmetic, without carry–propagation in addition, is possible.

---

[9]This leads to variable (i.e. operand-dependent) operational times, which might be considered undesirable.

All the preceding techniques are exemplified by the high-speed division algorithms of Section 2.3, and there are very close similarities between the division algorithms and the algorithms here. For that reason, we shall, for brevity, sometimes just refer to aspects of the division algorithms, and the reader might find it helpful to quickly review that material.

We shall consider radix-2 and radix-4 algorithms. In each case, we shall first consider the use of redundant representation outside the arithmetic and then make a few remarks on the use of such representation in the arithmetic. The brief discussions on convergence and error will be limited to the radix-4 cases, the general approaches being equally applicable to the radix-2 cases.

5.6.2.1 *Logarithm*

The starting point for the algorithm is the set of recurrences of Equations 5.33–5.38, in which $X_i \to 1$ and $Y_i \to \ln x$ as $i \to \infty$. For the radix-2 computation, with the digit set $\{\bar{1}, 0, 1\}$, we now need to make the digit selection on the basis of three intervals. So the basic algorithm is

$$X_1 = x \qquad\qquad 1/2 \leq x < 1$$

$$Y_1 = 0$$

$$c_i = 1 + s_i 2^{-i}$$

$$X_{i+1} = c_i X_i$$

$$Y_{i+1} = Y_i - \ln c_i$$

$$s_i = \begin{cases} 1 & \text{if } X_i \leq 1 - k \\ 0 & \text{if } 1 - k < X_i < 1 + k \qquad\qquad i = 1, 2, 3, \ldots \\ \bar{1} & \text{if } X_i \geq 1 + k \end{cases}$$

where k is a suitably small value.

The basic idea in the normalization step is as follows. In step i, if X_i is "much smaller" than one, then, to force it towards one, it is multiplied by a value (i.e. $1 + 2^{-i}$) that is slightly larger than one. If it is "much larger" than one, then, to force it towards one, it is multiplied by a value (i.e. $1 - 2^{-i}$) that is slightly smaller than one. (In both cases, the magnitude of the multiplier diminishes as X_i gets closer to one.) And if for that iteration X_i is "sufficiently close" to one, then no action is taken.

$$x = 0.55 \qquad \ln x = -0.597837\cdots \qquad \alpha = 1/2$$

i	s_i	c_i	X_i	Y_i
1	1	1.1000000000000000	0.1000110011001100	0.0000000000000000
2	1	1.0100000000000000	0.1101001100110011	- 0.0110011111001100
3	0	1.0000000000000000	1.0000100000000000	- 0.1010000011101100
4	0	1.0000000000000000	1.0000100000000000	- 0.1010000011101100
5	-1	0.1111100000000000	1.0000100000000000	- 0.1010000011101100
6	0	1.0000000000000000	0.1111111111000000	- 0.1001100011001011
7	0	1.0000000000000000	0.1111111111000000	- 0.1001100011001011
8	0	1.0000000000000000	0.1111111111000000	- 0.1001100011001011
9	1	1.0000000010000000	0.1111111111000000	- 0.1001100011001011
10	-1	0.1111111111000000	1.0000000000111111	- 0.1001100101001011
11	0	1.0000000000000000	0.1111111111111111	- 0.1001100100001011
12	0	1.0000000000000000	0.1111111111111111	- 0.1001100100001011
13	0	1.0000000000000000	0.1111111111111111	- 0.1001100100001011
14	0	1.0000000000000000	0.1111111111111111	- 0.1001100100001011
15	0	1.0000000000000000	0.1111111111111111	- 0.1001100100001011
16	0	1.0000000000000000	0.1111111111111111	- 0.1001100100001011

$$\ln 0.55 \approx -0.5978$$

Table 5.10: Normalization computation of $\ln x$, $s_i \in \{\bar{1}, 0, 1\}$

Two factors influence the choice of k. The first is that for the process to continue when X_i is in the middle interval but not close enough to one for the iterating to be terminated, the value of k must be adjusted with the iterations. Second, k must be easily computable. A good, easy choice is $k = \alpha 2^{-i}$ at step i, with α a small constant. The s_i-selection rule is then

$$s_i = \begin{cases} 1 & \text{if } X_i - 1 \le -\alpha 2^{-i} \\ 0 & \text{if } -\alpha 2^{-i} < X_i - 1 < \alpha 2^{-i} \\ \bar{1} & \text{if } X_i - 1 \ge \alpha 2^{-i} \end{cases}$$

The choice of a value for α will be determined by several considerations. An obvious one is how easily the value can be represented in binary; another might be the desire to have a value that will optimize the probability of $s_i = 0$, if the objective in that is to avoid arithmetic; and the particular value can also affect the initializations of the variables. (We shall below see the last quite clearly in the radix-4 case.)

The algorithm will converge if $0 < \alpha < 1$, with appropriate initializations,[10] and $\alpha = 1/2$ is a good, easy value. Table 5.10 gives an example computation that corresponds to that of Table 5.4.

In implementing the algorithm, it is convenient to keep the values of the comparison variables within a fixed range and so avoid having to adjust the values against which the comparisons are made. Fixed comparison values can be obtained by using the auxiliary variable $U_i = 2^i(X_i-1)$ instead of X_i, which scaling has the effect of removing leading 0s (1s) in the representation of a positive (negative) number, so that the most significant bits are always in the same position.

With the aforementioned changes, the recurrence for X_i is then replaced with one in terms of of U_i, and 2^{-i} is eliminated from the selection rules:

$$U_{i+1} = 2(U_i + s_i + s_i 2^{-i} U_i) \tag{5.69}$$

$$s_i = \begin{cases} 1 & \text{if } U_i \leq -\alpha \\ 0 & \text{if } -\alpha < U_i < \alpha \\ \bar{1} & \text{if } U_i \geq \alpha \end{cases}$$

The above algorithm can easily be extended to a radix-4 one, and we next consider such an algorithm, with the minimally redundant digit set [7]. We proceed as for the radix-2 case above, except that with two more intervals determined by the larger digit set, an additional comparison constant is required. The starting recurrences are

$$X_1 = x$$
$$Y_1 = 0$$
$$c_i = 1 + s_i 4^{-i}$$
$$X_{i+1} = c_i X_i$$
$$Y_{i+1} = Y_i - \ln c_i$$

---

[10] Apply similar reasoning to that of the radix-4 case below.

$$s_i \begin{cases} 2 & \text{if } X_i - 1 \le -\beta 4^{-i} \\ 1 & \text{if } -\beta 4^{-i} < X_i - 1 \le -\alpha 4^{-i} \\ 0 & \text{if } -\alpha 4^{-i} < X_i - 1 < \alpha 4^{-i} \\ \bar{1} & \text{if } \alpha 4^{-i} \le X_i - 1 < \beta 4^{-i} \\ \bar{2} & \text{if } X_i - 1 \ge \beta 4^{-i} \end{cases}.$$

and by substituting the scaled variable $U_i \overset{\triangle}{=} 4^i(X_i - 1)$, we obtain

$$U_{i+1} = 4\left(U_i + s_i + s_i U_i 4^{-i}\right) \tag{5.70}$$

$$s_i = \begin{cases} 2 & \text{if } U_i \le -\beta \\ 1 & \text{if } -\beta < U_i \le -\alpha \\ 0 & \text{if } -\alpha < U_i < \alpha \\ \bar{1} & \text{if } \alpha \le U_i < \beta \\ \bar{2} & \text{if } U_i \ge \beta \end{cases}$$

Equation 5.70 is exactly the same as Equation 2.9, and a similar analysis, as $i \to \infty$, yields the same results: in summary, for convergence it suffices to have $|U_i| \le 8/3$, and this will be the case if the constants α and β are chosen according to Table 5.11, which gives the selection-interval bounds. The effect of the redundancy in the digit set is evident in the overlapping of the intervals. Within a region of overlap, either of the corresponding s values may be chosen. So the constants may be chosen to be any easily computable values in the ranges $[1/3, 2/3]$, for α, and $[4/3, 5/3]$, for β.

U_i bounds		s_i
lower	uppper	
$-8/3$	$-4/3$	2
$-5/3$	$-1/3$	1
$-2/3$	$2/3$	0
$1/3$	$5/3$	$\bar{1}$
$4/3$	$8/3$	$\bar{2}$

Table 5.11: Digit selection in radix-4 multiplicative normalization

The same considerations as in the analysis of the division algorithm apply here. Since the analysis is for the limiting case, care must be taken with small values of i, and the results are similar. Within the regions $[1/3, 2/3]$ and $[4/3, 5/3]$, the most convenient values are $\alpha = 1/2$ and $\beta = 3/2$; but for these, convergence is assured only from $i = 3$, and a complex initialization is required to ensure that $|U_i| \leq 8/3$. The next best choices are $\alpha = 5/8$ and $\beta = 13/8$. These will give convergence from $i = 1$, provided $|U_1| < 13/8$ and the bounds on U_i are changed to $|U_i| < 21/8$. Given that Equation 5.70 is exactly Equation 2.9, the convergence proof of Section 2.3.1.2 is directly applicable here, the only difference being in the replacement of the bound $8/3$ with $21/8$.

The initializations to get U_1 in the right range are

$$c_0 = \begin{cases} 2 & \text{if } 1/2 \leq x < 5/8 \\ 1 & \text{if } 5/8 \leq x < 1 \end{cases}$$

$$U_1 = 4(c_0 x - 1)$$
$$Y_1 = -\log c_0$$

and $|U_1| < 13/8$, as required for convergence.

The s_i-selection rule is

$$s_i = \begin{cases} 2 & \text{if } U_i \leq -13/8 \\ 1 & \text{if } -13/8 < U_i \leq -5/8 \\ 0 & \text{if } -5/8 < U_i < 5/8 \\ \bar{1} & \text{if } 5/8 \leq U_i < 13/8 \\ \bar{2} & \text{if } U_i \geq 13/8 \end{cases}$$

That the algorithm converges follows from the remarks above, in relation to the similarities with division.

Reasoning as for the radix-2 case in Section 5.3.2, we conclude that after n iterations, the bound on the magnitude of the absolute approximation error is

$$|\ln x - Y_{n+1}| = |\log X_{n+1}|$$

$$< |X_{n+1} - 1|$$

and from the discussion above on the choice of comparison constants

$$|U_{n+1}| = |4^{n+1}(X_{n+1} - 1)| \leq \frac{21}{8}$$

So

$$|\log X_{n+1}| < |X_{n+1} - 1| \le \frac{21}{8} 4^{-(n+1)} < 4^{-n} = 2^{-2n}$$

which shows that after n iterations, the result will be correct to about $2n$ bits, provided that, as indicated above, a sufficient number of guard digits are included in the datapath to take care of errors generated and propagated during the iterations.

In order to take into account generated errors, the datapath needs to be of a precision that is greater than that of the final results. On the basis of the discussions in Sections 3.5 and 5.3.2, we may conclude that $\lceil \log_4(n+1) \rceil + 1$ guard digits will suffice for n-bit results.

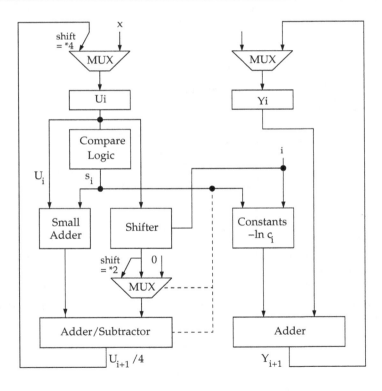

Figure 5.3: Hardware organization for radix-4 computation of $\ln x$

In implementation, fast arithmetic can be realized by using carry–save representation and selecting s_i on the basis of an approximation, $\widehat{U}_i$, of U_i, with the approximation obtained by assimilating a few leading bits of the carry–save representation of U_i. Alternatively, if the use of carry–save arithmetic is not an option, then better performance than would otherwise be the case is possible by if

$$\widehat{U}_{i+1} = 4(U_i + s_i)$$

is used as an approximation to Equation 5.70 and using low-precision truncations of those values. In either case, the fact that Equation 5.70 is just Equation 2.9 means that the considerations, including required precisions, are the same as in the case of division.

A sketch of hardware architecture for the algorithm is shown in Figure 5.3. This arrangement consists of two loops: one for U_i and one for Y_i. A lookup table holds the constants $\{\ln(1 + s_i 4^{-i})\}$. The initial value of U_i is either $4(2x - 1)$ or $4(x - 1)$, according to value of c_0 and is easily formed in the U_i loop. The initial value of Y_i is either 0 or $-\ln 2$ (a constant that can be computed beforehand).

The operation of the Y_i loop is self-explanatory. In the U_i loop, one iteration consists of these steps:

- The formation of s_i by the Compare Logic.
- The addition of U_i and s_i in the Small Adder, which adds one bit in either of the two most significant bits of U_i.
- Shifting U_i right by i places to obtain $U_i 4^{-i}$.
- Forming $|s_i| U_i 4^{-i}$ in the multiplexor, whose output is effectively multiplication by 0, or 1, or 2 (by wired shifts, indicated in slanted lines).
- The addition, or subtraction, according to the sign of s_i, of $|s_i| U_i 4^{-i}$ to, or from, $U_i + s_i$.
- A multiplication by four, accomplished by a two-bit wired left shift, to produce U_{i+1}.

Note that for sufficiently large i—approximately $i > n/2$—it is the case that $\ln(1 + s_i 4^{-i}) = s_i 4^{-i}$, to within machine precision (Equation 5.65); so no constants need be stored for such i. We leave it to the reader to modify Figure 5.3 accordingly, noting that 4^{-i} can be computed as running value, in a shift-register that shifts by two bit positions in each iteration.

The architecture of Figure 5.3 is largely similar to that of Figure 3.4 (for CORDIC), and similar considerations apply with respect to the design-space: one can devise "unrolled" implementations (as in Figure 3.5), "shared pipelines" (as in Figure 3.6), and so forth.

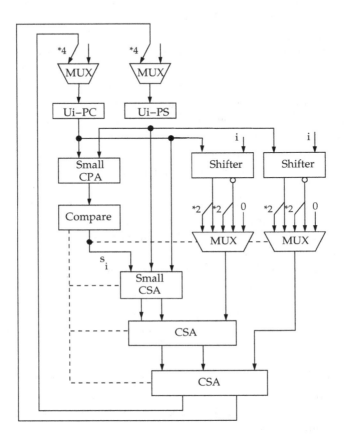

Figure 5.4: U_i loop for radix-4 computation of $\ln x$ (CS)

A high-performance version of the architecture of Figure 5.3 is readily obtained by having the arithmetic in carry–save form. The U_i recurrences here are the same as those in multiplicative-normalization division (Equations 2.7 and 2.9); so the changes required correspond to those made in changing from Figure 2.4 to 2.5, except that for radix-4 computation some of the wired shifts are for multiplication by four and the multiplexors have more inputs. For the latter, we observe that $s_i 4^{-i} U_i \in \{0, \pm 4^{-i}, \pm 2 \times 4^{-i}\}$, which values can be computed by no shifts, one-bit shifts, and two-bit shifts. The U_i-loop architecture is therefore as shown in Figure 5.4; the carry–propagate adder/subtractor (CPA) has now been replaced with carry–save adders (CSAs) The changes for the Y_i loop are as shown in Figure 5.5.

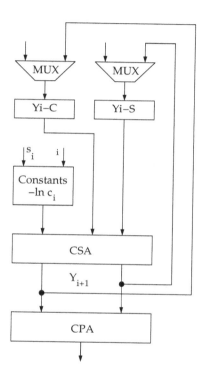

Figure 5.5: Y_i loop for radix-4 computation of $\ln x$ (CS)

5.6.2.2 *Exponential*

To obtain a radix-2 algorithm that uses the digit set $\{\bar{1}, 0, 1\}$, we start with the algorithm of Equations 5.33–5.38 and proceed in a manner similar to that above for the logarithm function, to get

$$x = 0.5 \qquad e^x = 1.648721 \cdots$$

i	s_i	c_i	X_i	Y_i
1	1	1.100000000000000	0.100000000000000	1.000000000000000
2	0	1.000000000000000	0.000110000011001	1.100000000000000
3	1	1.001000000000000	0.000110000011001	1.100000000000000
4	0	1.000000000000000	- 0.000001011111001	1.101100000000000
5	-1	0.111110000000000	- 0.000001011111001	1.101100000000000
6	1	1.000001000000000	0.000000100010110	1.101000101000000
7	-1	0.111111100000000	- 0.000000011100101	1.101010010000101
8	0	1.000000000000000	0.000000000011011	1.101001011011011
9	0	1.000000000000000	0.000000000011011	1.101001011011011
10	1	1.000000000100000	0.000000000011011	1.101001011011011
11	0	1.000000000000000	- 0.000000000000100	1.101001100010000
12	-1	0.111111111111000	- 0.000000000000100	1.101001100010000
13	1	1.000000000000100	0.000000000000011	1.101001100000011
14	0	1.000000000000000	- 0.000000000000000	1.101001100001010
15	0	1.000000000000000	- 0.000000000000000	1.101001100001010
16	-1	0.111111111111111	- 0.000000000000000	1.101001100001010

$$e^x \approx 1.6487$$

Table 5.12: Normalization computation of e^x, $s_i \in \{\overline{0}, 0, 1\}$

$$X_1 = x$$

$$Y_1 = 1$$

$$c_i = 1 + s_i 2^{-i}$$

$$X_{i+1} = X_i - \ln c_i$$

$$Y_{i+1} = c_i Y_i$$

$$s_i = \begin{cases} 1 & \text{if } X_i \geq \alpha 2^{-i} \\ 0 & \text{if } -\alpha 2^{-i} < X_i < \alpha 2^{-i} \\ \overline{1} & \text{if } X_i \leq -\alpha 2^{-i} \end{cases}$$

The algorithm will converge with $\alpha \in (0,1)$, and $\alpha = 1/2$ is a good value.

An example computation is given in Table 5.12; this corresponds to the examples of Tables 5.3 and 5.8.

As usual, the comparisons can be made against constant values, if scaled values of X_i are used: $U_i \triangleq 2^i X_i$ gives

$$U_1 = 2x$$

$$Y_1 = c_1$$

$$U_{i+1} = 2\left[U_i - 2^i \ln\left(1 + s_i 2^{-i}\right)\right]$$

$$Y_{i+1} = Y_i + s_i Y_i 2^{-i}$$

$$s_i = \begin{cases} 1 & \text{if } U_i \geq 1/2 \\ 0 & \text{if } -1/2 < U_i < 1/2 \\ \bar{1} & \text{if } U_i \leq -1/2 \end{cases}$$

The radix-4 algorithm is similarly derived [7]. The recurrence for X is $X_{i+1} = X_i - \ln(1 + s_i 4^{-i})$, and the scaled variable is $U_i \triangleq 4^i X_i$. Bounds for the comparison constants can be determined in a straightforward manner, as is done above for the radix-4 logarithms.

The recurrence for U_{i+1} is

$$U_{i+1} = 4\left[U_i - 4^i \ln\left(1 + s_i 4^{-i}\right)\right]$$

and (Equation 5.65)

$$\ln\left(1 + s_i 4^{-i}\right) = \left(s_i 4^{-i}\right) - \frac{\left(s_i 4^{-i}\right)^2}{2} + \frac{\left(s_i 4^{-i}\right)^3}{3} - \cdots$$

So for large i

$$U_{i+1} \approx 4(U_i - s_i)$$

Considering the possible values of s_i, except for sign, this equation has the same form as the "large-i" version of Equation 2.9 (for division), and grinding through the different values of s_i produces similar bounds for the s_i intervals. Here too, care is required in the initialization.

The comparison constants, 3/8 and 11/8, result in an algorithm that is convergent for iteration steps $i \geq 1$, and with these values $|U_i| \leq 5/2$ for all $i \geq 2$. The algorithm requires $|U_1| < 11/8$, and this dictates the initialization. All this is verified below, in the additional remarks on convergence.

The complete radix-4 algorithm with the digit set $\{\bar{2}, \bar{1}, 0, 1, 2\}$ is

$$U_1 = 4(x - \mu)$$

$$Y_1 = e^\mu$$

$$\mu = \begin{cases} 1/2 & \text{if } x \geq 1/4 \\ 0 & \text{if } -1/4 \leq x < 1/4 \\ -1/2 & \text{if } x < -1/4 \end{cases}$$

$$U_{i+1} = 4\left[U_i - 4^i \ln\left(1 + s_i 4^{-i}\right)\right]$$

$$Y_{i+1} = Y_i + s_i 4^{-i} Y_i$$

$$s_i = \begin{cases} 2 & \text{if } 11/8 \leq U_i < 5/2 \\ 1 & \text{if } 3/8 \leq U_i < 11/8 \\ 0 & \text{if } -3/8 < U_i < 3/8 \\ \bar{1} & \text{if } -11/8 \leq U_i < -3/8 \\ \bar{2} & \text{if } -5/2 < U_i \leq -11/8 \end{cases}$$

Y_1 represents only two values that need computing, and these can be computed beforehand and stored.

We now consider convergence and errors. To show convergence, we use the Taylor expansion

$$U_{i+1} = 4\left[U_i - 4^i \ln\left(1 + s_i 4^{-i}\right)\right]$$

$$= 4\left[U_i - 4^i \left(s_i 4^{-i} - \frac{(s_i 4^{-i})^2}{2} + \frac{(s_i 4^{-i})^3}{3} - \cdots\right)\right]$$

$$= 4\left(U_i - s_i + \frac{s_i 4^{-i}}{2} - \frac{s_i^2 4^{-2i}}{3} + \cdots\right)$$

for an interval-by-interval analysis and show that, under the right conditions, $|U_i| \leq 5/2$, for all i. (That $|U_i|$ being bounded implies convergence is explained in Section 2.3.1.2.).

The different cases are as follows.

- $s_i = 0$: Since $-3/8 < U_i < 3/8$ and $U_{i+1} = 4U_i$, we have $|U_{i+1}| < 3/2$.
- $s_i = 1$: $3/8 \leq U_i < 11/8$.

At the lower extreme

$$4\left(\frac{3}{8} - 1 + \frac{4^{-i}}{2} - \frac{4^{-2i}}{3} + \cdots\right)$$

$$= -\frac{5}{2} + \frac{4^{-i+1}}{2} - \frac{4^{-2i+1}}{3} + \cdots$$

$$> -\frac{5}{2}$$

At the upper extreme, we have

$$4\left(\frac{11}{8} - 1 + \frac{4^{-i}}{2} - \frac{4^{-2i}}{3} + \cdots\right)$$

$$< \frac{3}{2} + \frac{4^{-i+1}}{2} - \frac{4^{-2i+1}}{3} + \cdots$$

$$< \frac{3}{2} + \frac{4^{-(i-1)}}{2}$$

$$< 2 \qquad \text{for all } i \geq 1$$

So $|U_{i+1}| < 5/2$.

- $s_i = 2$: $11/8 \leq U_i < 5/2$.
  At the lower extreme

$$4\left(\frac{11}{8} - 2 + 2 \cdot \frac{4^{-i}}{2} - 2^2 \cdot \frac{4^{-2i}}{3} + \cdots\right)$$

$$= -\frac{5}{2} + 4^{-i+1} - \frac{4^{-2i+2}}{3} + \cdots$$

$$> -\frac{5}{2}$$

At the upper extreme, we have

$$4\left(\frac{5}{2} - 2 + 2 \cdot \frac{4^{-i}}{2} - 2^2 \cdot \frac{4^{-2i}}{3} + \cdots\right)$$

$$< 2 + 4^{-i+1} - \frac{4^{-2i+2}}{3} + \cdots$$

$$< \frac{5}{2} \qquad \text{for all } i \geq 2$$

So, again, $|U_{i+1}| < 5/2$, provided $i \geq 2$.

Because of the symmetry in the s_i-selection rule, the results will be similar—with changes of sign in some places—for $s_i = \bar{1}$ and $s_i = \bar{2}$.

To get convergence from $i = 1$, it is necessary to ensure that the possibility of for $s_1 = \bar{1}$ or $s_1 = \bar{2}$ does not arise, i.e. that $|U_1| < 11/8$. That is accomplished by the initialization.

Applying the same reasoning as in the radix-2 case of Section 5.3.1, for the magnitude of the absolute approximation error after K iterations is

$$|e^x - Y_{K+1}| < 2\,|X_{K+1}|$$

And from the discussion above on convergence

$$|U_{K+1}| = |4^{K+1}X_{K+1}| \leq 5/2$$

Therefore,

$$|e^x - Y_{K+1}| < 2 \cdot \frac{5}{8}4^{-K} < 2^{-2K+1}$$

which shows that after $n+1$ iterations, the result will be correct to $2n$ bits. To ensure that error bound, guard digits are required in the datapath, to take care of errors generated and propagated during the iteration. $\lceil \log_4(n+1)\rceil + 1$ radix-4 digits will suffice for that.

A sketch of hardware architecture for the algorithm is shown in Figure 5.6. The operational procedure should be self-explanatory, but the reader may find it useful to refer to the notes on Figure 5.5 (for logarithm-computation). The other comments made on architectures for the logarithm computation also here as well: "unrolled" and "shared pipeline" architectures, similar to those of Figures 3.5 and 3.6, are possible. An additional note is that the shifter in the U_i loop can be eliminated, and the loop made faster, by storing the constants $\{-4^i \ln(1 + s_i4^{-i})\}$ instead of $\{-\ln(1 + s_i4^{-i})\}$.

For fast computation, carry–save arithmetic may be used, with the comparisons based on an approximation, $\widehat{U}_i$, of U_i; the considerations are as above for the algorithms for logarithms, and we leave it to the reader to make the required modifications of Figure 5.6. As in the case of the algorithm for logarithms, if the arithmetic is in non-redundant representation, an arrangement that is faster than that of Figure 5.6 is possible, if s_i is determined on the basis of low-precision values obtained from using

$$\widehat{U}_{i+1} = 4(U_i - s_i)$$

as an approximation[11] to U_{i+1}. The considerations, including precision requirements, are similar to those for division (Section 2.3.1.2) and are left to the reader.

---

[11]This is based on the Taylor expansion, given above, of U_{i+1}.

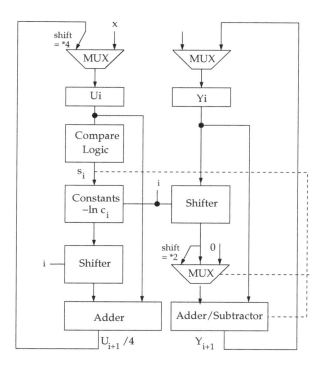

Figure 5.6: Hardware organization for radix-4 computation of e^x

5.6.3 *Very-high-radix computation*

As formulated above, the algorithms for logarithms and exponentials cannot be easily extended to high-radix computation—at least not directly. For logarithms, the radix-r normalization recurrence is

$$U_{i+1} = r \left(U_i + s_i + s_i U_i r^{-i} \right)$$

and for exponentials, the radix-r result recurrence is

$$Y_{i+1} = Y_i + s_i Y_i r^{-i}$$

The terms in $s_i U_i$ and $s_i Y_i$ are evidently problematic with the maximally-redundant radix-4 digit set and with any radix larger than four, because of the need to compute multiples of three, five, seven, and so forth. The interval-by-interval selection of s_i also gets more complex with large radices, and a replacement is in order.

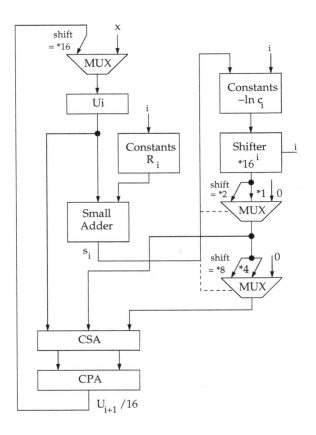

Figure 5.7: Hardware organization for radix-16 computation of $\ln x$ (U_i)

If r is of moderate size, then an "awkward" digit set can be effected indirectly, by cascading "nicer" digit sets and forming multiples accordingly—for example, $\{\bar{3},\bar{2},\bar{1},0,1,2,3\}$ from $\{\bar{2},\bar{1},0,1,2\}$ and $\{\bar{1},0,1\}$. Accordingly, [15] proposes the use of the radix-16 digit set $\{\overline{10},\bar{9},\ldots,\bar{1},0,1,\ldots,9,10\}$ from $\{\bar{8},\bar{4},0,4,8\}$ and $\{\bar{2},\bar{1},0,1,2\}$. The selection of s_i is by rounding: a value, T_i, obtained from six leading bits of U_i, is added to a six-bit, iteration-dependent rounding constant, R_i, and the result then used to form s_i. A sketch of the hardware architecture for the exponential-evaluation U_i loop is shown in Figure 5.7; we leave it to the reader to make appropriate radix-16 modifications of the Y_i loop of Figure 5.6.

The implications on performance of the cascaded digit sets is apparent in Figure 5.7: increased levels of cascading, for higher radices, will increase both the hardware costs and the operational times. There is, however, a different approach to the computation of multiples: if the radix is sufficiently large that only a very small number of iterations suffice to obtain a result of a given precision, then direct multiplication might be worthwhile. That is the basis of *selection by rounding* for very-high-radix division (Section 2.3.4), and the idea can be applied to the evaluation of other functions. Very-high-radix algorithms have been proposed for the computation of several functions, including logarithms and exponentials, and we next describe two of these [13, 14].

5.6.3.1 *Logarithm*

Generalizing from the radix-2 and the radix-4 recurrences, the basic recurrences for radix-r computation are

$$U_{i+1} = r\left(U_i + s_i + s_i r^{-i} U_i\right) \qquad\qquad i = 1, 2, 3, \ldots \qquad (5.71)$$

$$Y_{i+1} = Y_i - \ln\left(1 + s_i r^{-i}\right)$$

If the arguments are x and y, so that $U_1 = r(x - 1)$ and $Y_1 = y$, then Y_i converges to $y + \ln x$ as U_i converges to one. The values of s_i are determined as follows.

From U_i, an approximation, $\widehat{U}_i$, that has p fraction bits is obtained.[12] $\widehat{U}_i$ is then rounded to an integer, from which s_i is obtained:

$$s_i = -\left\lfloor \widehat{U}_i + \frac{1}{2} \right\rfloor$$

This implies that

$$-\frac{1}{2} - 2^{-p} \leq U_i + s_i < \frac{1}{2} \qquad\qquad (5.72)$$

Assuming that the maximally-redundant radix-r digit set is used, $|s_i| \leq r - 1$; so

$$-r + \frac{1}{2} \leq \widehat{U}_i < r - \frac{1}{2}$$

---

[12]In redudant signed-digit representation, simply truncate to p fractional bits; in carry–save representation, add 1 at position $p + 1$ and then truncate.

which gives these constraints on U_{i+1}:

$$-r + \frac{1}{2} \leq U_{i+1} < r - \frac{1}{2} - 2^{-p} \qquad (5.73)$$

Rewriting Equation 5.71 into

$$U_{i+1} = r(U_i + s_i) + s_i r^{-i+1}[(U_i + s_i) - s_i]$$

and combining this with Inequations 5.72–5.73 gives

$$r\left(-\frac{1}{2} - 2^{-p}\right) + s_i r^{-i+1}\left(-\frac{1}{2} - 2^{-p} - s_i\right) \leq U_{i+1} < \frac{r}{2} - \frac{1}{2} - 2^{-p} \quad (5.74)$$

We also must have

$$Q_{i+1} \leq U_{i+1} \leq P_{i+1} \qquad (5.75)$$

where P_{i+1} and Q_{i+1} are the extremes of the positive and negative ranges for convergence in iteration $i + 1$. Since $|s_i| \leq r - 1$, $X_i = x\prod_{k=i}(1 + s_k r^{-k})$, and $U_i = r^i(X_i - 1)$, taking the largest possible value of $|s_i|$, we have

$$P_{i+1} = r^{i+1}\left(\prod_{j=i+1}^{\infty}\left[1 + (r-1)r^{-j}\right] - 1\right)$$

$$Q_{i+1} = r^{i+1}\left(\prod_{j=i+1}^{\infty}\left[1 - (r-1)r^{-j}\right] - 1\right)$$

Combining Inequations 5.74 and 5.75, for convergence we require

$$\frac{r}{2} + s_i r^{-i+1}\left(\frac{1}{2} - s_i\right) < \min\left(r - \frac{1}{2} - 2^{-p},\ P_{i+1}\right)$$

$$(5.76)$$

$$r\left(-\frac{1}{2} - 2^{-p}\right) + s_i r^{-i+1}\left(-\frac{1}{2} - 2^{-p} - s_i\right) \geq \max\left(-r + \frac{1}{2},\ Q_{i+1}\right)$$

$$(5.77)$$

Now (and noting Inequations 5.73)

$$P_{i+1} > r - \frac{1}{2} - 2^{-p}$$

$$Q_{i+1} < -r - \frac{1}{2}$$

so the conditions for convergence are reduced to

$$r - \frac{1}{2} - 2^{-p} + s_i^2 r^{-i+1} + \frac{1}{2} s_i r^{-i+1} > 0$$

$$r - \frac{1}{2} - 2^{-p} r - s_i r^{-i+1} \left(\frac{1}{2} - 2^{-p} - s_i \right) \geq 0 \qquad (5.78)$$

The first condition is satisfied with

- $i \geq 1$, $p \geq 0$, $r \geq 2$

and the second is satisfied with

- $i \geq 3$, $p \geq 2$, $r \geq 8$

For iterations $i = 1$ and $i = 2$, some exceptional arrangement must be made. A straightforward one is to use lookup tables that are addressed with some leading bits of the argument and which return the values of s_1 and s_2. It is, however, possible to use selection by rounding if the possible values of s_2 are limited: with $i = 2$ and $p = 2$, the worst case of Inequation 5.78 is

$$\frac{r}{4} - \frac{1}{2} - \frac{3}{4} s_2 r^{-1} - s_2^2 r^{-1} \geq 0$$

which, solving for equality, gives

$$s_2 = -\frac{3}{8} \pm \frac{1}{8} \sqrt{16 r^2 - 32 r + 9}$$

Therefore selection by rounding is possible at $i = 2$, provided

$$|s_2| \leq \frac{\sqrt{3}}{2} \frac{r}{2} - \frac{3}{8}$$

The value of s_1 that is obtained by table lookup should then be such as to ensure that this constraint is satisfied. A different solution to the problem of initial iterations will be found in [13], as will discussions on matters of implementation.

5.6.3.2 *Exponential*

The very-high-radix algorithm for the computation of exponentials is an *online* algorithm [14]. The essence of such an algorithm is that:

- The operation is most significant digit first and is digit serial.
- Computation starts before all digits of the operand(s) are available as input.[13]
- The result is produced a digit at a time, starting from the most significant digit.

More detailed and general discussons of such algorithms, in the context of computer arithmetic, will be found in [11].

The algorithm for the exponential has an online delay, δ, of two. So, with digit-serial input, the first digit of the result is produced on the basis of an "input" based on the first two digits (x_1 and x_2) of the argument:

$$\widetilde{x} = x_1 r^{-1} + x_2 r^{-2} \qquad \text{radix } r$$

and thereafter in each iteration the next digit of the argument is accepted as input and the next digit of the result is produced as output.

Generalizing from the radix-2 and radix-4 recurrences for exponentials, the recurrences for radix-r computation are

$$Y_{i+1} = Y_i + s_i Y_i r^{-i}$$

$$U_{i+1} = r \left[U_i - r^i \ln\left(1 + s_i r^{-i}\right) \right] + x_{i+\delta} r^{-\delta+1} \qquad (5.79)$$

$$= r U_i - W_i + x_{i+\delta} r^{-\delta+1}$$

where

$$W_i = r^{i+1} \ln\left(1 + s_i r^{-i}\right)$$

If $U_1 = r\widetilde{x}$ and $Y_1 = y$, then Y_i converges to ye^x as U_i converges to one. With $r = 2^k$ and an n-bit result, there are $N \triangleq \lceil n/k \rceil$ iterations, as follows.

- Iteration 1:

$$U_1 = r^2 \widetilde{x} - W_1 + x_3$$

$$Y_1 = y + s_1 r^{-1} y$$

$$W_1 = r^2 \ln\left(1 + s_1 r^{-1}\right)$$

---

[13]If $\delta + 1$ digits are required before computation can start, then the algorithm is said to have an *online delay* of δ.

- Iteration 2 to $\lceil N/2 \rceil$:

$$U_{i+1} = rU_i - W_i + x_{i+2}$$

$$Y_i = y + s_i r^{-1} Y_i$$

$$W_1 = r^{i+1} \ln(1 + s_i r^{-i})$$

- Iteration $\lceil N/2 \rceil + 1$ to N:

$$U_{i+1} = rU_i - s_i r + x_{i+2}$$

$$Y_i = y + s_i r^{-1} Y_i$$

$$W_1 = r^{i+1} \ln(1 + s_i r^{-i})$$

For these iterations, $\ln(1 + s_i r^{-i})$ to n-bit machine precision—see Equation 5.65—so $W_i = s_i r$.

The digits s_i are obtained in a manner similar to that for the logarithms, i.e. by rounding a p-fraction-bits approximation, $\widehat{U}_i$, of U_i:

$$s_i = \left\lfloor \widehat{U}_i + \frac{1}{2} \right\rfloor$$

Then

$$-\frac{1}{2} - 2^{-p} \le U_i - s_i < \frac{1}{2}$$

Since $|s_i| \le r - 1$, if we assume a maximally-redundant digit set, then

$$-r + \frac{1}{2} < \widehat{U}_i < r - \frac{1}{2}$$

and

$$-r + \frac{1}{2} < U_i < r - \frac{1}{2} - 2^{-p}$$

Combining the expressions above, the conditions required for convergence are

$$r\left(\frac{1}{2} + s_i\right) - W_i + x_{i+\delta} r^{-\delta+1} < \min\left(r - \frac{1}{2} - 2^{-p}, P_{i+1}\right)$$

$$r\left(-\frac{1}{2} - 2^{-t} + s_i\right) - W_i + x_{i+\delta} r^{-\delta+1} > \max\left(-r + \frac{1}{2}, Q_{i+1}\right)$$

where P_{i+1} and Q_{i+1} are the extremes of the positive and negative ranges for convergence in iteration $i + 1$. Since, $|s_i| \le r - 1$, $X_i =$

$x - \sum_{k=i} \ln(1 + s_k r^{-i})$, and $U_i = r^i X_i$, taking the largest possible value of $|s_i|$, we have

$$P_{i+1} = -r^{i+1} \sum_{j=i}^{\infty} \ln(1 - (r-1)r^{-j}) + r^{i+1-\delta} \sum_{j=i}^{K} (r-1)r^{-j}$$

$$Q_{i+1} = -r^{i+1} \sum_{j=i}^{\infty} \ln(1 + (r-1)r^{-j}) - r^{i+1-\delta} \sum_{j=i}^{K} (r-1)r^{-j}$$

Since

$$P_{i+1} > r - \frac{1}{2} - 2^{-p}$$

$$Q_{i+1} < -r - \frac{1}{2}$$

the convergence conditions are

$$\frac{r}{2} - \frac{1}{2} - rs_i + W_i - x_{i+\delta} r^{-\delta+1} > 0 \qquad (5.80)$$

$$\frac{r}{2} - \frac{1}{2} - r2^{-t} - W_i + x_{i+\delta} r^{-\delta+1} > -r + \frac{1}{2} \qquad (5.81)$$

The first condition is satisfied with

- $\delta \geq 2,\ i \geq 1,\ p \geq 2,\ \geq 8$

and the second is satisfied with

- $\delta \geq 2,\ i \geq 3,\ p \geq 0,\ r \geq 4$

As with the algorithms for logarithms, here too convergence can be guaranteed with selection by rounding from $i = 2$ if the possible values of s_2 are constrained. With the values $i = 2$, $p = 2$, and $\delta = 2$, Inequation 5.81 becomes

$$\frac{r}{2} - \frac{3}{4} - s_2 r + r^3 \ln(1 + s_2 r^{-2}) - x_4 r^{-1} > 0$$

which gives the constraints on s_2 as

$$-(r-3) \leq s_2 \leq (r-2)$$

Further details, including discussions on implementation, will be found in [14].

Chapter 6

Polynomial and Rational-Function Approximations

Polynomial approximations are good for computer function approximations, in so far as they can be evaluated with reasonable efficiency. A polynomial of a given degree can be evaluated using a fixed number of additions and multiplications, and there exist algorithms that will keep the number optimally low. Nevertheless, on their own, or if used without sufficient care, they might be not particularly well suited to hardware implementation: in some cases—depending on the function, or the argument, or both—obtaining high accuracy will require a large number of terms and, hence, time-consuming operations. For hardware evaluation, the best uses of polynomials are in combinations of low-degree polynomials and lookup tables; that is the subject of Chapter 7. In this chapter we shall discuss polynomials in some generality, making few assumptions of the reader's background, or of what the reader might consider "low degree", or of what hardware functional units one might have in mind and how this might influence the choice of evaluation method.

The chapter also covers rational functions, which are quotients of polynomials. As a generalization of the basic polynomial—which is a rational function with a constant divisor—rational functions may be expected to be better than polynomials in terms of accuracy, and that is indeed the case. The main issue with the implementation of rational functions is that division is required, and, for the hardware evaluation of other functions, division is a costly operation that should generally be avoided, if possible.

For a given function, one can devise any number of polynomials as approximations. Some of these may be considered better than others, and so at the outset it is necessary to have some clear and objective criteria for such judgments; that is the subject of the first section of the chapter. The second section covers polynomials derived from standard Taylor series,

223

with a particular focus on their limitations. The third and fourth sections cover Chebyshev and Legendre polynomials, which, according to some of the criteria given in the first section, are better than Taylor series. The fifth section consists of a brief discussion on *interpolation*, which is a way of constructing an approximating polynomial that exactly matches the approximated function at certain points and, more generally, of evaluating between tabulated points. And the last section is on rational functions.

Some early work on the hardware evaluation of polynomials and rational functions will be found in [1–3]. More recent work includes [4–6].

6.1　Quality of approximation

In considering polynomial approximations, naturally the first question is whether we can always find a *good* approximation to a given function. Before we can answer this question, we obviously require some means of measuring "goodness", which, intuitively, we understand to to be a measure of the distance between the approximating function and the approximated function: the smaller the "distance", the better the approximation. We shall therefore start with a discussion of this distance. In what follows, we shall assume that $f(x)$ is a continuous function defined on a closed, finite interval, $[a, b]$, and that $P(x)$ is a polynomial on the same interval.

The *norm*, denoted $\| \cdots \|$, is a measure of "distance" contrived so that the smaller it is, the "better" the approximation; the definition also allows different interpretations of "distance". The L_p norm, denoted $\|f - P\|_p$, is defined as

$$L_p = \left[\int_a^b |f(x) - P(x)|^p dx \right]^{1/p}$$

It is sometimes useful to generalize this to include a weighting function, $w(x)$, in order to allow some flexibility in how the "goodness" of approximation, with a particular norm, is measured:

$$L_p = \left[\int_a^b |f(x) - P(x)|^p w(x) dx \right]^{1/p}$$

where $w(x)$ is an integrable function on $[a, b]$, $w(x) > 0$, and $\int_a^b w(x) dx$ is finite. In this book, we shall assume just the "plain" version.

In numerical computations, three norms tend to be of special interest:

$$L_1 = \int_a^b |f(x) - P(x)| dx$$

$$L_2 = \sqrt{\int_a^b |f(x) - P(x)|^2 dx}$$

$$L_\infty = \max_{a \leq x \leq b} |f(x) - P(x)|$$

Evidently, "closeness" in one norm does not necessarily imply "closeness" in another norm.

For discrete N points, x_i, the integrals are replaced with summations, and it is typical to use "l" instead of "L":

$$l_p = \left(\sum_{i=0}^N |f(x_i) - P(x_i)|^p dx \right)^{1/p}$$

and

$$l_1 = \sum_{i=1}^N |f(x_i) - P(x_i)|$$

$$l_2 = \sqrt{\sum_{i=1}^N |f(x_i) - P(x_i)|^2}$$

$$l_\infty = \max |f(x_i) - P(x_i)| \qquad 1 \leq i \leq N$$

With one exception of a relatively minor nature, throughout this book we shall concern ourselves with only the L norms.

Of the three norms, the last is the best, in that for given f and P:

$$\|f - P\|_1 \leq \|f - P\|_\infty$$

$$\|f - P\|_2 \leq \|f - P\|_\infty$$

So we usually strive to work with L_∞ whenever possible.[1] Approximations based on L_∞ are known as *minimax approximations*, as they seek to minimize the maximum magnitude of error. With the L_2 norm, the objective is,

---

[1] On the other hand, L_2 is much loved by mathematicians, especially numerical analysts, for reasons that are beyond the scope of this book.

essentially, to minimize $[f(x) - P(x)]^2$; so such approximations are known as *least-squares approximations*. The L_1 and L_2 norms are useful if we want to minimize "average" error. Unless otherwise specified, we shall assume that the norm to be used is L_∞.

Armed with the preceding definition of "goodness", we now return to the question of whether we can always find a good polynomial approximation, P, to a function, f, on the closed interval $[a, b]$. To the extent that "good" is measured by one of the norms above, the answer, via the following theorem, is YES.[2]

WEIERSTRASS APPROXIMATION THEOREM: *Let $f(x)$ be a continuous real-valued function defined on the interval $[a, b]$. Then for every $\varepsilon > 0$, there exists a polynomial, $P(x)$, of degree n_ε, such that $\|f - P\|_\infty < \varepsilon$.* (Note that the degree depends on the error bound.)

What this theorem tells us is that a continuous function on a bounded interval can be approximated arbitrarily closely by some polynomial. We shall, however, see that the polynomial might converge too slowly—that is, require an excessively large number of terms—to be useful in practice.

Suppose we now restrict ourselves to just the polynomials of degree at most n, a fixed integer. It is then natural to ask questions about the best one of these, if there is a particular one. The following theorem gives us a partial answer—that there is indeed a unique "best" polynomial for each of the three norms above. (The polynomial may differ according to the chosen norm.)

THEOREM: *Let $f(x)$ be a continuous real-valued function defined on the interval $[a, b]$ and n be a fixed integer. Then on that interval, there is a polynomial, $P(x)$, of degree at most n, such that for all polynomials, $Q(x)$, on the same interval and of degree at most n, it is the case that $\|f - P\| \leq \|f - Q\|$.*

For our *practical* purposes, the answer is "partial" because it does not give us the slightest idea of how to find the polynomial, and constructing "best" polynomial approximations can be a laborious process in some cases.[3] Of particular interest to us is the L_∞ norm. Minimax polynomial

---

[2]Note that, as indicated above, L_∞ is the "best" norm.

[3]Most of the relevant methods are outside the scope of this book. It is for only the L_2 norm that such polynomials can *always* be constructed explicitly.

approximations are not always easy to obtain,[4] but there are alternatives—based on the Chebyshev polynomials of Section 6.3—that are near-minimax and which are, in several respects, superior to standard Taylor and Maclaurin series.

6.2 Taylor series

The functions that we are interested in all have Taylor-series expansions, and truncations of these will readily provide polynomials for practical numerical computation. The Taylor-series expansion of $f(x)$ about a is

$$f(x) = f(a + (x - a)) = f(a) + \frac{f'(a)}{1!}(x - a) + \frac{f''(a)}{2!}(x - a)^2 + \cdots$$

$$+ \frac{f^{(n)}(a)}{n!}(x - a)^n + \cdots \qquad (6.1)$$

When $a = 0$, we get the Maclaurin-series expansion:

$$f(x) = f(0) + \frac{f'(0)}{1!}x + \frac{f''(0)}{2!}x^2 + \cdots + \frac{f^{(n)}(0)}{n!}x^n + \cdots$$

The error in a Taylor series after omitting all terms of degree $n + 1$ and above is given by the remainder expression

$$R_n(x) = \frac{f^{(n+1)}(\xi)}{(n + 1)!}(x - a)^{n+1} \qquad \xi \in [a, x] \qquad (6.2)$$

In general, we do not have any information on what ξ is; so for $f^{(n+1)}(\xi)/(n + 1)!$ we usually work with bounds on the magnitude over the interval at hand.

Two important observations can readily be made on the basis of Equation 6.2. First, excluding other factors, the closer x is to a, the smaller $|R_n(x)|$ is. That is, even when convergence is assured, the rate of convergence might be dependent on the value of x. For a simple, concrete example that also takes into account the other subterm in Equation 6.2, consider the Maclaurin expansion for e^x:

$$e^x = \sum_{n=0}^{\infty} \frac{x^n}{n!}$$

and consider the ratio of successive terms:

[4]The standard method is the *Remez algorithm* [11].

$$\left| \frac{x^{n+1}/(n+1)!}{x^n/n!} \right| = \left| \frac{x}{n+1} \right|$$

This tends to zero as $n \to \infty$; so the series will converge for all x. But as x increases, n must also increase in order to retain the same level of accuracy. Table 6.1 shows the number of terms required to reach an accuracy of six places after the decimal point for various values of x.

x	0.01	0.05	0.10	1.00	1.50	2.00	10.0
n	2	3	4	9	11	13	37

Table 6.1: Evaluation of e^x

A consideration of the preceding example shows how range reduction (Section 1.2) can be useful: we can partially deal with the aforementioned "difficulty" by reducing the range of the argument to a small region around the point of expansion, or by devising an expansion at the midpoint of the interval of interest, or both. There is also another, more significant possibility: instead of a single polynomial over a "large" interval, the interval is split into several "small" subintervals, with a separate, appropriately centered, polynomial for each subinterval; then every argument (in the initial interval) will be near the point of expansion for some polynomial. This, in several variations, is the underlying idea in all of Chapter 7, and such "splitting" can be, and often is, combined with range reduction.

The second observation in relation to Equation 6.2 is that provided $|f^{(n+1)}(\xi)|$ does not grow too quickly, we may expect the magnitude of the error to decrease with increasing n, because $(n+1)!$ grows faster than $|(x-a)^{n+1}|$ for given x and a. But matters are not so clear if the growth of the derivatives is rapid [19]. Although it seems reasonable to assume that errors will decrease as more terms are included in the polynomial, this is not always the case. For some functions $|f^{(n+1)}(\xi)|$ will indeed be bounded. Take, for example, $f(x) = \sin x$. Every derivative will be of the form $\pm \sin x$ or $\pm \cos x$. So $|f^{(n+1)}(\xi)| \le 1$ and

$$|R_n(x)| \le \left| \frac{(x-a)^{n+1}}{(n+1)!} \right|$$

$(n+1)!$ grows faster than $|(x-a)^{n+1}|$; so the errors decrease with increasing n. On the other hand, consider the case of $f(x) = \ln x$, $x > 0$. Here, we do not always have bounds, because the derivatives tend to be dominated by the growth of $n!$:

$$f^{n+1}(x) = \frac{(-1)^n n!}{x^{n+1}}$$

and we should not expect that modest increases in n will necessarily do much good. Also, the remainder term is

$$|R_n(x)| = \left| \frac{(x-a)^{n+1}}{(n+1)\xi^{n+1}} \right|$$

$$> \frac{(x-a)^{n+1}}{(n+1)a^{n+1}} \qquad \text{since } \xi \in [a, x]$$

and one can see that if, for example, $a = 1$, then for convergence we must not have $x - 1 > 1$; we require $x \le 2$, which defines a *radius of convergence* that is not necessary for some functions.

It should also be noted that for a given function, we may be able to devise different expansions, using Taylor series on their own or in combination with standard algebraic identities, and that the "obvious" series might not be the "best", depending on what one is after. As an example, take the case of the natural-logarithm function, for which the reader is likely to encounter different series used in approximations. Consider the first expansion in Table 6.3:

$$\ln x = (x-1) - \frac{(x-1)^2}{2} + \frac{(x-1)^3}{3} - \frac{(x-1)^4}{4} + \cdots$$

This is the "straightforward-and-obvious" expansion around the point $a = 1$. The expansion is evidently related to that for $\ln(1+x)$:

$$\ln(1+x) = x - \frac{x^2}{2} + \frac{x^3}{3} - \frac{x^4}{4} + \frac{x^2}{2} - \cdots$$

Replacing x with $-x$ in this series gives

$$\ln(1-x) = -x - \frac{x^2}{2} - \frac{x^3}{3} - \frac{x^4}{4} - \frac{x^2}{2} - \cdots$$

and subtracting, we get

$$\ln(1+x) - \ln(1-x) = \ln\left(\frac{1+x}{1-x}\right)$$

$$= 2\left(x + \frac{x^3}{3} + \frac{x^5}{5} + \cdots\right)$$

From the last expression—a handy one that we shall encounter again in Chapter 7—a suitable change of variables gives us the second expression in Table 6.3 for $\ln x$. Comparing the two series for $\ln x$, the second has both a better convergence rate and a wider range of convergence, although it might be considered more awkward to evaluate.

Tables 6.2–6.4 list some Taylor expansions for almost all of the functions we are interested in, and several others can be obtained through the use of standard identities. A large variety of such expansions will be found in [15–17].

$$\frac{1}{1-x} = 1 + x + x^2 + x^3 + \cdots + x^n + \cdots \qquad\qquad |x| < 1$$

$$\sqrt{1+x} = 1 + \frac{1}{2}x - \frac{1}{2\cdot 4}x^2 + \frac{1\cdot 3}{2\cdot 4\cdot 6}x^3 - \cdots$$
$$+ (-1)^{n+1}\frac{1\cdot 3\cdot 5\cdots(2n-3)}{2\cdot 4\cdot 6\cdots 2n}x^n + \cdots \qquad -1 < x \le 1$$

$$\frac{1}{\sqrt{1+x}} = 1 - \frac{1}{2}x + \frac{1\cdot 3}{2\cdot 4}x^2 - \frac{1\cdot 3\cdot 5}{2\cdot 4\cdot 6}x^3 - \cdots$$
$$+ (-1)^{n}\frac{1\cdot 3\cdot 5\cdots(2n-1)}{2\cdot 4\cdot 6\cdots 2n}x^n + \cdots \qquad -1 < x \le 1$$

$$\sqrt{x} = 1 + \frac{1}{2}(x-1) - \frac{1}{8}(x-1)^2 + \frac{1}{16}(x-1)^3 - \cdots \qquad a = 1$$
$$+ (-1)^{n-1}\frac{n(2n-2)!}{2^{2n-1}(n!)^2}(x-1)^n + \cdots$$
$$\qquad\qquad\qquad 0 \le x \le 2$$

$$\frac{1}{\sqrt{x}} = 1 - \frac{1}{2}(x-1) + \frac{3}{8}(x-1)^2 - \frac{5}{16}(x-1)^3 + \cdots \qquad a = 1$$
$$+ (-1)^{n}\frac{2n!}{2^{2n}(n!)^2}(x-1)^n + \cdots \qquad 0 < x \le 2$$

$$e^x = 1 + \frac{x}{1!} + \frac{x^2}{2!} + \frac{x^3}{3!} + \cdots + \frac{x^n}{n!} + \cdots$$

Table 6.2: Taylor series I

$$\ln x = (x-1) - \frac{(x-1)^2}{2} + \frac{(x-1)^3}{3} - \frac{(x-1)^4}{4} + \cdots \qquad a = 1$$

$$+ \frac{(-1)^{n+1}(x-1)^n}{n} + \cdots \qquad 0 < x \le 2$$

$$\ln\left(\frac{1+x}{1-x}\right) = 2\left(x + \frac{x^3}{3} + \frac{x^5}{5} + \cdots + \frac{x^{2n+1}}{2n+1} + \cdots\right)$$

$$\ln x = 2\left[\left(\frac{x-1}{x+1}\right) + \frac{1}{3}\left(\frac{x-1}{x+1}\right)^3 + \frac{1}{5}\left(\frac{x-1}{x+1}\right)^5 + \cdots \right.$$

$$\left. + \frac{1}{2n-1}\left(\frac{x-1}{x+1}\right)^{2n-1} + \cdots\right] \qquad x > 0$$

$$\ln(1+x) = x - \frac{x^2}{2} + \frac{x^3}{3} - \frac{x^4}{4} + \cdots + (-1)^{n+1}\frac{x^n}{n} + \cdots$$

$$-1 < x \le 1$$

$$\sin x = x - \frac{x^3}{3!} + \frac{x^5}{5!} - \frac{x^7}{7!} + \cdots + (-1)^n\frac{x^{2n+1}}{(2n+1)!} + \cdots \quad \text{for all } x$$

$$\cos x = 1 - \frac{x^2}{2!} + \frac{x^4}{4!} - \frac{x^6}{6!} + \cdots + (-1)^n\frac{x^{2n}}{(2n)!} + \cdots \qquad \text{for all } x$$

$$\tan x = x + \frac{1}{3}x^3 + \frac{2}{15}x^5 + \frac{17}{315}x^7 + \cdots$$

$$+ \frac{(-4^n(1-4^n)B_{2n}}{(2n)!}x^{2n-1} + \cdots \qquad |x| < \pi/2$$

where the Bs are the Bernoulli numbers:

$$B_m = \sum_{j=0}^{m}\sum_{k=0}^{j}(-1)^k\binom{j}{k}\frac{k^m}{j+1}$$

Table 6.3: Taylor series II

$$\sin^{-1} x = x + \frac{1}{2 \cdot 3} x^3 + \frac{1 \cdot 3}{2 \cdot 4 \cdot 5} x^5 + \frac{1 \cdot 3 \cdot 5}{2 \cdot 4 \cdot 6 \cdot 7} x^7 + \cdots$$

$$+ \frac{(2n)!}{(2^n n!)^2 (2n+1)} x^{2n+1} + \cdots \qquad |x| \le 1$$

$$\tan^{-1} x = x - \frac{x^3}{3} + \frac{x^5}{5} - \frac{x^7}{7} + \cdots + \frac{(-1)^n x^{2n+1}}{2n+1} + \cdots \qquad |x| \le 1$$

$$\cosh x = 1 + \frac{x^2}{2!} + \frac{x^4}{4!} + \cdots + \frac{x^{2n}}{(2n)!} + \cdots \qquad \text{for all } x$$

$$\sinh x = x + \frac{x^3}{3!} + \frac{x^5}{5!} + \cdots + \frac{x^{2n+1}}{(2n+1)!} + \cdots \qquad \text{for all } x$$

$$\tanh x = x - \frac{1}{3} x^3 + \frac{2}{15} x^5 - \frac{17}{315} x^7 + \cdots$$

$$+ \frac{4^n (4^n - 1) B_{2n}}{(2n)!} x^{2n-1} + \cdots \qquad |x| < \pi/2$$

where the Bs are the Bernoulli numbers:

$$B_m = \sum_{j=0}^{m} \sum_{k=0}^{j} (-1)^k \binom{j}{k} \frac{k^m}{j+1}$$

Table 6.4: Taylor series III

An efficient method for the evaluation of polynomials, assuming co-efficients have been computed beforehand or can be computed easily, is *Horner's method*, which consists of rearranging the polynomial $P_n(x) \triangleq \sum_{i=0}^{n} c_i x^i$ into

$$P_n(x) \triangleq c_0 + x(c_1 + x(c_2 + x(\cdots (c_{n-1} + c_n x) \cdots)))$$

and then performing the evaluation via the recurrences

$$Q_n = c_n$$
$$Q_k = c_k + xQ_{k+1} \qquad k = n-1, n-2, \ldots, 1$$
$$P_n(x) = Q_0$$

This takes n multiplications and n additions and is optimal. The number of required operations will be less if some terms have zero coefficients, and the method is easily extendible to a series in which successive powers of x differ by a factor other than x. It should be noted, and this is significant for implementation, that Horner's method transforms polynomial evaluation into a sequence of MULTIPLY-ADD operations.

A hardware polynomial evaluator may be implemented as a single direct derivation of Horner's method or, for higher performance, a modification of that. Several variants are possible, of which one is to partition the polynomial at hand into two polynomials, one consisting of terms of even power and the other of terms of odd power, use Horner's scheme to evaluate these concurrently, and finally add the results. So instead of the single set of recurrences given above, assuming n is odd, we would have two sets of recurrences:

$$Q'_n = c_{n-1}$$
$$Q'_k = c_k + x^2 Q'_{k+1} \qquad k = n-2, n-4, \ldots, 1$$
$$P'_n(x) = Q'_0$$

and

$$Q''_n = c_n$$
$$Q''_k = c_k + x^2 Q''_{k+1} \qquad k = n-1, n-3, \ldots, 0$$
$$P''_n(x) = xQ''_0$$

with the result obtained as $P_n(x) = P'_n(x) + P''_n(x)$. The concurrent evaluation can be carried out in two identical hardware units, each consisting of a multiplier and an adder, or even in a single pipelined unit; and the idea can be extended to more or different partitionings of the initial polynomial.

On the basis of Horner's method, the basic hardware required for polynomial evaluation consists of a multiplier and adder, arranged in series and used repeatedly. Such an arrangement can be implemented to be both faster and cheaper than a separate multiplier in conjunction with a separate adder, as follows. In a fast multiplier, all the multiplicand–multiples are added in a carry–save adder (CSA) array, of one or more CSAs, sequentially or in parallel, and the carry–save representation of the result is then converted, in a carry–propagate adder (CPA), into conventional form. In polynomial evaluation there is also a sequence of additions, and these too may be handled in a similar manner: CSA additions with a single CPA addition for conversion. The two nominal structures suggested may be combined so that there is only a single CPA used. Figure 6.1 shows the sketch of an evaluator designed on such a basis.

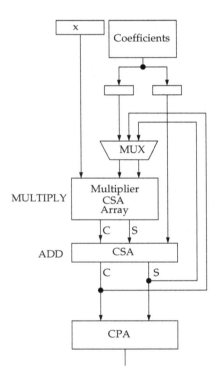

Figure 6.1: Polynomial evaluator

For high performance, the loop of Figure 6.1 may be unrolled and pipelined. An example is shown in Figure 6.2, for a cubic polynomial, $c_0 + c_1 x + c_2 x^2 + c_3 x^3$; evidently, such an arrangement is useful only if the frequency of use is sufficiently high to justify the high cost of replication.

A third, obvious, alternative is to take the polynomial as is and completely parallelize its evaluation, as shown in Figure 6.3 for a cubic polynomial; here we assume that squaring and cubing are done in specialized units of the type described in Section 2.2.2, with the outputs left in carry–save form, as with multiplication. A detailed description of such an implementation will be found in [22].

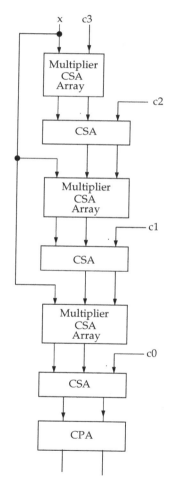

Figure 6.2: Unrolled polynomial evaluator

For the hardware evaluation of elementary functions, the polynomials are almost always of very low order, and so the designs of Figures 6.1–6.3 are quite practical as they are. Nevertheless, various other arrangements are possible: limited parallelism may be combined with limited sequential operation in various hybrids of the designs of Figures 6.1–6.3. Some variations on hardware polynomial evaluators will be found in [4–6, 14].

For high-precision or high-performance operations, Taylor series can be problematic, as may be (partially) deduced from the observations above. Other than the fact that very lengthy series might be required in some cases, Taylor series generally have poor errors distributions, and we next look at polynomials that are better in this regard. Nevertheless, Taylor series can be put to good use, if sufficient care is exercised. The typical arrangement in such cases consists of a combination of low-order Taylor series and lookup tables; we shall see examples in Chapters 7 and 8.

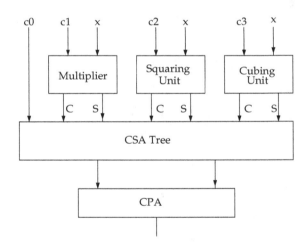

Figure 6.3: Parallel polynomial evaluator

6.3 Chebyshev polynomials

Approximations based on the Chebyshev polynomials[5] have found much use in hardware implementations. The polynomials are closely connected to the

---

[5]Strictly, these are Chebyshev polynomials *of the first kind*.

L_∞ norm,[6] in that they produce near-minimax approximations. Indeed, it has been shown in that for the type of *practical purposes* we are interested in, Chebyshev polynomials can be just as good as minimax ones [8], and, while not as good for "maximum errors", they will generally be better for "average error". Comprehensive discussions of Chebyshev polynomials will be found in [7, 21].

The interval of interest here is $[-1, 1]$. As indicated above, computing minimax coefficients for arbitrary intervals is not an easy task; but evaluation on any interval, $[a, b]$, can be transformed into evaluation on $[-1, -1]$, and for this interval the Chebyshev polynomials give an "optimal" result. (Of course, the interval translation means that the result will not necessarily be optimal for $[a, b]$, but in practice it will be close.)

The Chebyshev polynomials, $T_n(x)$, are defined as

$$T_n(x) = \cos(n\theta) \qquad \theta = \cos^{-1} x \qquad n = 0, 1, 2, \ldots \qquad (6.3)$$

From the identity

$$\cos(n+m)\theta + \cos(n-m)\theta = 2\cos n\theta \cos m\theta$$

we get

$$T_{n+m}(x) + T_{n-m}(x) = 2T_n(x)T_m(x)$$

which, with $m = 1$, gives

$$T_{n+1}(x) = 2xT_n(x) - T_{n-1}(x) \qquad (6.4)$$

From this we can generate all the polynomials. We can also observe that $T_n(x)$ is a polynomial of degree n, a point that will be useful later on.

The first six Chebyshev polynomials are

$$T_0(x) = 1$$

$$T_1(x) = x$$

$$T_2(x) = 2x^2 - 1$$

$$T_3(x) = 4x^3 - 3x$$

$$T_4(x) = 8x^4 - 8x^2 + 1$$

$$T_5(x) = 16x^5 - 20x^3 + 5x$$

---

[6]Chebyshev was the first to carry out a systematic study of the L_∞ norm, which, accordingly, is also sometimes referred to as the *Chebyshev norm*.

In general

$$T_n(x) = \sum_{k=0}^{\lfloor n/2 \rfloor} \left[(-1)^k \sum_{j=k}^{\lfloor n/2 \rfloor} \binom{n}{2j} \binom{j}{k} \right] x^{n-2k}$$

We will next proceed to a major property of these polynomials. But, first, some preliminaries:

From Equations 6.3 and 6.4, we can immediately deduce that on the interval $[-1, 1]$:

- $|T_n(x)| \leq 1$
- $T_n(x)$ has n zeroes, and these are at $n\theta = (k - 1/2)\pi$, $k = 1, 2, \ldots, n$; that is, $\theta = (k - 1/2)\pi/n$. So the roots are

$$\cos \frac{(k - 1/2)}{n}\pi \qquad k = 1, 2, \ldots, n$$

- $T_n(x)$ attains its maximum magnitude at $n + 1$ points—when $n\theta = k\pi$ $k = 0, 1, 2, \ldots, n$. That is, at the points

$$x_k = \cos\left(\frac{k\pi}{n}\right) \qquad k = 0, 1, 2, \ldots, n \qquad (6.5)$$

and these extrema alternate in sign:

$$T_n(x_k) = (-1)^k$$

Also, from Equation 6.4, it is evident—and easily proven, by induction—that

$$T_n(x) = 2^{n-1}x^n + c_{n-1}x^{n-1} + \cdots + c_1 x + c_0 \qquad \text{for some constants } c_i$$

and therefore, since $|T_n(x)| \leq 1$, that

$$\left| \frac{T_n(x)}{2^{n-1}} \right| \leq \frac{1}{2^{n-1}}$$

(That concludes the "preliminaries".)

Now, on the interval $[-1, 1]$, let P be any polynomial of the form

$$P_n(x) = x^n + a_{n-1}x^{n-1} + \cdots + a_1 x + a_0 \qquad \text{for some constants } a_i$$

and consider the error function

$$\varepsilon(x) = \frac{T_n(x)}{2^{n-1}} - P_n(x)$$

This is obviously a polynomial of degree $n - 1$, since the terms in x^n cancel out.

Suppose, then, that on the interval $[-1, 1]$, the maximum magnitudes attained by $|P_n(x)|$ are less than those of $|T_n(x)/2^{n-1}|$ at the points x_i of Equation 6.5. Because the extrema of $T_n(x)$ alternate in sign, we should have n alternations in sign:

$$\varepsilon(x_0) > 0$$
$$\varepsilon(x_1) < 0$$
$$\varepsilon(x_2) > 0$$

$$\cdots$$

Since $\varepsilon(x)$ changes sign in every interval $[x_i, x_{1+1}]$, it has a root in each such interval,[7] which implies that $\varepsilon(x) = 0$ at n points. But $\varepsilon(x)$ is a polynomial of degree $n - 1$, which implies that it has $n - 1$ roots.[8] So, it must be the case that $\varepsilon(x) = 0$ at *all* those points. Therefore, our initial supposition cannot be correct, and it must be the case that

$$\max \left| \frac{T_n(x)}{2^{n-1}} \right| \leq \max |P_n(x)| \qquad -1 \leq x \leq 1$$

We have thus arrived at a siginificant result:

OPTIMALITY OF CHEBYSHEV POLYNOMIALS: *Of all degree-n polynomials in which the coefficient of the term in x^n is 1, $T_n(x)/2^{n-1}$ has the smallest maximum magnitude on the interval* $[-1, 1]$.

There sometimes are cases where we wish to work with the interval $[0, 1]$, instead of $[-1, 1]$; in such cases one uses the *shifted* polynomials, $T_n^* \triangleq T_n(2x - 1)$. For an arbitrary interval, $[a, b]$, the translation between $t \in [-1, 1]$ and $x \in [a, b]$ is via the equations

$$u = 2\frac{x - a}{b - a} - 1$$

$$x = \frac{b - a}{2}u + \frac{a + b}{2}$$

and the polynomials, $\widetilde{T}_n(x)$, used are defined as

$$\widetilde{T}_n(x) = T_n(u)$$

---

[7]By the *Intermediate Value Theorem*: If $f(x)$ is a continuous function on the interval $[a, b]$, then it takes any value between $f(a)$ and $f(b)$ at some point within the interval. So if $f(a)$ and $f(b)$ are of opposite sign, then $0 = f(c)$ for some c in the interval.

[8]By the *Fundamental Theorem of Algebra*: A non-zero, single-variable polynomial of degree m has, counted with multiplicity, exactly m roots.

where, from Equation 6.4

$$\widetilde{T}_{n+1}(x) = 2uT_n(u) - T_{n-1}(u) \tag{6.6}$$

$$= 2\left[\frac{2(x-a)}{b-a} - 1\right]\widetilde{T}_n(x) - \widetilde{T}_{n-1}(x) \tag{6.7}$$

So

$$\widetilde{T}_{n+1}(x) = c_0 + c_1 x + c_2 x^2 + \cdots + c_{n+1} x^{n+1}$$

where

$$c_{n+1} = 2^n \left(\frac{2}{b-a}\right)^{n+1} \tag{6.8}$$

(This fact is used in Section 6.5.)

We next look at another especially useful aspect of Chebyshev polynomials—the *economization of power series*. In summary, this is the process of taking a finite power series, expressing it in terms of Chebyshev polynomials, truncating the result, and then converting back to a shorter power series with the same or better accuracy than the original. The details are as follows.

A large variety of functions can be approximated using Chebyshev polynomials. Of particular interest to us are those functions that have power-series expansions. For these, we can get Chebyshev expansions relatively easily, by expressing each power of x in terms of Chebyshev polynomials:

$$1 = T_0(x)$$

$$x = T_1(x)$$

$$x^2 = [T_0(x) + T_2(x)]/2$$

$$x^3 = [3T_1(x) + T_3(x)]/4$$

$$x^4 = [3T_0(x) + 4T_2(x) + T_4(x)]/8$$

$$x^5 = [10T_1(x) + 5T_3(x) + T_5(x)]/16$$

$$\text{and so forth}$$

These powers can be generated by "reversing" the application of Equation 6.4:

$$xT_n(x) = \frac{1}{2}[T_{n+1}(x) + T_{n-1}(x)]$$

$$xT_0(x) = T_1(x)$$

For example

$$x^3 = x[x(T_1(x))] \qquad \text{since } T_1(x) = x$$

$$= x\left[T_2(x) + T_0(x)\right]/2$$

$$= xT_2(x)/2 + xT_0/2$$

$$= \left[T_3(x) + T_1(x)\right]/4 + T_1(x)/2$$

$$= \left[3T_1(x) + T_3(x)\right]/4$$

In general

$$x^n = \frac{1}{2^{n-1}}\left[* \sum_{k=0}^{\lfloor n/2 \rfloor} \binom{n}{k} T_{n-2k}(x)\right]$$

where the "*" means that the kth term is to be halved if n is even and $k = n/2$.

The transformation of a power series into a series of Chebyshev polynomials can be quite useful, as we next show.

Consider the Taylor-series expansion above (Table 6.2) for $\ln(1+x)$, on the interval $[0,1]$:

$$\ln(1+x) \approx x - \frac{x^2}{2} + \frac{x^3}{3} - \frac{x^4}{4} + \frac{x^5}{5} + \cdots$$

If we drop all terms after the fourth, to get

$$\ln(1+x) \approx x - \frac{x^2}{2} + \frac{x^3}{3} - \frac{x^4}{4} \tag{6.9}$$

the maximum-magnitude error in the approximation is $1/5$. We next compare this with a Chebyshev-polynomial expansion.

Using the list given above to express the x^ks in terms of the T_js and rearranging the terms in the result, we get

$$\ln(1+x) \approx -\frac{11}{32}T_0(x) + \frac{11}{8}T_1(x) - \frac{3}{8}T_2(x) + \frac{7}{48}T_3(x)$$

$$-\frac{1}{32}T_4(x) + \frac{1}{80}T_5(x) \tag{6.10}$$

Since $|T_n(x)| \le 1$, the magnitudes of the errors due to the last three terms in this approximation are at most $7/48, 1/32$, and $1/80$, the sum of which is less than $1/5$. So the three-term approximation

$$\ln(1+x) \approx -\frac{11}{32}T_0(x) + \frac{11}{8}T_1(x) - \frac{3}{8}T_2(x)$$

is better than the four-term approximation of Equation 6.9. We can turn this back into a power series, by substitution from the list above that relates $\{x^i\}$ and $\{T_j\}$. After some algebraic manipulations, we end up with

$$\ln(1+x) \approx -\frac{11}{32} + \frac{11}{8}x - \frac{3}{4}x^2$$

which is of both lower degree and better accuracy than Equation 6.9.

The procedure just described is known as the *economization of a power series* and is one way in which the Chebyshev polynomials are particularly useful. Comparing Equations 6.9 and 6.10, we observe that the magnitudes of the coefficients in the latter tend to zero faster than those in the former. This will usually be the case and explains informally why economization works. A slightly more precise explanation is as follows.

On an interval $[a, b]$, it is possible to use the properties of Chebyshev polynomials to devise (as we show in Section 6.5) a degree-n polynomial approximation to a function $f(x)$ with error of magnitude

$$\frac{2(b-a)^{n+1}}{4^{n+1}(n+1)!} \max_{a \leq x \leq b} \left| f^{(n+1)}(x) \right| \tag{6.11}$$

On the interval $[-1, 1]$, this is equal to

$$\frac{1}{2^n(n+1)!} \max_{-1 \leq x \leq 1} \left| f^{(n+1)}(x) \right|$$

Comparing this with Equation 6.2 shows that, in general, the error magnitudes with the use of Chebyshev polynomials are much smaller than with the Taylor series.

There are instances where a Taylor series might give better results than a Chebyshev expansion, expecially for very small ranges and values of the argument, but even in such cases the Chebyshev expansion will have a better distribution of errors. As an example, consider the four-term Taylor for e^x:

$$e^x \approx 1 + \frac{x}{1!} + \frac{x^2}{2!} + \frac{x^3}{3!}$$

$$\approx 1 + x + 0.5x^2 + 0.1667x^3$$

and the four-term Chebyshev series:

$$e^x \approx 1.266T_0 + 1.130T_1 + 0.2715T_2 + 0.0443T_3$$

$$\approx 0.995 + 0.997x + 0.543x^2 + 0.177x^3$$

Table 6.5 shows a comparison of the two series for some values of x in the interval $[-1, 1]$. In the region near $x = 0$, the Taylor series has smaller errors. But these errors get larger away from the origin (the point of expansion) and are much larger at the ends of the interval, whereas the errors with the Chebyshev approximation have a more uniform distribution.

Chebyshev economization is especially useful when one starts with a series that converges slowly. Take, for example, the evaluation of $\ln(1+x)$ on the interval $[0, 1]$. The degree-six polynomial obtained through Chebyshev economization will have an error of maximum magnitude 1.6×10^{-6}. On the other hand, the Taylor series about the middle of the interval requires more than sixteen terms to get the same accuracy.

x	Absolute Error		Relative Error	
	Taylor	Chebyshev	Taylor	Chebyshev
-1.000000	0.034546	0.003879	0.093906	0.010545
-0.900000	0.023070	0.001927	0.056742	0.004740
-0.800000	0.014662	0.004967	0.032632	0.011054
-0.700000	0.008752	0.005874	0.017624	0.011828
-0.600000	0.004812	0.005236	0.008767	0.009541
-0.500000	0.002364	0.003594	0.003898	0.005926
-0.400000	0.000987	0.001432	0.001472	0.002136
-0.300000	0.000318	0.000827	0.000430	0.001117
-0.200000	0.000064	0.002827	0.000078	0.003453
-0.100000	0.000004	0.004284	0.000005	0.004735
-0.000000	0.000000	0.005000	0.000000	0.005000
0.100000	0.000004	0.004864	0.000004	0.004401
0.200000	0.000069	0.003867	0.000057	0.003166
0.300000	0.000359	0.002110	0.000266	0.001563
0.400000	0.001158	0.000183	0.000776	0.000123
0.500000	0.002888	0.002654	0.001752	0.001610
0.600000	0.006119	0.004793	0.003358	0.002631
0.700000	0.011586	0.005928	0.005753	0.002944
0.800000	0.020208	0.005203	0.009080	0.002338
0.900000	0.033103	0.001560	0.013459	0.000634
1.000000	0.051615	0.006282	0.018988	0.002311

Table 6.5: Comparison of Taylor and Chebyshev approximations

We have so far considered just the expression of specific functions in terms of Chebyshev polynomials. The general formulation is that a function, $f(x)$, that is continuous on the interval $[-1, 1]$ has a unique expresion in terms of Chebyshev polynomials:

$$e^{vx} = I_0(v) + 2\sum_{n=1}^{\infty} I_n(v)T_n(x)$$

$$\sin vx = 2\sum_{n=0}^{\infty} (-1)^n J_{2n+1}(v)T_{2n+1}(x)$$

$$\cos vx = J_0(v) + 2\sum_{n=1}^{\infty} J_{2n}(v)(-1)^n T_{2n}(x)$$

$$\sinh vx = 2\sum_{n=0}^{\infty} I_{2n+1}(v)T_{2n+1}(x)$$

$$\cosh vx = I_0(k) + 2\sum_{n=1}^{\infty} I_{2n}(v)T_{2n}(x)$$

$$\ln(1+x) = \ln\left(\frac{3+2\sqrt{2}}{4}\right) T_0(2x-1)$$
$$+2\sum_{n-1}^{\infty} (-1)^{n+1} \frac{(3-2\sqrt{2})^n}{n} T_n(2x-1) \qquad x \in [0,1]$$

$$\tan^{-1} x = \frac{\pi}{8} + 2\sum_{n=0}^{\infty} (-1)^n \frac{u^{2n+1}}{2n+1} T_{2n+1}(y) \qquad x \in [0,1]$$
$$\text{where } u = \tan\frac{\pi}{16} \text{ and } y = \frac{(\sqrt{2}+1)x-1}{(\sqrt{2}-1)x+1}$$

$$\sin^{-1} x = \frac{4}{\pi} \sum_{n=1}^{\infty} \frac{1}{(n+1)^2} T_{2n+1}(x)$$

where $J_m(v)$ is the order-n Bessel function of the first kind, and $I_m(v)$ is the order-n modified Bessel function of the first kind:

$$J_m(v) = \sum_{k=0}^{} \frac{(-1)^k (v/2)^{m+2k}}{k!(m+k)!} \qquad\qquad I_m(v) = \sum_{k=0}^{} \frac{((v/2)^{m+2k}}{k!(m+k)!}$$

Table 6.6: Chebyshev expansions of some functions

$$f(x) = \sum_{k=0}^{\infty} c_k T_k(x)$$

where

$$c_0 = \frac{1}{\pi} \int_{-1}^{1} \frac{f(x)}{\sqrt{1-x^2}} dx$$

$$c_k = \frac{2}{\pi} \int_{-1}^{1} \frac{f(x)T_k(x)}{\sqrt{1-x^2}} dx \qquad k \geq 1$$

$$= \frac{2}{\pi} \int_{0}^{\pi} f(\cos\theta)\cos(k\theta)d\theta$$

Table 6.6 gives a list of some Chebyshev-polynomial expansions,[9] and many more will be found in [15–17].

The Chebyshev polynomials also provide a different path to obtaining approximation polynomials. We shall see this in Section 6.5; here, we conclude with some remarks on the evaluation of such a polynomial.

A Chebyshev expansion

$$P_n(x) = \sum_{k=0}^{n} c_k T_k(x) \tag{6.12}$$

can be evaluated as follows (*Clenshaw's method*). Starting with $b_{n+2} = b_{n+1} = 0$, compute the sequence of constants $b_n, b_{n-1}, \ldots, b_0$ from the recurrence

$$b_k - 2x b_{k+1} + b_{k+2} = c_k$$

Substitution into Equation 6.12 gives

$$P_n(x) = \sum_{k=0}^{n} c_k T_k(x)$$

$$= \sum_{k=0}^{n} [(b_k - 2x b_{k+1} + b_{k+2}) T_k(x)]$$

---

[9]These have a less "user-friendly" appearance than Taylor series. But, fortunately, the reader who has practical computations in mind has other options: computed coefficients are readily available in the literature—for example, [16, 17] give them for all the functions of interest—and symbolic-mathematics software, such as MAPLE, can be put to good use if such tables are not readily available.

Whence:

$$P_n(x) = b_0 T_0(x) - b_1 2x T_0(x) + b_1 T_1(x)$$

$$+ \sum_{k=0}^{n-2} [b_{k+2}(T_k(x) - 2x T_{k+1}(x) + T_{k+2}(x))]$$

$$+ b_{n+1} T_{n-1}(x) + (b_{n+2} - 2x b_{n+1}) T_n(x)$$

$$= (b_0 - 2x b_1) T_0(x) + b_1 T_1(x)$$

$$\text{since } T_{i+1}(x) - 2x T_i(x) - T_{i-1}(x) = 0$$

$$\text{by Equation 6.4 and } b_{n+1} = b_{n+2} = 0$$

$$= b_0 - b_1 x$$

From which we obtain the recurrences for the evaluation:

$$Q_n = c_n$$
$$Q_{n+1} = 0$$
$$Q_k = 2x Q_{k+1} - Q_{k+2} + c_k \qquad\qquad k = n-1, n-2, \ldots, 1$$
$$Q_0 = x Q_1 - Q_2 + c_0$$
$$P_n(x) = Q_0$$

Lastly, if $P_n(x)$ is of the form $\sum_{i=0}^{n} c_i \prod_{j=0}^{i}(x - x_i)$, for some constants x_i—a form that is frequently found in some formulations of the solution to the interpolation problem (Section 6.5)—then the evaluation can be carried out in n multiplications and $2n$ additions, through the recurrences:

$$Q_n = c_n$$
$$Q_k = (x - x_k) Q_{k+1} + c_k \qquad\qquad k = n-1, n-2, \ldots, 0$$
$$P_n(x) = Q_0$$

Apart from their special properties, from a hardware perspective Chebyshev polynomials are like any other polynomial; so their implementation does not require anything special. Some examples of the use of Chebyshev polynomials in hardware evaluation will be found in [12, 13, 18, 20].

6.4   Legendre polynomials

Legendre polynomials, which we shall denote $L_n(x)$, are good for approximations in the L_2 norm. And for that norm, on the interval $[-1, 1]$, we can get a "minimization" result similar to that for the Chebyshev polynomials and the L_∞ norm.

The Legendre polynomials are defined as

$$L_0(x) = 1$$

$$L_1(x) = x$$

$$L_n(x) = \frac{1}{2^n n!} \frac{d^n}{dx^n} \left(x^2 - 1\right)^n$$

and can be obtained by using the recurrence

$$L_{n+1}(x) = \frac{1}{n+1} \left[(2n+1)x L_n(x) - n L_{n-1}(x) \right]$$

The first few Legendre polynomials are

$$L_0(x) = 1$$

$$L_1(x) = x$$

$$L_2(x) = \frac{1}{2} \left(3x^2 - 1\right)$$

$$L_3(x) = \frac{1}{2} \left(5x^3 - 3x\right)$$

$$L_4(x) = \frac{1}{8} \left(35x^4 - 30x^2 + 3\right)$$

$$L_5(x) = \frac{1}{8} \left(63x^5 - 70x^3 + 15x\right)$$

Using these, we can construct an approximating polynomial as $P(x) = \sum_i c_i L_i(x)$. If the polynomial so constructed is of order n, then the error on the interval $[-1, 1]$ is proportional to $1/[2^{n+1}(n+1)!]$, which is similar to that of a Chebyshev approximation.

6.5 Interpolation

The general *interpolation* problem is that we have the tabulated values of a function, f, at some points, $\{x_i\}$, and we wish to determine (or at least approximate) its values at other points. In general, the underlying function may or may not be known, but in our case it is always known. The interpolation problem can be related to our function-approximation problem in two ways.

The first is that for a given x, we compute $f(x)$ in terms of $f(x_i)$ at the x_i nearest to x. There is no specific or implied requirement on how the computation is to be done, but one can see the general idea suggested by standard Taylor series, in which evaluation (expansion) is relative to a specific point. We shall see interpolation in this form applied in Section 7.1.3.

The second is more directly related to our business here of devising polynomials to approximate certain functions. In this case we select some function points and then find a polynomial that fits through them. The following is a brief discussion of interpolation in this sense.

In the present context, we wish to construct a degree-n polynomial, $P_n(x)$, to approximate some function $f(x)$, on the interval $[a, b]$. Let $\langle x_0, f(x_0) \rangle$, $\langle x_1, f(x_1) \rangle$, ..., $\langle x_n, f(x_n) \rangle$ be $n + 1$ distinct points in the interval. Then the interpolation problem is to find $P_n(x)$ such that $P_n(x_i) = f(x_i), 0 \le i \le n$.

The interpolating polynomial is unique,[10] and it can be obtained through a variety of means and expressed in a variety of forms. An obvious, but generally not recommended, way to formulate the polynomial is the *method of undetermined coefficients*, which consists of solving for the cofficients, c_i, in

$$P_n(x) = c_0 + c_1 x + c_2 x^2 + \cdots + c_n x_n = f(x)$$

at the tabulated points. That is, solving the $n + 1$ equations

$$c_0 + c_1 x_0 + c_2 x_0^2 + \cdots + c_n x_0^n = f(x_0)$$
$$c_0 + c_1 x_1 + c_2 x_1^2 + \cdots + c_n x_1^n = f(x_1)$$
$$\vdots$$
$$c_0 + c_1 x_n + c_2 x_n^2 + \cdots + c_n x_n^n = f(x_n)$$

If the x_is are distinct, then evidently there is a unique solution that yields $P_n(x)$.

Another well-known, and much better, method for formulating the interpolating polynomial is through its *Lagrange form*:

$$P_n(x) = \sum_{j=0}^{n} f(x_j) l_j(x) \qquad (6.13)$$

---

[10]Consider the *Fundamental Theorem of Algebra*: Suppose $P_n(x) = c_0 + c_1 + \cdots + c_n x^n$ is a polynomial, with $n \ge 0$ and $c_n \ne 0$. Then $P_n(x)$ has n roots, $\{r_i: P_n(x) = c_n(x - r_1)(x - r_2) \cdots (x - r_n)\}$.

where

$$l_j(x) = \prod_{i=0,\ j\neq i}^{n} \frac{x - x_i}{x_j - x_i}$$

We shall henceforth assume, unless otherwise specified, that the interpolating polynomial is in Lagrange form. As noted above, however, there are other forms—most notably those derived from *difference schemes*[11]—and some of these have been used in hardware implementations (e.g. [18]).

Computationally, there are at least two obvious ways in which we can use Equation 6.13. The first is to explicitly construct the polynomial, arrange the terms in powers of x, and then apply it as needed, to each value of x; in this case the values x_i and $f(x_i)$ may be discarded once the polynomial has been constucted, but the coefficients of the resulting polynomial need to be stored. The other way is to construct the polynomial "on the fly", as it were, by evaluating Equation 6.13 for each argument; in this case, the constants $\langle x_i, f(x_i)\rangle$—in practice, just $f(x_i)$—are stored and the coefficients of the polynomial are computed "on the fly". The choice between the two methods will depend on the trade-off between memory used and computation required: *in general*, the latter requires less memory but more computation.[12] For hardware evaluations, the former is the more commonly used method, but there are interesting exceptions. For example, [18] describes a hardware evaluator that combines both approaches, the basic idea being that some polynomial coefficients will be computed beforehand and others will be computed on the fly.

We next consider the issues of error and the choice of the interpolation points, $\{x_i\}$.

The error from Equation 6.13 is

$$\varepsilon_n(x) = f(x) - P_n(x)$$

$$= \frac{f^{(n+1)}(\xi)}{(n+1)!} \prod_{i=0}^{n} (x - x_i) \qquad (6.14)$$

$$= \frac{f^{(n+1)}(\xi)}{(n+1)!} Q_n(x)$$

---

[11]See standard texts on numerical analysis.
[12]It should be noted that for the latter there are other forms of the interpolation polynomial that are computationally more efficient than the expression of Equation 6.13.

where

$$Q_n(x) = \prod_{i=0}^{n}(x - x_i)$$

and ξ is some value in the smallest interval that contains $x, x_0, x_1, \ldots, x_n$. Evidently, the derivative $Q_n^{(n+1)} = (n+1)!$. We next show that Equation 6.14 holds.

Suppose x is arbitrary but fixed. Then $[f(x) - P_n(x)]/Q_n(x)$ is constant. If $x = x_i$, for some $0 \leq i \leq n$, then $f(x) = P_n(x)$, and Equation 6.14 is clearly the case. Otherwise, consider the function

$$g(u) = f(u) - P_n(u) - \frac{f(x) - P_n(x)}{Q_n(x)}Q_n(u)$$

We have

$$g(x) = g(x_0) = g(x_1) = \cdots g(x_n) \tag{6.15}$$

and

$$g^{(n+1)}(u) = f^{(n+1)}(u) - \frac{f(x) - P_n(x)}{Q_n(x)}(n+1)! \tag{6.16}$$

Now, let I be the smallest interval that contains $x, x_0, x_1, \ldots, x_n$. Applying Rolle's Theorem[13] to Equations 6.15, we see that $g'(u)$ has at least $n+1$ distinct zeroes in I, $g''(u)$ has at least n distinct zeroes in I, $\ldots$, and $g^{(n+1)}(u)$ has at least one zero, ξ, in I. So with Equation 6.16:

$$f^{(n+1)}(\xi) - \frac{f(x) - P_n(x)}{Q_n(x)}(n+1)! = 0 \tag{6.17}$$

which gives Equation 6.14.

Considering Equation 6.14, in trying to minimize the magnitude of error, in general there is not much we can do about the derivative. But we can try to minimize the magnitude of $|Q_n(x)|$, and that means choosing the interpolation points, $\{x_i\}$, carefully. As a rough rule, interpolation at uniformly spaced points will not yield the best results, although it can be computationally convenient; typically, we are interested in optimizing some aspect of error, and this should be taken into account. Thus, for example, if the objective is to minimize the maximum magnitude of error on the interval $[-1, 1]$, then, noting that $Q_n(x)$ is a polynomial of degree $n+1$, a

---

[13] *Rolle's Theorem*: If $f(x)$ is continuous on the interval $[a, b]$, differentiable in (a, b), and $f(a) = f(b)$, then there is at least one $c \in (a, b)$ such that $f'(c) = 0$.

good choices for the set of interpolation points consists of the roots of the Chebyshev polynomial $T_{n+1}(x)$:

$$x_i = \cos\left[\frac{(2i+1)\pi}{2(n+1)}\right] \qquad i = 0, 1, 2, ...n$$

(Similarly, if we wish to miminize the value of the L_2 norm, then the interpolation points should be taken to be the roots of the Legendre polynomials.) The explanation for the use of Chebyshev polynonmials is as follows.

From Equation 6.14, the bound on the magnitude of error on the interval $[-1, 1]$ is

$$|\varepsilon_n(x)| \le \frac{1}{(n+1)!} \max_{-1 \le x \le 1} \left|f^{(n+1)}(x)\right| \max_{-1 \le x \le 1} |Q_n(x)| \qquad (6.18)$$

To minimize this, we should select interpolation points that minimize $\max |Q_n(x)|$, for $-1 \le x \le 1$, and we know, from the Chebyshev "optimality" result above, that the best choice is

$$Q_n(x) = \frac{T_{n+1}(x)}{2^n}$$

in which case $\max |\varepsilon_n(x)| = 1/2^n$. So, if λ is the bound on $|f^{(n+1)}(x)|$, then the bound on the magnitude of the error will be

$$\left|\frac{\lambda}{2^n(n+1)!}\right|$$

For an arbitrary interval, $[a, b]$, translation is required, relative to $[-1, 1]$. Therefore, to obtain the interpolation points, $\{x_i\}$, we first obtain (on $[-1, 1]$)

$$u_i = \cos\left[\frac{(2i+1)\pi}{2(n+1)}\right] \qquad i = 0, 1, 2, ..., n$$

and then obtain (on $[a, b]$)

$$x_i = \frac{b-a}{2}u_i + \frac{a+b}{2} \qquad i = 0, 1, 2, ..., n$$

That is, the interpolation points are the roots of the polynomial $\widetilde{T}_{n+1}(x)$ (Equations 6.6–6.8). So

$$Q_n(x) = \frac{1}{2^n}\left(\frac{b-a}{2}\right)^{n+1} \widetilde{T}_{n+1}(x)$$

and

$$\max_{a \le x \le b} |Q_n(x)| = \frac{1}{2^n}\left(\frac{b-a}{2}\right)^{n+1} \qquad (6.19)$$

If the bound on $\left|f^{(n+1)}(x)\right|$ is λ, then

$$|\varepsilon_n(x)| \leq \frac{2\lambda}{(n+1)!}\left(\frac{b-a}{4}\right)^{n+1} \tag{6.20}$$

Instead of the Lagrange form, we may also directly construct a Chebyshev interpolation polynomial approximation

$$\sum_{k=0}^{n} c_k T_k(x) \approx f(x)$$

by computing the interpolation points and coefficients as

$$x_i = \cos\left[\frac{(2i+1)\pi}{2(n+1)}\right] \qquad i = 0,1,2,...,n$$

$$c_0 = \frac{1}{n+1}\sum_{k=0}^{n} f(x_k)$$

$$c_j = \frac{2}{n+1}\sum_{k=0}^{n} f(x_k)T_j(x_k) \qquad j = 1,2,...,n$$

$$= \frac{2}{n+1}\sum_{k=0}^{n} f(x_k)\cos\left[\frac{j(2k+1)\pi}{2(n+1)}\right]$$

and then formulating a "normal" expression in terms of powers of x.

EXAMPLE. For a degree-3 Chebyshev polynomial, $P_3(x)$, approximation to $f(x) = e^x$ on $[-1,1]$, the interpolation points are

$$x_k = \cos\left[\frac{(2k+1)\pi}{8}\right] \qquad k = 0,1,2,3$$

and (in five decimal figures)

$$c_0 = \frac{1}{4}\sum_{k=0}^{3} e^{x_k} = 1.2660$$

$$c_1 = \frac{1}{2} \sum_{k=0}^{3} e^{x_k} x_k = 1.1303$$

$$c_2 = \frac{1}{2} \sum_{k=0}^{3} e^{x_k} \cos\left[\frac{2(2k+1)\pi}{8}\right] = 0.2715$$

$$c_3 = \frac{1}{2} \sum_{k=0}^{3} e^{x_k} \cos\left[\frac{3(2k+1)\pi}{8}\right] = 0.0438$$

So

$$P_3(x) = 1.266T_0(x) + 1.1303T_1(x) + 0.2715T_2(x) + 0.0438T_3(x)$$

$$= 0.9946 + 0.9989x + 0.5429x^2 + 0.1712x^3$$

END EXAMPLE.

The description of a hardware evaluator designed on the basis of Chebyshev interpolation will be found in [18], and there are many others in the published literature.

A note on segmentation

We conclude this section with a note that clarifies and emphasizes a point made earlier and which helps "set the stage" for what is to come in Chapter 7.

We saw in Section 6.2 that high-order Taylor-series polynomials are not necessarily good in terms of accuracy (as well as computational cost) and that instead of a single high-order polynomial over a given interval, it is better to divide the interval of evaluation into smaller *segments* (or *pieces*) and apply a low-order polynomial to each segment. The same considerations apply here too, as can be seen from an examination of Equation 6.14:

$$\varepsilon_n(x) = \frac{f^{(n+1)}(\xi)}{(n+1)!} \prod_{i=0}^{n}(x - x_i)$$

Consider the bounds on the two main terms in this equation. For some functions, e.g. $\sin x$, the values of

$$\frac{\left|f^{(n+1)}(\xi)\right|}{(n+1)!}$$

will decrease rapidly. (In the case of sine, the magnitudes of the derivatives are each bounded by one.) For other functions, the value of the expression may decrease only slowly or not at all: for example, $1/x$ on the interval $[1/2, 1]$. So, in general, we also need to ensure that

$$\max \left| \prod_{i=0}^{n} (x - x_i) \right|$$

is small. If we wish to mimimize the maximum magnitude of absolute error, then, as indicated above, the interpolation points would be taken as the roots of the Chebyshev polynomials. In this case, from Equation 6.19, the last expression becomes

$$2 \left(\frac{b - a}{4} \right)^{n+1}$$

and the effect of the interval size is evident.

For the most part, what we should like is to ensure that any argument, x, is not far from an interpolation point. That can be achieved by dividing $[a, b]$ into small segments, $\{[u_i, v_i]\}$ and then applying a separate interpolating polynomial on each segment. The errors are then

$$2 \left(\frac{v_i - u_i}{4} \right)^{n+1}$$

and we can control the maximum magnitudes by properly choosing the segment sizes. That is one of the main topics in Chapter 7.

6.6   Rational functions

A rational function, $R_{n,m}(x)$, is the ratio of a degree-n polynomial, $P_n(x)$, and a degree-m polynomial, $Q_m(x)$:

$$R_{n,m}(x) \overset{\triangle}{=} \frac{P_n(x)}{Q_m(x)} = \frac{p_0 + p_1 x + p_2 x^2 + \cdots + p_n x^n}{q_0 + q_1 x + q_2 x^2 + \cdots + q_n x^m} \qquad (6.21)$$

where $P_n(x)$ and $Q_m(x)$ have no common factors.

If $R_{n,m}(x)$ is used to approximate some function, then $Q_m(x)$ should not have a root in the interval of approximation. For a given value of $m+n$, the magnitude of errors will be smallest when $n = m$ or $n = m + 1$.

Rational functions can be useful if we wish to use polynomials on their own but those of the types discussed above are of limited practicality. For example, for $\cos^{-1} x$ on the interval $[-1, 1]$, a Taylor-series polynomial of degree 10,000 is required to obtain an accuracy of 10^{-8}, whereas lower-degree polynomials will be required with a rational function. Generally, rational functions will give better approximations than polynomials, which is as we should expect, given that polynomials are just a special case (with $m = 0$) of rational functions. "Visually", the graphs of rational functions can assume shapes that those of polynomials cannot and so are more likely to better match the graphs of the functions being approximated. Another useful property of rational functions is that they can work beyond the radii of convergence of the corresponding Taylor series. And a third, significant, property is that they tend to balance the extremes of the error curve in an approximation; we shall take another look at this type of *balanced-error property* in Chapter 7. Probably the best-known type of rational-function approximation is the *Padé approximation*, which is obtained as follows.

With reference to Equation 6.21: Since $R_{n,m}(x)$ is unchanged if both $P_n(x)$ and $Q_m(x)$ are divided by a constant, q_0 is set to 1, and $f(x)$ and $R_{n,m}(x)$ are required to agree at $x = 0$ and on the first k derivatives at that point, where k is as large as possible.[14] The choice of $q_0 = 1$ ensures the uniqueness (for given n and m) of the approximation; without it, uniqueness is up to a multiplicative-constant factor. And the condition on derivatives means that the Maclaurin-series expansions agree on the first k terms. Ideally, we should have $k = m + n + 1$, but this cannot be guaranteed. We can, however, ensure that k is at least $n + 1$, simply by choosing $Q_m(x) = 1$. We shall therefore assume that $n+1 \leq k \leq n+m+1$. It should also be noted that the choice of $x = 0$ for the point of agreement is somewhat arbitrary, and its primary justification is that it simplifies matters. In general, one may start with Taylor series about any point, a:

$$P_n(x) = \sum_{i=0}^{n} p_i(x - a)^i$$

$$Q_m(x) = \sum_{i=0}^{m} q_i(x - a)^i$$

Indeed, even Taylor series are not the only possibility. As an example of an alternative, the general techniques used in Padé approximations (i.e.

---

[14]Other alternatives to a Padé approximation are to choose $R_{n,m}(x)$ so that $R(x_i) = f(x_i)$ at as many points as possible or to seek to minimize $\sum_i [f(x_i) - R(x_i)]^2$, i.e. a least-squares approximation. The interested reader will find details in good books on numerical analysis.

with MacLaurin series) can be applied to Chebyshev series, and the resulting *Chebyshev–Padé approximation* should yield even better results. We leave it to the interested reader to consult the relevant literature.

Getting back on track: Suppose $f(x)$ has a Maclaurin-series expansion

$$f(x) = \sum_{i=0}^{\infty} a_i x^i$$

and suppose we can find $P_n(x)$ and $Q_m(x)$ such that $R_{n,m}(x) \triangleq P_n(x)/Q_m(x)$ has a Maclaurin expansion $\sum_{i=0}^{\infty} r_i x^i$. Then the Padé approximation consists of choosing $P_n(x)$ and $Q_m(x)$ so that

$$f(x) - R_{n,m}(x) = \sum_{i=k}^{\infty} c_i x^i \tag{6.22}$$

where k is as large as possible; that is, $f(x)$ and $R_{n,m}(x)$ agree on as many terms as possible. From Equation 6.22:

$$f(x)Q_m(x) - P_n(x) = Q_m(x) \sum_{i=k}^{\infty} c_i x^i$$

$$= \sum_{i=k}^{\infty} d_i x^i$$

and

$$f(x)Q_m(x) - P_n(x) = \left(\sum_{i=0}^{\infty} a_i x^i \right) \left(\sum_{i=0}^{m} q_i x^i \right) - \sum_{i=0}^{n} p_i x^i$$

$$= (a_0 q_0 - p_0) + (a_0 q_1 + a_1 q_0 - p_1)x \tag{6.23}$$

$$+ (a_0 q_2 + a_1 q_1 + a_2 q_0 - p_2)x^2 + \cdots$$

For the best aproximation $f(x)Q_m(x) - P_n(x) = 0$. So for a good approximation we want as many terms as possible to vanish on the right-hand side of Equation 6.23. We therefore choose

$$\sum_{i=0}^{j} a_i q_{j-i} = \begin{cases} p_j & \text{for } 0 \le j \le n \\ 0 & \text{for } n+1 \le j \le k \end{cases}$$

with $q_{j-i} = 0$ for $j - i > m$. This gives a set of linear $n + m + 1$ equations to be solved for the p_is and q_is.

EXAMPLE: Let $f(x) = \cos x$. The Maclaurin series is

$$1 - \frac{x^2}{2!} + \frac{x^4}{4!} - \frac{x^6}{6!} + \frac{x^8}{8!} - \cdots$$

Take the case $m = n = 4$:

$$R_{4,4}(x) = \frac{p_0 + p_1 x + p_2 x^2 + p_3 x^3 + p_4 x^4}{1 + q_1 x + q_2 x^2 + q_3 x^3 + q_4 x^4}$$

Choosing $k = n + m = 8$, the equations to be solved are

$$1 = p_0$$

$$q_1 = p_1$$

$$-\frac{1}{2} + q_2 = p_2$$

$$-\frac{q_1}{2} + q_2 = p_3$$

$$\frac{1}{4!} - \frac{q_2}{2} + q_4 = p_4$$

$$\frac{q_1}{4!} - \frac{q_3}{2} + q_4 = 0$$

$$-\frac{1}{6!} - \frac{q_2}{4!} - \frac{q_4}{2} = 0$$

$$-\frac{q_1}{6!} + \frac{q_3}{4!} = 0$$

$$-\frac{1}{8!} - \frac{q_2}{6!} + \frac{q_4}{4!} = 0$$

whose solutions are $p_0 = 1$, $p_1 = 0$, $p_2 = 115/252$, $p_3 = 0$, $p_4 = 313/15120$, $q_1 = 0$, $q_2 = 11/252$, $q_3 = 0$, and $q_4 = 13/15120$. So

$$R_{n,m}(x) = \frac{1 + (115/252)x^2 + (313/15120)x^4}{1 + (11/252)x^2 + (13/15120)x^4}$$

$$= \frac{15120 - 6900x^2 + 313x^4}{15120 + 660x^2 + 13x^4}$$

With this approximation, on the interval $[-1, 1]$, the errors of largest magnitude occur at the end of the intervals and the magnitudes are approximately

3.599×10^{-7}. By way of contrast, consider the Maclaurin series with the same number of parameters:

$$1 - \frac{x^2}{2!} + \frac{x^4}{4!} - \frac{x^6}{6!} + \frac{x^8}{8!}$$

On the same interval, this polynomial has a maximum magnitude in error of about 2.453×10^{-5}. And the Padé approximation is even better on smaller intervals.

END EXAMPLE

Numerous examples of rational functions for the approximation of elementary functions will be found in [15–17].

There are several ways to evaluate a rational function, none of which is particularly cheap. The most direct way is to use Horner's method to evaluate each of the polynomials and then carry out a division. There are other methods, but there is no getting around the division, and given the high cost of division (relative to the cost of other basic arithmetic operations), it is not surprising that rational functions have not found much use in the hardware evaluation of elementary functions. Nevertheless, the actual cost of division will depend on the particular implementation. Therefore, at some level, matters must be taken on a "case-by-case" basis, and it is not entirely unreasonable to imagine the use of rational functions in hardware implementations. An early example will be found in [3], in which the criteria for the choice of the polynomial coefficients is to minimize the maximum relative error on the interval in question; that is, to minimize

$$\max \left| \frac{f(x) - R_{n,m}(x)}{f(x)} \right|$$

Despite the, perhaps-justifiable, "lack of interest" in the hardware use of rational functions, the area is not entirely moribund. There has been some relatively recent work, such as [9, 10], that has taken an entirely different approach from that in earlier efforts. This later work is based on the use of *continued fractions*, which are expressions of the form

$$b_0 + \cfrac{a_1}{b_1 + \cfrac{a_2}{b_2 + \cfrac{a_3}{b_3 + \cfrac{a_4}{b_4 + \ldots}}}}$$

which is often abbreviated as

$$b_0 + \frac{a_1}{b_1+} \; \frac{a_2}{b_2+} \; \frac{a_3}{b_3+} \; \frac{a_4}{b_4+} \; \ldots$$

Some examples of continued fractions are

$$e^x = \frac{1}{1-} \; \frac{x}{1+} \; \frac{x}{3+} \; \frac{x}{4-} \ldots$$

$$\ln x = \frac{x-1}{1+} \; \frac{1^2(x-1)}{2+} \; \frac{1^2(x-1)}{3+} \; \frac{2^2(x-1)}{4+} \; \frac{2^2(x-1)}{5+} \ldots$$

$$\tan^{-1} x = \frac{x}{1+} \; \frac{x^2}{3+} \; \frac{(2x)^2}{5+} \; \frac{(3x)^2}{7+} \ldots$$

Several other examples of continued-fraction expressions for elementary functions will be found in [17].

The continued fraction

$$P = b_0 + \frac{a_1}{b_1+} \; \frac{a_2}{b_2+} \; \frac{a_3}{b_3+} \; \frac{a_4}{b_4+} \; \ldots \; \frac{a_n}{b_n}$$

can be evaluated through the recurrences

$$P_n = 1$$
$$P_{n-1} = b_n$$
$$P_i = b_{i+1}P_{i+1} + b_{i+2}P_{i+2} \qquad i = n-2, n-1, \ldots, 0$$
$$P = a_1 P_1 / P_0$$

Continued fractions have in fact long been studied for the hardware evaluation of elementary functions, but there has not been much progress in a practical direction. The more recent work in [9, 10] considers the optimal digit representations of continued fractions, how to convert between such representations and conventional binary, and how to control errors in computations with continued fractions. On the basis of this, hardware designs are proposed for both binary and high-radix computations (with redundant signed digit sets). The collective work embodies many novel ideas that perhaps will be refined with time. But, as they stand, it is doubtful that what is proposed can compete—in practical cost:performance terms—with more conventional ways of doing things.

That the rational-function approach has not yielded much fruit, for hardware implementations, does not necessarily mean that it does not have much value. Just as memory requirements increase over time, so do accuracy requirements, and for hardware evaluation, the most fruitful (in the short term) use of rational functions is probably in computations that require results of very high accuracy or where a large number of such computations are required. In some of such cases, parallelism and pipelining in the hardware would be worthwhile: at the highest level, the numerator and denominator polynomials can be evaluated concurrently—with varying degrees of parallelism—and the division carried out in, say, a fast Newton–Raphson/Goldschmidt divider.

Chapter 7

Table Lookup and Segmented Polynomial Approximations

A computer can represent only a finite number of the real numbers. So, in principle, the simplest method for the evaluation of a function, f, at an argument, x, is to use a table that is addressed with values of x and whose outputs are the corresponding values of $f(x)$. This also ought to be fast, as the single step involves no arithmetic computations. In practice, however, this simple method is of limited worth. If there are m possible values of x, then a table of 2^m elements is required, which is impractical, except for small values of m. So in practice the essential idea is typically combined with some other technique that involves some arithmetic operations. One way to do so is to partition the bits[1] of x into groups, use the groupings to access tables that contain some partial information on $f(x)$, and then, with some arithmetic operations, combine the outputs of these tables to obtain the full $f(x)$. We thus have a whole range of methods that involve the use of a variety of tables and arithmetic operations, with the latter ranging from one or two additions to more complex polynomial evaluation.

From the preceding chapter, we know that many of the functions we are interested in will have "polynomial-like" behavior on relatively small intervals. To get good single-polynomial approximations over "large" intervals, costly-to-evaluate high-order polynomials must be used. One standard way to avoid the use of a high-order polynomial over a large interval is the use of several low-order polynomials over subintervals of the interval of evaluation. With proper choices, it is possible to achieve with the latter the same order of accuracy that one would with a single high-order polynomial but with much lower computational costs.

---

[1] For brevity, and where no confusion is possible, we sometimes write "*the bit(s) of ...*" instead of the more accurate "*the bit(s) of the representation of ...* ".

261

The remainder of this introduction gives a quick overview of the general methods.

Let us suppose that the interval of evaluation, $[a, b]$, is split into m *segments*, identified by some *breakpoints*, $\{x_i\}$; that is, the segments are $[x_0 = a, x_1], [x_1, x_2], \ldots, [x_{m-1}, x_m = b]$. And, for simplicity, let us assume that the segments are of the same size, Δ. Now, suppose that on the interval $[x_i, x_{i+1}]$ we apply the truncated Taylor expansion

$$f(x) \approx f(x_i + (x - x_i)) \qquad\qquad x \in [x_i, x_{i+1}] \qquad\qquad (7.1)$$

$$= f(x_i) + \frac{f'(x_i)}{1!}(x - x_i) + \frac{f''(x_i)}{2!}(x - x_i)^2 + \cdots + \frac{f^{(k)}(x_i)}{k!}(x - x_i)^k$$

and recall (from Chapter 6) that such a series is generally good around the point of expansion but problematic farther away. Given that the x_is are finite in number, only a finite number of $f(x_i)$ and $f^{(j)}(x_i)$ values are required. And x will be represented in finite machine precision, so there is only a finite number of $(x - x_i)^j$ values. Therefore, in principle, we could tabulate all the possible values of the terms—say, one term per table—and evaluation would then consist of just table lookups followed by addition. Of course, we do not want to tabulate a large number of terms; but if Δ is small enough and the values are represented in sufficient precision, then just two or three terms may suffice. Also, as just described, each of the tables would have to be addressed with all the bits of the argument, which of course is exactly the sort of thing we should like to avoid. So the practical "trick" required is to arrange matters so that each table is addressed with just a subset of those bits.

The description just given is, somewhat roughly, the essential idea in what, for want of better terminology, we shall refer to as *polynomial-based table lookup* methods; the first section of the chapter covers such methods. Noting that small Δ means large tables, we should therefore expect that such methods will be problematic for high-precision[2] operations.

Keeping table sizes small inevitably leads to the classic trade-off between memory and computation: fewer breakpoints are used but more terms of Equation 7.1 are evaluated. The more general view then is that of interpolation, in the sense of evaluating between tabulated entries (Section 6.5), and the following is a first cut at describing the more computational of the "table and-polynomial" methods.

---

[2] "High" is a relative term, and its specification will change over time and with improvements in technology. Around 2015, we may consider it, as, roughly, above the range of 24-bit to 28-bit results.

Consider a polynomial obtained from a standard Taylor expansion, e.g. one of the Maclaurin series of Tables 6.2–6.4. Such a polynomial may have a limited convergence range, and maintaining accuracy is also an issue for "large" arguments (i.e. those not close to the point of expansion). With good segmentation, there need not be any "large" arguments, and such a polynomial can be used effectively. Here is a simplified description of how that can be done: Function values, $f(x_i)$, are stored for selected segment breakpoints. Then suppose the argument is x, and the nearest breakpoint is x_k. A new argument, $\tilde{x}$, is obtained from x and x_k; with a sufficient number of breakpoints, $\tilde{x}$ will be small and sufficiently close to x_k. The polynomial at hand is then applied to $\tilde{x}$, to yield $f(\tilde{x})$. Lastly, $f(x)$ is constructed from $f(\tilde{x})$ and $f(x_k)$. The arrangement therefore consists of the memory of some values—a smaller number than with the polynomial-based table lookup methods—and the core of the evaluation involves a polynomial approximation. (In principle any type of polynomial may be used.) The second section of the chapter deals with such *table-driven polynomial approximation* methods.

A further step in the "less memory but more computation" direction involves not storing any function values at all. Each segment has associated with it a distinct polynomial that is used for evaluation on the interval, and only the polynomial coefficients are stored. The computation of $f(x)$ then consists of identifying the segment into which x falls and applying the polynomial associated with that segment. For want of better terminology, we shall refer to this arrangement as *segmented polynomial approximation*[3] (or *piecewise polynomial approximation*). The polynomials in such cases are usually low-order ones, typically of degree no higher than three.

The three-group classification above is somewhat arbitrary—in so far as all three cases involve the use of memory, the evaluation of polynomials, and segmentation of the interval for evaluation—but, apart from the organizational benefits in the exposition, it is useful as a way of indicating significant markers in a broad spectrum that ranges from "much memory, little computation", at one end, to "little memory, much computation", at the other end. Storage requirements can be reduced by having more arithmetic operations or increasing the degrees of polynomials used, and this is likely to be necessary for high-precision operations.

In concluding this introduction, we remark that there are numerous

---

[3]This is is actually near-standard terminology, although it may be regarded as not particularly distinctive, given that the preceding two classes also involve segmentation, if in a somewhat less explicit manner.

variations on the tables-and-polynomials theme, and the reader will readily find these in the published literature. What we have included in the following are those methods that have something *fundamental*, and the reader might well find that many other methods in the literature consist of no more than minor variations on what is discussed here.

7.1   Polynomial-based table lookup

At present, nearly all of the best of such methods are based on two-term Taylor expansions. In *essence*, two tables are used: one for function values and one for first-derivative values; we will refer to these as the f *table* and the f' *table* .   The key aspects that make the methods worthwhile are that the values are not obtained directly from Equation 7.1, as the rough description there suggests, and the addressing of the tables is also carefully tailored to result in smaller tables than would otherwise be the case. In all cases, the argument is partitioned[4] into several pieces, combinations of which are then used address the tables of stored values.

The simplest arrangement is that of the *Bipartite Table Method* (two table method). The *Multipartite Table Methods* (many table methods) are extensions of the basic idea that use more than one f' table, in ways that further reduce the memory requirements. In all these arrangements, there is no arithmetic on the pieces of the argument; evaluation consists of table lookup followed by additions of partial function values.

On the other hand, in the ATA (*addition–table–addition*) methods there are arithmetic operations (additions) on parts of the arguments; so evaluation consists of additions (on argument bits), followed by table lookup, followed by additions (of partial function values). In addition to function values and first-derivative values, the ATA methods also include certain error-correcting terms that are based on second-order derivatives (i.e. the remainder terms from the truncated Taylor expansions).

Most of the methods are based on two-term Taylor expansions; but, in principle, there is no reason more than two terms cannot be used. So we shall, by way of example, also briefly discuss one method that involves the use of degree-five Taylor expansions [28]. Nor is there anything particularly special about Taylor expansions: other types of polynomials, e.g. Chebyshev or minimax polynomials, may be used, and we shall also briefly discuss

---

[4]As indicated above, strictly, such a phrase refers to the sequence of bits that comprise the representation of the operand.

one method that involves the use of minimax polynomials [29]. The design space is therefore quite large.

Unless otherwise specified, we shall assume that the argument, x, is in the range $[0, 1)$. Other ranges can be accommodated through range reduction (Section 1.2).

7.1.1 *Bipartite tables*

The Bipartite Table Method was originally devised for the evaluation of reciprocals, but has since been extended to other functions and to more than two tables [1-5, 27]. We next give a brief description of the basic Bipartite Table Method and then follow with the more detailed description of a refinement.

The bits of the operand, x, are partitioned[5] into three groups, consisting of the high-order, middle-order, and low-order bits. We shall use x_0, x_1, and x_2 to denote the values represented by these groups and n_0, n_1, and n_2 to denote the numbers of bits that make up the groups. So

$$0 \leq x_i \leq 1 - 2^{-n_i} \qquad i = 0, 1, 2$$

and

$$x = x_0 + \lambda_1 x_1 + \lambda_2 x_2 \qquad \text{where } \lambda_1 = 2^{-n_0} \text{ and } \lambda_2 = 2^{-(n_0+n_1)}$$

Now, take the Taylor expansion of $f(x)$ about $x_0 + \lambda_1 x_1$:

$$f(x) = f(x_0 + \lambda_1 x_1) + f'(x_0 + \lambda_1 x_1)(\lambda_2 x_2) + \frac{f''(\xi)}{2}(\lambda_2 x_2)^2$$

$$\xi \in [x_0 + x_1, x]$$

and consider a table lookup approximation, $\widehat{f}(x)$, based on the first two terms; that is, $\widehat{f}(x)$ is to be computed by reading two values from two tables, one for each term, and adding those values. The "reading" is straightforward with the first term: it involves only the bits of x_0 and x_1—i.e. only a part of the argument—and these are used to access a table that holds the values of $f(x_0 + \lambda_1 x_1)$. The second term involves the bits of x_0, x_1, and x_2, i.e. the entire argument, and it would clearly be unhelpful to have to use all for a table address. Some of these bits must be excluded, and the most logical candidates are the bits of x_1. The exclusion is done by taking $f'(x_0)$

---

[5]The best partitioning will depend on the particular function being approximated.

as an approximation to $f'(x_0 + \lambda_1 x_1)$; then only the bits of x_0 and x_2 are required to access the other table. We therefore end up with

$$f(x) \approx \widehat{f}(x) = f(x_0 + \lambda_1 x_1) + f'(x_0)(\lambda_2 x_2)$$

$$\stackrel{\triangle}{=} h_0(x_0, x_1) + h_1(x_0, x_2)$$

The bits corresponding to the pair $\langle x_0, x_1 \rangle$ are used to address the f table, and bits corresponding to the pair $\langle x_0, x_2 \rangle$ are used to address the f' table. The outputs, $h_0(x_0, x_1)$ and $h_1(x_0, x_2)$, of the two tables are then added together to obtain, $\widehat{f}(x)$, an approximation to $f(x)$. Figure 7.1 shows this in a diagram.

For p-bit results, the sizes of the two tables are approximately $2^{n_0+n_1}$ words $\times$ p bits and $2^{n_0+n_2}$ words $\times$ p bits. In contrast, the size of a single table would be $2^{n_0+n_1+n_2}$ words $\times$ p bits—a substantial difference.

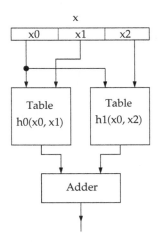

Figure 7.1: Bipartite table approximation

The *Symmetric Bipartite Table Method* is a variant of the basic idea, also based on a two-term Taylor expansion, but devised so as to take advantage of certain patterns in the representations of the values to be stored: leading 0s (positive values), leading 1s (negative values in complement representation), and symmetry in one of the two tables [2]. Here, the Taylor expansion is about the point $x_0 + \lambda_1 x_1 + \delta_2$, where δ_2 is the midpoint in the range of $\lambda_2 x_2$:

$$\delta_2 = 2^{-(n_0+n_1+1)} - 2^{-(n_0+n_1+n_2+1)}$$

So the initial two-term Taylor expansion is

$$f(x_0 + \lambda_1 x_1 + \lambda_2 x_2) = f(x_0 + \lambda_1 x_1 + \delta_2 + (\lambda_2 x_2 - \delta_2))$$
$$= f(x_0 + \lambda_1 x_1 + \delta_2) + f'(x_0 + \lambda_1 x_1 + \delta_2)(\lambda_2 x_2 - \delta_2) + \varepsilon$$

$$(7.2)$$

where

$$\varepsilon = \frac{f''(\xi)}{2}(\lambda_2 x_2 - \delta_2)^2 \qquad \xi \in [x_0 + \lambda_1 x_1 + \delta_2, x]$$

In order to make the second term of Equation 7.2 independent of x_1, $f'(x_0 + x_1 + \delta_2)$ is replaced with $f'(x_0 + \delta_1 + \delta_2)$, where

$$\delta_1 = 2^{-(n_0+1)} - 2^{-(n_0+n_1+1)}$$

i.e. halfway between the minimum and maximim possible values for $\lambda_1 x_1$. The working approximation to $f(x)$ is then

$$\widehat{f} = \widehat{f}(x_0 + \lambda_1 x_1 + \lambda_2 x_2)$$
$$= f(x_0 + \lambda_1 x_1 + \delta_2) + f'(x_0 + \delta_1 + \delta_2)(\lambda_2 x_2 - \delta_2) \qquad (7.3)$$

and functions for the two tables are

$$h_0(x_0, x_1) = f(x_0 + \lambda_1 x_1 + \delta_2)$$

$$h_1(x_0, x_2) = f'(x_0 + \delta_1 + \delta_2)(\lambda_2 x_2 - \delta_2)$$

Since $|x_2 - \delta_2| < 2^{-(n_0+n_1+1)}$, we have

$$|h_1(x_0, x_2)| < |f'(\xi_1)| 2^{-(n_0+n_1+1)}$$

where ξ_1 is the point at which $|f'(x)|$ has its maximum value in $[0, 1)$. If, in that interval, $|f(x)|$ has its maximum value at ξ_0, then

$$|f(\xi_0)| < |f'(\xi_1)| 2^{-(n_0+n_1+1)}$$

After some algebraic manipulation, we may conclude that the binary representation of $h_1(x_0, x_2)$ will have approximately

$$n_0 + n_1 + 1 + \log_2 \frac{|f(\xi_0)|}{|f'(\xi_1)|}$$

leading 0s or leading 1s, according to whether $h(x_0, x_2)$ is positive or negative. These bits may therefore be regarded as sign bits, and only one need be stored; the omitted bits are regained through sign extension during the arithmetic.

Table size can be reduced further by taking advantage of symmetry, on the basis that:

- $2\delta_2 - \lambda_2 x_2$ is the ones' complement of $\lambda_2 x_2$.
- $h_1(x_0, 2\delta_2 - \lambda_2 x_2)$ is the ones' complement of $h_1(x_0, x_2)$.

Table 7.1 gives an example of this symmetry in the table for $h_1(x_0, x_2)$. Since the table is symmetrical about the middle, its size need be only half the nominal size of the corresponding table in the plain bipartite method. And, as only the positive values need be stored, the sign bit too may be omitted; the bits to be stored are underlined in the table. Also, as we shall see below (under "Errors"), the least significant bit of $h_1(x_0, x_2)$ is always 1 and so need not be stored. Similarly, the least significant bit of $h_0(x_0, x_1)$ is always 0 and need not be stored. Both bits are reinserted during the arithmetic.

x		$h_1(x_0, x_2)$	
decimal	binary	decimal	binary
0.500000	0.1000000	0.0166016	0.0000010001
0.507812	0.1000001	0.0107422	0.0000001011
0.515625	0.1000010	0.0068359	0.0000000111
0.523438	0.1000011	0.0029297	0.0000000011
0.531250	0.1000100	-0.0029297	1.1111111101
0.539062	0.1000101	-0.0068395	1.1111111001
0.546875	0.1000110	-0.0107422	1.1111110101
0.554688	0.1000111	-0.0166016	1.1111101111

Table 7.1: Example entries in a symmetric bipartite table

The values of $h_1(x_0, x_2)$ are accessed as follows. If the leading bit of x_2 is 0, then the remaining bits are used as the address to obtain the value stored. Otherwise, those bits are complemented before being used to access the table, and the value read out is complemented. The resulting hardware arrangement is shown in Figure 7.2; the XOR gates do the conditional complementing.

The errors in the method are[6]:

- Approximation error, arising from the approximation of $f(x)$ with a truncated Taylor series.
- Propagated error,[7] arising from the replacement of $f'(x_0 + \lambda_1 x_1 + \delta_2)$,

---

[6]See Equation 1.2.

[7]Awkward terminology here, but consistent with the definitions given in Chapter 1.

in Equation 7.2, with $f'(x_0 + \delta_1 + \delta_2)$, to produce Equation 7.3.
- Representation errors in the stored values of $h_0(x_0, x_1)$ and $h_1(x_0, x_2)$.
- Computation errors (i.e. arithmetic and representation errors) in the addition of table entries and the rounding to produce the final result.

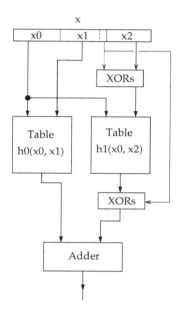

Figure 7.2: Symmetric bipartite table approximation

The magnitude of the approximation error is bounded by (Equation 7.2)

$$\varepsilon_a = \frac{\left| f''(\xi_2) \right|}{2} (x_2 - \delta_2)^2$$

So

$$\varepsilon_a < \frac{\left| f''(\xi_2) \right|}{2} 2^{-2(n_0 + n_1 + 1)} \qquad \text{since } |x_2 - \delta_2| < 2^{-(n_0 + n_1 + 1)}$$

$$= \left| f''(\xi_2) \right| 2^{-(2n_0 + 2n_1 + 3)}$$

where ξ_2 is the point at which $|f''(x)|$ has maximum value in the interval of evaluation.

For the propagated error:

$$\varepsilon_p = |f(x_0 + \lambda_1 x_1 + \delta_2)(\lambda_2 x_2 - \delta_2) - f(x_0 + \delta_1 + \delta_2)\lambda_2(x_2 - \delta_2)|$$

Taking the Taylor expansions, about $x_0 + \delta_2$, of each of the two subterms and subtracting:

$$\varepsilon_p \approx |f(x_0 + \delta_2)| \, (\lambda_1 x_1 - \delta_1)(\lambda_2 x_2 - \delta_2)$$

$$< \left| f''(\xi_2) \right| 2^{-(2n_0+n_1+2)}$$

since $|x_1 - \delta_2| < 2^{-(n_0+1)}$ and $|x_2 - \delta_2| < 2^{-(n_0+n_1+1)}$. Evidently, the choices of n_0 and n_1 are key in minimizing these errors.

The other errors are dealt with as follows. The addition can easily be made exact, so we may assume there is no arithmetic error; that leaves only representation errors. Assume that the representation of the final result includes p bits after the binary point that are obtained by rounding to the nearest representable number. Then $h_0(x_0, x_1)$ and $h_1(x_0, x_2)$ are each represented with g guard bits after the p bits, i.e. in a total of $p+g$ bits that are obtained by rounding to the nearest representable number; bit $p+g+1$ after the binary point in $h_0(x_0, x_1)$ is set to 0, and the corresponding bit of $h_1(x_0, x_2)$ is set to 1. So the magnitude of the error in each of $h_0(x_0, x_1)$ and $h_i(x_0, x_2)$ is bounded by

$$2^{-(p+g+1)}/2$$

and the value of g is key in minimizing such errors. With round to nearest, the error in the rounding to p bits (after addition) is at most $2^{-(p+1)}$. Therefore, the total representation error is bounded by

$$\varepsilon_r = 2^{-(p+1)} + 2^{-(p+g+1)}$$

The best possible result with p fractional bits is one with error less than 2^{-p}, so we want

$$\varepsilon_a + \varepsilon_p + \varepsilon_r < 2^{-p}$$

i.e.

$$\left| f''(\xi_2) \right| 2^{-(2n_0+n_1+2)} \left[1 + 2^{-(n_1+1)} \right] + 2^{-(p+g+1)} \leq 2^{-(p+1)}$$

from which:

$$2n_0 + n_1 \geq p - 1 + \log_2 \left[\frac{\left| f''(\xi_2) \right| \left(1 - 2^{-(n_1+1)} \right)}{1 - 2^{-g}} \right]$$

The bound is met through the judicious choice of n_0, n_1, and g. With $n_1 \geq 1$, we may choose $g = 2$, to get

$$2n_0 + n_1 \geq p + \log_2 \left| f''(\xi_2) \right| \qquad (7.4)$$

EXAMPLE: Suppose we wish to evaluate $f(x) = \cos x$ on the interval $[0, 1)$ with $n = p = 24$. $|f''(x)| = |\cos x|$, which has a maximum value of 1. Inequation 7.4 then becomes

$$2n_0 + n_1 \geq 24$$

which can be satisfied, with minimal memory requirements, by choosing $n_0 = n_1 = n_2 = 8$.

With two guard bits, each entry for $h_0(x_0, x - 1)$ and $h_1(x_0, x_2)$ nominally requires 26 fractional bits; where $h_0(x_0, x - 1)$ attains it maximum value of 1, the value stored is $1 - 2^{-26}$. But $h_1(x_0, x_2) < 2^{-17}$; so only 10 bits, including the sign bit, need be stored; the other bits are obtained by sign extension. So the size of the table for $h_0(x_0, x_1)$ is 2^{16} words $\times$ 26 bits and the nominal size of that for $h_1(x_0, x_2)$ is 2^{16} words $\times$ 10 bits. Exploiting symmetry, as outlined above, reduces the size of the latter table to 2^{15} words $\times$ 9 bits. In contrast, a single table would be of size 2^{24} words $\times$ 26 bits; and in the basic Bipartite Table Method, the second table would be of 2^{16} words $\times$ 16 bits.　　　　END EXAMPLE.

We next look at extensions of the Symmetric Bipartite Table Method to more than two tables. In these extensions, the essential idea is to reduce memory requirements by permitting more additions.

7.1.2　*Multipartite tables*

We have seen that, with good design, going from one table to two will, with judicious choices, reduce memory requirements. So we may reasonably expect that going from two tables to three or more tables can produce further reductions. That is indeed the case, and, accordingly, *multipartite table methods* have been proposed [3, 4, 27]. Increasing the number of tables also means that more additions are required; therefore, with such methods memory size alone is not the primary consideration.

7.1.2.1　*Symmetric table addition*

The *Symmetric Table Addition Method* [27] is a straightforward extension of the Symmetric Bipartite Table Method. The n-bit argument, x, is partitioned into $m + 1$ pieces, $x_0, x_1, \ldots, x_m$, represented in $n_0, n_1, \ldots, n_m$ bits, with $n = \sum_{i=0}^{m} n_i$. So

$$x = x_0 + \sum_{i=1}^{m} \lambda_i x_i \qquad\qquad \lambda_i = 2^{-(n_0 + n_1 + \cdots + n_{i-1})}$$

i.e.

$$0 \le\ x_0\ \le 1 - 2^{-n_0}$$

$$0 \le \lambda_i x_i \le 2^{-(n_0 + n_1 + \cdots + n_{i-1})} - 2^{-(n_0 + n + 1 + \cdots + n_i)} \qquad i = 1, 2, \ldots, m$$

We will use δ_i to denote the midpoint of the range for $\lambda_i x_i$.

The approximation, $\widehat{f}(x)$, of $f(x)$ is then obtained from a Taylor expansion about $x_0 + \lambda_1 x_1 + \delta$, where $\delta = \sum_{i=0}^{m} \delta_i$:

$$\widehat{f}(x) = f(x_0 + \lambda_1 x_1 + \delta) + f'(x_0 + \lambda_1 x_1 + \delta) \left(\sum_{i=2}^{m} x_i - \delta \right)$$

$$= f(x_0 + \lambda_1 x_1 + \delta) + \sum_{i=2}^{m} \left[f'(x_0 + \lambda_1 x_1 + \delta)\,(x_i - \delta_i) \right] \qquad (7.5)$$

and replacing $\lambda_1 x_1$ with δ_1:

$$\widehat{f}(x) = f(x_0 + \lambda_1 x_1 + \delta) + \sum_{i=2}^{m} \left[f'(x_0 + \delta_1 + \delta)\,(x_i - \delta_i) \right]$$

$$\triangleq h_0(x_0, x_1) + \sum_{i=2}^{m} h_{i-1}(x_0, x_i)$$

This gives one f table and $m - 1$ f' tables.

Figure 7.3 is a sketch of an architecture for the symmetric table addition method. The techniques used to minimize table sizes in the symmetric-bipartite table method are equally applicable here.

The errors here are similar to those in the symmetric table addition method, except that there are now $m - 1$ tables that contribute to the representation errors. That factor therefore changes to

$$\varepsilon_r = 2^{-(p+1)} + (m - 1)2^{-(p+g+1)}$$

and the requirement that total error be less than 2^{-p} will be satisfied if

$$2n_0 + n_1 \ge p + \log_2 |f''(\xi)|$$

$$g \ge 2 + \log_2(m - 1)$$

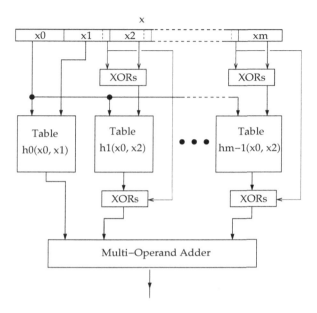

Figure 7.3: Symmetric table addition approximation

7.1.2.2 *Tripartite tables*

A somewhat different approach from the preceding is given in [4], where the starting point is a *tripartite* (three-part) table that consists of one f table and two f' tables.

In the tripartite table method, the argument, x, is split into five k-bit pieces, x_0, x_1, x_2, x_3, and x_4:

$$x = x_0 + \lambda x_1 + \lambda^2 x_2 + \lambda^3 x_3 + \lambda^4 x_4$$

where $\lambda = 2^{-k}$ and $0 \leq x_i \leq 1 - 2^{-k}$.

The approximation is then obtained through a Taylor expansion about $x_0 + \lambda x_1 + \lambda^2 x_2$:

$$f(x) \approx f\left(x_0 + \lambda x_1 + \lambda^2 x_2\right) + \left(\lambda^3 x_3 + \lambda^4 x_4\right) f'\left(x_0 + \lambda x_1 + \lambda^2 x_2\right) \quad (7.6)$$

with an error of magnitude

$$\varepsilon_0 = \left| \frac{f''(\xi_1)}{2} \left(\lambda^3 x_3 + \lambda^4 x_4\right)^2 \right| \qquad \xi_1 \in [x_0 + \lambda x_1 + \lambda^2 x_2, \ x]$$

$$\leq \frac{2^{-6k}}{2} \max |f''(\xi)| \qquad\qquad \xi \in [0, 1)$$

Consider now the first part of the second term in Equation 7.6, Taylor-expanded around $x_0 + \lambda x_1$:

$$\lambda^3 x_3 f'(x_0 + \lambda x_1 + \lambda^2 x_2) = \lambda^3 x_3 f'(x_0 + \lambda x_1) + \lambda^5 x_2 x_3 f''(\xi_2)$$

$$\xi_2 \in [x_0 + \lambda x_1, \ x_0 + \lambda x_1 + \lambda^2 x_2]$$

So if $\lambda^3 x_3 f'(x_0 + \lambda x_1 + \lambda^2 x_2)$ is replaced with $\lambda^3 x_3 f'(x_0 + \lambda x_1)$, then there is an error of magnitude

$$\varepsilon_1 = \left| \lambda^5 x_2 x_3 f''(\xi_2) \right| \qquad\qquad \xi_2 \in [x_0 + \lambda x_1, \ x_0 + \lambda x_1 + \lambda^2 x_2]$$

$$\leq 2^{-5k} \max \left| f''(\xi) \right|$$

Similarly, if the second part of the second term in Equation 7.6, i.e., $\lambda^4 x_4 f'(x_0 + \lambda x_1 + \lambda^2 x_2)$, is Taylor-expanded around x_0 and then replaced with $\lambda^4 x_4 f'(x_0)$, there is an error of magnitude

$$\varepsilon_2 = \left| \lambda^4 x_4 f''(\xi_3) \left(\lambda x_1 + \lambda^2 x_2 \right) \right| \qquad\qquad \xi_3 \in [x_0, \ x_0 + \lambda x_1 + \lambda^2 x_2]$$

$$\leq 2^{-5k} \max \left| f''(\xi) \right|$$

Putting together all of the above, we obtain the tripartite approximation formula:

$$\widehat{f}(x) = h_0(x_0, x_1, x_2) + h_1(x_0, x_1, x_3) + h_2(x_0, x_4)$$

where

$$h_0(x_0, x_1, x_2) = f\left(x_0 + \lambda x_1 + \lambda^2 x_2\right)$$

$$h_1(x_0, x_1, x_3) = \lambda^3 x_3 f'(x_0 + \lambda x_1)$$

$$h_2(x_0, x_4) = \lambda^4 x_4 f'(x_0)$$

with a total error bound of magnitude

$$\varepsilon_0 + \varepsilon_1 + \varepsilon_2 \leq \left(\frac{2^{-6k}}{2} + 2 \times 2^{-5k}\right) \max |f''(\xi)| \qquad \xi \in [0,1)$$

$$\approx 2^{-5k+1} \max |f''(\xi)|$$

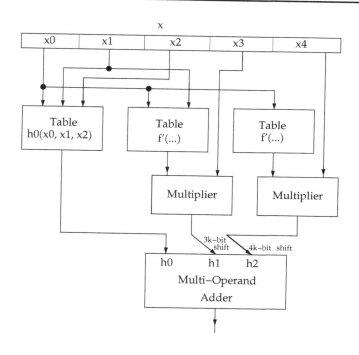

Figure 7.4: Tripartite table approximation

The sketch of a corresponding hardware architecture is shown in Figure 7.4. A nominal multiplication by λ is just a k-bit wired shift, and the nominal additions to form $x_0 + \lambda x_1$ and $x_0 + \lambda x_1 + \lambda x_2$ are just concatenations of the bits that form x_0 and x_1, in the first case, and those that form x_0, x_1, and x_2, in the second case.

In Figure 7.4 we have shown a "direct implementation" of the expressions that make up $h_1(x_0, x_1, x_3)$ and $h_2(x_0, x_4)$. The multiplications will, however, be low-precision ones. Therefore, each table–multiplier combination may be replaced with a table that stores all the shifted products, to give an all table (plus adder) organization.

7.1.2.3 *Unified multipartite tables*

The generalization from tripartite to multipartite tables is straightforward. The argument, x, is split into $2m + 1$, k-bit pieces, $x_0, x_1, \ldots, x_{2m}$:

$$x = x_0 + \sum_{i=1}^{2m} \lambda^i x_i \qquad \text{where } \lambda = 2^{-k} \text{ and } 0 \le x_i \le 1 - 2^{-k}$$

and the approximation is obtained from a Taylor expansion about $x_0 + \lambda x_1 + \lambda^2 x_2 + \cdots + \lambda^m x_m$:

$$f(x) = f\left(\sum_{i=0}^{m} \lambda^i x_i\right) + f'\left(\sum_{i=0}^{m} \lambda^i x_i\right)\left(\sum_{i=m+1}^{2m} \lambda^i x_i\right) + \varepsilon_0 \qquad (7.7)$$

where

$$\varepsilon_0 = \frac{f''(\xi)}{2}\left(\sum_{i=m+1}^{2m} \lambda^i x_i\right) \qquad \xi \in \left[\sum_{i=m+1}^{2m} \lambda^i x_i,\ x\right]$$

Taylor-expanding the subterms of the second term in Equation 7.7 about the points $\sum_{i=0}^{j} \lambda^i x_i, j = m, m-1, \ldots, 0$, we get

$$f(x) = f\left(\sum_{i=0}^{m} \lambda^i x_i\right) + \varepsilon_0 + \lambda^{m+1} x_{m+1} f'\left(\sum_{i=0}^{m} \lambda^i x_i\right) + \varepsilon_1$$

$$+ \lambda^{m+2} x_{m+2} f'\left(\sum_{i=0}^{m-1} \lambda^i x_i\right) + \varepsilon_2$$

$$+ \lambda^{m+3} x_{m+3} f'\left(\sum_{i=0}^{m-2} \lambda^i x_i\right) + \varepsilon_3$$

$$+ \cdots$$

$$+ \lambda^{2m} x_{2m} f'(x_0) + \varepsilon_m$$

with

$$|\varepsilon_i| \le 2^{-2mk} \max \left| f''(\xi) \right|$$

Excluding the error terms, the last equation gives $m + 1$ expressions that are used to address $m + 1$ tables.

For the approximation error, we have

$$\sum_{i=1}^{m+1} |\varepsilon_i| \leq \left(\frac{2^{-2mk}}{2} + m \times 2^{-(2m-1)k+1} \right) \left| f''(\xi) \right| \qquad \xi \in [0, 1]$$

$$\approx 2^{-2m+1} \left| f''(\xi) \right|$$

to which should be added representation errors in the table entries and computation errors. We may reasonably assume that the arithmetic is exact; so the latter consist of just the error in final rounding to get the result. Assuming the final result is of n bits, that g guard bits are used for each table entry, that the adders are appropriately extended, and that round to nearest is used for both the table entries and the result, these errors add up to

$$(m + 2)2^{-(n+g+1)}$$

For the best n-result, the total error should be less than 2^{-n}; so we should have

$$2^{-2m+1} \left| f''(\xi) \right| + (m + 2)2^{-(n+g+1)} < 2^{-n}$$

The *Unified Multipartite Table Method* (UMTM) is a unification of all of the above methods[8] [3]. The details are as follows.

In the methods above, the argument is split into $m + 1$ pieces, x_0, x_1, ... ,x_m. The f table is addressed with some leading bits of x, say, x_0, x_1, ... , x_j; and each f' table is addressed with x_0 and some combination of the x_is. Thus, in the bipartite table method, $m = 2$, the f table is addressed with x_0 and x_1 (i.e. $j = 1$), and the one f' table is addressed with x_0 and x_2. And in the tripartite table method, $m = 4$, the f table is addressed with $x_0, x_1,$ and x_2 (i.e. $j = 2$), one f' table is addressed with the bits of $x_0, x_1,$ and x_3, and the other f' table is addressed with x_0 and x_4.

In UMTM, the argument, x, is split into two parts, A and B, of α and β bits. A (which is equivalent to $x_0, x_1, \ldots, x_j$ above) is used to address the f table. The B part is further split into m parts, $B_{m-1}, B_{m-1}, \ldots ,$ B_0, in order of decreasing significance, of precisions $\beta_{m-1}, \beta_{m-2}, \ldots , \beta_0$; part B_i starts at bit position p_i, so $p_0 = 0$ and $p_{i+1} = p_i + \beta_i$. The address for f' table i consists of γ_i bits of A and the β_i bits that comprise B_i.

---

[8] Assume an all-table arrangement for Figure 7.4, as described above.

The preceding defines a very large design-space in which one has to find one or more points that satisfy some criteria of cost, performance, and accuracy, all of which are intimately related. The cost is determined by the total size of the tables (number of entries $\times$ precision) and the depth and width of the addition tree; the performance is determined by the memory access time and the depth of the adder tree; and the precisions of the table entries are determined by the total error bound. The overarching trade-off is between memory and computation, and that is a good starting point in the design-space exploration.

If we assume that memory-access time is constant,[9] regardless of memory size, then the "free variable" in performance is the depth of the addition tree, and this corresponds to the number of tables. So we may start by fixing a "reasonable" number[10] of tables and then exploring the design-space in terms of the other parameters, which are largely on the basis of the error bounds. All of this suggests the following algorithm:

(1) Determine the number of tables.
(2) Determine the possible decompositions of the argument.
(3) Compute the total error for each decomposition, and discard any decomposition for which the total error exceeds the desired error bound.
(4) Of the remaining decompositions, choose one that best satisfies the cost and performance constraints.

The second step appears problematic, given that there is (nominally) an exponential number of decompositions; but, in practice, the number that need be determined is much smaller:

• For f' table i, the approximation error depends on only the function being aproximated; the input precision; and p_i, β_i, and γ_i. So the approximation errors for these tables can be computed once and for all; for k-bit input precision, the total number of decompositions is k^3.
• For a given pair (p_i, γ_i), the approximation error grows as γ_i decreases; so there is a $\gamma_{\min}$ such that for any $\gamma_i \le \gamma_{\min}$, the error is larger than the accuracy required in the given output precision. Such $\gamma_{\min}$ too may be computed once and for all.
• The enumerations of (p_i, β_i) are limited by the relation $p_{i+1} = p_i + w_i$, and those of γ_i are limited by the relation $\gamma_{\min} < \gamma_i < \alpha$, where α is the number of bits that comprise A.

---

[9] In general, the assumption is not true, but it is for a given range of memory sizes.
[10] The "reasonable number" may be changed, but the range of possibilities will be small.

The details of the algorithm will be found in [3]. The error analysis is as for the other, related, methods above; and optimizations of the type used in the Symmetric Bipartaitetable Method are equally applicable.

7.1.2.4 *High-order polynomials*

All of the methods described above use very-low-order Taylor expansions, which raises the obvious question of whether they can be usefully extended to higher-order expansions. In principle, there is no reason why that should not be possible, and there has been some work in that direction. But relative to the basic method, the cost:performance ratios in such extensions can be problematic: in moving to higher-order expansions, table size is no longer the sole criterion for cost, given that multiplications (and more additions) will now be necessary, and multipliers are relatively expensive. The following is a description of the proposal in [28].

Suppose we have an n-bit argument, x, and assume that $n = 4k + p$ for some integers k and p, with $p < k$. Then x is split into five pieces: x_0, x_1, x_2, and x_3, each of k bits, and x_4, of p bits:

$$x = x_0 + \lambda x_1 + \lambda^2 x_2 + \lambda^3 x_3 + \lambda^4 x_4 \qquad (7.8)$$

where $\lambda = 2^{-k}$ and $0 \leq x_i \leq 1 - 2^{-k}$.

For the approximation, $\widehat{f}(x)$, to $f(x)$, the Taylor expansion is about x_0:

$$\widehat{f}(x) = f(x_0) + \frac{f'(x_0)}{1!}(x - x_0) + \frac{f''(x_0)}{2!}(x - x_0)^2 + \frac{f'''(x_0)}{3!}(x - x_0)^3$$

$$+ \frac{f^{(4)}(x_0)}{4!}(x - x_0)^4 + \frac{f^{(5)}(x_0)}{5!}(x - x_0)^5 \qquad (7.9)$$

with an error

$$\varepsilon_1 = \frac{f'^{(6)}(\xi)}{6!}\left(x_1 2^{-k} + x_2 2^{-2k} + x_3 2^{-3k} + x_4 2^{-4k}\right) \qquad \xi \in [x_0, x]$$

The magnitude of this is bounded by

$$2^{-6k} \max \left|f''(\xi)\right| \qquad \xi \in [0, 1)$$

Substituting from Equation 7.8 into Equation 7.9, and excluding terms in powers higher than λ^5 (because they are of negligible magnitude), the second to the sixth subterms are

$$t_1 = x_1 2^{-k} f'(x_0) + x_2 2^{-2k} f'(x_0) + x_3 2^{-3k} f'(x_0) + x_4 2^{-4k} f'(x_0)$$

$$t_2 = x_1^2 2^{-2k} \frac{f''(x_0)}{2} + x_1 x_2 2^{-3k} f''(x_0) + x_1 x_3 2^{-4k} f''(x_0)$$

$$+ x_2^2 2^{-4k} \frac{f''(x_0)}{2} + x_2 2^{-5k} \frac{f''(x_0)}{2} + x_1 2^{-5k} \frac{f''(x_0)}{4} + \varepsilon_2$$

$$t_3 = x_1^3 2^{-3k} \frac{f'''(x_0)}{6} + x_1^2 x_2 + 2^{-4k} \frac{f'''(x_0)}{2} x_1^2 x_3 2^{-5k} \frac{f'''(x_0)}{2}$$

$$+ x_1 x_2^2 2^{-5k} \frac{f'''(x_0)}{2} + \varepsilon_3$$

$$t_4 = x_1^4 2^{-4k} \frac{f^{(4)}(x_0)}{24} + x_1^3 x_2 2^{-5k} \frac{f^{(4)}(x_0)}{24} \varepsilon_4$$

$$t_5 = x_1^5 2^{-5k} \frac{f^{(5)}(x_0)}{120}$$

with the magnitudes of the error bound

$$|\varepsilon_2| < \frac{2^{-5k}}{2} \max \left| f''(\xi) \right|$$

$$|\varepsilon_3| < \frac{2^{-6k}}{3} \max \left| f'''(\xi) \right|$$

$$|\varepsilon_4| < \frac{2^{-6k}}{24} \max \left| f^{(4)}(\xi) \right|$$

$$|\varepsilon_5| < \frac{2^{-6k}}{120} \max \left| f^{(5)}(\xi) \right|$$

From these expanded terms, the expressions for the approximation formulae are obtained as

$$h_1(x_0, x_1) = f(x_0) + x_1 2^{-k} f'(x_0) + x_1^2 2^{-2k} \frac{f''(x_0)}{2} + x_1^3 2^{-3k} \frac{f'''(x_0)}{6}$$

$$+ x_1^4 2^{-4k} \frac{f^{(4)}(x_0)}{24} + x_1^5 2^{-5k} \frac{f^{(5)}(x_0)}{120}$$

$$h_2(x_0, x_2) = x_2 2^{-2k} f'(x_0) + x_2^2 2^{-4k} \frac{f''(x_0)}{2} + x_2 2^{-5k} \frac{f''(x_0)}{2}$$

$$h_3(x_0, x_3) = x_3 2^{-3k} f'(x_0)$$

$$h_4(x_0, x_4) = x_4 2^{-4k} f'(x_0)$$

$$h_5(x_0, x_1) = x_1 2^{-3k} f''(x_0) + x_1^2 x_2 2^{-4k} \frac{f'''(x_0)}{2} + x_1^3 2^{-5k} \frac{f^{(4)}(x_0)}{6}$$

$$+ (x_1/2) 2^{-5k} \frac{f''(x_0)}{2}$$

The full approximation formula is then

$$\widehat{f}(x) = h_1(x_0, x_1) + h_2(x_0, x_2) + h_3(x_0, x_3) + h_4(x_0, x_4)$$

$$+ x_2 h_5(x_0, x_1) + x_3 2^k h_5(x_0, x_1)$$

with an error whose magnitude is bounded by $\sum_{i=1}^{5} |\varepsilon_i|$. This is just the approximation error. The total error includes the representation errors in the tables and the computational errors in the additions and subsequent rounding, all of which can be taken care of with a sufficient number of guard digits in the table entries and the arithmetic. Further details are straightforward and are left to the reader.

A sketch of hardware architecture for the approximation is shown in Figure 7.5. The higher-order-polynomial method requires smaller tables, but the reductions in memory must be considered against the additional cost (hardware and operational latency) introduced by the multiplications.

A more modest, and perhaps more practical method—based on second-degree polynomials, but readily extendible to higher order ones—is described in [32]. An underlying idea in the method is that of segmented polynomial approximation, which is the subject of detailed discussion in Section 7.3. In this case, however, the focus is on the table lookup; so it is more appropriate to have the following discussion here. What follows is a summary.

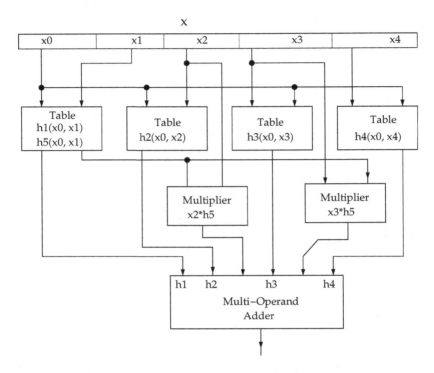

Figure 7.5: Hardware organization for high-order multipartite method

Suppose the argument, x, is split into two parts: u, of k bits, and w, of m bits. So $x = u + 2^{-k}w$, and the Taylor expansion about u is

$$f(x) = f(u) + f'(u)(2^{-k}w) + \frac{f''(\xi)}{2}(2^{-k}w)^2 \qquad \xi \in [u, x] \quad (7.10)$$

With basic segmentation, the values of u determine one of 2^k segments, each of which has stored coefficients that correspond to a polynomial, as per Equation 7.10. This is the starting point for the method described in [31], the details of which are as follows.

Equation 7.10 suggests a general form for second-degree polynomials applied to partitioned operands, and it can be used directly. But any other type of polynomial may be used, and in [31] the polynomial is

$$f(x) \approx c_0(u) + c_1(u)(2^{-k}w) + c_2(u)(2^{-k}w)^2 \qquad (7.11)$$

where, for each segment identified by a value of u, the constants c_0, c_1, and c_2 are determined through a Remez algorithm [22]; that is, the polynomials are minimax ones. This is then refined by further splitting w into two parts: w_0 of p_0 bits and w_1 of the remaining bits. So the working formula for the approximation is

$$\widehat{f}(x) = c_0(u) + c_1(u)2^{-k}w_0 + c_1(u)2^{-k-p_0}w_1 + c_2(u)2^{-2k}w^2 \qquad (7.12)$$

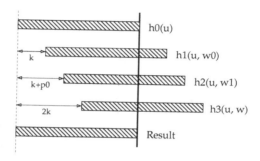

Figure 7.6: Values in second-order approximation

The multiplications in Equations 7.12 may be traded off against memory, and the choice has been made to have only one multiplication—for the second term. On that basis, four tables are used for the approximation:

- A table, addressed with the bits of u, that holds the values c_0.
- A table, addressed with the bits of u and w_0, that holds the values $c_1 2^{-k}w_0$.
- A table, addressed with the bits of u and w_1, that holds the values $c_1 2^{-k-p_0}w_1$.
- A table, addressed with the bits of u and w, that holds the values $c_2 2^{-2k}w^2$.

Using h_i for the table addressing functions that correspond to the terms of Equation 7.12, we may express the approximation formula as

$$\widehat{f}(x) = h_0(u) + h_1(u, w_0) + h_2(u, w_1) + h_3(u, w) \qquad (7.13)$$

For the implementation, two aspects of Equation 7.12 are exploited. The first is that it is possible to have a "degradation of accuracy", which may be explained as follows. The last three terms of Equation 7.12 involves right shifts (multiplications by powers of 2^{-k}), and these give values that are strictly more accurate than is necessary; this is depicted in Figure 7.6. If we consider truncating these values to the bold line in that figure, then it is evident that the tables can be addressed with fewer bits and so will be smaller. Accordingly, the three tables are addressed with shorter substrings of u and w—say u_0, u_1, and u_2 of u and w_2 of w, of precisions k_0, k_1, k_2, and p_2 (Figure 7.7)—and Equation 7.13 is replaced with

$$\widehat{f}(x) = h_0(u) + h_1(u_0, w_0) + h_2(u_1, w_1) + h_3(u_2, w_2) \qquad (7.14)$$

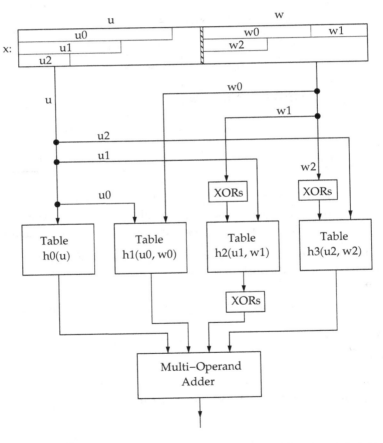

Figure 7.7: Hardware organization for second-order approximation

The second improvement is to exploit symmetry and so store only half the nominal values in two of the tables:

- $h_2(u_1, -w_1) = -h_2(u_1, w_1)$
- $h_3(u_2, -w_2) = h_3(u_2, w_2)$

The sketch of a hardware architecture is shown in Figure 7.7. The symmetry exploitation is implemented using XOR gates as done in the case of the Symmetric Bipartite Table Method. Storage may be traded off against multiplication; in [32], instead of a table for the second term in the approximation, a table and multiplier are used: the table stores the values of $c_1(u_0)2^{-k}$, and the multiplication is by w_0.

The errors in the approximation consist of:

- Approximation error, ε_a, from approximating f with a truncated polynomial.
- Approximation error, ε_d, from degrading table accuracy.
- Representation error (total), ε_r, in (each set of) the table entries.
- Computation error, ε_c, in the arithmetic and representation error from the final rounding.

The arithmetic consists of just a few additions, and there is little cost in making it exact. We may therefore assume that to be the case, and the computation error may be taken to be just the representation error.

ε_a is just the error in truncating a Taylor series at the third term. Degrading accuracy effectively imposes a constant value over an interval, and so ε_d is half the difference between that value and the extremal function values on the interval.

If g guard bits are used for each table entry, and round to nearest is used for the table entries and in the arithmetic, then for an n-bit final result:

$$\varepsilon_r < 4 \times 2^{-(n+g+1)} + 2^{-(n+g+1)}$$

$$\varepsilon_c < 2^{-(n+1)}(1 - 2^{-g})$$

7.1.3 *Addition–Table lookup–Addition*

Addition–Table lookup–Addition (ATA), is, as the name implies, a method in which function evaluation is realized in terms of additions, followed by table lookups, followed by additions [25]. The procedure for obtaining an approximation of $f(x)$ consists of additions of various bit groups of the argument (i.e. of its binary representation) to form lookup table addresses, followed by table lookups that yield partial function values, and finally the additions of those to obtain the result. The original proposal is for single-precision operands in the IEEE-754 standard for floating-point arithmetic, i.e. 24-bit significands. The details are as follows.

If the argument, x, is partitioned into four, 6-bit pieces, of values x_0, x_1, x_2, and x_3, then

$$x = x_0 + \lambda x_1 + \lambda^2 x_2 + \lambda^3 x_3 \qquad \text{where } \lambda = 2^{-6}$$

and the Taylor expansion of f about $x_0 + \lambda x_1$ is

$$f(x) = f(x_0 + \lambda x_1) + f'(x_0 + \lambda x_1) \left(\lambda^2 x_2 + \lambda^3 x_3 \right)$$

$$+ \frac{f''(x_0 + \lambda x_1)}{2} \left(\lambda^4 x_2^2 + 2\lambda^5 x_2 x_3 + \lambda^6 x_3^2 \right) + \varepsilon \qquad (7.15)$$

where

$$\varepsilon = \frac{f'''(\xi)}{6} \left(\lambda^2 x_2 + \lambda^3 x_3 \right)^3 \qquad \xi \in [x_0 + \lambda x_1, \, x]$$

The approximation consists of neglecting all terms of magnitude smaller than λ^5, as these are effectively zero to within the target precision. The terms include ε, $|\varepsilon| < \lambda^5$ for the chosen argument ranges, which are given in Table 7.2.

Function	Range
$1/x$	$[1, 2)$
e^x	$[0, 1]$
$\sin x$	$[0, \pi/2)$
$\sqrt{x}$	$[1, 4)$
$\ln x$	$[1/2, 2)$
$\tan^{-1} x$	$[0, 1)$

Table 7.2: Argument ranges for ATA method

The approximation to $f(x)$ is based on a central-difference formulation.[11] Corresponding to the subterm $f'(x_0 + \lambda x_1)\lambda^2 x_2$ of Equation 7.15, the central difference used is

---

[11]In a *central-difference* formulation, the derivative $f'(x)$ is approximated by $[f(x+h) - f(x-h)]/(2h)$, and high-order derivatives are similarly derived. See standard texts on numerical analysis.

$$\frac{\lambda}{2} [f(x_0 + \lambda x_1 + \lambda x_2) - f(x_0 + \lambda x_1 - \lambda x_2)]$$

and corresponding to the subterm $f'(x_0 + \lambda x_1)\lambda^3 x_3$ of Equation 7.15, the central difference is

$$\frac{\lambda^2}{2} [f(x_0 + \lambda x_1 + \lambda x_3) - f(x_0 + \lambda x_1 - \lambda x_3)]$$

The Taylor expansion about $x_0 + \lambda x_1$ of the first central difference is

$$\frac{\lambda}{2} [f(x_0 + \lambda x_1 + \lambda x_2) - f(x_0 + \lambda x_1 - \lambda x_2)]$$

$$=$$

$$\frac{\lambda}{2} \left[\left(f(x_0 + \lambda x_1) + f'(x_0 + \lambda x_1)(\lambda x_2) + \frac{f''(x_0 + \lambda x_1)}{2!}(\lambda x_2)^2 \right. \right.$$

$$\left. + \frac{f'''(x_0 + \lambda x_1)}{3!}(\lambda x_2)^3 + \cdots \right)$$

$$- \left(f(x_0 + \lambda x_1) - f'(x_0 + \lambda x_1)(\lambda x_2) + \frac{f''(x_0 + \lambda x_1)}{2!}(\lambda x_2)^2 \right.$$

$$\left. \left. - \frac{f'''(x_0 + \lambda x_1)}{3!}(\lambda x_2)^3 - \cdots \right) \right]$$

$$= f'(x_0 + \lambda x_1)\lambda^2 x_2 + \frac{f'''(x_0 + \lambda x_1)}{6}\lambda^4 x_2^3 + \cdots \tag{7.16}$$

Similarly, for the second central difference

$$\frac{\lambda^2}{2} [f(x_0 + \lambda x_1 + \lambda x_3) - f(x_0 + \lambda x_1 - \lambda x_3)]$$

$$= f'(x_0 + \lambda x_1)\lambda^3 x_3 + \frac{f'''(x_0 + \lambda x_1)}{6}\lambda^5 x_3^3 + \cdots \tag{7.17}$$

On the basis of Equations 7.16 and 7.17, the difference between Equation 7.15 and the expression

$$f(x_0 + \lambda x_1) + \frac{\lambda}{2}\left[f(x_0 + \lambda x_1 + \lambda x_2) - f(x_0 + \lambda x_1 - \lambda x_2)\right]$$

$$+\frac{\lambda^2}{2}\left[f(x_0 + \lambda x_1 + \lambda x_3) - f(x_0 + \lambda x_1 - \lambda x_3)\right] \quad (7.18)$$

is

$$\frac{f''(x_0 + \lambda x_1)}{2}\left(\lambda^4 x_2^2 + 2\lambda^5 x_2 x_3 + \lambda^6 x_3^2\right) - \frac{f'''(x_0 + \lambda x_1)}{6}\left(\lambda^4 x_2^3 + \lambda^5 x_3^3\right)$$

$$(7.19)$$

So to use Equation 7.18 as the basis of an approximation to Equation 7.15 (without the remainder, ε), the terms with values smaller than λ^5 may be ignored, but, in principle, two correction terms should then be added, these being the "leftovers" from Equation 7.15:

$$\frac{f''(x_0 + \lambda x_1)}{2}\left(\lambda^4 x_2^2\right)$$

and

$$-\frac{f'''(x_0 + \lambda x_1)}{6}\left(\lambda^4 x_2^3\right)$$

Instead of the aforementioned corrections, approximations to these are used, in order to keep small the required table size: x_1 is eliminated as an argument, by using $f''(x_0)$ and $-f'''(x_0)$ as approximations to $f''(x_0 + \lambda x_1)$ and $-f'''(x_0 + \lambda x_1)$. It is therefore the effects of these approximations that dominate the final errors in the approximation, which is

$$\widehat{f}(x) = f(x_0 + \lambda x_1) + \frac{\lambda}{2}\left[f(x_0 + \lambda x_1 + \lambda x_2) - f(x_0 + \lambda x_1 - \lambda x_2)\right]$$

$$+\frac{\lambda^2}{2}\left[f(x_0 + \lambda x_1 + \lambda x_3) - f(x_0 + \lambda x_1 - \lambda x_3)\right]$$

$$+\lambda^4\left[\frac{f'''(x_0)}{2}x_2^2 - \frac{f''(x_0)}{6}x_2^3\right] \quad (7.20)$$

$$\triangleq f(t_0) + \frac{\lambda}{2}f(t_1) - \frac{\lambda}{2}f(t_2) + \frac{\lambda^2}{2}f(t_3) - \frac{\lambda}{2}f(t_4) + \lambda^4 g(x_0, x_2)$$

(The last term is essentially an error-correction term, based on the preceding discussions.)

For the functions and ranges of Table 7.2, it has been shown that this approximation has a maximum absolute error of at most 0.5 ulps.

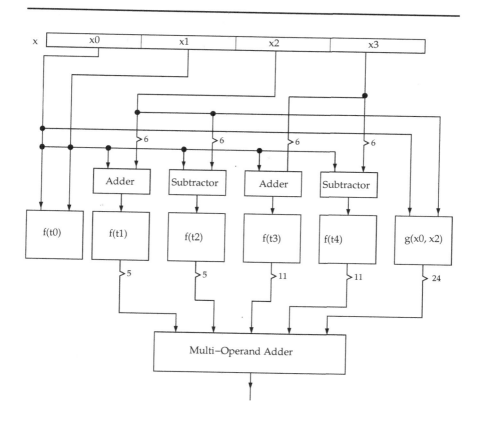

Figure 7.8: Hardware organization for ATA method

A sketch of hardware architecture for the ATA method is shown in Figure 7.8. The value $x_0 + \lambda x_1$ is just a concatenation of the bits that compromise x_0 and x_1, but additions and subtractions are required to obtain $x_0 + \lambda x_1 + \lambda x_2$, $x_0 + \lambda x_1 - \lambda x_2$, $x_0 + \lambda x_1 + \lambda x_3$, and $x_0 + \lambda x_1 + \lambda x_2$. The values are then used to address lookup tables that yield the corresponding function values; the error-correction value is obtained from a sixth lookup table that is addressed with the values of x_0 and x_2. The nominal multiplications by $\lambda, \lambda/2, \lambda^2/2$, and λ^4 are just 6-bit, 5-bit, 11-bit, and 24-bit wired shifts; in Figure 7.8, these are shown as "line breaks" with the corresponding numbers attached.

The *Improved ATA* (iATA) method is a recent modification of the ATA method, devised so as to significantly reduce the memory requirements [26].

The iATA method includes four main modifications to the basic ATA method:

- Splitting the input argument into pieces of unequal size.
- Elimination of the use of central differences. (This produces the largest reduction in table sizes.)
- Reduction in table addresses, by one bit each, through the handling of borrows-in during subtractions to form the addresses. (Similar additions in the ATA method are avoided.)
- Exploitation of symmetry, in a manner that has some similarities with the arrangement in Symmetric Bipartite Table Method.

Elimination of central differences: The second term in Equation 7.15 contains the subterm

$$f'(x_0 + \lambda x_1) \left(\lambda^2 x_2 \right)$$

which in the ATA method is obtained via the expressions

$$\frac{\lambda}{2} f(x_0 + \lambda x_1 + \lambda x_2) \qquad \text{and} \qquad \frac{\lambda}{2} f(x_0 + \lambda x_1 - \lambda x_2)$$

The two corresponding tables constitute about 24% of the total table size. The iATA approximation is based on only the second term and so requires less memory.

Similarly, for the other part of the second term in Equation 7.15, i.e.

$$f'(x_0 + \lambda x_1) \left(\lambda^3 x_3 \right)$$

the ATA approximation is obtained from the expressions

$$\frac{\lambda}{2} f(x_0 + \lambda x_1 + \lambda x_3) \qquad \text{and} \qquad \frac{\lambda}{2} f(x_0 + \lambda x_1 - \lambda x_3)$$

which account for about 19% of the total table size. Again, the corresponding iATA approximation involves only the second term, so there is a substantial reduction in table size.

Carry/borrow handling: The additions and subtractions to form the arguments in Equations 7.20 can generate carries from the most significant bit positions, and borrows into the most significant bit positions. In the basic ATA method, the carries and borrows are handled by including an additional bit in the addresses of the lookup tables, which, accordingly are larger than would be the case if the borrows/carries were not a possibility. On the other hand, in the iATA method matters are arranged so that only subtractions are necessary. Therefore, only the borrows are of concern, and it is proposed that these be handled by either preventing their occurrence or by splitting the table to be addressed into two parts and using any borrow-in to select one of the two. In the latter case, the conditions under which borrows occur are such that the second table is significantly smaller than half a single table without the use of the technique; so there is a a reduction of table size. One or the other technique is used, according to whether or not symmetry-exploitation is also employed.

We next look at some of the details of the iATA approximation.

The n-bit input argument, x, is split into four unequal parts, x_0, x_1, x_2, and x_3, represented in n_0, n_1, n_2, and n_3 bits. So

$$x = x_0 + \lambda_0 x_1 + \lambda_0 \lambda_1 x_2 + \lambda_0 \lambda_1 \lambda_2 x_3$$

where $0 \leq x_i \leq 1 - 2^{-n_i}$, $\lambda_i = 2^{-n_i}$, and $n_0 + n_1 + n_2 + n_3 = n$.

The basis of the approximation is the Taylor-series expansion around $x_0 + \lambda_0 x_1$:

$$f(x) = f(x_0 + \lambda_0 x_1) + f'(x_0 + \lambda_0 x_1)\lambda_0 \lambda_1 x_2 \tag{7.21}$$

$$+ f'(x_0 + \lambda_0 x_1)\lambda_0 \lambda_1 \lambda_2 x_3$$

$$+ \frac{1}{2} f''(x_0 + \lambda_0 x_1) \left[(\lambda_0 \lambda_1 x_2)^2 + 2(\lambda_0 \lambda_1)^2 \lambda_2 x_2 x_3 + (\lambda_0 \lambda_1 \lambda_2)^2 x_3^2 \right]$$

$$+ \cdots$$

Now, consider the expression

$$t_1 \triangleq -\lambda_a f(x_0 + \lambda_0 x_1 - \lambda_b x_2) \tag{7.22}$$

The corresponding Taylor-series expansion around $x_0 + \lambda_0 x_1$ is

$$t_1 = -\lambda_a f(x_0 + \lambda_0 x_1) + f'(x_0 + \lambda_0 x_1)\lambda_a \lambda_b x_2 - \cdots$$

So t_1 may be used as an approximation to $f'(x_0 + \lambda_0 x_1)\lambda_0 \lambda_1 x_2$ in Equation 7.21, provided that the first term (of t_1) and all terms in the second, third, and fourth derivatives are somehow cancelled out. Terms in the fifth and higher derivatives may be ignored, on the same basis as in the basic ATA approximation.

Similarly, the Taylor-series expansion for

$$t_2 \overset{\triangle}{=} -\lambda_c \lambda_d f(x_0 + \lambda_0 x_1 - \lambda_e x_3) \tag{7.23}$$

is

$$t_2 = -\lambda_c \lambda_d f(x_0 + \lambda_0 x_1) + f'(x_0 + \lambda_0 x_1) \lambda_c \lambda_d \lambda_e x_3 - \cdots$$

and this may be used to approximate $f'(x_0 + \lambda_0 x_1) \lambda_0 \lambda_1 \lambda_2 x_3$ in Equation 7.21, provided that the first term (of t_2) and all terms in the second, third, and fourth derivatives are somehow cancelled out.

(The values of λ_a, λ_b, λ_c, and λ_d are "internal" parameters whose values are determined by precisions that are chosen according to the desired table sizes and error bounds.)

If we start with t_1 and t_2, and the first terms to be excluded are taken care of by adding $\lambda_a f(x_0 + \lambda_0 x_1)$ and $\lambda_c \lambda_d f(x_0 + \lambda_0 x_1)$, then the starting approximation is

$$\widehat{f}(x) = t_0 + t_1 + t_2$$

where

$$t_0 = f(x_0 + \lambda_0 x_1) + \lambda_a f(x_0 + \lambda_0 x_1) + \lambda_c \lambda_d f(x_0 + \lambda_0 x_1) \tag{7.24}$$

If we then assume that $\lambda_0 \lambda_1 = \lambda_a \lambda_b$ and $\lambda_0 \lambda_1 \lambda_2 = \lambda_c \lambda_d \lambda_e$ and ignore terms that include five or more λs, we get

$$f(x) - \widehat{f}(x) \approx \frac{1}{2} f''(x_0 + \lambda_0 x_1) \left[(\lambda_0 \lambda_1)^2 x_2^2 \right] + \frac{1}{2} f''(x_0 + \lambda_0 x_1) \left[\lambda_1 (\lambda_a \lambda_b^2 x_2^2) \right]$$

$$- \frac{1}{6} f'''(x_0 + \lambda_0 x_1) \left[\lambda_a \lambda_b^3 x_2^3 \right] + \frac{1}{2} f''(x_0 + \lambda_0 x_1) \left[\lambda_c \lambda_d \lambda_e^2 x_3^2 \right]$$

$$\tag{7.25}$$

These may be considered errors terms that must be "removed", i.e. added to $\widehat{f}(x)$, to improve the approximation.

To obtain a better approximation than $\widehat{f}(x)$ above, $\lambda_0 x_1$ is replaced with $\delta_1 \overset{\triangle}{=} (1 - 2^{-n_1})/2$, which is halfway between the minimum and maximum possible values of x_1. The approximation is then

$$\widehat{f} = t_0 + t_1 + t_2 + t_3 + t_4 + t_5 + t_6 \tag{7.26}$$

where the first three terms are as given in Equations 7.22–7.24, and

$$t_3 = \frac{1}{2} f''(x_0 + \lambda_0 \delta_1) \left[(\lambda_0 \lambda_1)^2 x_2^2 \right]$$

$$t_4 = -\frac{1}{6} f'''(x_0 + \lambda_0 \delta_1) \left[\lambda_a \lambda_b^3 x_2^3 \right]$$

$$t_5 = \frac{1}{2} f''(x_0 + \lambda_0 \delta_1) \left[\lambda_1 \lambda_b^2 x_2^2 \right]$$

$$t_6 = \frac{1}{2} f''(x_0 + \lambda_0 \delta_1) \left[\lambda_c \lambda_d \lambda_e^2 x_3^2 \right]$$

In the bipartite method, there is symmetry that arises "naturally" and explicitly from the mathematical formulation. On the other hand, in the approximation of Equation 7.26, there is symmetry in the use of x_2 and x_3 in the last four terms, but the symmetry is implicit, and several changes are required to expose and exploit it. The starting point for these changes is the replacement of x_2 and x_3 with $x_2 - \delta_2$ and $x_3 - \delta_3$, where

$$\delta_2 = (1 - 2^{-n_2})/2$$

and

$$\delta_3 = (1 - 2^{-n_3})/2$$

these being the midpoints between the minimum and maximum possible values of x_2 and x_3. Although the primary target for the changes are the terms t_3 through t_6 in Equation 7.26, the replacements also directly affect t_1 and t_2, and this in turn affects t_0.

The exploitation of symmetry and the manner in which borrows (in forming table addresses) are handled mean that the final approximation formula is slightly different from that of Equation 7.26. The final formula is obtained by a Taylor expansion about

$$x_m = x_0 + \lambda_0 x_1 + \delta$$

where

$$\delta = \lambda_0 \lambda_1 \delta_2 + \lambda_0 \lambda_1 \lambda_2 \delta_3$$

That formula is

$$\widehat{f} = t_0 + t_1 + t_2 + t_3 + t_4 + t_5 + t_6 \tag{7.27}$$

where

$$t_0 = (1 + \lambda_a + \lambda_c \lambda_d) f(x_m)$$

$$t_1 = -\lambda_a f(x_0 - \lambda_0 x_1 - \lambda_b x_2 + 2\lambda_b \delta_2 + \delta)$$

$$t_2 = -\lambda_c \lambda_d f(x_0 - \lambda_0 x_1 - \lambda_e x_3 + 2\lambda_e \delta_3 + \delta)$$

$$t_3 = \frac{1}{2} f''(x_p) \left[(\lambda_0 \lambda_1)^2 (x_2 - \delta_2)^2 \right]$$

$$t_4 = -\frac{1}{6} f'''(x_p) \left[\lambda_a \lambda_b^3 (x_2 - \delta_2)^3 \right]$$

$$t_5 = \frac{1}{2} f''(x_p) \left[\lambda_a \lambda_b^2 (x_2 - \delta_2)^2 \right]$$

$$t_6 = \frac{1}{2} f''(x_p) \left[\lambda_c \lambda_d \lambda_e^2 (x_3 - \delta_3)^2 \right]$$

with

$$x_p = x_0 + \lambda_0 \delta_1 + \lambda_0 \lambda_1 \delta_2 + \lambda_0 \lambda_1 \lambda_2 \delta_3$$

The details of how all this is derived are straightforward—they are largely similar to the derivation of Equation 7.14—but are extremely tedious, and we leave it to the interested reader to plough through [26]. If n_* denotes the number of bits used to represent λ_*, where $* = 0, 1, 2, 3, a, b, c, d, e$, then the proposed design parameters for n-bit arguments are of the sets

$$\{n_0 = n/4, n_1 = n/4 - 1, n_2 = n/4, n_3 = n/4 + 1,$$
$$n_a = n/4, n_b = n/4 - 1, n_c = n/4, n_d = n/4, n_e = n/4 - 1\}$$

and

$$\{n_0 = n/4 + 1, n_1 = n/4 - 1, n_2 = n/4, n_3 = n/4 + 1,$$
$$n_a = n/4 - 1, n_b = n/4 + 1, n_c = n/4, n_d = n/4 - 1, n_e = n/4\}$$

according to the functions to be evaluated. The first set produces smaller tables than the second but requires smaller values of derivatives in order to achieve the same accuracy.

For implementation, the base architecture for Equation 7.27 consists of six tables : one for each term. Including symmetry exploitation and carry/borrow handling then necessitates the addition of two extra tables, some arithmetic on tables addresses, and the use of XOR gates in a manner similar to their use for symmetry exploitation in other methods above.

An issue of immediate interest is whether the method leads to better hardware than the basic ATA method and the various multipartite methods. On the face of it—on the basis of some of the results given in [26]—the answer is *YES*, in so far as table sizes are generally smaller. But there are gaps in those results;[12] so, as things stand, the answer may be considered partial or inconclusive.

7.2 Table-driven polynomial approximation

The basis of table-driven polynomial evaluation is that a table holds function values at a set of selected *breakpoints* (segment boundaries), and these values are then used for evaluation at arbitrary points within the interval covered by the breakpoints, i.e. between the breakpoints. The evaluation of $f(x)$ consists of four steps:

- The breakpoint, x_k, closest to x is located in the table.
- A value, $\tilde{x}$, is obtained from x and x_k.
- $f(\tilde{x})$ is computed, through some polynomial.
- Finally, $f(x)$ is obtained from $f(\tilde{x})$.

These are similar to the steps involved in range reduction as described in Section 1.2 but should not be confused with those: throughout this chapter, we assume that any required range reduction of that type is dealt with separately, thus placing all the methods discussed discussed in the chapter on a uniform level.

Ideally, the value of $\tilde{x}$ will be sufficiently small that a polynomial of low degree can be used with good results, and such a polynomial may be obtained in any one of the ways discussed in Chapter 6, according to the objectives at hand.

We next describe three algorithms that exemplify table-driven polynomial evaluation [24]. The algorithms are for the functions 2^x, $\ln x$, and $\sin x$, but the basic idea can be extended to other functions, the main consideration in such extension being the ease with which the computation of

---

[12]See, for example, Tables 3 and 4 in [26]. Also take into account that (i) the cost is not due to just table size, as there are arithmetic operations as well, and (ii) some of the results are only for FPGAs, and particular ones at that.

$\tilde{x}$ and, especially, the computation of $\tilde{x}$ in the secound step and the re-construction in the fourth step above can be carried out. For the general forms of the polynomials below, the reader might find it it useful to refer to Tables 6.2–6.4; in [24], however, the Remez algorithm is used to obtain the coefficients, which corresponds to minimax error.

The following is a description of the algorithms as given in [24]. It will, however, be apparent that the number of breakpoints (i.e. segment bound-aries) and their location are somewhat arbitrary. That is, it is possible to retain the essential aspects of the algorithms if other breakpoints are used and there are more or fewer of them, according to available memory and desired error bounds. (The number of breakpoints is related to the degree of polynomial required to achieve a given accuracy.)

Evaluation of 2^x

To evaluate 2^x on the interval $[-1, 1]$, the lookup table holds the function values at thirty-two breakpoints, $x_k \triangleq k/32, k = 0, 1, 2, \ldots, 31$. The point of evaluation is then determined by finding the breakpoint, x_k, such that

$$|x - (m + x_k)| \leq 1/64 \qquad\qquad m \in \{-1, 0, 1\}$$

and then computing

$$\tilde{x} = [x - (m + x_k)] \ln 2$$

which gives $|\tilde{x}| \leq (\ln 2)/64$.

The third step (in the list above) then consists of the application of a polynomial to approximate $e^{\tilde{x}} - 1$:

$$P(u) = u + c_1 u^2 + c_2 u^3 + \cdots + c_n u^{n+1} \qquad\qquad c_i \text{ constants}$$

In the last step, 2^x is obtained as

$$2^x = 2^{m + x_k} e^{\tilde{x}}$$

$$= 2^m \left[2^{x_k} + 2^{x_i} \left(e^{\tilde{x}} - 1 \right) \right]$$

$$\approx 2^m [2^{x_k} + 2^{x_k} P(\tilde{x})]$$

$$\approx 2^m [T_k + P(\tilde{x}) T_i]$$

where $T_k \approx 2^{x_k}$ is a tabulated value.

Evaluation of ln x

The evaluation of $\ln x$ is on the interval $[1, 2]$. For "small" arguments, defined as $x < e^{1/16}$, a simple polynomial approximation, designed for the interval $[1, e^{1/16}]$, is used. The evaluation for other arguments is table driven, and the details as follows.

The breakpoints are set at $x_k \overset{\triangle}{=} 1 + k/64, k = 0, 1, 2, \ldots, 64$, and the point of evaluation is determined by finding a breakpoint, x_k, such that

$$|x - x_k| \leq 1/128$$

and then computing

$$\tilde{x} = 2 \left(\frac{x - x_k}{x + x_k} \right) \tag{7.28}$$

So

$$\frac{x}{x_k} = \frac{1 + \tilde{x}/2}{1 - \tilde{x}/2}$$

and $|\tilde{x}| \leq 1/128$

The polynomial for the evaluation is

$$P(u) = u + c_1 u^3 + c_2 u^5 + \cdots + c_n u^{2n+1} \qquad c_i \text{ constants}$$

and the evaluation is of $\ln(x/x_k)$:

$$\ln \left(\frac{x}{x_k} \right) = \ln \left(\frac{1 + \tilde{x}/2}{1 - \tilde{x}/2} \right)$$

The value of $\ln x$ is then obtained as

$$\ln x = \ln[x_k(x/x_k)] = \ln x_k + \ln(x/x_i)$$

$$\approx \ln x_k + P(\tilde{x})$$

$$\approx T_k + P(\tilde{x})$$

where $T_k \approx \ln x_k$ is a tabulated value.

Evaluation of sin x

The argument, x, is in the interval $[0, \pi/4]$. If $|x| < 1/16$, then the evaluation is through a simple polynomial. Otherwise, it is based on the breakpoints (for both sine and cosine)

$$x_{jk} \overset{\triangle}{=} 2^{-j}(1 + k/8) \qquad\qquad j = 1, 2, 3, 4 \quad \text{and} \quad k = 0, 1, 2, \ldots, 7$$

with the point of evaluation determined as

$$\widetilde{x} = x - x_{jk}$$

So $|\widetilde{x}| \leq 1/32$.

The core of the evaluation consists of approximations of $\sin \widetilde{x} - \widetilde{x}$ and $\cos \widetilde{x} - 1$, through the polynomials

$$P(u) = u + c_1 u^3 + c_2 u^5 + \cdots + c_n u^{2n+1} \qquad\qquad c_i \text{ and } c_i' \text{ constants}$$

$$Q(u) = u + c_1' u^2 + c_2' u^4 + \cdots + c_n' u^{2n}$$

$\sin x$ is then obtained as

$$
\begin{aligned}
\sin x &= \sin(x_{jk} + \widetilde{x}) \\
&= \sin(x_{jk}) \cos \widetilde{x} + \cos(x_{jk}) \sin \widetilde{x} \\
&= \sin x_{jk}(\cos \widetilde{x} - 1) + \sin x_{jk} + \cos x_{jk}(\sin \widetilde{x} - \widetilde{x}) + \widetilde{x} \cos x_{jk} \\
&\approx T_{s,jk} + \widetilde{x} T_{s,jk} + T_{c,jk} Q(\widetilde{x}) + T_{c,jk} P(\widetilde{x})
\end{aligned}
$$

where $T_{s,jk}$ and $T_{c,jk}$ are tabulated sine and cosine values.

Errors

There will be errors in all three steps in the computation of $f(x)$:

- Nominally, computation error (i.e. arithmetic and representation errors) in obtaining $\widetilde{x}$, but the arithmetic can easily be made exact.
- Approximation error, since $p(\widetilde{x})$ only approximates $f(\widetilde{x})$.
- Computation error in the evaluation of $p(\widetilde{x})$.
- Computation error in finally obtaining (an approximation to) $f(x)$ from $p(\widetilde{x})$.

A detailed analysis of these errors will be found in [24]. A summary of the results is that for double-precision representation in the IEEE-754 standard on floating-point arithmetic, i.e. a working significand of 53 bits, the total error need not exceed 0.556 ulps, if the approximation polynomials are chosen properly.

More on table-driven polynomial evaluation, along the lines of the preceding, will be found in [30].

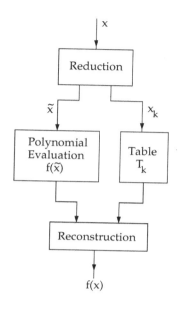

Figure 7.9: Table-driven polynomial approximation

Hardware implementation

The practicality of a hardware implementation depends on the sizes of the tables, and these depend on the precision used and the accuracy desired; the numbers above—for breakpoints and, therefore, table size—have been chosen to be sufficient for IEEE-754 Double Precision. Figure 7.9 shows the generic structure for an approximator. Given that the numbers of breakpoints are small, the Reduction is best implemented in the form of a lookup table. For the polynomial evaluation, the numbers of polynomial coefficients are $n = 5$ for 2^x, $n = 2$ for $\ln x$, and $n = 3$ and $m = 3$ for $\sin x$. The evaluation can be implemented in the manner described at the end of Section 6.2.

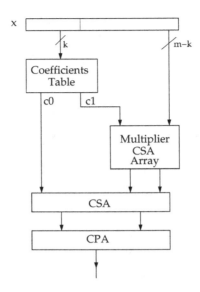

Figure 7.10: Segmented linear approximator

7.3   Segmented polynomial approximation

We now consider segmented approximation with several low-order polynomials instead of a single high-order one and without thestorage of function values. As indicated in Chapter 6 and the introduction to this chapter, we can get the same accuracy as with a high-order polynomial, but with much lower computational costs, if the range of evaluation is subdivided into several small segments and a low-order polynomial is then used on each segment. This observation is suggested by the theorem[13] at the end Section 1.2 and shown more directly by the remarks at the end of Section 6.5.

A low-order polynomial used may be a simple truncated Taylor series; and, indeed, when of low degree and if used properly, these are not too bad. But it could be that it is desirable to optimize some particular measure of error, in which case other choices are better—for example, a Chebyshev

---

[13]For example, assume a Chebyshev approximation, so that K in that theorem is determined according to Equation 6.11, and consider the effect of splitting the interval into two segments of equal size.

polynomial, if the objective is to minimize maximum error, and so on. In principle, it is also possible to have polynomials of different degrees on different segments—for example, a linear one where a function shows little variation and one of a higher order where the function has more variation—but from a hardware perspective, this is likely to be awkward, and increasing the level of segmentation would be a better practical alternative. We shall therefore assume that polynomials of the same degree are used on all the segments of an interval. This assumption is not unreasonable, given the basic premise that increasing segmentation may replace increasing polynomial degree.

Uniform segmentation, i.e. approximation with segments of the same size, is a straightforward arrangement. The first part of this section is a brief discussion of such segmentation, and it concludes with a summary of the limitations of such approximation. The remainder of the section is then devoted to non-uniform segmentation and consists of a clarification of some of the fundamental difficulties in such approximation followed by a discussion of solutions (as exemplifed in some implementations).

7.3.1   *Uniform segmentation*

The most straightforward form of segmented polynomial approximation is one with segments of the same size, an arrangement in which:

- The interval of evaluation is divided into 2^k segments, k an integer.
- The per-segment polynomial coefficients are stored in a table of 2^k entries.
- For an argument of m bits, the most significant k bits are used to locate entries in the table.
- An approximation is obtained by using the remaining $m - k$ bits of the original argument as an argument to the polynomial whose coefficients are the aforementioned table entries.

The design of hardware for uniform segmented approximation is straightforward, on the basis of the discussion at the end of Section 6.2; the structures generally consist of tables for the coefficients, arrays of carry–save adders (CSAs) for the multiplications, a CSA tree for the additions, and a carry–propagate adder (CPA) for conversion from of the result carry–save representation to conventional representation. Figure 7.10 shows such a structure for linear approximation, and Figure 7.11 shows one for quadratic approximation. We assume that the "squaring array" consists of the equivalent of a multiplier and a specialized squaring unit, of the type described in Section 2.2. (Good and detailed descriptions of quadratic approximators will be found in [6, 12].)

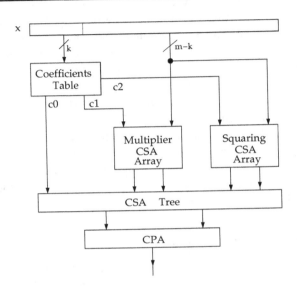

Figure 7.11: Segmented quadratic approximator

Historically, segmented polynomial approximation has most often been implemented as just described; and in many cases such usage was of a limited fashion, to provide initial approximations for use with other methods. That is a reflection of the historical costs of memory. As the cost of memory has dropped and density increased, it has become practical to use such approximations on their own. At the same time, however, demands on accuracy have increased, which, in turn, implies an increased demand for memory. So although it is now possible to use segmented polynomial approximations to a greater degree than used to be possible, it is still necessary to have methods that can achieve high accuracy but with reasonable memory requirements.

One way in which memory requirements can be reduced is to have some constraints on the relationships between the polynomials for different segments. As described above, each segment is associated with an independent polynomial. On the other hand, *constrained segmentation*, the underlying idea is that some of the "independence" may be given up in return for a reduction in table sizes [14].

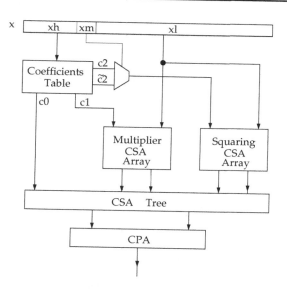

Figure 7.12: Constrained quadratic polynomial approximator

The basic arrangement in constrained segmentation is that the interval of evaluation is divided into several segments of the same size, adjacent segments are paired, and constraints are imposed on the approximations for each pair. The constraints are the requirement of continuity on up to the kth derivatives. That is, if the adjacent segments are $[u, v]$ and $[v, w]$, with $v = (u + w)/2$, and the approximation polynomials on the two are $p(x)$ and $q(x)$, then it is required that $p(v) = q(v)$, $p'(v) = q'(v)$, ..., $p(v) = q(v)$, $p^{(k)}(v) = q^{(k)}(v)$. This reduces memory requiremens because some constants will now be shared between segments. Thus, for example, with third-degree polynomials and $k = 2$, the number of required coefficients would be five, whereas with unconstrained segmentation it would be eight—a substantial reduction. The results in [14]—for 12-bit to 42-bit results and polynomials of degrees one, two, and three—show that substantial reductions in table sizes are possible relative to unconstrainted segmentation.

Figure 7.12 shows the sketch of an architecture for second-degree constrained segmentation. The polynomial coefficients are the same for the first two terms (c_0 and c_1), but differ for the third terms (c_2 and $\widehat{c}_2$). The high-order m bits, x_H, of the argument, x, are used to identify a segment-pair of which the segments share coefficients; bit x_M indicates which half of the pair the argument is in; and the remaining bits, x_L, are the argument to a third-degree polynomial.

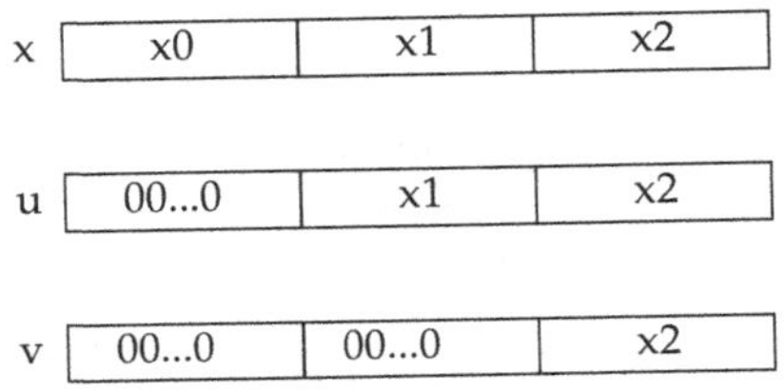

x	x0	x1	x2

u	00...0	x1	x2

v	00...0	00...0	x2

Figure 7.13: Argument partitioning for two-level approximation

The "extraneous" constraints are obviously in conflict with the fundamental criteria of choosing the polynomials so as to minimize errors, and we should expect that errors will be greater than with independent polynomials. In general, that is indeed the case, but the specifics vary. If n, the degree of the approximating polynomial is odd, and the constraints do not involve derivatives, then there is no increase in error. Otherwise, if the kth derivative is involved, then there is a small increase that is minimal when k is odd and n is even or k is even and n is odd. Such error can be kept low by using high precision for the coefficients, thus reducing the representation errors and what they contribute to the overall error.

A different approach in the implementation of uniform segmentation is *Two-Level Evaluation*, as described in [33]. The evaluation for a function, $f(x)$, is in two levels. The first level consists of "coarse" uniform segmentation with linear interpolation. In the second level, each of the "coarse" segments is subdivided into finer uniform segments and linear interpolation is again applied. The second level takes into account errors from the first-level approximations and so refines those approximations. Some of the details are as follows.

Assume that the argument, x, is fractional and is represented in n bits. It is divided into three pieces, x_0, x_1, and x_2, represented in n_0, n_1, and n_2 bits. Let u denote what is obtained by setting to 0s the bits that correspond to x_0, and let v denote what is obtained by setting to 0s the bits that correspond to x_0 and x_1, as shown in Figure 7.13.

Then

$$0 \le u < 2^{-n_0}$$

$$0 \le v < 2^{-(n_0+n_1)}$$

The bits that comprise x_0 are used to address a table that contains function values for 2^{n_0} segments, and the first level of the approximation is the computation of $f(u)$. For each segment, $[s_i, s_{i+1})$, two values are stored: $f(s_i)$ and $f(s_{i+1})$, which are used to approximate, by linear interpolation, $f_i(u)$, which is the value of $f(u)$ in that segment. With $[f(s_{i+1}) - f(s_i)]/(s_{i+1} - s_i)$ as an approximation to the first derivative, the interpolation formula is

$$f_i(u) = f(s_i) + \frac{f(s_{i+1}) - f(s_i)}{s_{i+1} - s_i} u \qquad i = 0, 1, 2, \ldots, 2^{n_0} - 1$$

$$= f(s_i) + \frac{f(s_{i+1}) - f(s_i)}{2^{-n_0}} u$$

$$\triangleq f(s_i) + [f(s_{i+1}) - f(s_i)]\Delta u$$

So on the interval $[s_i, s_{i+1})$, the value of $f_i(u)$ is computed as an approximation to that of $f(s_i + u)$. The difference between the two, i.e.

$$\varepsilon_i(u) = f(s_i + u) - f_i(u)$$

is then used in the second level of approximation, to obtain a "correction" value that is added to $f_i(u)$, to get a more accurate approximation.

For a given function, f, the functions ε_i are all very similar, because they represent similar high-order terms, and so the graphs have the same shape but differ in maximum magnitude. Therefore, if E_i is the value of e_i at its maximum magnitude, and $\varepsilon_i(u)$ is normalized to

$$p_i(u) = \frac{\varepsilon_i(u)}{E_i}$$

then the resulting $p_i(u)$ graphs will be nearly identical, and one of them, $P(u)$, may be used to represent all of them. $P(u)$ may be selected in a variety of ways, of which a straightforward one is to find

$$E_k = \max |E_i| \qquad i = 0, 1, 2, \ldots, 2^{n_0} - 1$$

and then choose

$$P(u) = P_k(u) = \frac{\varepsilon_k(u)}{E_k}$$

For the second-level, refining approximation, each first-level segment is subdivided into 2^{n_1} segments, $\{[w_j, w_{j+1})\}$, addressed with the bits that comprise x_1. The linear interpolation formula gives the values of $P(v)$ in segment j:

$$P_j(v) = P(s_j) + \frac{P(w_{j+1}) - P(w_j)}{w_{j+1} - w_j} v \qquad i = 0, 1, 2, \ldots, 2^{n_1} - 1$$

$$\triangleq P(s_j) + [P(w_{j+1}) - P(w_j)]\, \Delta v$$

The value of $\widehat{f}(x)$, an approximation to $f(x)$, is then obtained as

$$f(x) = f_i(u) + E_i * P_j(v)$$

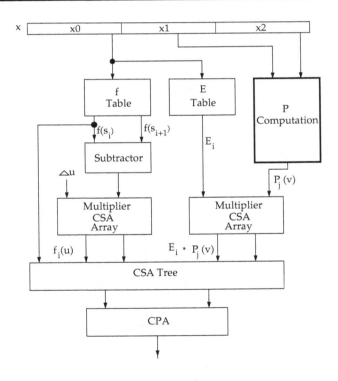

Figure 7.14: Hardware organization for 2-level segmented approximation

Figure 7.14 shows the sketch of hardware architecture for the evaluation. Multiplications are carried out in carry–save-adder (CSA) arrays, as are the additions of the outputs of those arrays and the first terms in the interpolation formulae, and a final carry–propagate adder (CPA) is used to convert from the carry–save representation into conventional representation. The first-level approximation is carried out in the Table–Subtractor–Multiplier on the left. The second-level refinement is carried out in the P-Computation module, whose design is similar to that of the first-level approximator: considering the corresponding equations, with exactly similar hardware structure, w_j replaces s_i, w_{j+1} replaces s_{i+1}, P replaces f, v replaces u, and P_j replaces f_i. For higher performance, the Subtractors may be replaced with CSAs, with subsequent units modified appropriately.

As the arrangement of Figure 7.14 is largely similar to that for a second-degree evaluator (Figure 7.11), that is a reasonable basis for comparison. The results of such a comparison show a cost:performance trade-off: For the functions $\log_2 x$, 2^x, $1/x$, $\sqrt{x}$, $1/\sqrt{x}$, and $\sin x$, and comparing with other second-degree evaluators (Chebyshev and minimax) on 24-bit results (IEEE Single Precision), the main results are that the tables are smaller with the two-level evaluator, and the total cost too is smaller, by factors ranging from 1.13 to 1.98; but the operational delay is larger with the two-level evaluator, by factors ranging from 1.23 to 1.37.

Uniform segmentation does not take into account the nature of the particular function being approximated and so will not, in general, yield the best results (considering cost, accuracy, etc.). Ideally we should have more segments where a function varies rapidly than where it varies slowly. Segment sizes are also related to errors and to the number of segments: for a given error bound, the size of the smallest segment will be determined by where the magnitude of error is likely to be greatest, which means that with uniform segmentation there may be unnecessary segments where errors are of small magnitude, thus leading to a waste of memory. Indeed, for a function whose graph varies rapidly, the number of segments required to attain high accuracy may be too large to be practical if uniform segments are used. On the other hand, simply fixing the total number of segments can result in a poor approximation. Variable-sized segments are therefore attractive, but realizing them is not without difficulty: allowing arbitrary-sized segments tends to complicate the design of the corresponding addressing circuits, with the end result being relatively high costs, or poorer performance than would otherwise be the case, or both. As we shall see below, one way to deal with this difficulty is to impose some constraints on how segment sizes may vary.

On the basis of the preceding remarks, we can identify three inter-related main issues with variable-size segmentation:

- The choice of segment broundaries (breakpoints).
- The optimal number of segments.
- The addressing of segments.

In what follows, we shall make some general remarks on these issues and then consider in detail how they are dealt with in three types of implementations: *Hierarchical Segmentation, LUT Casacades*, and *Address Remapping*, named after key aspects of the implementations.

7.3.2   *Segment boundaries and numbers*

In [18], Lawson considered two questions:

- How can a given interval be partitioned into segments so that the (magnitude of maximum) error in approximating a given continuous function by m different polynomials or rational functions[14] of specified degrees will be as small as possible?
- What is the smallest integer m such that a given continuous function on a given interval can be approximated by m different polynomials or rational functions of specified degrees and to within a specified error tolerance?

To answer these, the *segmented rational minimax approximation problem* is defined as follows.

Let f be a continuous function on the interval $[a, b]$ and $m \geq 2$ be the number of segments into which $[a, b]$ is partitioned, with $m - 1$ segment boundaries, u_i, such that

$$a = u_0 \leq u_1 \leq u_2 \leq \cdots \leq u_{m-1} \leq u_m = b$$

And let R_i be the set of rational functions with numerators and denominators of given degrees.

For u_{i-1} and u_i, the minimax error function on the ith segment is defined as

$$h(u_{i-1}, u_i) = \min_{r_i \in R_i} \max_{u_{i-1} \leq x \leq u_i} |f(x) - r_i(x)| \qquad i = 1, 2, \ldots, m$$

---

[14] A polynomial is just a special case of a rational function (Chapter 6).

The problem then is to determine $\underline{u} \stackrel{\triangle}{=} (u_0, u_1, \ldots, u_m)$ so as to minimize

$$\mu(\underline{u}) = \max h(u_{i-1}, u_i) \qquad i = 1, 2, \ldots, m$$

i.e. a sort of "minimax–minimax" problem that can be formulated as a dynamic programming problem.

In general, a rational minimax approximation has the property—the *balanced-error property*—of a tendency to balance the extremes of the error curve. In the present context, "balanced" means that $\mu(\underline{u}) = h(u_{i-1}, u_i), i = 1, 2, \ldots, m$. It is shown in [18] that this property is a sufficient condition for the existence of a solution to the segmented rational minimax approximation problem and that there is such a solution. To find a solution, an iterative approach is proposed, based on the assumptions that:

- For small changes in u_{i-1} and u_i, the value of $h(u_{i-1}, u_i)$ depends on only the (*small*) size, $s_i \stackrel{\triangle}{=} u_i - u_{i-1}$, of the segment.
- The aforementioned dependency is of the form $k_i s_i^{c_i}$, where k_i is a positive constant, $c_i = n_i + d_i + 1$; and n_i and d_i and are the degrees of the numerator and denominator of r_i, the rational approximation on that interval.

(The latter assumption is derived from some experimental results with a few elementary functions.)

Another approach to determining segment boundaries is given in [19]; this too produces an approximation to a balanced solution. Here, the iterations have the form

$$u_{i,j+1} = u_{i,j} + k \left(\varepsilon_{i+1,j} - \varepsilon_{i+1,j} \right)$$

where $u_{i,j}$ is the value of the ith point in iteration j, $e_{i,j}$ is the error on $(u_{i-1,j}, u_{i,j})$, and k is a small positive number. The final number of segments is fixed, and this determines the maximum error. It is, however, possible to use the algorithm to determine a segmentation that matches a desired accuracy, by starting at one end of the interval ($[a, b]$ above) and proceeding in small increments until satisfaction is obtained.

On the basis of the assumptions stated above [18], the error, ε, on a small segment, $[a, b]$, is determined approximately by the equation

$$\varepsilon = k(b - a)^m \tag{7.29}$$

where, k is some positive constant, $m = 2$ for a linear approximation, and $m = 3$ for a second-degree approximation. An obvious problem with

Equation 7.29 is that, in general, we do not know what k is, and the equation does not explicitly take into account the function being approximated. More recent work on the best number of segments has come up with the following results [7].

Suppose we wish to obtain a segmented linear approximation of a function, $f(x)$, on the interval $[a, b]$, such that the approximation is accurate to within ε. Then the optimum number of segments is approximately

$$\frac{1}{4\sqrt{\varepsilon}} \int_a^b \sqrt{|f''(x)|} dx$$

for non-uniform segmentation and

$$\frac{b-a}{4\sqrt{\varepsilon}} \sqrt{\max_{a \leq x \leq b} |f''(x)|}$$

for uniform segmentation.

Table sizes, for varying precisions, are given in [7] for several functions, including all those of interest in this book. What they show is that under the reasonable assumption that $\varepsilon = 0.5$ ulps, the table sizes are practical for, say, IEEE Single Precision (24-bit significands) but not for much beyond that and certainly not for IEEE Double Precision (53-bit significands).

7.3.3 *Hierarchical segmentation*

The problem of variable-sized segments with first-order polynomials has been considered in [10, 11, 15], with respect to the minimax error. The objective in these works is to arrange things so that at least *relatively* simple circuits are feasible for the determination of segment addresses. The essence of the solution is to constrain segment sizes so that they increase or decrease by a factor of two. This idea is applied as follows.

Suppose, for example, that we have four bits for addressing and that the segment sizes increase. Consider all the possible bit patterns of the segment-element addresses, i.e. $00 \cdots 0$ to $11 \cdots 1$. The partitioning is as shown in Table 7.3, with the segment start addresses underlined. (The first address is not used.) These patterns show that the addresses of a segment can be determined by counting the *number* of leading 0s. The design of a circuit to do that is a simple, straightforward affair.

With the same four addressing bits and decreasing segment sizes, a segment is identified by the number of leading 1s, as shown in Table 7.4.

Lastly, we can have an arrangement that consists of both increasing and decreasing segment sizes; and it is also possible to generalize the above by having further levels of segmentation (i.e. nesting) in which a segment is further partitioned into variable or fixed-sized "subsegments". Suppose, for example, that we have an 8-bit argument and that five bits are used for one level of variable-sized-segment addressing and the other bits to address fixed-sized segments within the former segments. Then the partitioning of addresses is as shown in Table 7.5. The segment addresses are underlined, and the "size" is computed from the range of addresses covered.

Element Address	Segment Size	Leading 0s
0000	—	—
<u>0001</u>	1	3
<u>0010</u> 0011	2	2
<u>0100</u> 0101 0110 0111	4	1
<u>1000</u> 1001 1010 1011 1100 1101 1110 1111	8	0

Table 7.3: Addressing with increasing-size segments

A consideration (and "extrapolation") of Table 7.5 shows that it is possible to have segmentation vary according to a "nesting level". For example, one may have uniformly sized "super segments" at the first level, and the sizes of each of those may then vary, by increasing or decreasing; and the basic idea can be extended to several levels, whence the term *hierarchical*.

Element Address	Segment Size	Leading 1s
<u>0000</u> 0001 0010 0011 0100 0101 0110 0111	8	0
<u>1000</u> 1001 1010 1011	4	1
<u>1100</u> 1101	2	2
<u>1110</u>	1	3
1111	—	—

Table 7.4: Addressing with decreasing-size segments

A closer examination of the addressing shown in Tables 7.3–7.5 shows that with k bits used for segment identication, the maximum possible number of segments is $2k$, which is much smaller than with uniform segmentation, for which the number would be 2^k. The expectation is that reduction in the number of possible segments will be more than made up for by a better quality of segmentation (and, therefore, better accuracy).

Although variable segmentation is qualitatively superior to uniform segmentation, in that far fewer segments (and, therefore, less memory) will be required, it does not "come for free": in the implementation, the addressing implies penalties in hardware cost and operational time. For the type of segmentation just described, the circuits will not be particularly complicated—they will consist of cascades of basic gates to determine prefixes and adders of multiple one-bit operands—but the operational time is likely to be a major consideration. Therefore, the choice between variable segmentation and uniform segmentation must be determined on a case-by-case basis, according to the function at hand, the desired level of accuracy, the constraints on cost and operational time, and so forth.

Segment	Address Range		Size
	Start	**End**	
0	00000000	00000111	8
1	00001000	00001111	8
2	00010000	00011111	16
3	00100000	00111111	32
4	01000000	01111111	64
5	10000000	10111111	64
6	11000000	11011111	32
7	11100000	11101111	16
8	11110000	11110111	8
8	11111000	11111111	8

Table 7.5: Addressing with hierarchical segmentation

The segmentation method just described may be applied so that fewer or more segments are used according to how the function varies in different regions (subintervals) of the interval of evaluation. The starting point is the determination of the subinterval boundaries. In [10], that is done according to how the function varies and closest power-of-two sizes. The algorithm:

(1) Determine optimal placement of segment boundaries. This includes dividing the interval of evaluation into regions such that in each region the function either monotonically increases or decreases.
(2) For a non-linear region, if the non-linearity is monotonically increasing, then increase segment size by a factor of two or more at each step; and if the non-linearity is monotonically decreasing, then reduce segment size by a factor of two or more at each step.
(3) Obtain the segment addresses by computing prefixes (as described above).
(4) If necessary, divide the function into several intervals, and repeat (1)–(3).
(5) If necessary, repeat the above steps with higher-order terms.

```
x₁ := a; x₂ := b; x̃₂ := 0;
oscillating := 0; done := 0;
while (¬ em done)
    ε := minimax(f, d, a, b, ulp);
    if (ε ≤ εₘₐₓ)
        if (x₂ = b)
            uᵢ := x₂;
            done := 1;
        else
            if (oscillating)
                uᵢ := x₂;
                x̃₂ := x₂;
                x₁ := x₂;
                x₂ := b;
                i := i + 1;
                oscillating := 0;
            else
                δ := |x₂ − x̃₂|/2;
                x̃₂ := x₂;
                if (δ > ulp)
                    x₂ := x₂ + δ;
                else
                    x₂ := x₂ + ulp;
                end-if
            end-if
        end-if
    else    /* ε > εₘₐₓ */
        δ := |x₂ − x̃₂|/2;
        x̃₂ := x₂;
        if (δ > ulp)
            x₂ := x₂ + δ;
        else
            x₂ := x₂ + ulp;
            if (x̃₂ = x₂)
                oscillating := 1;
            else
                x̃₂ := x₂
            end-if
        end-if
    end-if
end-while
```

Table 7.6: Segment-boundary algorithm

For the determination of the segment boundaries, a binary-search algorithm is used that does not produce a segmentation with the balanced-error property but which, for minimax error, is optimal in the number of segments for a given maximum-error target, ε_{max}, and machine precision[15] [11].

The basic steps of the segment-boundary algorithm:

(1) Start with a single segment on the interval of evaluation, $[a, b]$.
(2) Use the Remez algorithm [22] to find a polynomial approximation of degree at most d over the current interval, and determine the maximum error, ε, with that approximation.
(3) If $\varepsilon > \varepsilon_{max}$, then halve the segment size and repeat (2).
(4) When $\varepsilon \leq \varepsilon_{max}$, one end of the current interval is adjusted by a small amount. If that amount is an ulp, then the interval end will oscillate between a value such that ε is just below ε_{max} and one such that it is just above. The former is set as a segment boundary.
(5) Repeat from (2) until all segment boundaries, u_i, have been determined for the entire interval $[a, b]$.

The detailed algorithm is given in Table 7.6.

7.3.4 *LUT cascades*

The segmentation algorithm[16] used in [7] has some similarities with the "boundary-determination" procedure given above, in so far as segments are iteratively subdivided into smaller ones until a desired error level is attained. The approximation for each segment is a linear one: $\widehat{f}(x) = c_0 + c_1 x$. The name, "LUT cascades" is taken from the manner in which segments are addressed—using a cascade of lookup tables [7–9].

The inputs to the algorithm are a function, $f(x)$, an interval $[a, b]$ for the range of the argument, and an error bound, ε; the outputs are the boundaries of m segments, $[v_0, u_0], [v_1, u_1], \cdots, [v_{m-1}, u_{m-1}]$. The algorithm starts by first fitting a single line through the entire interval and then iterating as follows, taking each segment in turn. If the error over the "current segment" exceeds ε, the maximum error allowed over the entire interval, then the segment is split into two subsegments whose boundary is where the maximum error occurs, and each of the subsegments is made a "current segment". This process is repeated until the error over each of

---

[15]The boundaries are to within one ulp of the ideal.
[16]The algorithm is based on the Douglas–Peucker algorithm, which was devised for the rendering of curves for graphic displays [16].

the subsegments is within ε. The algorithm does not produce the smallest number of segments, but the results are close to optimal.

The algorithm consists of these steps:

(1) Set *current segment*, $[v_0, u_0]$, to $[a, b]$.
(2) Approximate $f(x)$ in the *current* segment $[v_i, u_i]$ with $\widehat{f}(x) = c_0 + c_1 x$, where $c_1 = [f(u_i) - f(v_i)]/(u_i - v_i)$ and $c_0 = f(v_i) - c_1 v_i$.
(3) Find p_{max}, a value of x, that maximizes $f(x) - \widehat{f}(x)$ in $[v_i, u_i]$, and set $\varepsilon_{max} = f(p_{max}) - \widehat{f}(p_{max})$.
(4) Find p_{min}, a value of x, that minimizes $f(x) - \widehat{f}(x)$ in $[v_i, u_i]$, and set $\varepsilon_{min} = f(p_{min}) - \widehat{f}(p_{min})$
(5) If $|\varepsilon_{max}| > |\varepsilon_{min}|$, then set $p = p_{max}$; otherwise set $p = p_{min}$.
(6) Set $\varepsilon_i = |\varepsilon_{max} - \varepsilon_{min}|/2$ and $\lambda_i = (\varepsilon_{max} + \varepsilon_{min})/2$.
(7) If $\varepsilon_i \leq \varepsilon$, then $[v_i, u_i]$ is a *complete* segment. Stop if all segments are complete.
(8) Partition any incomplete segment $[v_i, u_i]$ into two segments, $[v_{i+1} = v_i, u_{i+1} = p]$ and $[v_{i+2} = p, u_{i+2} = u_i]$ and make each a *current segment*.
(9) Change i and go to (2).
(10) Apply λ_i to each segment $[v_i, u_i]$. ("Apply" is explained in the next paragraph.)

For the last step, ε_{max} and ε_{min} in (6) are the positive and negative errors of the largest magnitudes, and they are equalized by a vertical shift through λ_i; this produces near-minimax approximations for the linear function $\widehat{f}(x)$, if $f(x)$ is concave or convex on the interval $[a, b]$. Seen another way, the algorithm aims for a balanced-error property.

Because, in many cases, the approximation accuracy of a polynomial generally improves with increases in degree,[17] we should expect that increases in degree will reduce the number of intervals required to achieve a given level of accuracy for a given function and interval of evaluation. That is indeed the case, and some confirming results, obtained for second-degree Chebyshev polynomials, will be found in [9, 12, 17].

For a second-degree Chebyshev approximation of $f(x)$ on the interval $[a, b]$, the maximum error is (Equation 6.11)

$$\varepsilon(a, b) = \frac{(b - a)^3}{192} \max_{a \leq x \leq b} \left| f^{(3)}(x) \right|$$

---

[17] Cases for which there might be exceptions are noted in Chapter 6.

The fact that this is a monotonically increasing function of $b - a$ may be used to partition the interval into s segments, $[v_0, u_0]$, $[v_1, u_1]$, ... , $[v_{s-1}, u_{s-1}]$, that are as wide as possible but with the magnitude of approximation error less than some specified value, ε_{max}.

The algorithm:

(1) Set $v_0 = 0$ and $i = 0$.
(2) Find a value u such that $u \geq v_i$ and $\varepsilon(v_i, u) = \varepsilon_{max}$, where $\varepsilon(v_i, u)$ is the largest error over $[v_i, u]$.
(3) If $u > b$ then set $u = b$.
(4) Set $u_i = u$ and increment i.
(5) If $u = b$ then set $s = i$ and stop. Otherwise set $v_i = u$ and go to (2)

It is not easy to find a u that satisfies the conditon in (2); so, instead, a value $\widehat{u}$ is found such that $\varepsilon(v_i, \widehat{u}) \leq \varepsilon_{max}$. The value of $\widehat{u}$ can be found by an exhaustive search through the 2^n possible values of an n-bit argument, or by a linear search, if it is possible to specify the bits of the argument that can yield values that satisfy that condition. The value of $\max \left| f^{(3)}(x) \right|$, where $v_i \leq x \leq \widehat{u}$, is found through linear programming.

The main problem with the method we have just described is in the proposed address-encoding scheme that transforms an argument into a segment address. That design is for a linear cascade of lookup tables. Although the total size of the tables will be small, the arrangement will no doubt contribute substantially to the operational delay: for S segments, $\lceil \log_2 S \rceil$ lookup tables are required. It does, however, appear possible to replace the lookup tables with fast combinational-logic circuits, if the operand precision is not large; and in either case pipelining might be of some value.

7.3.5   *Address remapping*

The *Addressing Remapping* scheme is one in which non-uniform segments are constructed in such a way that relatively simple addressing is possible [13]. The scheme has some similarities with the hierarchical-segmentation scheme, in that non-uniform segments are constructed from basic segments whose sizes are powers of two. The segmentation for an approximation on an interval $[a, b)$ and with error bound ε is in four phases:

(i) *Uniform segmentation*, in which the interval of evaluation is divided into 2^m segments, $\{U_i\}$ ($i = 0, 1, 2, \ldots$) of uniform width, $\Delta \overset{\triangle}{=} (b - a)/2^m$, such that the per-segment error does not exceed ε. (In what follows, "size" will be in units of Δ.)

(ii) *Non-uniform segmentation*, in which the segments from the preceding phase are grouped into non-uniform segments, $\{S_j\}$, that satisfy certain constraints.

(iii) *Grouping*, in which non-uniform segments that are adjacent to each other and are of equal size are collected into groups, $\{G_k\}$, and each group is assigned an address. The grouping simplifies subsequent addressing.

(iv) *Remapping*, in which the groups are sorted according to size, and new addresses are assigned. The process ensures that the address of each non-uniform segment can be obtained by simply concatenating the address of a group and some offset bits that are extracted from the original segment address.

The second phase consists of starting with segment U_0 and repeatedly constructing (until all the U_i are covered) non-uniform segments, $\{S_j\}$, that satisfy three constraints:

(i) The approximation error over each S_j does not exceed ε.
(ii) The number of merged segments is a power of two.
(iii) All the segments, U_i, in S_j can be addressed with just some leading bits of the function argument.

The effect of (a) is that the segmentation "automatically" takes into account the nature of the function being approximated: there will be many small segments where the function varies rapidly and a few large segments where there is little variation.

The grouping phase consists of two main steps. In the first step, all S_j of the same size are placed into the same group, G_k; this may produce groups whose sizes are not powers of two. So in the second step each such group is split into two groups, G_k' and G_k'', such that G_k' is as large as possible and has a size that is a power of two. G_k' is then taken as a final group, while G_k'' is taken as an "ordinary" group and subjected to the same process.

The tree of Figure 7.15 shows an example of a construction in which the nature of the function is such that the final segmentation gives the sizes shown in the shaded circles. Table 7.7 shows the addresses (j index) of the non-uniform segments relative to the addresses (i index) of the original uniform segments. Examination of the addresses shows that the address of a non-uniform segment can be obtained by adding an offset (the underlined bits in the "original address") to a base (the underlined bits in the "new address"). The grouping in the second phase is indicated by the k index, which corresponds to the leading bits of the S_i address.

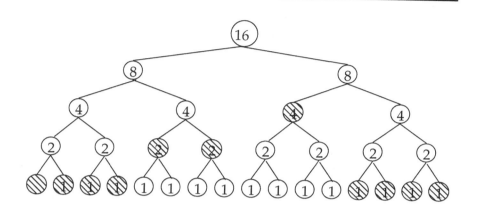

Figure 7.15: Non-uniform-segment construction

i	j	k	Segment (size)	Original (U_i) Address	New (S_j) Address
0	0	0	1	00<u>00</u>	0000
1	1		1	000<u>1</u>	0001
2	1		1	00<u>1</u>0	0010
3	3		1	00<u>11</u>	0011
4	4	1	2	01<u>00</u>	01<u>00</u>
6	5		2	01<u>1</u>0	0101
8	6	2	4	1000	0110
12	7	3	1	11<u>00</u>	01<u>11</u>
13	8		1	11<u>01</u>	1000
14	9		1	11<u>1</u>0	1001
15	10		1	11<u>11</u>	1010

Table 7.7: Non-uniform segment addresses

The size-based sorting and remapping of addresses does away with the need for the aforementioned addition of a base to an offset. Table 7.8 shows the results of sorting the segments of Table 7.7 according to size and then remapping the addresses. It can be seen that now an address is obtained by nominally adding a k-bit offset to a base address (underlined) in which the least siginificant k bits are all 0s. That is, there need not be an actual addition: a concatenation or bit replacement suffices. This is the novel aspect of the remapping scheme.

If the argument, x, for the function evaluation consists of n bits and 2^m uniform segments are constructed, then up to m bits may be used to address a table that contains polynomial coefficients, and at least $n - m$ bits may be used as argument to the selected polynomial. Where the argument is in a segment that is larger than one, fewer than m bits are required (for remapping) to obtain the coefficients, and more bits, s, are available as additional bits for the argument to the selected polynomial; the maximum value of s is $\log_2 b_{max}$, where b_{max} is the size of the largest possible non-uniform segment. Thus for a second-degree approximations, the basic architecture is as shown in Figure 7.16.

j	Segment Size	Original Offset	Remapped Address
0	1	00	<u>0000</u>
1	1	01	0001
2	1	10	0010
3	1	11	0011
4	1	00	<u>0100</u>
5	1	01	0101
6	1	10	0110
7	1	11	0111
8	2	0	<u>1000</u>
9	2	1	1001
10	4	-	<u>1010</u>

Table 7.8: Remapped non-uniform segment addresses

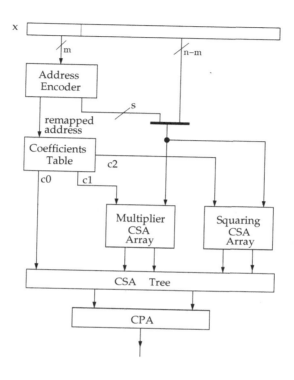

Figure 7.16: Address-remapping evaluator

7.3.6 *Errors*

We next make make some general remarks on errors and then describe a simple, straightforward technique than can be used to obtain a balanced-error property or at least come close to it.

7.3.6.1 *Basic bounds*

In segmentation, the polynomial on a segment is almost always of low degree. So it should be possible to easily carry out an exact (or almost-exact) error analysis that would be similar to those in Section 7.1. Let us suppose, for example, that we have a second-degree approximation:

$$\widehat{f}(x) = c_0 + c_1 x + c_2 x^2$$

Then, in general, the errors are:

- Approximation errors arising from the trunction of an infinite series to a series of three terms.
- Representation errors in the representation of the coefficients and all computed values (and the consquent propagation of such errors).
- Arithmetic errors in the additions and multiplications.

Having determined these—basic formulae for bounds are given in Section 1.1—steps are then taken to ensure that their sum is within some required accuracy.

The approximation error will depend on the particular function and how the second-degree approximation—specifically, the set of coeffients, c_i—has been obtained. For example, in several of the cases discussed earlier in the chapter, the second-degree polynomial in question is obtained by truncating a Taylor series, and the approximation error is just the remainder after the truncation.

Considering the initial errors and their propagation in each of the three terms of the second-degree polynomial above, the bounds on the magnitudes of the absolute errors are:

- For the three coefficients, representation errors: $|\varepsilon_{c_0}|, |\varepsilon_{c_1}|$, and $|\varepsilon_{c_2}|$.
- For the second term: $|\varepsilon_{c_1} x| + |\varepsilon_x c_1| + |\varepsilon_{c_1} \varepsilon_x|$, where ε_x is the representation error in x.
- For the third term: $|\varepsilon_{c_2} x^2| + |\varepsilon_{x^2} c_2| + |\varepsilon_{c_2} \varepsilon_{x^2}|$, where ε_{x^2} is the representation error in the computed value of x^2.

In this case, in which x is an "original" argument, ε_x would be the error between the user-provided argument and what is actually represented. Given that we have no information on the former, it is reasonable to take the value as it is and assume the representation is exact; that is, that $\varepsilon_x = 0$. Then for the second term, we have just $|\varepsilon_{c_1} x|$.

For the third term, even if there is no error in x, the result of the squaring–multiplication will most likely—in order to keep hardware costs and performance reasonable—be truncated before the additions. We may therefore reasonably assume that $\varepsilon_{x^2} \neq 0$.

We may also reasonably assume that the products of the multiplications with the coefficients will be truncated to a reasonable precision before the final additions; this will then produce representation errors ε_{r2} in the second term and ε_{r3} in the third term. And with the products thus truncated, the additions can easily be made exact; so there are no further errors.

On the basis of the above, the bound on the magnitude of total error is

$$|\varepsilon_{c_0}| + |\varepsilon_{c_1}x| + |\varepsilon_{c_2}x^2| + |\varepsilon_{x^2}c_2| + |\varepsilon_{c_2}\varepsilon_{x^2}| + |\varepsilon_{r2}| + +|\varepsilon_{r2}|$$

In most cases, the precision of the final result and intermediate values will be no less than the precision of the initial argument. If that is so, and each error is properly controlled, then $\varepsilon_{c_2}\varepsilon_{x^2}$ will be negligible and may be considered zero.

7.3.6.2 *Error balance*

Once we have obtained a bound on the errors, what is then of interest beyond the sum is their distribution and in particular of the maximum magnitudes. We next briefly consider one aspect of this; other aspects have been addressed above, for example in the discussion of Chebyshev polynomials.

We have noted above that rational minimax approximations tend to balance errors at the extremes of an interval. In hardware segmented approximations, the polynomials are of sufficiently low order that such balance can be sought directly. Indeed, in the above modified Douglas–Peucker algorithm (Section 7.3.4), the adjustment, by λ_i, in step (6) aims to do exactly that. We next describe how the basic underlying idea there can be applied in a slightly more general way that first found its way into hardware approximation through a segmented approximation of the reciprocal function[18] [20]. We shall here discuss only the case of a linear approximation, $\widehat{f}(x)$, to a function $f(x)$, on a segment $[x_i, x_j]$.

Consider the function $f(x)$ of Figure 7.17 and, for simplicity, assume symmetry around the midpoint, x_m, of the interval, $[x_i, x_j]$. The simplest approximation is to take $\widehat{f}(x)$ as a constant. For that, there are three obvious possibilities:

$$\widehat{f}_1(x) = f(x_i)$$
$$\widehat{f}_2(x) = f(x_j)$$
$$\widehat{f}_3(x) = f(x_m)$$

With $\widehat{f}_1(x)$ all the errors are negative and have the largest magnitude at $x = x_j$; and with $\widehat{f}_2(x)$, all the errors are positive and have the largest magnitude at $x = x_i$. That the errors in either case are of the same sign means that in repeated computations (say, at random points) over the

---

[18]And used well before that in software approximations, e.g. in the Ferranti Mercury, a machine of the 1950s.

interval, we should expect an accumulation of errors, which would not be the case if there were alternations in sign. On the other hand, with $\widehat{f}_3(x)$, the errors are of different signs on either side of x_m, and the largest magnitude of error occurs at either end of the interval and is only half the largest magnitude in the other two cases.

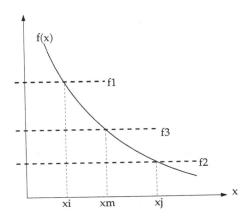

Figure 7.17: Constants approximation on a segment

In general, for a function $f(x)$ and approximation $\widehat{f}(x)$, we should like the graph of the the error function

$$\varepsilon(x) = f(x) - \widehat{f}(x) \tag{7.30}$$

to be anti-symmetrical about the x axis and, in the ideal case, symmetrical about the midpoint[19] of the interval of evaluation, $[x_i, x_j]$. We can achieve this, or come close to it, if we make equal the errors at the extremes—the main objective—by imposing the condition

$$|\varepsilon(x_i)| = |\varepsilon(\alpha)| = |\varepsilon(x_j)| \tag{7.31}$$

where α is the point at which $\varepsilon(x)$ has an extremum in the interval $[x_i, x_j]$. (The equation is for absolute error, but one may equally well use relative error instead.)

---

[19]This is a nice, easy choice. Depending on the function, a different point might be better.

For an example, consider the function $f(x) \triangleq 1/x$ on the interval $[x_i, x_j]$ with

$$\widehat{f}(x) = c_0 + c_1 x \tag{7.32}$$

and suppose that $\widehat{f}(x)$ is to be obtained by simple interpolation, i.e. $f(x_i) = \widehat{f}(x_i)$ and $f(x_j) = \widehat{f}(x_j)$. Then substitution into Equation 7.31 gives

$$1/x_i = c_0 + c_1 x_i$$
$$1/x_j = c_0 + c_1 x_j$$

the solution of which is

$$\widehat{f}(x) = \left(\frac{1}{x_i} + \frac{1}{x_j} \right) - \frac{1}{x_i x_j} x$$

A sixteen-segment example, on the interval $[1/2, 1)$, together with the corresponding error function, is shown in Figure 7.18.

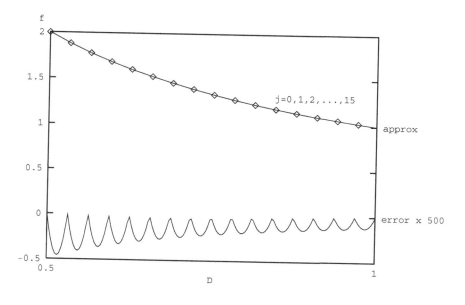

Figure 7.18: Simple segmented linear approximation of $1/x$

Let us now consider an approximation derived on the basis of Equation 7.31, with error measured through the relative-error function, $\varepsilon_r(x)$:

$$\varepsilon_r(x) = \frac{1/x - c_0 - c_1 x}{1/x}$$

$$= 1 - c_0 x - c_1 x^2$$

into which substitution of x_i and x_j, with Equation 7.31, gives

$$1 - c_0 x_i - c_1 x_i^2 = 1 - c_0 x_j - c_1 x_j^2$$

Whence $c_1 = -c_0/(x_i + x_j)$ and

$$\varepsilon_r(x) = 1 - c_0 x + \frac{c_0}{x_i + x_j} x^2$$

$$\varepsilon'(x) = -c_0 + \frac{2c_0}{x_i + x_j} x$$

$$\varepsilon''(x) = \frac{2c_0}{x_i + x_j}$$

From which we conclude that $\varepsilon_r(x)$ has a minimum at $\alpha = (x_i + x_j)/2$. Therefore

$$\varepsilon_r(\alpha) = 1 - c_0 \alpha + \frac{c_0}{x_i + x_j} \alpha^2 \tag{7.33}$$

We also have

$$\varepsilon_r(x_i) = 1 - c_0 x_i + \frac{c_0}{x_i + x_j} x_i^2 \tag{7.34}$$

Taking absolute values of the right-hand sides of Equations 7.33 and 7.34 and applying Equation 7.31, straightforward algebraic manipulations yield

$$c_0 = \frac{4\alpha}{\alpha^2 + x_i x_j}$$

$$c_1 = \frac{2}{\alpha^2 + x_i x_j}$$

Figure 7.19 shows the results for sixteen segments. Compared with Figure 7.18, the maximum magnitude of error has been halved, and the errors have some alternation in sign.

The basic idea is easily applied to other functions, the main difference being in the quantity of algebraic grind required. So, for example, for $f(x) = \sqrt{x}$ and $\widehat{f}(x) = c_0 + c_1 x$, the local extremum is a maximum, at

$$\alpha = \sqrt{x_i x_j}$$

and

$$c_0 = \frac{2\alpha}{2\sqrt{\alpha} + \sqrt{x_i} + \sqrt{x_j}}$$

$$c_1 = \frac{2}{2\sqrt{\alpha} + \sqrt{x_i} + \sqrt{x_j}}$$

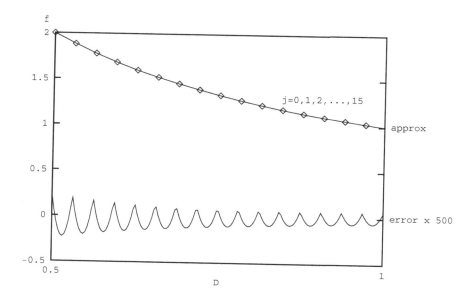

Figure 7.19: Improved segmented linear approximation of $1/x$

And for $f(x) = e^x$ and $\widehat{f}(x) = c_0 + c_1 x$, the local extremum is a minimum, at

$$\alpha = 1 + \frac{x_j e^{x_i} - x_i e^{x_j}}{e^i - e^{x_j}}$$

and

$$c_0 = \frac{2e^\alpha (1 - \alpha)\left(-e^{x_i} + e^{x_j}\right)}{-e^{x_i} + e^{x_j} - e^\alpha (x_i - x_j)}$$

$$c_1 = \frac{2e^\alpha \left(-e^{x_i} + e^{x_j}\right)}{-e^{x_i} + e^{x_j} - e^\alpha (x_i - x_j)}$$

Chapter 8

Reciprocals, Square Roots, and Inverse Square Roots

The first section of this chapter is a short one on the use of polynomials to compute all three functions; we have separated this from the other two sections because of the "unified approach" of the particular work on which the section is based [9]. The second section covers the computation of reciprocals. And the third covers the computation of square roots and their inverses; square roots are especially important given their place in the IEEE standard on floating-point arithmetic. Most of the algorithms discussed in the latter two sections are based on one or another form of normalization. Other algorithms can be obtained directly or indirectly on the basis of the discussions of Chapters 6 and 7; for example, the bipartite-table method (Section 7.1) was invented specifically for reciprocals [1].

Without loss of generality, and unless otherwise specified, we shall assume that the argument for the reciprocal function is in the range $[1/2, 1)$ and that the argument for the square root function is in the range $[1/4, 1)$.

As regards rounding, the issues here are as for division.[1] In general, the "subtractive" algorithms will leave a "remainder" that can be used to provide information that is critcical to the rounding. So, to obtain a final result of n bits, the preliminary result to be rounded does not have to be computed to a much higher precision than the final result; $n + 3$ bits will be sufficient for such algorithms. On the other hand, "multiplicative" algorithms do not produce a "remainder", r, and so more bits of the preliminary results are required—at least $2n + 1$ bits for reciprocal, $2n + 3$ bits for square root, and $3n + 2$ for inverse square root [20, 21, 26]. There is, however, the alternative of computing a "remainder", by performing an

---

[1] We assume that the reader is familiar with the rounding modes in the IEEE standard on floating-point arithmetic and how they can be implemented for the basic arithmetic operations. If not, a good reference is [17].

inverse operation and then using that: if $\widehat{y}$ is the computed approximation to $\sqrt{x}$, then compute $r = x - \widehat{y} \times \widehat{y}$.

8.1   Polynomial approximations

In this chapter we have not included much on the direct use of polynomials, but one can readily devise a variety of such approximations, starting with the standard expressions of Chapter 6. Consider, for example, the reciprocal function. If $1/2 \le x < 1$, then we may evaluate $1/x$ by finding a u such that $0 < u \le 1/2$ and then applying the Taylor series:

$$\frac{1}{x} = \frac{1}{1-u} = 1 + u + u^2 + u^3 + \cdots$$

We shall see below (Sections 8.2 and 8.3) that the series can be the basis of an algorithm with very fast convergence.

For another example, consider the square root function, and let Y_0 be an approximation to $\sqrt{x}$, obtained from, say, a lookup table. Then, if Y_0 is sufficiently close to $\sqrt{x}$, the Taylor series of Chapter 6 may be used carry out the evaluation as

$$\sqrt{x} = \frac{Y_0}{\sqrt{1-u}} \qquad\qquad u = 1 - Y_0^2/x$$

$$= Y_0 \left(1 + \frac{u}{2} + \frac{3u^2}{8} + \frac{5u^3}{16} + \cdots \right)$$

or

$$\sqrt{x} = Y_0\sqrt{1+u} \qquad\qquad u = x/Y_0^2 - 1$$

$$= Y_0 \left(1 + \frac{u}{2} - \frac{u^2}{8} + \frac{u^3}{16} - \frac{5u^4}{128} \cdots \right)$$

or

$$\sqrt{x} = \frac{1}{Y_0}\sqrt{1-u} \qquad\qquad u = 1 - xY_0^2$$

$$= \frac{1}{Y_0} \left(1 + \frac{u}{2} + \frac{3u^2}{8} + \frac{5u^3}{16} + \cdots \right)$$

These examples are given as "interesting side bits", but they are actually not too shabby in practice. As an example, a hardware implementation based on the last of these is described in [19].

Numerous variations are possible in the hardware use of polynomials, including non-Taylor-series ones; the latter includes Chebyshev polynomials, of which [22] is a good example. We shall not give a comprehensive discussion. Instead, the remainder of this section is devoted to a sufficiently exemplary use of Taylor series, in a manner that treats uniformly all three functions of interest here. As indicated in Chapter 6, Taylor series can be useful if applied in a limited way and with sufficient care, a typical arrangement being the use of short series in combination with some form of table lookup.

There are at least two straightforward ways in which to improve the performance of an otherwise-straightforward Taylor-series implementation. One, at the algorithm level, is to limit the arguments to a small area near the point of expansion;[2] the other, at the implementation level, is to aim for fast, low-cost arithmetic operations. The design of [9] exemplifies this combination: the first aspect is in the use of Taylor series with arguments near the origin, and the second is in the use of small multipliers.

The general form of a Taylor expansion for a function f is

$$f(x) = c_0 + c_1 x + c_2 x^2 + c_3 x^3 + \cdots \tag{8.1}$$

This can be used fruitfully as follows. Obtain a sufficiently small x from the original argument, $\widetilde{x}$, for which evaluation is sought; use a such a series to compute $f(x)$; and then obtain $f(\widetilde{x})$ from $f(x)$. The following discussions show this procedure as applied in [9].

Assume that x has been obtained as indicated above—the actual details are given below—and that it is fractional. To compute $f(x)$ using small multipliers, the bits that represent the n-bit argument are split into four[3] k-bit pieces, so $k = n/4$. If the values represented by those pieces are x_1, x_2, x_3, and x_4, then $|x_i| \le 2^k - 1$ and

$$x = x_1 2^{-k} + x_2 2^{-2k} + x_3 3^{-3k} + x_4 4^{-4k}$$

$$= x_1 \lambda + x_2 \lambda^2 + x_3 \lambda^3 + x_4 \lambda^4 \qquad \lambda = 2^{-k} \tag{8.2}$$

The value of x is determined so that $|x| < 2^{-k}$, which means $x_1 = 0$. With this, substitution from Equation 8.2 into Equation 8.1 gives

---

[2]Chapter 6 shows that such series are problematic as one moves farther away from that point.

[3]This could be any number, and four is just a convenient design compromise.

$$f(x) = c_0 + c_1 \left(x_2\lambda^2 + x_3\lambda^3 + x_4\lambda^4\right) + c_2 \left(x_2\lambda^2 + x_3\lambda^3 + x_4\lambda^4\right)^2$$

$$+ c_2 \left(x_2\lambda^2 + x_3\lambda^3 + x_4\lambda^4\right)^3 c_4 \left(x_2\lambda^2 + x_3\lambda^3 + x_4\lambda^4\right)^4$$

With $k = n/4$ and a result precision of n bits, a term of value less than or equal to 2^{-4k} is effectively zero, and such terms may be dropped, to get

$$f(x) \approx c_0 + c_1 x + c_2 x_2^2\lambda^4 + 2c_2 x_2 x_3\lambda^5 + c_3 x_2^3\lambda^6 \qquad (8.3)$$

To use this expression for the evaluation of reciprocals, square roots, and inverse square roots, the c_is are determined by equating the expression with each of the appropriate standard Taylor series[4]:

$$\frac{1}{1+x} = 1 - x + x^2 - x^3 + x^4 - \cdots$$

$$\sqrt{1+x} = 1 + \frac{1}{2}x - \frac{1}{8}x^2 + \frac{1}{16}x^3 - \frac{5}{128}x^4 + \cdots$$

$$\frac{1}{\sqrt{1+x}} = 1 - \frac{1}{2}x + \frac{3}{8}x^2 - \frac{5}{16}x^3 + \frac{35}{128}x^4 - \cdots$$

The justification for the choice of these particular series—i.e. expansions in terms of $1 + x$—among the various possibilities, will become apparent below, in how x is obtained from an original argument that is in a larger range.

The application of Equations 8.2 and 8.3 then gives

$$\frac{1}{1-x} \approx 1 - x_2\lambda^2 - x_3\lambda^3 + \left(-x_4 + x_2^2\right)\lambda^4 + 2x_2 x_3\lambda^5 - x_2^3\lambda^6$$

$$= 1 - x + x_2^2\lambda^4 + 2x_2 x_3\lambda^5 - x_2^3\lambda^6$$

$$\sqrt{1+x} = 1 + \frac{1}{2}x - \frac{1}{8}x_2^2\lambda^4 - \frac{1}{4}x_2 x_3\lambda^5 + \frac{1}{16}x_2^3\lambda^6$$

$$\frac{1}{\sqrt{1+x}} = 1 - \frac{1}{2}x + \frac{3}{8}x_2^2\lambda^4 - \frac{3}{4}x_2 x_3\lambda^5 - \frac{5}{16}x_2^3\lambda^6$$

---

[4] See Table 6.2.

It is shown in [9] that the approximation errors do not exceed 8.31×2^{-4k} for the reciprocal, 0.94×2^{-4k} for the square root, and 2.93×2^{-4k} for the inverse square root.

The original argument, $\widetilde{x}$, is assumed to be a normalized significand in the IEEE standard on floating-point arithmetic [40], i.e. in the range $[1, 2)$. From this, x is obtained such that $|x| < 2^{-k}$ and

$$x = r\widetilde{x} - 1$$

where r is a tabulated $(k + 1)$-bit, rounded-down approximation of $1/y$. Then

$$r\widetilde{x} = 1 + x$$

(The form of $r\widetilde{x}$ explains the choice of Taylor series that are in terms of $1 + x$.) The value of $\widehat{r}$ is such that $1 - 2^{-k} < r\widetilde{x} < 1 + 2^{-k}$.

So for the reciprocal we have

$$\frac{1}{r\widetilde{x}} = \frac{1}{1 + x}$$

$$\frac{1}{\widetilde{x}} = r\frac{1}{1 + x}$$

For the square root we have

$$\sqrt{r\widetilde{x}} = \sqrt{1 + x}$$

$$\sqrt{\widetilde{x}} = \frac{1}{r}\sqrt{1 + x}$$

And for the inverse square root

$$\frac{1}{\sqrt{r\widetilde{x}}} = \frac{1}{\sqrt{1 + x}}$$

$$\frac{1}{\sqrt{\widetilde{x}}} = r\frac{1}{\sqrt{1 + x}}$$

In summary, given $\widetilde{x}$, the process of computing $f(\widetilde{x})$ consists of three steps that correspond to standard range reduction (Section 1.2):

(1) Reduction: obtain x from the argument $\widetilde{x}$.
(2) Evaluation: use the series for the function at hand to compute an approximation to $f(x)$.
(3) Postprocessing: multiply the result from (2) with the appropriate factor to obtain $f(\widetilde{x})$.

There are some errors from the postprocessing, and if these are added to the approximation errors, the total errors do not exceed 9.31×2^{-4k} for the reciprocal, 2.39×2^{-4k} for the square root, and 3.68×2^{-4k} for the inverse square root. The values for k are seven for single-precison operands for all three operations, fourteen for double-precision square roots and inverse square roots, and fifteen for double-precision reciprocals.

For the implementation, it is proposed that the arithmetic be in redundant signed-digit representation. Carry–save representation is an alternative possibility, but a brief consideration of possible hardware architectures for high-performance implementations will reveal several difficulties in accommodating the subtractions if that representation is used; this may be considered a problematic aspect of the method.

8.2   Reciprocals

The first algorithm we consider is based on the well-known Newton–Raphson root-finding procedure; as we shall see, the algorithm can also be reformulated into a normalization algorithm. The second algorithm is a "proper" normalization algorithm, i.e. one that is explicitly derived as such.

8.2.1   *Newton–Raphson method*

The Newton–Raphson formula is a standard method for approximating the root of a real non-linear function f. Suppose Y_i is an approximation to the root of f and that we wish to obtain a better approximation, $Y_{i+i} \stackrel{\triangle}{=} Y_i + h$. Taking the Taylor-series expansion about Y_i, i.e.

$$f(Y_i + h) = f(Y_i) + hf^{'}(Y_i) + \frac{h^2}{2!} f^{''}(Y_i) + \cdots$$

truncating at the first term, and setting to 0

$$f(X_i) + hf^{'}(Y_i) = 0$$

whence

$$h = -\frac{f(Y_i)}{f'(Y_i)}$$

and the Newton–Raphson root-finding formula:

$$Y_{i+1} = Y_i - \frac{f(Y_i)}{f'(Y_i)} \tag{8.4}$$

8.2.1.1 *Algorithm*

To apply Equation 8.4 to the computation of $1/x$, we take $f(Y) = x - 1/Y$. Then, $f'(Y) = 1/Y^2$, at the root of f we have $Y = 1/x$, and the recurrence is

$$Y_{i+1} = Y_i - \frac{x - 1/Y_i}{1/Y_i^2}$$

$$= 2Y_i - xY_i^2$$

$$= Y_i(2 - xY_i) \tag{8.5}$$

$$x = 0.65 \qquad 1/x = 1.5384615\cdots$$

i	xY_i	Y_i
0	0.97500000000	1.50000000000
1	0.99937500000	1.53750000000
2	0.99999960938	1.53846093750
3	1.00000000000	1.53846153846

(a) $Y_0 = 1.5$

i	xY_i	Y_i
0	1.95000000000	3.00000000000
1	0.09750000000	0.15000000000
2	0.18549375000	0.28537500000
3	0.33657956871	0.51781472109
4	0.55987333135	0.86134358669
5	0.80628851554	1.24044387006
6	0.96247586079	1.48073209352
7	0.99859193898	1.53629529073
8	0.99999801736	1.53845848825
9	1.00000000000	1.53846153846

(b) $Y_0 = 3.0$

Table 8.1: Newton–Raphson computations of $1/x$

The values of Y_i will, under the right conditions (given below), converge to $1/x$. Two example computations are given in Table 8.1. The example in (a) shows very rapid convergence. We shall show below that the convergence is *quadratic*; that is, if X_i is correct to k digits, then X_{i+1} will be correct to about $2k$ digits. On the other hand, the convergence in (b) is effectively linear, if averaged over all the iterations. The difference between (a) and (b) is the starting point, Y_0, and how close it is to $1/x$; indeed, it can be seen that the convergence in (b) becomes quite rapid when Y_i is close enough, which highlights the importance of starting with a sufficiently good approximation, Y_0. The reader will also observe that the rapid convergence appears to arise from the fact that $2 - xY_i$ converges rapidly to one; so such convergence may be used as a stopping criterion in the iterating.

If, for Equation 8.5, Y_0 is chosen appropriately (as discussed below), then, for the argument range of interest, xY_i will be fractional[5] which means that in binary $2 - xY_i$ is just the two's complement of Y_i. Forming that complement requires a proper addition (subtraction), but in practice that operation may be replaced with the faster ones' complement approximation, with only a small amount of additional error. This small error need not cause much concern because the algorithm is *self-correcting*; that is, an error at any given step gets "cancelled" out in the much more accurate values that are computed in subsequent steps.[6] This is shown in Section 8.2.1.2, on convergence and errors.

Equation 8.5 may be rewritten into, and implemented as

$$Y_{i+1} = Y_i + Y_i(1 - xY_i) \tag{8.6}$$

Equations 8.5 and 8.6 are mathematically equivalent but not computationally equivalent[7] [2]. If Y_i approximates $1/x$ to $n/2$ bits, then $Y_i(1-xY_i)$ need be computed to only $n/2$ bits to get an n-bit Y_{i+1}. On the other hand, $Y_i(2-xY_i)$ must be computed to n bits. But there is no such thing as a free lunch: Equation 8.6 implies a reduction in costs (hardware and operational delay) in the multiplications, but there is the cost of the extra addition. Ultimately, which of the two forms is better will depend on the precise details of the implementations.

We conclude this introduction with a brief discussion of an aspect that we shall return to: the relationship between the Newton–Raphson method and multiplicative normalization. Equation 8.5 can be reformulated as a normalization algorithm, as follows. Rewrite the equation into two recur-

---

[5]Strictly, it will not exceed one. See Table 8.1.

[6]See also the remarks in Section 1.1.3.

[7]They are computationally equivalent only if all computations are carried out exactly.

rences:

$$c_{i+1} = 2 - xY_i \tag{8.7}$$
$$Y_{i+1} = c_{i+1}Y_i \tag{8.8}$$

Let $c_0 = Y_0$, and unwind the recurrences:

$$c_{i+1} = 2 - x \prod_{k=0}^{i} c_k$$

$$Y_{i+1} = \prod_{k=0}^{i} c_k$$

Now, define

$$X_i = x \prod_{k=0}^{i} c_k$$

Then

$$c_{i+1} = 2 - X_i \tag{8.9}$$
$$X_{i+1} = c_{i+1}X_i \tag{8.10}$$
$$Y_{i+1} = c_{i+1}Y_i \tag{8.11}$$

Evidently, $Y_i \to 1/x$ as $c_i \to 1$ and $X_i \to 1$; so we have the general form of a multiplicative-normalization algorithm.

8.2.1.2 *Convergence and errors*

The following analysis is general, in that it does not specify a range for the argument, x, but the reader should recall the range restriction given at the start of the chapter, i.e. $1/2 \leq x < 1$, and consider its implications.

To determine the rate of convergence, we ignore generated errors and consider just the propagation of error from one iteration to the next of Equation 8.5.

Let ε_i denote the absolute error at iteration i. Then

$$\varepsilon_{i+1} = \frac{1}{x} - Y_{i+1}$$

$$= \frac{1}{x} - (2Y_i - xY_i^2)$$

$$= x\left(\frac{1}{x^2} - \frac{2Y_i}{x} + Y_i^2\right)$$

$$= x\left(\frac{1}{x} - Y_i\right)^2$$

$$= x\varepsilon_i^2 \qquad (8.12)$$

which shows quadratic convergence. So provided $|\varepsilon_0| < 1$, the absolute error at step $i+1$ is approximately the square root of the error at step i. Therefore, if Y_0 is correct to k bits, then approximately $\lceil \log_2 n/k \rceil$ iterations are required to obtain an n-bit reciprocal.

To find bounds for Y_0 that will ensure convergence, we unwind Equation 8.12:

$$\varepsilon_i = x^{2^{i-1}} \varepsilon_0^{2^i}$$

$$= x^{2^{i-1}} \left(\frac{1}{x} - Y_0\right)^{2^i}$$

$$= \frac{1}{x}(1 - xY_0)^{2^i}$$

For convergence, we want $\varepsilon_i \to 0$ as $i \to 0$, which will be the case if $|1 - xY_0| < 1$; that is, if $0 < xY_0 < 2$. As indicated above, we may want to ensure that xY_i is fractional, in which case we should impose a more restrictive condition: $0 < xY_0 < 1$.

Let us now consider the effect of generated error. If the magnitude of the generated error at each step is bounded by b_{gen}, then for the error at step $i+1$, we have (by extending Equation 8.12)

$$|\varepsilon_{i+1}| = |x\varepsilon_i^2| + b_{gen} \qquad (8.13)$$

and for convergence we require $|\varepsilon_{i+1}| < |\varepsilon_i|$. If we assume that computations are stopped as soon as this condition no longer holds, i.e. when $|\varepsilon_{i+1}| = |\varepsilon_i|$, then a bound on the magnitude of error after many iterations is obtained by solving that equation, which corresponds to the quadratic equation

$$|x||\varepsilon_i^2| - |\varepsilon_i| + b_{gen} = 0$$

the solution of which is

$$|\varepsilon_i| = \frac{1 - \sqrt{1 - 4|x|b_{gen}}}{2|x|}$$

If $4|x|b_{gen}$ is sufficiently small, then we may express this in terms of a convergent Taylor series:

$$\frac{1}{2|x|} \left\{ 1 - \left[1 - 2\left(|x|b_{gen}\right) + 2\left(|x|b_{gen}\right)^2 - 4\left(|x|b_{gen}\right)^3 + \cdots \right] \right\}$$

which is approximately b_{gen}. (The justification for the Taylor series is given in the next paragraph.)

Y_{i+1} is computed as $Y_i(2 - xY_i)$, and it is reasonable to assume that the "inner" multiplication is carried out exactly but that the result of the outer one is reduced to some precision, of m bits, before being used as input to the next iteration. We may also reasonably assume that the two's complement operation generates no error.[8]

From Section 1.1, the bound on the generated error depends on the rounding method used, but we may take the worst case; assuming radix-2 computation, $b_{gen} \approx 2^{-m}$. For practical values, m will be large enough to ensure that, with the bounds on $|x|$, it is the case that $4|x|b_{gen}$ is sufficiently small to justify the Taylor-series approximation above. So the approximate error after i iterations is

$$\varepsilon_i = \varepsilon_0^{2^i} + 2^{-m}$$

It will be observed from Equation 8.13 that the generated error from one iteration goes into the next iteration as propagated error, and in the process that generated error is diminished quadratically. In other words, the propagation of error is such that it "cancels" the generation of error.[9] Therefore, the effect of generated error can be overcome by (a) determining the nominal number of iterations required to achieve a desired level of accuracy—that is, by assuming no generated error—and then running the

---

[8] If the two's complement is replaced with the ones' complement, as indicated above, then the error would have to be taken into account. Because of the rapid convergence, such error is not problematic.

[9] See also the earlier remark on *self-correction*.

algorithm with one or two more iterations; or (b) by performing the arithmetic with a greater precision[10] than is nominally required for the result, i.e. for a result of n bits, have $m > n$; or (c) doing both.

In the preceding, we have assumed the number of iterations is "sufficiently large", and, therefore, that some value is "sufficiently small". If the number of iterations is small—say, three or four—then the preceding analysis is somewhat "rough-and-ready"; it should, and can, be replaced with a more precise one. In such a case, one should simply take a "muscular" approach and grind through the computation graph. Suppose, for example, that we have three iterations. Let $\varepsilon_{i,gen}$ and $\varepsilon_{i,prop}$ denote the generated and propagated absolute errors out of iteration i. The error in Y_0 is ε_0, and the error from each iteration is

$$\varepsilon_i = \varepsilon_{i,gen} + \varepsilon_{i,prop}$$

The error out of the first iteration is

$$\varepsilon_1 = x\varepsilon_0^2 + \varepsilon_{1,gen}$$

This goes into the second iteration as propagated error, so

$$\varepsilon_2 = x\left(x\varepsilon_0^2 + \varepsilon_{1,gen}\right)^2 + \varepsilon_{2,gen}$$

and for the third iteration

$$\varepsilon_3 = x\left[x\left(x\varepsilon_0^2 + \varepsilon_{1,gen}\right)^2 + \varepsilon_{2,gen}\right]^2 + \varepsilon_{3,gen}$$

The error analysis is then completed on the basis of bounds on the magnitudes of x, ε_0, and $\varepsilon_{i,gen}$. An example of this type of more precise analysis will be found in [3].

8.2.1.3 *Starting value, Y_0*

The number of iterations required to obtain a result of given accuracy and precision will depend on how close the starting value, Y_0, is to the final result sought; a comparison of the two examples of Table 8.1 shows this. Therefore, the value should be an approximation, however crude, to $1/x$; so it is, in general, a function of x. For a hardware implementation, speed and cost are the main issues in choosing a particular method to produce starting values.

The simplest possible approximation is to assume that $Y_0(x)$ is constant; for example, for $x \in [1/2, 1)$, take $Y_0(x) = 3/2$, i.e. halfway between $f(1/2) = 2$ and $f(1) = 1$. This is a simple straight line on the interval of

---

[10]This will already be the case, to some extent, prior to rounding.

evaluation and is as simple and as fast as one can get. But, for anything other than very-low-precision results, it is likely to be inadequate, given the number of iterations that are likely to be required. Nevertheless, such approximations have been used in a few machines.

A better single, straight line is one that fits the ends of the interval. The general form of such a function is $Y_0(x) = c_0 + c_1 x$, which, for the endpoints $[1/2, 1)$ and $(1, 2]$, gives $Y_0(x) = 3 - 2x$. This is an improvement on $Y_0(x) = 3/2$, but it is nonetheless still a crude approximation; however, the implementation cost is low: a single shift (to compute $2x$) and an addition (i.e. subtraction). A slightly better linear approximation[11] is $Y_0(x) = 4(\sqrt{3} - 1) - 2x$, which was implemented in the Ferranti Mercury computer, a machine of the early 1950s. The term $4(\sqrt{3} - 1)$ is a constant that can be precomputed and stored; so the implementation cost is still an addition and a shift.

There are numerous other possibilities that have been used over the years, but the costs of hardware are now such that crude methods need not be used, unless cost is absolutely critical. The trend for some time now has been to use reasonably accurate table lookup methods and polynomial approximations, such as those of Chapter 7. In such cases, the approximation does not yield the final result; therefore, the requirements are less stringent than for the general case, in which the table lookup or polynomial approximation is used to compute a final result. We may therefore use segmented approximation, with a small number of segments, or the bipartite-table and related methods; indeed, the bipartite-table method was invented to provide approximations in just such a case. If the per-segment approximation function is a constant function, then $Y_0(x)$ is obtained simply by using a few bits of x to address a lookup table of approximation values. For a linear approximation, fewer segments will be required than with constant approximation; and even fewer will be required for a quadratic approximation.

Very good approximations are necessary for high-precision and fast computations. An "extreme" example will be found in [5], in which a segmented second-degree minimax polynomial is used to obtain an initial approximation of fairly high accuracy—up to half the required final precison, which means that just one or two iterations are required to obtain the final result.

Pure combinational logic can also be used to obtain approximations.

---

[11]The approximation is obtained as follows: Take a linear approximation, $c_0 + c_1 D$ to $1/D$, that cuts the $1/D$ at two points in $[1/2, 1)$. The value of c_1 will be approximately two; make it two for easy computation. Then apply the error-balancing technique of Section 7.3.6.2 to relative error.

Partial product arrays (PPAs), similar to those used in ordinary multiplication can be devised to obtain good approximations at low cost. For example, [6] shows that 16-bit accuracy in the initial approximation can be achieved with a logic cost of about 1000 gates and a time cost of about one multiplication.

Additional, detailed discussions on various methods for obtaining Y_0 will be found in [27, 28].

8.2.2   *Goldschmidt normalization*

Goldschmidt's algorithm, which is a normalization algorithm, is mathematically equivalent to the Newton–Raphson algorithm; but we shall see that there are important computational differences. The basic normalization is that described at the start of Section 5.2 and consists of the recurrences

$$X_{i+1} = c_i X_i \qquad X_0 = x \qquad (8.14)$$
$$Y_{i+1} = c_i Y_i \qquad Y_0 = 1 \qquad (8.15)$$

where $X_i \to 1$ and $Y_i \to 1/x$, but the multipliers, c_i, are different from those of Section 5.2. The normalizing multipliers here are determined as follows.

If $1/2 \le x < 1$, then it may be expressed as $1 - u$, where $0 < u \le 1/2$. Now, consider the Maclaurin-series expansion for $1/x = 1/(1 - u)$:

$$\frac{1}{1-u} = 1 + u + u^2 + u^3 + \cdots + u^k + \cdots$$

Repeatedly factoring, we get

$$\frac{1}{1-u} \approx 1 \times (1+u)(1+u^2)(1+u^4)(1+u^8) \cdots (1+u^{2^i}) \qquad (8.16)$$

the first term of which is $Y_0 \stackrel{\triangle}{=} 1$, and

$$(1-u)(1+u)(1+u^2)(1+u^4)(1+u^8) \cdots (1+u^{2^i}) \approx 1 \qquad (8.17)$$

where the first term is $X_0 \stackrel{\triangle}{=} x$.

Equation 8.16 corresponds to Equation 8.15, and Equation 8.17 corresponds to Equation 8.14; so we may take the normalizing multipliers to be

$$c_i = 1 + u^{2^i}$$

With these values, unwinding Equation 8.14 yields

$$X_i = 1 - u^{2^i}$$

whence

$$c_i = 2 - X_i \tag{8.18}$$

which in binary is just the two's complement of X_i, since X_i is fractional. An example computation with these choices of is given in Table 8.2.

$$x = 0.65 \qquad 1/x = 1.5384615\cdots$$

i	X_i	c_i	Y_i
0	0.65000000000	1.35000000000	1.00000000000
1	0.87750000000	1.12250000000	1.35000000000
2	0.98499375000	1.01500625000	1.51537500000
3	0.99977481246	1.00022518754	1.53811509609
4	0.99999994929	1.00000005071	1.53846146045
5	1.00000000000	1.00000000000	1.53846153846

Table 8.2: Goldschmidt computation of $1/x$

We now look the rate of convergence. Consider a few iterations of Equations 8.14, and recall that the normalization is $X_i \to 1$. For the first iteration:

$$c_0 = 1 + u$$
$$X_1 = (1 - u)(1 + u)$$
$$= 1 - u^2$$

which has the binary representation

$$0 \cdot \overbrace{11}^{2 \text{ 1s}} * * \cdots * \qquad \text{since } X_1 \ge 3/4$$

For the second iteration:

$$c_1 = 1 + u^2$$
$$X_2 = (1 - u^2)(1 + u^2)$$
$$= 1 - u^4$$

which has the binary representation

$$0 \cdot \overbrace{1111}^{4 \text{ 1s}} * * \cdots * \qquad \text{since } X_2 \ge 15/16$$

For the third iteration:

$$c_2 = 1 + u^4$$
$$X_3 = (1 - u^4)(1 + u^4)$$
$$= 1 - u^8$$

which has the binary representation

$$0 \cdot \overbrace{11111111}^{8 \ 1s} * * \cdots * \qquad \text{since } X_3 \geq 255/256$$

And so on, and so forth.

From the per-iteration doubling of the number of 1s as X_i converges to one, we may conclude that the convergence is quadratic. That is indeed the case, and it is confimed in the fact, which we next show, that the Goldschmidt algorithm is, mathematically, just a reformulation of the Newton–Raphson algorithm of Equation 8.5.

From Equations 8.14 and 8.15

$$X_i = x \prod_{k=0}^{i-1} c_k$$

$$Y_i = \prod_{k=0}^{i-1} c_k$$

so

$$X_i = xY_i$$

and combining this with Equations 8.15 and 8.18

$$Y_{i+1} = c_i Y_i$$
$$= (2 - X_i)Y_i$$
$$= Y_i(2 - xY_i)$$

which is just Equation 8.5.

We can also arrive at the same conclusion by unwinding Equation 8.5:

$$Y_1 = Y_0 \left[1 + (1 - xY_0) \right]$$

$$Y_2 = Y_0 \left[1 + (1 - xY_0) \right] \left[1 + (1 - xY_0)^2 \right]$$

$$\vdots$$

$$Y_{i+1} = Y_0 \left[1 + (1 - xY_0) \right] \left[1 + (1 - xY_0)^2 \right] \cdots \left[1 + (1 - xY_0)^{2^i} \right]$$

Setting $1 - xY_0 = u$ and $Y_0 = 1$, we get

$$Y_{i+1} = (1 + u)(1 + u^2)(1 + u^4)(1 + u^8) \cdots (1 + u^{2^i})$$

which is just Equation 8.16.

Notwithstanding the mathematical equivalence we have just shown between the Newton–Raphson procedure and the Goldschmidt algorithm, there are some noteworthy computational differences.[12]

First, if we view the latter as just an instance of the former, then the difference is that (with the latter) we have a crude approximation to $1/x$, i.e. $Y_0(x) = 1$. So, even with its quadratic convergence, we should expect that more iterations will be required to reach a specified level of accuracy.

Second, and of substantial significance for performance, is that the two multiplications of Equations 8.14 and 8.15 can be carried out in parallel, whereas those of Equation 8.5 must be carried out sequentially. The former does not necessarily require two multipliers: the two multiplications can proceed concurrently in a single pipelined multiplier.

Third, the Newton–Raphson process is *self-correcting*; that is, an error in one iteration need not cause concern since it is "cancelled" in subsequent iterations that greatly increase the number of correct bits. On the other hand, the Goldschmidt is not self-correcting; any errors generated in the Y_i computations will not be cancelled out in propagation. The practical implication of this is that the computations in the Goldschmidt iterations must be carried with a few extra bits of precision and an increasing number of bits retained from each iteration; therefore, the operands get wider as the iterations proceed. We shall see, however, that not all the multiplications need be in full precision [16].

To facilitate a "visual" comparison, let us rewrite the Newton–Raphson Equation 8.5 into

$$X_i = xY_i$$
$$Y_{i+1} = Y_i(2 - X_i)$$

The Goldschmidt recurrences are

$$X_{i+1} = X_i(2 - X_i)$$
$$Y_{i+1} = Y_i(2 - X_i)$$

and in both pairs of recurrences $X_i \to 1$. But the fact that in the first pair both recurrences depend on each other has a significant, positive effect on the propagation of errors.

---

[12]They would be computationally equivalent if all arithmetic operations were exact.

We have determined above that the Newton–Raphson process converges quadratically; because of the dependence between X_i and Y_i, that convergence is tied directly to the convergence in Y_i. We may express this as

$$\varepsilon_{i+1,\,y} = \varepsilon_{i,\,y}^2 + \varepsilon_{gen,y}$$

in which $\varepsilon_{gen,\,y}$ includes the error generated in all the arithmetic operations of one iteration.

On the other hand, in the Goldschmidt case, the quadratic convergence of Y_i values may be viewed as a "side-effect" of the quadratic convergence in X_i. The latter aspect is easily seen: $X_i \to 1$, and for the absolute error, we have

$$\begin{aligned} \varepsilon_{i+1} &= 1 - X_{i+1} \\ &= 1 - (2 - X_i)X_i \\ &= (1 - X_i)^2 \\ &= \varepsilon_i^2 \end{aligned}$$

Including the generated error, denoted by $\widetilde{\varepsilon}_{i,\,x}$, we end up with an error equation that is similar to that for the Newton–Raphson algorithm:

$$\varepsilon_{i+1,\,x} = \varepsilon_{i,\,x}^2 + \widetilde{\varepsilon}_{i,\,x}$$

The generated error becomes quadratically smaller in subsequent iterations as it is propagated out.

The Y_i recurrence is where "complications" arise: the generated errors there are separate from those generated in the X_i-computation and are not quadratically reduced in subsequent iterations; they accumulate. Let us suppose there are no generated errors in the Y_i computations and consider just the propagated error, ε. Then we have

$$\begin{aligned} \varepsilon_{i+1,\,y} &= \frac{1}{x} - Y_{i+1} \\ &= \frac{1}{x} - Y_i(2 - X_i) \\ &= \left(\frac{1}{x} - Y_i\right) - (1 - X_i)Y_i \\ &= \varepsilon_{i,\,y} - \varepsilon_{i,\,x}Y_i \end{aligned}$$

Given that $X_0 = x \in [1/2, 1)$ and $X_i \to 1$, we have $\varepsilon_{i,\,x} \geq 0$. Likewise, $Y_1 = 1$ and $Y_i \to 1/x \in [1, 2)$; so $\varepsilon_{i,\,y} \geq 0$. Therefore $|\varepsilon_{i+1,\,y}| < |\varepsilon_{i,\,y}|$. The computations converge and in a way directly linked to the convergence in X_i.

If we now include generated error, $\widetilde{\varepsilon}_{i,y}$, the error from one Y iteration to another is

$$\varepsilon_{i+1,y} = \varepsilon_{i,y} + \varepsilon_{i,x}Y_i + \widetilde{\varepsilon}_{i,y}$$

The quadratic convergence in X_i means that the second term will diminish rapidly, but the errors generated overall in Y_i will accumulate and not be propagated out (as are such errors in X_i); this is because $|\varepsilon_{i,x}Y_i| \leq |\varepsilon_{i\,y}|$. Clearly, the generated errors must be kept as small as possible. If all the bits produced in each iteration are retained (and not truncated/rounded for the next iteration), then there will be no such errors. Whether or not this is too costly (in hardware or operational time) will depend on the particular implementation; but it is worth noting—and we show it below—that not all iterations require full-precision operations. Various other proposals have been made to deal with this problem; they include changes to the formulation of the algorithm, switching to Newton–Raphson iterations in the last one or two iterations, and so forth.

The computation of Goldschmidt's algorithm can be speeded up by starting the iterations with values that are the (approximate) products of the first few terms of Equation 8.17. (Given the quadratic convergence, the first few iterations are not as significant as the later ones.) This essentially starts the iterations with a better approximation to $1/x$ than $Y_0 = 1$.

For a given x, let $\widehat{Y}$ be the aforementioned approximation, obtained from a lookup table or by other means. Then, from Equations 8.14 and 8.15, the recurrences are now

$$X_0 = x\widehat{Y}$$
$$Y_0 = \widehat{Y}$$
$$X_{i+1} = c_iX_i$$
$$Y_{i+1} = c_iY_i$$

If the table entries are each accurate to k bits, then the number of iterations required to obtain a result that is correct to n bits will now be $\lceil \log_2(n/k) \rceil + 1$ instead of $\lceil \log_2 n \rceil$. This therefore addresses the first difference above with respect to the Newton–Raphson algorithm.

We have so far implicitly assumed that all the multiplications are full-length ones. That need not be so.[13] We next show that if X_i is correct to

---

[13] What follows is similarly applicable to Newton–Raphson computations.

m bits, then for the next multiplication it[14] may be truncated to $2m$ bits and X_{i+1} will still be correct to $2m$ bits.

From the expressions above

$$X_i = 1 - u^{2^{i-1}}$$
$$\stackrel{\triangle}{=} 1 - u_i$$

and

$$c_i = 2 - X_i$$
$$\stackrel{\triangle}{=} 1 + u_i$$

So with full multiplication

$$X_{i+1} = c_i X_i$$
$$= 1 - u_i^2 \tag{8.19}$$

If $\widehat{X}_i$ is obtained by truncating X_i to $2m$ bits and $\widehat{u}_i$ is similarly defined as an approximation to u_i, then

$$2 - \widehat{X}_i = 1 + \widehat{u}_i$$
$$= 1 + u_i + (\widehat{u}_i - u_i)$$
$$\stackrel{\triangle}{=} 1 + u_i + \varepsilon_i$$

with $0 \leq \varepsilon_i < 2^{-2m}$.

Using the truncated value in the next multiplication:

$$X_{i+1} = X_i(1 + \widehat{u}_i)$$
$$= (1 - u_i)(1 + \widehat{u}_i)$$
$$= 1 + (\widehat{u}_i - u_i) - u_i\widehat{u}_i$$
$$= 1 + \varepsilon_i - u_i(u_i + \varepsilon_i)$$
$$= 1 - u_i^2 + \varepsilon_i(1 - u_i) \tag{8.20}$$

Comparing Equations 8.19 and 8.20, we see that for the error in computing X_{i+1} from the truncated values:

$$\varepsilon_i(1 - u_i) < 2^{-2m} \qquad \text{since } 1 - u_i < 1 \text{ and } \varepsilon_i < 2^{-2m}$$

which is within the range required for $2m$-bit accuracy when starting with values of m-bit accuracy. Therefore, the approximation $\widehat{X}_i$ is sufficient.

---

[14]The "sloppy" language is in the interests of brevity: in such cases it is to be understood that it is the *representation of* ... that is truncated.

The practical implications of using the approximate values is that the hardware multipliers used may start out as small, fast ones and then increasingly get larger, by doubling in size with each iteration—an arrangement that would be faster than using full-sized multipliers for all iterations. In the implementation, this can be realized by configuring what is nominally a single multiplier so that parts of it operate as smaller multipliers, as needed.

The first implementation on the preceding basis was that in the IBM 360/91 [4]; a later, very-high-performance one is described in [5].

8.3 Square root and inverse

There exist numerous simple "paper-and-pencil" algorithms for the computation of square roots. As an example, the additive-normalization algorithm given in Section 5.5 is a modification of the well-known *"completing-the-square"* algorithm. Simple paper-and-pencil algorithms are ill–suited to high-speed computation, but they do have the advantage that only a small amount of additional control logic would be required for implementation, if use is made of functional units that would already exist in even the most basic arithmetic unit. Other than versions of the basic additive-normalization algorithm, we shall not consider such algorithms; the reader will find several others in the published literature.

The first two algorithms discussed in this section are Newton–Raphson and Goldschmidt-normalization ones, and we largely proceed as we have done above for the reciprocal function. The two algorithms after that are versions of the normalization algorithms of Chapter 5; the algorithms here use redundant representations, for high-speed arithmetic and high-radix computations.

8.3.1 *Newton–Raphson method and variations*

Several algorithms for the evaluation of square roots can be derived on the basis of the Newton–Raphson formula of Equation 8.4 [8]. The best known of these algorithms starts with the function $f(Y) = Y^2 - x$, which in the Newton–Raphson formula gives

$$Y_{i+1} = Y_i - \frac{Y_i^2 - x}{2Y_i}$$

$$Y_{i+1} = \frac{1}{2}\left(Y_i + \frac{x}{Y_i}\right) \tag{8.21}$$

This formula was known (as *Heron's Method*) to the early Greeks,[15] who derived it by reasoning that if Y_0 is an approximation by defect (excess) to $\sqrt{x}$, then x/Y_0 is an approximation by excess (defect); so the average of the two, i.e. $Y_1 = (Y_0 + x/Y_0)/2$, is a better approximation than either. The general formula is then obtained by iterating.

$$x = 0.53 \qquad Y_0 = 1.0$$

i	x/Y_i	Y_i
0	0.53000000000	1.00000000000
1	0.69281045752	0.76500000000
2	0.72711784617	0.72890522876
3	0.72801044039	0.72801153747
4	0.72801098893	0.72801098893
5	0.72801098893	0.72801098893
		$\sqrt{x}$

Table 8.3: Newton–Raphson computation of $\sqrt{x}$

Table 8.3 shows a computation on the basis of Equation 8.21. It can be seen that convergence is very rapid, and we shall show below that it is *quadratic*; that is, the number of correct digits obtained of $\sqrt{x}$ is doubled at each step.

Equation 8.21 may be rewritten into and implemented as

$$Y_{i+1} = Y_i + \frac{1}{2Y_i}\left(x - Y_i^2\right) \tag{8.22}$$

This has certain useful properties, but whether or not it is practically better than Equation 8.21 depends on the details of the implementation.[16]

An alternative recurrence for the computation of $\sqrt{x}$ can be obtained by starting with $f(Y) = x/Y^2 - 1$. This yields

---

[15]It appears to have been devised by the Babylonians well before that.
[16]See the comments above on Equations 8.5 and 8.6.

$$Y_{i+1} = \frac{Y_i}{2} \left(3 - \frac{Y_i^2}{x} \right) \tag{8.23}$$

which may be rewritten into, and implemented as[17]

$$Y_{i+1} = Y_i + \frac{Y_i}{2} \left(1 - \frac{Y_i^2}{x} \right)$$

Direct implementation of Equations 8.21–8.23 requires addition, shifting, and division; and division can be a slow and costly operation. We next consider variants that avoid division. These variants replace division with multiplication, but it will be apparent that division must be slower than multiplication by a factor of at least two if the division-free algorithms are to be worthwhile replacements for the original. That is usually the case.

Even if reciprocals are not required for themselves, there are division algorithms[18], also based on the Newton–Raphson formula, in which the operation is realized as a multiplication by a reciprocal. In such cases, there will be facilities for quickly computing or approximating reciprocals. Use may be made of these, by replacing Equation 8.21 with

$$Y_{i+1} = Y_i + \frac{r(Y_i)}{2} \left(x - Y_i^2 \right) \tag{8.24}$$

where r is the reciprocal function. This eliminates the explicit division, but convergence will be less than quadratic if $r(Y_i)$ is not of very high accuracy.

We can also obtain a different algorithm more directly by starting with the Newton–Raphson algorithm for the computation of reciprocals. For the reciprocal of Y_i, we have (Equation 8.5)

$$Z_{k+1} = Z_k(2 - Y_i Z_k) \tag{8.25}$$

Combining Equations 8.21 (with a change in variables) and 8.25 then yields a pair of intertwined recurrences for the division-free computation of square roots:

$$Z_{i+1} = Z_i(2 - Y_i Z_i) \tag{8.26}$$

$$Y_{i+1} = \frac{1}{2} \left(Y_i + x Z_{i+1} \right) \tag{8.27}$$

where $Z_i \to 1/\sqrt{x}$ and $Y_i \to \sqrt{x}$.

---

[17]See the comments above on Equations 8.5 and 8.6.
[18]Related algorithms of this type are discussed in Section 2.3.1.

$$x = 0.53 \qquad Y_0 = 1.0 \qquad Z_0 = 1.0$$

i	Z_i	Y_i
0	1.00000000000	1.00000000000
1	1.00000000000	0.76500000000
2	1.23500000000	0.70977500000
3	1.38743342562	0.72255735779
4	1.38396452277	0.72802927743
5	1.37349249018	0.72799014861
6	1.37364494504	0.72801098474
7	1.37360564626	0.72801098863
8	1.37360564005	0.72801098893
9	1.37360563949	0.72801098893
10	1.37360563949	0.72801098893
	$1/\sqrt{x}$	$\sqrt{x}$

Table 8.4: Divsion-free Newton–Raphson computation of $\sqrt{x}$

Equation 8.26 has the same form as Equation 8.5, as they both compute reciprocals. So one advantage of this algorithm is that, with appropriate control, the same hardware may be used for square root, inverse square root, and division, with the last is accomplished as multiplication of the dividend by the reciprocal of the divisor, which reciprocal is obtained by setting Y_i to the divisor. The convergence of this algorithm is less than quadratic but better than linear. The example of Table 8.3 is repeated in Table 8.4.

Another division-free algorithm for the computation of $\sqrt{x}$ consists of first computing $1/\sqrt{x}$ and then multiplying that by x. Here, the function whose root is to be found is $f(Y) = 1/Y^2 - x$. So $f'(Y) = -2/Y^3$, and the Newton–Raphson recurrence for the algorithm is

$$Y_{i+1} = Y_i - \frac{1/Y_i^2 - x}{-2/Y_i^3}$$

$$= \frac{3}{2} Y_i - \frac{Y_i^3}{2} x$$

$$= \frac{Y_i}{2} \left(3 - x Y_i^2 \right) \tag{8.28}$$

Given the relative costs of multiplication and division, this algorithm will most likely be better than the preceding ones. An example computation is given in Table 8.5.

$$x = 0.53 \qquad Y_0 = 1.0$$

i	$\mathbf{x Y_i^2}$	$\mathbf{Y_i}$
0	0.53000000000	1.00000000000
1	0.80836925000	1.23500000000
2	0.97069895914	1.35333198813
3	0.99934979764	1.37315900606
4	0.99999968286	1.37360542167
5	1.00000000000	1.37360563949
		$1/\sqrt{x}$

Table 8.5: Division-free Newton–Raphson computation of $1/\sqrt{x}$

Equation 8.28 may be rewritten into, and implemented as

$$Y_{i+1} = Y_i + \frac{1}{2} \left(1 - x Y_i^2 \right) \tag{8.29}$$

This has certain useful properties, but whether or not it is practically better depends on the details of the implementation.[19] In [7], a hardware implementation is proposed for Equation 8.29, on the basis of optimizations for three equations:

$$U_i = Y_i^2$$
$$V_i = 1 - x U_i$$
$$Y_{i+1} = Y_i + V_i Y_i / 2$$

The optimizations are that:

----

[19] See the comments above on Equations 8.5 and 8.6.

- U_i is computed in a specialized squaring unit.[20]
- V_i is approximated by a ones' complement operation;[21]
- the value of V_i is close to one and so has either leading 0s (positive) or leading 1s (negative), so not all bits need be computed.
- Truncated, rather than full-precision, multiplication is used to compute xU_i.
- Truncated multiplication is used to compute V_iY_i.

Convergence and errors

We shall now consider convergence and error in the use of Equation 8.21, leaving to the reader the analysis of the other iteration formulae. We shall first show that, under the right conditions, the computations will converge to $\sqrt{x}$. We shall then determine what starting values are required to ensure convergence. After that, we shall consider the rate of convergence.

From Equation 8.21

$$Y_i - \sqrt{x} = \frac{1}{2}\left(Y_{i-1} - 2\sqrt{x} + \frac{x}{Y_{i-1}}\right)$$

$$= \frac{Y_{i-1}^2 - 2Y_{i-1}\sqrt{x} + x}{2Y_{i-1}}$$

$$= \frac{(Y_{i-1} - \sqrt{x})^2}{2Y_{i-1}}$$

Similarly

$$Y_i + \sqrt{x} = \frac{(Y_{i-1} + \sqrt{x})^2}{2Y_{i-1}}$$

so

$$\frac{Y_i - \sqrt{x}}{Y_i + \sqrt{x}} = \left(\frac{Y_{i-1} - \sqrt{x}}{Y_{i-1} + \sqrt{x}}\right)^2$$

$$= \left(\frac{Y_0 - \sqrt{x}}{Y_0 + \sqrt{x}}\right)^{2^i} \triangleq \rho^{2^i}$$

---

[20]See Section 2.2.2.
[21]The non-fractional part is discarded.

and

$$Y_i - \sqrt{x} = Y_i \rho^{2^i} + \sqrt{x}\rho^{2^i}$$

$$Y_i(1 - \rho^{2^i}) = \sqrt{x} + \sqrt{x}\rho^{2^i}$$

$$Y_i = \frac{\sqrt{x} + \sqrt{x}\rho^{2^i}}{1 - \rho^{2^i}}$$

Therefore

$$Y_i - \sqrt{x} = \frac{\sqrt{x} + \sqrt{x}\rho^{2^i} - \sqrt{x}(1 - \rho^{2^i})}{1 - \rho^{2^i}}$$

$$= \frac{2\sqrt{x}\rho^{2^i}}{1 - \rho^{2^i}}$$

$$= 2\sqrt{x}\mu\left(1 + \mu + \mu^2 + \mu^3 \cdots\right) \qquad \text{where } \mu = \rho^{2^i}$$

For convergence, we want $\mu \to 0$ as $i \to \infty$, i.e. $|\rho| < 1$; so we require $Y_0 > 0$.

We next look at the rate of convergence, as usual under the assumption that there are no errors generated in the arithmetic operations.

Let ε_i denote the absolute error at step i. Then

$$\varepsilon_{i+1} = Y_{i+1} - \sqrt{x}$$

$$= \frac{1}{2}\left(Y_i + \frac{x}{Y_i}\right) - \sqrt{x}$$

$$= \frac{1}{2Y_i}\left(Y_i^2 - 2\sqrt{x}Y_i + x\right)$$

$$= \frac{1}{2Y_i}\left(Y_i - \sqrt{x}\right)^2$$

$$= \frac{\varepsilon_i^2}{2Y_i}$$

Our assumption, given at the start of the chapter, is that $x \in [1/4, 1)$, so $\sqrt{x} \in [1/2, 1)$. Therefore

$$\frac{\varepsilon_i^2}{2} < \frac{\varepsilon_i^2}{2Y_i} \leq \varepsilon_i^2$$

which shows that convergence will be quadratic if Y_0 is close to $\sqrt{x}$. If the latter is not the case, then the situation will be similar to that shown in Table 8.1, i.e. effectively linear convergence for some early iterations.

We leave it to the reader to work out a more detailed error analysis, along the lines of what has been done above for reciprocals.

Starting value, Y_0

The considerations here are as for the reciprocal computation (Section 8.2.1.3): the simplest choice is a constant, the next simplest is a value obtained from a linear approximation, and so forth. A variety of good linear approximations will be found in the literature [6, 11, 27, 35]. A good one obtained on the basis of a minimax approximation, and which requires just a SHIFT and ADD, is $Y_0(x) = \left(\sqrt[4]{8} - 1\right)^2 + x/2$. For fast, high-precision computation, the best initial-approximations methods are ones based on those of Chapter 7; that is, some (limited) form of table lookup or segmented polynomial approximation.

8.3.2   *Goldschmidt normalization*

The algorithm is the multiplicative-normalization algorithm of Section 5.5 (Equations 5.46–5.53), but with non-"CORDIC-like" normalizing multipliers. The basic recurrences are

$$X_{i+1} = c_i^2 X_i$$
$$Y_{i+1} = c_i Y_i$$
$$Z_{i+1} = c_i Z_i$$

If $X_0 = x$, $Y_0 = x$, and $Z_0 = 1$, then after n iterations $X_n \approx 1$, $Y_n \approx \sqrt{x}$, and $Z_n \approx 1/\sqrt{x}$. In general, the algorithm computes $Z_n \approx y/\sqrt{x}$, if $Y_0 = y$.

We can observe that the square root algorithm has the same general form as the reciprocal algorithm of Equations 8.14 and 8.15, but with some normalizers of the form c_i^2 instead of c_i. The multipliers, c_i, are also different; here, $c_i = (3 - X_i)/2$, on the basis of the following reasoning.

Since $c_i^2 X_i \approx 1$, we have $c_i \approx 1/\sqrt{X_i}$. Noting that X_i is fractional, let u_i denote $1 - X_i$. Then

$$c_i \approx \frac{1}{\sqrt{X_i}}$$

$$= \frac{1}{\sqrt{1 - u_i}}$$

$$= 1 + \frac{u_i}{2} + \frac{3u_i^2}{8} + \frac{5u_i^3}{16} + \cdots$$

$$\approx 1 + \frac{u_i}{2}$$

$$= (3 - X_i)/2$$

As with the Goldschmidt algorithms for reciprocals (Section 8.2.2), here too we may consider the rate of convergence in terms of the rate of increase in the number of 1s in the binary representation of $X_i = 1 - u_i$:

$$1 - u_i = 1 \cdot 0 - 0 \cdot \overbrace{00 \cdots 0}^{j \text{ 0s}} * * \cdots *$$

$$= 0 \cdot \overbrace{11 \cdots 1}^{j \text{ 1s}} * * \cdots *$$

We next show that convergence here is slightly faster than that for the reciprocals-algorithms and therefore quadratic.

In the Goldschmidt reciprocal algorithm, with X_i of the form $1 - u_i$, the normalizing multiplier used to the make X_i converge to one is $1 + u_i$. In that algorithm, if X_i has the binary representation

$$0 \cdot \overbrace{11 \cdots 1}^{j \text{ 1s}} * * \cdots *$$

then

$$X_{i+1} = (1 - u_i)(1 + u_i)$$

$$= 1 - u_i^2$$

will have the binary representation

$$0 \cdot \overbrace{11 \cdots 1}^{2j \text{ 1s}} * * \cdots *$$

The result is much closer to one than is $1 - u_i$, and that the number of 1s has been doubled in a single step suggests quadratic convergence. For the square root algorithm, if X_i is expressed as $1 - u_i$, then

$$X_{i+1} = (1 - u_i)(1 + u_i/2)^2$$

$$= 1 - \frac{3u_i^2}{4} - \frac{u_i^3}{4}$$

The result is much closer to one than is either $1 - u_i$ or $1 - u_i^2$, from which we conclude quadratic convergence to one and at a slightly faster rate than with the multipliers $1 + u_i$ used in the reciprocal-algorithm. Quadratic convergence was also confirmed for reciprocal computation by showing that the Newton–Raphson algorithm for reciprocals converges quadratically and is mathematically equivalent to the corresponding Goldschmidt algorithm. A similar procedure is equally applicable here; we leave it to the reader to work out the details.

An example computation is given in Table 8.6. A very-high-performance implementation of such algorithm is described in [5].

$$x = 0.53$$

i	X_i	Y_i	Z_i
0	0.53000000000	0.53000000000	1.00000000000
1	0.80836925000	0.65455000000	1.23500000000
2	0.97069895914	0.71726595371	1.35333198813
3	0.99934979764	0.72777427321	1.37315900606
4	0.99999968286	0.72801087349	1.37360542167
5	1.00000000000	0.72801098893	1.37360563949
6	1.00000000000	0.72801098893	1.37360563949
		$\sqrt{x}$	$1/\sqrt{x}$

Table 8.6: Goldschmidt computation of $\sqrt{x}$ and $1/\sqrt{x}$

The Goldschmidt algorithm for square root may be compared with the Newton–Raphson algorithm (above) that computes $\sqrt{x}$ by computing $1/\sqrt{x}$ and then multiplying that by x. The conclusions are largely similar to those above for the computation of reciprocals; that is, the multiplications in the

Goldschmidt algorithm can proceed in parallel, but the process is not self-correcting, and so forth.[22]

As with the Goldschmidt algorithm for reciprocals, the process here can be speeded up in various ways. The most direct of these is to start with a better approximation to $1/\sqrt{x}$ than $c_0 = (3-X_0)/2$, which is a rough linear approximation that can easily be improved upon. Additional discussion on Goldschmidt computations will be found in [10].

8.3.3 *Multiplicative normalization: non-redundant digit set*

The techniques described in Section 5.6.1 to speed up the simple "non-performing" algorithms for exponentials and logarithms are equally applicable to the same type of algorithm for square roots [36].

The basic algorithm is that given in Section 5.5. for the computation of $\sqrt{x}$ and $1/\sqrt{x}$:

$$X_1 = x \qquad\qquad\qquad\qquad 1/4 \le x < 1 \qquad (8.30)$$

$$Y_1 = x \qquad\qquad\qquad\qquad\qquad\qquad\qquad (8.31)$$

$$Z_1 = 1$$

$$s_i = \begin{cases} 1 & \text{if } X_i \left(1 + 2^{-i}\right)^2 < 1 \qquad i = 1, 2, 3, \ldots \\ 0 & \text{otherwise} \end{cases} \qquad (8.32)$$

$$c_i = 1 + s_i 2^{-i} \qquad\qquad\qquad\qquad\qquad (8.33)$$

$$X_{i+1} = X_i c_i^2 \qquad\qquad\qquad\qquad\qquad (8.34)$$

$$Y_{i+1} = Y_i c_i \qquad\qquad\qquad\qquad\qquad (8.35)$$

$$Z_{i+1} = Z_i c_i \qquad\qquad\qquad\qquad\qquad (8.36)$$

At the end of n iterations, $X_{n+1} \approx 1$, $Y_{n+1} \approx \sqrt{x}$, and $Z_{n+1} \approx 1/\sqrt{x}$, with convergence at a rate of one bit per iteration. (In what follows, it is sufficient for our purposes to consider just the square root, i.e. Y_i, computation.)

The normalization may also be viewed as a process of driving $1 - X_i$ to zero, by converting to 0s any 1s in the binary representation. That indeed is exactly what happens most in iterations, and it is the basis of the "*early termination*" that we describe next.

---

[22]See the remarks just near the end of Section 8.1.

Suppose k is the position of the leading 1 in $1 - X_i$. Then

$$1 - X_i = 2^{-k} + u_i \qquad \text{where } 0 \le u_i < 2^{-k} \qquad (8.37)$$

i.e.

$$X_i = 1 - 2^{-k} - u_i$$

If for the normalizing multiplier we take $c_i = 1 + 2^{-p}$, then

$$X_{i+1} = \left(1 - 2^{-k} - u_i\right)\left(1 + 2^{-p}\right)^2$$

and

$$1 - X_{i+1} = 2^{-k} - 2^{-p+1} + u_i + u_i 2^{-p+1} + 2^{-k+1}2^{-p} - 2^{-2p}$$
$$+ 2^{-k}2^{-2p} + u_i 2^{-2p} \qquad (8.38)$$

Comparing Equations 8.37 and 8.38, we see that if the choice is made of $p = k + 1$, then in computing X_{i+1}, the leading 1 in the representation[23] of $1 - X_i$ is turned into a 0 in $1 - X_{i+1}$.

It is evident[24] that in Equation 8.38 it will be the case that $p \ge i$ for all $i \ge 1$. Now, suppose $i > n/2$. Then, for n-bit precision, all but the first three terms in Equation 8.38 will be effectively zeros; that is, to machine precision, we have

$$1 - X_{i+1} = 2^{-k} - 2^{-p+1} + u_i$$

A comparison of this equation and Equation 8.37. shows that in this case $1 - X_i$ and $1 - X_{i+1}$ will then differ only in the altered bit. Therefore, the normalizing operations in iteration $i = n/2 + 1, n/2 + 2, \ldots$ correspond exactly to the 1s in $1 - X_{n/2+1}$. In particular, there will be a normalizing operation in iteration i only if bit $i - 1$ of $1 - X_{n/2+1}$ is a 1, and that bit is the same as bit i of $1 - X_{n/2+1}$ shifted to the right (i.e. divided by two). So the iterating can be terminated immediately by taking s_i to be bit $i - 1$ of $X_{n/2+1}$, for all $i = n/2 + 1, \ldots, n$. (See the values of $s_9, s_{10}, \cdots$ relative to the underlined bits of $1 - X_i$ in Table 8.7.) No additional iterations are required for the normalization, since the nominal termination operation is

$$X_{n+1} = X_k - X_k \qquad k = n/2 + 1$$

but the result computation must be completed.

---

[23] For brevity, and where no confusion can arise, in what follows we frequently write "in ..." or "of ... " instead of "in the binary of representation of ... ".
[24] Reason inductively from $i = 1$.

$$x = 0.65 \qquad \sqrt{x} = 0.80622\cdots$$

i	s_i	c_i	X_i	Y_i
1	0	1.0000000000000000	0.1011101011100001 *0.0100010100011110*	0.1011101011100001
2	0	1.0000000000000000	0.1011101011100001 *0.0100010100011110*	0.1011101011100001
3	1	1.0010000000000000	0.1011101011100001 *0.0100010100011110*	0.1011101011100001
4	0	1.0000000000000000	0.1110110010000101 *0.0001001101111010*	0.1101001000111101
5	1	1.0000100000000000	0.1110110010000101 *0.0001001101111010*	0.1101001000111101
6	0	1.0000000000000000	0.1111101110001000 *0.0000010001110111*	0.1101100011001111
7	1	1.0000001000000000	0.1111101110001000 *0.0000010001110111*	0.1101100011001111
8	0	1.0000000000000000	0.1111111101111010 *0.0000000010000101*	0.1101101010000000
9	0	1.0000000000000000	0.1111111101111010 *0.0000000010000101*	0.1101101010000000
10	1	1.0000000001000000	0.1111111101111010 *0.0000000010000101*	0.1101101010000000
11	0	1.0000000000000000	0.1111111111111010 *0.0000000000000101*	0.1101101010110111
12	0	1.0000000000000000	0.1111111111111010 *0.0000000000000101*	0.1101101010110111
13	0	1.0000000000000000	0.1111111111111010 *0.0000000000000101*	0.1101101010110111
14	0	1.0000000000000000	0.1111111111111010 *0.0000000000000101*	0.1101101010110111
15	1	1.0000000000000010	0.1111111111111010 *0.0000000000000101*	0.1101101010110111
16	0	1.0000000000000000	0.1111111111111110 *0.0000000000000001*	0.1101101010111001
				$(\sqrt{0.65} \approx 0.8062)$

$1 - X_i$ values in italics under X_i values

Table 8.7: Multiplicative-normalization computation of $\sqrt{x}$

On termination, the result to be computed is

$$Y_{n+1} = Y_k \prod_{i=k} \left(1 + s_i 2^{-i}\right) \qquad\qquad k = n/2 + 1$$

$$= Y_k \left[1 + s_k 2^{-k} + s_{k+1} 2^{-(k+1)} + \cdots + s_n 2^{-n}\right]$$

$$= Y_k + Y_k \left[s_k 2^{-k} + s_{k+1} 2^{-(k+1)} + \cdots + s_n 2^{-n}\right]$$

where smaller powers have been omitted, because they are zero to within n-bit machine precison.

Now, s_i is taken to be bit $i - 1$ of $X_{n/2+1}$, which is equivalent to taking it to be bit i of $1 - X_{n/2+1}$. And all of the leading $n/2$ bits of $1 - X_{n/2+1}$ are 0s; so

$$s_k 2^{-k} + s_{k+1} 2^{-(k+1)} + \cdots + s_n 2^{-n} = (1 - X_k)/2$$

We may therefore conclude that the effect of what would have been the last $n/2$ iterations can be achieved with a single addition (subtraction) and a single multiplication:

$$Y_{n+1} = Y_k + Y_k (1 - X_k)/2 \qquad\qquad k = n/2 + 1$$

In the example computation of Table 8.7, $1 - X_k \approx 0.0046, Y_k \approx 0.8043$, so on early termination $Y_{n+1} \approx 0.8062$.

The basic algorithm will, because of the non-redundancy, be implemented using only carry–propagate adders. On the other hand a good multiplier—even a sequential one—will carry out multiplication as a sequence of carry–save additions and a terminating carry–propagate addition. So the replacement of the $n/2$ original iterations should be worthwhile; moreover, even a rudimentary arithmetic unit will most likely have a multiplier, which means there should not be any additional cost.

8.3.4   *Multiplicative normalization: redundant digit set*

We next describe the use of redundant representation to obtain faster versions of the square root normalization algorithms of Section 5.5. Much of the foundational work here is due to [12, 13, 14, 25], on which the following discussions are based. We shall first discuss the non-arithmetic use of redundant representation (redundant signed-digit) and then make some remarks on the use of such representation (carry–save representation) in the arithmetic as well. The former facilitates the latter.

The algorithms here have similarities with the division algorithms of Section 2.3.1.2, and we rely on that keep the discussions at a reasonable length. Therefore, the reader might find it helpful to review the division algorithms.

A radix-2 algorithm that uses the digit set $\{\bar{1}, 0, 1\}$ is obtained by taking the algorithm of Equations 5.41–5.43 and changing the s_i-selection rule:

$$X_1 = x$$

$$Y_1 = x$$

$$Z_1 = 1$$

$$s_i = \begin{cases} \bar{1} \text{ if } X_i \geq 1 + k \\ 0 \text{ if } 1 - k \leq X_i < 1 + k \qquad\qquad i = 1, 2, 3, \ldots \\ 1 \text{ if } X_i < 1 - k \end{cases}$$

$$c_i = 1 + s_i 2^{-i}$$

$$X_{i+1} = X_i c_i^2$$

$$Y_{i+1} = Y_i c_i$$

$$Z_{i+1} = Z_i c_i$$

where k is a suitable constant, and c_i is chosen so that the nominal multiplications are just SHIFT–AND-ADD operations. Recall that we want $X_i \to 1$ as $Y_i \to \sqrt{x}$ and $Z_i \to 1/\sqrt{x}$.

The idea in the modification of selection rules is that to get X_i to converge to one, we should do the following. If X_i is "much larger" than one, then the multiplier, $1 + s_i 2^{-i}$, should be smaller than one; if X_i is "much smaller" than one, then the multiplier should be larger than one; and if, for that iteration, X_i is "sufficiently close" to one, then there should be no multiplication in that iteration. As X_i gets closer to one, the value of k needs to change in order to ensure that the process continues to converge. A good, easily computed value for k is $\alpha 2^{-i}$, where α is a small constant.

We shall here skip the details of how the value for α is determined, as similar details are given below for the radix-4 case. Taking a similar approach will show that α should be in the range $(0, 2)$. We may therefore take $\alpha = 1$. An example computation is given in Table 8.8.

Rather than work with $\alpha 2^{-i}$, which implies scaling the comparison values in every iteration, it is better to modify the recurrences above by substituting the scaled variable $U_i \triangleq 2^i(X_i - 1)$, i.e. $X_i = 1 + 2^{-i}U_i$. The effect of this is to remove leading 1s (0s) in the representation of a positive (negative) X_i so that the significant digits to be examined are always in the same position. The X_i recurrence is therefore transformed into

$$1 + 2^{-(i+1)}U_i = (1 + 2^{-i}U_i)(1 + 2s_i2^{-i} + s_i^2 2^{-2i})$$

whence the new recurrences

$$U_{i+1} = 2(U_i + 2s_i) + 2^{-i}(4s_iU_i + 2s_i^2) + 2^{-2i}2s_i^2 U_i \qquad (8.39)$$

$$Y_{i+1} = Y_i(1 + s_i2^{-i})$$

$$= Y_i + s_i2^{-i}Y_i$$

$$s_i = \begin{cases} \overline{1} \text{ if } U_i \geq \alpha \\ 0 \text{ if } -\alpha \leq U_i < \alpha \\ 1 \text{ if } U_i < -\alpha \end{cases}$$

$$x = 0.53 \qquad\qquad \alpha = 1.0$$

i	s_i	X_i	Y_i	Z_i
1	0	00.100001111010111	00.100001111010111	01.000000000000000
2	1	00.100001111010111	00.100001111010111	01.000000000000000
3	1	00.110101000000000	00.101010011001100	01.010000000000000
4	0	01.000011000101000	00.101111101100110	01.011010000000000
5	-1	01.000011000101000	00.101111101100110	01.011010000000000
6	1	00.111110111100111	00.101110001101011	01.010111001100000
7	-1	01.000000111011110	00.101110111011100	01.011000100011001
8	0	00.111111111011000	00.101110100100001	01.010111110110111
9	0	00.111111111011000	00.101110100100001	01.010111110110111
10	1	00.111111111011000	00.101110100100001	01.010111110110111
11	-1	01.000000000011000	00.101110100111000	01.010111111100011
12	0	00.111111111111000	00.101110100101100	01.010111111001101
13	1	00.111111111111000	00.101110100101100	01.010111111001101
14	0	01.000000000000000	00.101110100101111	01.010111111010010
15	0	01.000000000000000	00.101110100101111	01.010111111010010
16	-1	01.000000000000000	00.101110100101111	01.010111111010010
			$\sqrt{x} \approx 0.7280$	$1/\sqrt{x} \approx 1.3736$

Table 8.8: Radix-2 computation of $\sqrt{x}$ and $1/\sqrt{x}$

For faster operation, the arithmetic may be carried out in redundant representation; this may be redundant signed-digit or carry–save form, but we shall henceforth assume the latter, as this is the more widely used form. The redundancy in the digit set for f s_i means that the comparisons need not be exact; so with redundant-representation arithmetic, the selection of s_i may be on the basis of an approximation, $\widehat{U}_i$, to U_i. The approximation is obtained by assimilating a few leading bits of the carry–save form of U_i; four bits will suffice for radix-2 computation. The corresponding hardware architectures, with and without the use of redundant arithmetic, will be similar to those for the radix-4 computation (of which one is shown below).

We now consider the radix-4 algorithm with the minimally redundant digit set, i.e. $\{\overline{2}, \overline{1}, 0, 1, 2\}$. The multipliers here are $c_i = 1 + s_i 4^{-i}$; so substituting the scaled variable $U_i \triangleq 4^i(X_i - 1)$ in the equation for X_i yields

$$U_{i+1} = 4(U_i + 2s_i) + 4^{-i}(8s_i U_i + 4s_i^2) + 4^{-2i} 4s_i^2 U_i \qquad (8.40)$$

and the Y_i recurrence is now

$$Y_{i+1} = Y_i + s_i 4^{-i} Y_i$$

For the s_i-selection rules, we now have two more intervals and so require an additional constant. The starting point is

$$s_i = \begin{cases} \overline{2} \text{ if } & U_i \geq \beta \\ \overline{1} \text{ if } & \alpha \leq U_i < \beta \\ 0 \text{ if } & -\alpha \leq U_i < \alpha \\ 1 \text{ if } & -\beta \leq U_i < -\alpha \\ 2 \text{ if } & U_i < -\beta \end{cases}$$

We next proceed to determine the ranges from which to select the constants α and β and then discuss the selection of particular values in those ranges. The general approach is as for the division algorithm of Section 2.3.1.2.

For convergence, the worst of Equation 8.40 is when $U_{i+1} = U_i = \gamma$ and $s_i = \overline{2}$. If we consider that case as $i \to \infty$, then we get

$$4(\gamma - 4) = \gamma$$

$$\gamma = \frac{16}{3}$$

Similarly, on the other side, with $s_i = 2$, we get a bound of $-16/3$. So for convergence, we want $|U_i| \leq 16/3$. An interval-by-interval analysis, substituting for s_i, and with $i \to \infty$, shows that:

- For $s_i = 0$, we want $|4U_i| \leq 16/3$, i.e. $-4/3 \leq U_i \leq 4/3$.
- For $s_i = \bar{1}$, we want $|4(U_i - 2)| \leq 16/3$, i.e. $2/3 \leq U_i \leq 10/3$.
- For $s_i = \bar{2}$, we want $|4(U_i - 4)| \leq 16/3$, i.e. $8/3 \leq U_i \leq 16/3$.

(Because of the symmetry, an analysis of the other cases yields bounds that are of a similar magnitude but of opposite sign.) The ranges are summarized in Table 8.9. The values of α and β may be any convenient values within the regions of overlap, i.e. $[2/3, 4/3]$ and $[8/3, 10/3]$. The simplest values are $\alpha = 1$ and $\beta = 3$.

With $\alpha = 1$ and $\beta = 3$, it can be easily shown[25] that the algorithm will converge for all $i \geq 3$ and that $|U_i| < 5$ for these values of i. It is, however, possible to start iterations at $i = 2$, provided $|U_2| < 3$. This is equivalent to the condition that $|X_2 - 1| < 3/16$, and, therefore, the initialization problem is then one of finding such an X_2. Since $X_2 = xc_1^2$, one solution is to divide the domain of the argument, $[1/4, 1)$, into several intervals, each with a constant, c, such that if each argument is multiplied by the c^2 for the interval that contains the argument, then the result lies in the interval delimited by $1 \pm 3/16$, i.e. $(13/16, 19/16)$. If the number of intervals is considered unacceptably large, then a different solution is to use the above radix-2 algorithm (which would use exactly the same hardware) to perform iterations until some stage, i, is reached where $|X_i - 1| < 3/16$ and then continue from that point with radix-4 iterations. It is straightforward to show that $i = 5$ is sufficient for all cases. One may choose either of these two solutions depending on the cost-versus-performance trade-offs to be made.

U_i bounds		
Lower	**Upper**	s_i
$-16/3$	$-8/3$	2
$-10/3$	$-2/3$	1
$-4/3$	$4/3$	0
$2/3$	$10/3$	$\bar{1}$
$8/3$	$16/3$	$\bar{2}$

Table 8.9: Digit selection in radix-4 multiplicative normalization

---

[25] Assume that $|U_i|$ is within the given bounds. Take each value of s_i in turn, and show that $|U_{i+1}|$ is within the same bounds.

Because of the algorithmic similarities in many cases, square root evaluation and division are often implemented on the same hardware.[26] That can be done here too, but there are two minor complications that must be taken care of. The first has to do with the range of constants and other values, and the other has to do with the form of the recurrences. We next briefly discuss these for the radix-4 algorithms, but the considerations are evidently applicable to the radix-2 algorithms as well.

The normalizing recurrence for multiplicative-normalization division with a redundant signed-digit digit set is (Equation 2.9)

$$U_{i+1} = 4(U_i + s_i + s_i 4^{-i} U_i)$$

and that for square root evaluation is

$$U_{i+1} = 4(U_i + 2s_i) + 4^{-i}(8s_i U_i + 4s_i^2) + 4^{-2i} 4s_i^2 U_i$$

Considering the magnitude of the leading terms (Equations 2.10 and 8.42):

$$U_{i+1,\text{ div}} \approx 4(U_i + s_i)$$
$$U_{i+1,\text{ sqrt}} \approx 4(U_i + 2s_i)$$

we see that the values of U_i in the square root algorithm will be about twice those in the division algorithm, and this can be seen in the ranges for the comparison constants (Tables 2.13 and 8.9). This is the first minor complication, and it can be dealt with by modifying the square root recurrences, in one of two ways that both have exactly the same effect. One way is to keep $s_i \in \{\bar{2}, \bar{1}, 0, 1, 2\}$ but scale down the contribution of the terms in s_i, by changing the normalizing constants from

$$c_i = 1 + s_i 4^{-i}$$

to

$$c_i = 1 + (s_i/2)4^{-i}$$

The other is to scale the values of s_i, by changing the digit set to $\{\bar{1}, \overline{1/2}, 0, 1/2, 1\}$.

The second complication is that the square root recurrence has a form that appears to be very different from that for division, and, for hardware implementation, we should like them to be the same or at least very similar. We can get that similarity by rewriting Equation 8.40 into two recurrences:

$$V_i = U_i + s_i + s_i U_i 4^{-i}$$
$$U_{i+1} = 4\left(V_i + s_i + s_i V_i 4^{-i}\right)$$

[26]Such combinations affect the choice and details of square root algorithms.

The last recurrence has exactly the same form as that for division, and the recurrence for V_i also has the same form, except for the absence of the multiplication by four (i.e. a two-bit wired shift). So exactly the same hardware arrangement may be used for both division and square root evaluation. It is, however, apparent that the price for using the same hardware in such a case would be a relative loss in the performance for square root evaluation: the modified recurrences require two cycles for a single iteration; therefore, square root evaluation will be half as fast as division. This is a case where pipelining would help greatly in getting good performance.

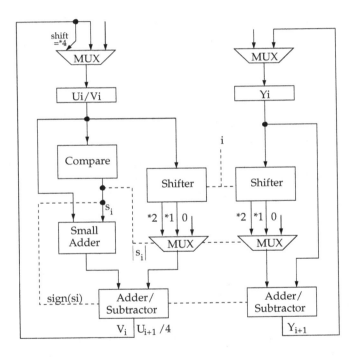

Figure 8.1: Radix-4 multiplicative-normalization $\sqrt{x}$ evaluator

Multiplicative-normalization algorithms of the type just described above are more complex than other algorithms that used redundant signed-digit representation in the operation selection—consider, for example, the requirement for shifters in the implementation—and should not be considered a first choice if square root alone is to be computed. The attractive aspect of such an algorithm is that the general form is similar to that of algorithms for several other functions (described in Chapters 2, 3, and 5), and so the same hardware may be used for all. An description of such implementation will be found in [13].

The sketch of a hardware architecture on the basis of the last two recurrences is shown in Figure 8.1. For carry–save arithmetic, the modifications required would be similar to those made in going from Figure 2.4 to Figure 2.5, with appropriate changes also made for the Y loop.

8.3.5   *Additive normalization: redundant digit set*

The following covers additive-normalization algorithms that use redundant signed-digit representations. Additive-normalization algorithms for the computation of square roots are very similar to those for division, which has the beneficial consequence that essentially the same hardware can be used for both operations. Square root algorithms, like division algorithms, may be formulated in a general additive form (Section 2.3.2) or in the SRT style (Section 2.3.3). We shall in what follows consider both. As with division, the two approaches may be regarded as just a difference in syntactic formulation, but the differences lead to two algorithms that differ in a critical aspect—how the initial iterations are handled—and it is therefore instructive to look at both, as they show how the same problem is solved in different ways.

Just as additive-normalization division is more commonly implemented on the basis of the SRT formulation, rather than the generic formulation, so too is the case with corresponding square root algorithms; and this is especially the case when both division and square root evaluation are implemented with the same hardware [23, 29, 32, 33, 34, 41]. Accordingly, we shall focus on the "SRT" type of algorithm, but we first discuss the more general form.

The starting point for the algorithms here is the algorithm of Equations 5.49–5.56, in which the values of X_i are driven to zero.:

$$X_0 = x \qquad\qquad 1/4 \le x < 1$$

$$Y_0 = 0$$

$$s_i = \begin{cases} 1 & \text{if } X_i \geq 0 \\ -1 & \text{otherwise} \end{cases} \qquad i = 0, 1, 2, \ldots \tag{8.41}$$

$$c_i = s_{i+1} 2^{-i}$$

$$\begin{aligned} X_{i+1} &= X_i - 2 c_i Y_i - c_i^2 \\ &= X_i - s_i 2^{-i} \left(2 Y_i + s_i 2^{-i} \right) \end{aligned} \tag{8.42}$$

$$\begin{aligned} Y_{i+1} &= Y_i + c_i \\ &= Y_i + s_i 2^{-i} \end{aligned} \tag{8.43}$$

To use the digit set $\{\overline{1}, 0, 1\}$, these recurrences are modified as follows.

The value of s_i for each iteration is chosen so that $|X_{i+1}| \leq |X_i|$, and the X_is therefore tend to zero. In iteration i, if X_i is much larger than zero, then it is to be reduced; if X_i is much smaller than zero, then it is to be increased; and if X_i is close to zero, then no action is taken. We therefore have the base algorithm

$$X_0 = x$$

$$Y_0 = 0$$

$$s_i = \begin{cases} 1 \text{ if } X_i \geq k \\ 0 \text{ if } -k \leq X_i < k \\ \overline{1} \text{ if } X_i < -k \end{cases}$$

$$X_{i+1} = X_i - s_i 2^{-i} \left(2 Y_i + s_i 2^{-i} \right) \tag{8.44}$$

$$Y_{i+1} = Y_i + s_i 2^{-i}$$

where k is some suitable value.

To ensure continued convergence when the values of X_i fall into the middle range, k should be adjusted with increasing i, and it should also be easily computable. A good choice is $k = \alpha 2^{-i}$:

$$s_i = \begin{cases} 1 \text{ if } X_i \geq \alpha 2^{-i} \\ 0 \text{ if } -\alpha 2^{-i} \leq X_i < \alpha 2^{-i} \\ \overline{1} \text{ if } X_i < -\alpha 2^{-i} \end{cases}$$

To avoid the need to rescale the comparison constants at every iteration, the recurrences above are modified by substituting the scaled variable $U_i \stackrel{\triangle}{=} 2^i X_i$; that is, X_i is replaced with $2^{-i} U_i$. The effect of this is to remove leading 0s (1s) in the representation of a positive (negative) X_i, so that the significant digits to be examined are always in the same position. With the scaling, normalizing recurrence is

$$U_{i+1} = 2(U_i - 2s_i Y_i - s_i^2 2^{-i})$$

$$s_i = \begin{cases} 1 \text{ if } U_i \geq \alpha \\ 0 \text{ if } -\alpha \leq U_i < \alpha \\ \overline{1} \text{ if } U_i < -\alpha \end{cases}$$

$$x = 0.53 \qquad \alpha = Y_i/2$$

i	s_i	U_i	Y_i
0	1	00.1000011110101110	00.0000000000000000
1	-1	-00.1111000010100011	01.0000000000000000
2	1	01.0001111010111000	00.1000000000000000
3	0	-00.0100001010001111	00.1100000000000000
4	-1	-00.1000010100011110	00.1100000000000000
5	1	01.1101010111000010	00.1011000000000000
6	1	00.1101101110000101	00.1011100000000000
7	-1	-01.0011000011110101	00.1011110000000000
8	1	00.1000101000010100	00.1011101000000000
9	-1	-01.1101010111010111	00.1011101100000000
10	-1	-00.1100000010101110	00.1011101010000000
11	1	01.0110100000100011	00.1011101001000000
12	0	-00.0001100011111000	00.1011101001100000
13	0	-00.0011000111110000	00.1011101001100000
14	-1	-00.0110001111100001	00.1011101001100000
15	1	10.0010000110110101	00.1011101001011100

$$\sqrt{x} \approx 0.7280$$

Table 8.10 : Radix-2 additive-normalization computation of $\sqrt{x}$

The manner in which the range for α is determined is subsumed in the radix-4 case below, and we shall therefore skip the details here. The method described below will show that the range is $(0, Y_i)$, and $\alpha = Y_i/2$ is a reasonable choice; an example computation with that value is given in Table 8.10. The s_i selection rule as given implies full-precision comparisons; however, the redundancy allows some "tolerance", and so low-precision comparisons (of six fraction bits) will suffice. This also means that after $i = 6$, for the purposes of the comparisons, Y_i is effectively constant; so the comparisons may be made against constant values. The manner in which this can be done is exemplified by the radix-4 algorithm below.

We will now consider the direct extension of the preceding algorithm to radices larger than two; for practical reasons, this boils down to just radix 4.

Generalizing from the radix-2 algorithm, the main recurrences for radix-r computation are

$$U_{i+1} = r(U_i - 2s_iY_i - s_i^2 r^{-i})$$

$$Y_{i+1} = Y_i + s_i r^{-i}$$

which present an obvious problem: If the digit set used is the maximally redundant radix-4 one (and therefore includes the digit 3), or the radix is larger than four, then s_iY_i consists of difficult-to-form multiples that must be computed in each iteration. So the maximally redundant radix-4 digit set is not practical for a square root algorithm or for a combined division–square root unit, even though it may be used for just division. The following is therefore limited to the minimally redundant radix-4 algorithm; where nominally large radices are used, the implementations will be of multiple radix-4 units, as described in Section 8.3.7.

The general approach here is as for the multiplicative-normalization algorithm, and the details will be found in [14, 15]. With $U_i \triangleq 4^i X_i$, we may suppose that the radix-4 algorithm is

$$U_0 = x$$

$$Y_0 = 0$$

$$Y_{i+1} = Y_i + s_i 4^{-i}$$

$$U_{i+1} = 4\left(U_i - 2s_iY_i - s_i^2 4^{-i}\right)$$

$$s_i = \begin{cases} \overline{2} & \text{if } U_i \leq -\beta \\ \overline{1} & \text{if } -\beta \leq U_i < -\alpha \\ 0 & \text{if } -\alpha \leq U_i < \alpha \\ 1 & \text{if } \alpha \leq U_i < \beta \\ 2 & \text{if } U_i \geq \beta \end{cases}$$

To determine the values for α and β, we proceed in the general manner that has been done for the radix-4 redundant signed-digit division algorithm of Section 2.3 and the radix-4 square root multiplicative-normalization algorithm above. If we take limits as $i \rightarrow \infty$ in the above equations for Y_{i+1} and U_{i+1}, then

$$Y_i = \sqrt{x}$$
$$U_{i+1} = 4\left(U_i - 2s_i\sqrt{x}\right) \tag{8.45}$$

For positive values, the worst case of Equation 8.45 is with $U_{i+1} = U_i = \gamma$ and $s_i = 2$. This gives

$$4\left(\gamma - 4\sqrt{x}\right) = \gamma$$

$$\gamma = \frac{16}{3}\sqrt{x}$$

Similarly, for the largest possible negative value of U_i and $s_i = 2$, we get $-16\sqrt{x}/3$ as the bound on the negative side. Therefore, convergence will be assured for large values of i, if $|U_i| \leq 16\sqrt{x}/3$.

An interval-by-interval analysis, with respect to Equation 8.45 then shows that:

- For $s_i = 0$, we want $|4U_i| \leq 16\sqrt{x}/3$, i.e. $-4\sqrt{x}/3 \leq |U_i| \leq 4\sqrt{X}/3$.
- For $s_i = 1$, we want $|4(U_i - 2\sqrt{x})| \leq 16\sqrt{x}/3$, i.e. $2\sqrt{x}/3 \leq U_i \leq 10\sqrt{x}/3$.
- For $s_i = 2$, we want $|4(U_i - 4\sqrt{x})| \leq 16\sqrt{x}/3$, i.e. $8\sqrt{x}/3 \leq U_i \leq 16\sqrt{x}/3$.

(Because of the symmetry, the other intervals produce similar values but of opposite sign.) The overlaps in the intervals give $[2\sqrt{x}/3, 4\sqrt{x}/3]$ as the range in which to choose a value α and $[8\sqrt{x}/3, 10\sqrt{X}/3]$ as the range for β. Conveniently computable values within these ranges are $\alpha = \sqrt{x}$ and $\beta = 3\sqrt{x}$.

There are, however, two problems with the preceding determination. The first is that the analysis has been carried out in the limiting case, and it might not be—and in fact it is not—applicable with small values of i. The second is that the nominal comparison values are functions of $\sqrt{x}$, which is exactly what we wish to compute.

The first problem can be solved by replacing the bound $16\sqrt{x}/3$ with a tighter bound $(5\sqrt{x})$ and the second by replacing $\sqrt{x}$ with Y_i, which (presumably) will be converging to $\sqrt{x}$. The two comparison values are then $\alpha = Y_i$ and $\beta = 3Y_i$. It is, however, desirable that the comparison values be constants, and this can be achieved by starting the computation at some point other than $i = 1$. The justification for this is that as i increases, the changes in Y_i decrease, and at some point the value will be good enough for all remaining iterations, given that the redundancy allows some inexactness in the comparisons. If the iterations are started with $i = 3$, and α and β are chosen to be Y_3 and $3Y_3$, then the computation will converge, with $|U_i| \leq 5Y_3$, for all $i \geq 3$. This can be shown through straightforward induction.[27]

The complete radix-4 algorithm for an argument x:

$$U_3 = 4^3 \left(x - Y_3^2 \right)$$

$$Y_{i+1} = Y_i + s_i 4^{-i} \qquad\qquad i = 3, 4, 5, \ldots$$

$$U_{i+1} = 4 \left(U_i - 2s_i Y_i - s_i^2 4^{-i} \right)$$

$$s_i = \begin{cases} \bar{2} & \text{if } U_i < -3Y_3 \\ \bar{1} & \text{if } -3Y_3 \leq U_i < -Y_3 \\ 0 & \text{if } -Y_3 \leq U_i < Y_3 \\ 1 & \text{if } Y_3 \leq U_i < 3Y_3 \\ 2 & \text{if } U_i \geq 3Y_3 \end{cases}$$

In implementation, since only a limited accuracy is required—Y_3 is accurate to only six (fraction) bits—the number of values that have to be stored need not be large: the range of $\sqrt{x}$ can be divided into intervals and one set of constants stored for each interval. For 64-bit results, sixteen intervals are sufficient, with Y_3 in the middle of an interval. The value of $3Y_3$ may be obtained by a low-precision addition (of Y_3 and $2Y_3$), but a probably better alternative is to also store these values (and possibly of

---

[27]Assume $|U_i|$ is in the range for convergence; take each value of s_i in turn; and show that the resulting $|U_{i+1}|$ too is in the range for convergence.

$-3Y_3$ too.) The values of Y_3^2, which are required in the initialization, can similarly be obtained by a low-precision multiplication or stored, with the latter probably better. The comparisons will also include two integer bits (to cover the range of U_i) and one sign bit.

The use of a redundant digit set allows fast evaluation, since the comparisons may be based on an approximation, $\widehat{U}_i$, of U_i instead of using U_i itself. With the arithmetic in conventional non-redundant form, such an approximation can be obtained by truncating the terms in the equation for U_{i+1}: the values of

$$\widehat{U}_{i+1} = 4\,(U_i - 2s_iY_i)$$

instead of those of U_{i+1} are used in the comparisons, and only a few most significant bits of each of $\widehat{U}_{i+1}$ and the comparison constants are required. The main advantage of this is that $\widehat{U}_{i+1}$ can be produced much faster than U_{i+1}; so s_{i+1} will be available by the time U_{i+1} is available, thus giving a type of "lookahead". The details are left to the reader to work out, but will also be found in [15]. They are similar to those in Section 2.3.1.2; and the U_{i+1} recurrence here is roughly similar to Equation 2.9, except for the different signs and that $s_i^2 4^{-i}$ replaces $s_i U_i 4^{-i}$ as the "missing term".

A sketch of hardware architecture for the radix-4 algorithm is shown in Figure 8.2. Wired shifts, which accomplish multiplications, are indicated by slanted lines, with the direction of slant indicating the direction of shifting and the attached number indicating the shift length in bit positions. The values 4^{-i} are formed in a shift register that is initialized to 4^{-3} and which shifts by two bit positions in each cycle. The constants assumed to be stored are $Y_3, 3Y_3$ and $16Y_3^2$, and for each argument the relevant constants are selected by decoding leading bits of the argument; the values $16Y_3^2$ are stored instead of Y_3^2 because the organization makes it conevenient to compute U_3 as $4(16x - 16Y_3^2)$. With the digit set $\{\overline{2}, \overline{1}, 0, 1, 2\}$, we have $s_i^2 4^{-i} \in \{0, 4^{-i}, 4 \times 4^{-i}\}$, which values are formed by shifting and selection in MUX A; $2|s_i|Y_i \in \{0, 2Y_i, 4Y_i\}$, which values are formed by shifting and selection in MUX B; and $|s_i|4^{-i} \in \{0, 4^{-i}, 2 \times 4^{-i}\}$, which values are formed by shifting and selection in MUX C. Two's complement representation is assumed; so a subtractions is by taking the ones' complement and adding 1, with the latter included in the carry–save adder (CSA) and the carry–propagate adder (CPA). A much faster arrangement can be readily obtained by removing all carry propagations in the two main loops.

A faster implementation would use carry–save arithmetic throughout the loops, and for that the changes required of Figure 8.2 are similar to those made in the changes[28] from Figure 2.4 to Figure 2.5.

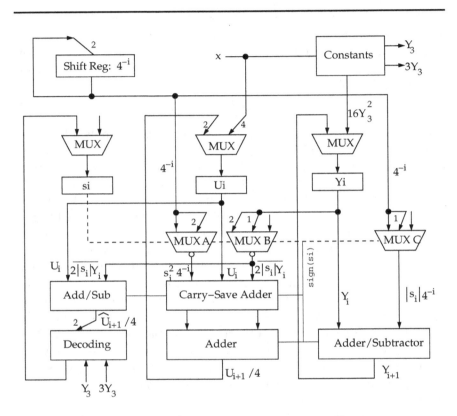

Figure 8.2: Radix-4 additive-normalization $\sqrt{x}$ evaluator

In the modifications, each of U_i and Y_i will now be in partial-carry/partial-sum form; so the CSA and CPA in the U_i loop gets replaced with three CSAs, as there are five inputs that are to be reduced to two outputs. The Adder/Subtractor in the Y_i loop gets replaced with a single CSA, with a final (outside-the-loop) CPA for conversion of the result to conventional form. Lastly, the manner in which s_i is determined also

---

[28]The main issues here are similar to those in division, and the reader might find it helpful to review the relevant parts of Chapter 2.

changes: with the much faster arithmetic, there is no advantage in using an approximation, $\widehat{U}_i$, of the type above. s_i will now be determined from a nominal comparison between U_i and the constants. U_i is not available in the right form, but the redundancy in the digit set means that it suffices to use an approximation that is obtained by assimilating a few leading bits (two integer, one sign, and seven fraction) of the partial-carry/partial-sum form. The reader will find the relevant details in [15].

We next take a look at more common alternatives for additive-normalization algorithms for square root evaluation.

8.3.6 *"SRT" algorithms*

The algorithms here too are variations of the "completing-the-square" algorithms of Section 5.5 (Equations 5.49–5.56). We shall refer to them as "SRT" algorithms because they have a general form that is similar to the SRT division algorithms of Chapter 2; advantageous use is often made of this, to implement both division and square root evaluation on the same hardware. The reader might therefore find it helpful to review the SRT division algorithms.

The recurrence for the diminishing of the partial remainder in radix-r SRT division is (Equation 2.20)

$$U_{i+1} = rU_i - s_{i+1}D \tag{8.46}$$

where U_i is the partial remainder at the end of step i, D is the divisor, and s_{i+1} is the next quotient digit. To obtain a similar recurrence for radix-r square root evaluation, the starting point is the recurrence (generalizing from Equation 8.44, with a syntactic change in the s indices):

$$X_{i+1} = X_i - s_{i+1}r^{-i}\left(2Y_i + s_{i+1}r^{-i}\right)$$

Substituting the scaled variable $U_i \triangleq r^i X_i$, we get

$$U_{i+1} = rU_i - s_{i+1}\left(2Y_i + s_{i+1}r^{-(i+1)}\right) \tag{8.47}$$

$$\triangleq rU_i - s_{i+1}\widetilde{D}$$

where s_{i+1} is a next "quotient digit" and $\widetilde{D} = 2s_{i+1}Y_i - s_{i+1}r^{-(i+1)}$ is a "divisor".

The result is computed as

$$Y_{i+1} = Y_i + s_{i+1}2^{-(i+1)} \qquad Y_0 = 0$$

The general similarities between Equations 8.46 and 8.47 are evident, and they allow the use of a single hardware unit, for which the details of the square root component are derived on a similar basis to that for the division.

There is, however, the one complicating difference: in the division algorithm, the comparisons to determine the next quotient digit involve a divisor that is constant; for the square root algorithm, the "divisor" is a function of the very value that is to be computed. This is not very problematic for radix-2 computation, but it is for larger radices. We next look at the radix-2 and radix-4 algorithms. For the latter, we shall especially rely on the similarity above of SRT division and square root evaluation.

8.3.6.1   *Radix 2*

The s_i-selection rule is derived on the basis that if $s_i \in \{\bar{1}, 1\}$ and s_i is chosen to have the same sign as U_{i-1}, then [39]

$$-2\left(Y_i - 2^{-i-1}\right) \leq U_i \leq 2\left(Y_i + 2^{-i-1}\right) \qquad i \geq 1 \qquad (8.48)$$

This is easily proved by induction. Note that $|U_i| < 2$.

For the base case, $U_0 = X_0 = x \in [1/4, 1)$ and $s_1 = 1$, which gives $Y_1 = s_1 = 1/2$. So Inequations 8.48 are reduced to

$$0 \leq U_1 \leq 3/2$$

and computing U_1 from Equation 8.47 shows that the bounds are satisfied.

Now, assume that Inequations 8.48 hold for i. For $i + 1$, if we take the upper bound in Inequations 8.48, then Equation 8.47, with $s_{i+1} = 1$, gives

$$U_{i+1} = 2U_i - \left(2Y_i + 2^{-i-1}\right)$$

$$= 2\left(2Y_i + 2 \times 2^{-i-1}\right) - 2Y_i - 2^{-i-1} \qquad \text{by hypothesis}$$

$$= 2Y_i + 3 \times 2^{-i-1}$$

$$= 2\left(Y_i + 2^{-i-1}\right) + 2^{-i-1}$$

$$= 2\left(Y_{i+1} + 2^{-i-2}\right)$$

And the last expression is the upper bound in Inequations 8.48 for $i + 1$. Similarly, if we take the lower bound in Inequations 8.48 and apply Equation 8.47 with $s_{i+1} = \bar{1}$, then we get the lower bound in Inequations 8.48 for $i + 1$.

If $s_{i+1} = 0$, then Equation 8.47 gives $U_{i+1} = 2U_i$, and Inequations 8.48 become

$$-\left(Y_i - 2^{-i-1}\right) \leq U_i \leq \left(Y_i + 2^{-i-1}\right) \qquad (8.49)$$

Putting together Inequations 8.48 and 8.49 and Equation 8.43, we end up with an "analogue" of Equation 2.18:

$$s_{i+1} = \begin{cases} 1 & \text{if } 0 \le U_i \le 2\left(Y_i + 2^{-i-1}\right) \\ 0 & \text{if } -\left(Y_i - 2^{-i-1}\right) \le U_i \le \left(Y_i + 2^{-i-1}\right) \\ \bar{1} & \text{if } -\left(Y_i + 2^{-i-1}\right) \le U_i \le 0 \end{cases}$$

Between $s_{i+1} = 0$ and $s_{i+1} = 1$, the overlap is $\left[0, Y_i + 2^{-(i+1)}\right]$; and, since $Y_i \ge 1/2$, in that interval we may take $1/2$ for the comparison constant. Similarly, to choose between $s_{i+1} = 0$ and $s_{i+1} = \bar{1}$, we may take $-1/2$ for the comparison constant. We then end up with

$$s_{i+1} = \begin{cases} 1 & \text{if } U_i \ge 1/2 \\ 0 & \text{if } -1/2 \le U_i < 1/2 \\ \bar{1} & \text{if } U_i < -1/2 \end{cases}$$

which corresponds to Equation 2.19.

The complete algorithm:

$$U_0 = x \qquad\qquad\qquad 1/4 \le x < 1$$

$$Y_0 = 0$$

$$s_{i+1} = \begin{cases} 1 & \text{if } U_i \ge 1/2 \\ 0 & \text{if } -1/2 \le U_i < 1/2 \qquad\qquad i = 0, 1, 2, \ldots \\ \bar{1} & \text{if } U_i < -1/2 \end{cases}$$

$$Y_{i+1} = Y_i + s_{i+1} 2^{-(i+1)}$$

$$U_{i+1} = 2U_i - s_{i+1}\left(2Y_i + s_{i+1} 2^{-(i+1)}\right)$$

An example computation is given in Table 8.11. Figure 8.3 shows the sketch of an architecture for the algorithm. This design is for a result that is generated in conventional representation; redundant signed-digit representation may be used, as discussed for the radix-4 case below. The primary arithmetic is in non-redundant representation and is carried out in carry–propagate adders (CPAs), with a carry–save adder (CSA) used to reduce three operands to two in the U_i loop. The values $2^{-(i+1)}$ are generated in a shift register that shifts by one bit position in each cycle. Twos' complement representation is assumed; so subtractions are by taking the ones' complements and adding 1s, with the latter included in the CSA and the CPAs. With $s_i \in \{\bar{1}, 0, 1\}$, we have $2s_{i+1}Y_i \in \{0, -2Y_i, 2Y_i\}$, for which values are formed in MUX A; $s_{i+1}^2 2^{-(i+1)} \in \{0, 2^{-(i+1)}\}$, for which values are formed in MUX B; and $|s_{i+1}|2^{-(i+1)} = s_{i+1}^2 2^{-(i+1)}$. Slanted lines indicate a one-bit shift, with the direction of slant corresponding to the direction of shift.

$$x = 0.53$$

i	s_i	U_i	Y_i
0	1	0.1000011110101110	0.0000000000000000
1	1	0.1000111101011100	0.1000000000000000
2	0	-0.0010000101000111	0.1100000000000000
3	0	-0.0100001010001111	0.1100000000000000
4	-1	-0.1000010100011110	0.1100000000000000
5	0	0.0110110111000010	0.1011100000000000
6	1	0.1101101110000101	0.1011100000000000
7	0	0.0100010100001010	0.1011101000000000
8	1	0.1000101000010100	0.1011101000000000
9	0	-0.0110000001010111	0.1011101010000000
10	-1	-0.1100000010101110	0.1011101010000000
11	0	-0.0000110001111100	0.1011101001100000
12	0	-0.0001100011111000	0.1011101001100000
13	0	-0.0011000111110000	0.1011101001100000
14	0	-0.0110001111100001	0.1011101001100000
15	-1	-0.1100011111000010	0.1011101001100000
			$\sqrt{x} \approx 0.7280$

Table 8.11: Radix-2 "SRT" computation of $\sqrt{x}$

For faster computation, the arithmetic will be in carry–save representation. An architecture for that is described for the radix-4 case; the considerations are largely the same for radix 2, but there is one noteworthy aspect in the latter: with cary-save arithmetic, s_i selection can be made on the basis of just the integer bits of $2U_i$. The following explains this.

Let $\widetilde{U}_i$ be the result of truncating[29] each of the sum and carry parts

---

[29]The "sloppiness" is for brevity. In such statments we mean truncating the representations.

of $2U_i$ to two fraction bits and then assimilating the two. Then $\widetilde{U}_i$ will be less than $2U_i$ by up to $1/2$. (Recall from Section 2.3.3.1 that in such truncation, magnitude is decreased for a positive value and increased for a negative value.)

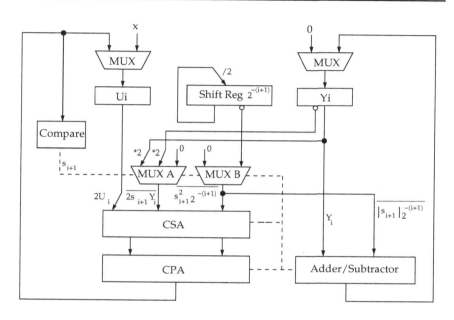

Figure 8.3: Hardware organization for radix-2 "SRT" $\sqrt{x}$

Rewriting the selection rule in terms of $2U_i$:

$$s_{i+1} = \begin{cases} 1 & \text{if } 2U_i \geq 1 \\ 0 & \text{if } -1 \leq U_i < 1/2 \\ \overline{1} & \text{if } 2U_i < -1 \end{cases}$$

and we may imagine that, in terms of $\widetilde{U}_i$, this (because of the error reductions by $1/2$) is

$$s_{i+1} = \begin{cases} 1 & \text{if } \widetilde{U}_i \geq 1/2 \\ 0 & \text{if } -3/2 \leq \widetilde{U}_i < 1/2 \\ \overline{1} & \text{if } \widetilde{U}_i < -3/2 \end{cases}$$

Since $|U_i| < 2$, we have $|2U_i| < 4$, and $|\widetilde{U}_i| < 9/2$, the last of which requires four integer bits (including a sign bit, assuming two's complement) for representation. For $s_{i+1} = 1$, the binary patterns for values in the corresponding U_i range have the form $0000 \cdot * * * \cdots$, the integer part of which represents zero; for $s_{i+1} = \bar{1}$, the binary patterns have the form $1110 \cdot * * * \cdots$, the integer part of which represents negative two; and for $s_{i+1} = 0$, the binary patterns have the form $1111 \cdot * * * \cdots$ or $0000 \cdot * * * \cdots$, which correspond to negative one and zero. So, if $\widehat{U}_i$ denotes the integer part of $\widetilde{U}_i$, then for the selection rule we may take

$$s_{i+1} = \begin{cases} 1 & \text{if } \widehat{U}_i \geq 0 \\ 0 & \text{if } \widehat{U}_i = -1 \\ \bar{1} & \text{if } \widehat{U}_i \leq -2 \end{cases}$$

(Note that the symmetry in the original rule is for convenience and is not a necessity; so the "splitting" in the 0 case is acceptable.)

Since $-4 < 2U_i < 4$, we have $-9/2 < \widetilde{U}_i < 3/2$. The binary patterns for the ends of the latter range are 1011.10 and 0011.10, the integer parts of which represent negative five and three; so $-5 \leq \widehat{U}_i \leq 3$.

8.3.6.2   Radix 4

In the SRT division algorithms, there is a leap in complexity in going from radix 2 to radix 4. A similar situation exists here and with an additional complication: the dependency of the "divisor" on the value, Y_i, being computed (Equation 8.47). That dependency complicates the task of finding a single set of comparison constants. The problem can be dealt with in several ways, all of which have the same basis—that the comparison constants need not be of high precision, and only a few leading bits of Y_i are required. So there is an iteration after which Y_i is effectively constant for the comparisons. The iteration in question is the third one; after that, "normal" iterations with a constant "divisor"—i.e. with a single set of comparison constants—are possible. For the iterations before that, special actions are required, and these will generally be of one of three types:

- The use of a lookup table to obtain the few bits of the root that would be determined in the first three iterations.
- The use of a radix-2 algorithm for the first three iterations.
- The (nominal) use of different sets of constants for each of those itera-

tions and the ones after.[30]

We shall focus on the last of these.

The radix-4 algorithm has the general form

$$U_0 = x \qquad\qquad\qquad 1/4 \leq x < 1$$

$$Y_0 = 0$$

$$s_{i+1} = S(U_i) \qquad\qquad\qquad i = 0, 1, 2, \ldots$$

$$Y_{i+1} = Y_i + s_{i+1}4^{-(i+1)}$$

$$U_{i+1} = 4U_i - s_{i+1}\left(2Y_i + s_{i+1}4^{-(i+1)}\right)$$

and the main problem is to determine S.

The first of the three types of solutions is exemplified by the implementation described in [23]. Since the first three iterations would produce six bits of the result, and one bit is known to be 1—because $x \in [1/4, 1)$ implies $\sqrt{x} \in [1/2, 1)$—five bits are required to start the iterations. These are obtained from a lookup table (a PLA) that is addressed with six bits of the argument; not all combinations of the input bits, and the table is of 28 words × 5 bits. Thereafter, s_{i+1} is obtained by comparisons against mutiples of Y_3; the implementation uses another PLA (of 19 terms) for this, but this may be replaced with combinational logic. Arithmetic is in carry–save representation, and the result is produced in redundant signed-digit form and then converted into conventional form.

The third of the three types of solutions does not use an initial lookup table and is as follows. Based on the general similarity between division and square root evaluation, we shall examine Equation 8.47 (with $r = 4$) as was done for the radix-4 SRT division algorithm, i.e. by taking similar steps, but with the "divisor" taken to be $2s_{i+1}Y_i + s_{i+1}r^{-(i+1)}$. So corresponding to Equations 2.21 and 2.22, the starting point here is the pair of equations

$$U_i^{\max} = 2(s_{i+1} + \rho)Y_i + (s_{i+1} + \rho)^2 4^{-(i+1)} \qquad (8.50)$$

$$U_i^{\min} = 2(s_{i+1} - \rho)Y_i + (s_{i+1} - \rho)^2 4^{-(i+1)} \qquad (8.51)$$

---

[30]In practice, the sets are combined into a single set, but different initializations are necessary.

where ρ is the redundancy of the digit set used, and the selection of s_{i+1} must be such that

$$U_i^{\max} \leq 4U_i \leq U_i^{\min}$$

We now consider the radix-4 algorithm with the minimally redundant digit set.[31] Details of this algorithm will be found in [33, 34].

s_{i+1}	$U_i{}^{\min}$	$U_i{}^{\max}$
2	$2\left(\frac{4}{3}\right)Y_i + \left(\frac{4}{3}\right)^2 4^{-(i+1)}$	$2\left(\frac{8}{3}\right)Y_i + \left(\frac{8}{3}\right)^2 4^{-(i+1)}$
1	$2\left(\frac{1}{3}\right)Y_i + \left(\frac{1}{3}\right)^2 4^{-(i+1)}$	$2\left(\frac{5}{3}\right)Y_i + \left(\frac{5}{3}\right)^2 4^{-(i+1)}$
0	$-2\left(\frac{2}{3}\right)Y_i + \left(\frac{2}{3}\right)^2 4^{-(i+1)}$	$2\left(\frac{2}{3}\right)Y_i + \left(\frac{2}{3}\right)^2 4^{-(i+1)}$
$\bar{1}$	$-2\left(\frac{5}{3}\right)Y_i + \left(\frac{4}{3}\right)^2 4^{-(i+1)}$	$-2\left(\frac{1}{3}\right)Y_i + \left(\frac{1}{3}\right)^2 4^{-(i+1)}$
$\bar{2}$	$-2\left(\frac{8}{3}\right)Y_i + \left(\frac{8}{3}\right)^2 4^{-(i+1)}$	$-2\left(\frac{4}{3}\right)Y_i + \left(\frac{4}{3}\right)^2 4^{-(i+1)}$

Table 8.12: Comparison parameters for a radix-4 square root

For the mininally-redundant radix-4 algorithm, i.e., $\rho = 2/3$, and the selection of $s_i = k$, Equations 8.50 and 8.51 give

$$U_i^{\max} = 2\left(k + \frac{2}{3}\right)Y_i + \left(k + \frac{2}{3}\right)^2 4^{-(i+1)} \qquad (8.52)$$

$$U_i^{\min} = 2\left(k + \frac{2}{3}\right)Y_i + \left(k + \frac{2}{3}\right)^2 4^{-(i+1)} \qquad (8.53)$$

---

[31] As explained in the case of division, there is no great loss in considering just this special case. Practical algorithms of this type do not use radices larger than four; nominally higher radices are implemented by using multiple radix-4 units (as described below). Maximally redundant radix-4 algorithms are also very rare but can readily be obtained from straightforward extensions to what is given here. The reader who seeks a general formulation should consult [33].

which correspond to Equations 2.24 and 2.25, but differ in the inclusion of the second term in each equation.

Substituting the different values of k into Equations 8.52 and 8.53, we get Table 8.12, which corresponds to Table 2.17.

Table 8.12 shows how the comparison values depend on i and suggests that it is not possible to have a single set of comparisons for all i, although (as indicated above) it is straightforward for all $i \geq 3$. So in the "SRT" square root algorithm, the different values of i must first be considered separately: $i = 0$, $i = 1$, $i = 2$, and $i \geq 3$. (The reader might find it useful before proceeding to quickly review Section 2.3.3, especially the "staircase construction" used in the determination of comparison constants.)

- $i = 0$: The result after n iterations is

$$Y = s_0 + \sum_{i=1}^{n} s_i 4^{-i} \qquad 1/2 \leq Y_n < 1$$

of which the largest possible value is with $s_i = 2$, for all i. That gives

$$Y = s_0 + \frac{2}{3} - \frac{2}{3 \times 4^n}$$

In order to allow for a result $Y > 2/3$, it is necessary to have $s_0 = 1$, which in turn gives $Y_0 = 1$. And in order to ensure that $Y < 1$, it is necessary to have $s_1 \in \{0, \bar{1}, \bar{2}\}$. Applying these values to the parameters of Table 8.12 gives two intervals of overlap from which two comparison constants are determined.

- $i = 1$: With $s_0 = 1$ and $s_1 \in \{0, \bar{1}, \bar{2}\}$, the possible values of Y_1 are $1/2, 3/4$, and 1. The parameters of Table 8.12, with $s_2 \in \{\bar{2}, \bar{1}, 0, 1, 2\}$, give ten intervals of overlap and ten constants.

- $i = 2$: The values of Y_i can be anywhere within the range $[1/2, 1)$, and the construction of similar tables is easiest done via a "staircase" in the P–D diagram of $4U_2$ against Y_2. By following the example given in Section 2.3.3 for division (with respect to Figure 2.11), the reader can readily verify that here a granularity of 2^{-3} for U_2 and 2^{-4} for Y_2 will suffice to determine the comparison constants.

- $i \geq 3$: Here too a staircase constuction is used, with a granularity of 2^{-4} for each of $4U_i$ and Y_i. In order to make the selection independent of i, the bound for $4U_i^{\min}$ is replaced with a smaller value:

$$2Y_i \left(k - \frac{2}{3} \right) + \left(k - \frac{2}{3} \right)^2 \triangleq L + \frac{(k - 2/3)^2}{256} \qquad k = \bar{2}, \bar{1}, 0, 1, 2$$

And given that the last term is negligible within a granularity of 2^{-4}, L is used instead, and the bound for $U_i^{\min}$ is replaced with a larger value:

$$2Y_i \left(k - \frac{2}{3} \right)$$

The "staircase construction then yields the required intervals and constants.

	Constants			
Y_i **Interval**	$s_i = 2/$ $s_i = 1$	$s_i = 1/$ $s_i = 0$	$s_i = 0/$ $s_i = -1$	$s_i = -1/$ $s_i = -2$
$[8/16, 9/16)$	$3/2$	$1/2$	$-1/2$	$-13/8$
$[9/16, 10/16)$	$7/4$	$1/2$	$-5/8$	$-7/4$
$[10/16, 11/16)$	2	$1/2$	$-3/4$	-2
$[11/16, 12/16)$	2	$3/4$	$-3/4$	$-17/8$
$[12/16, 13/16)$	$9/4$	$3/4$	$-3/4$	$-9/4$
$[13/16, 14/16)$	$5/2$	$3/4$	-1	$-5/2^*$
$[14/16, 15/16)$	$5/2$	1	-1	$-11/4$
$[15/16, 16/16)$	$11/2$	1	-1	$-23/8$

Table 8.13: Comparison constants for radix-4 "SRT" square root

The tables so constructed—the details will be found in [34]—are then combined, to the extent possible, into a single table; this is done by comparing the entries and, if possible, selecting different constants where they do not match. For carry–save arithmetic, the resulting table is given in Table 8.13. In combining the different tables, there is only one place[32] for which a common constant is not possible, and that is handled specially using a small amount of logic. The comparisons are basesd on approximations $\widehat{U}_i$ and $\widehat{Y}_i$ of $4U_i$ and Y_i, obtained from four integer bits (for range and sign) and four fraction bits of $4U_i$ and four fraction bits of Y_i. Additional discussion on s_i selection and the choice of comparison constants will be found in [38].

We now consider implementation issues beyond the aspects covered above in the radix-2 case; the following remarks are equally applicable for the latter. In the radix-2 case, we assumed arithmetic in conventional form,

---

[32] For the entry marked *, $Y_0 = 13/16$ is used instead of $Y_0 = 1$.

with the result also generated in conventional form. For high-performance (refer also to Figure 8.4):

- The arithmetic in the U_i-loop will be in carry–save (CS) representation.
- If the result is not produced in redundant signed-digit (RSD) form, then the Y_i arithmetic will be in CS form, with a final conversion to conventional form.
- If the result is produced in RSD form, then there is (in principle) no arithmetic in the Y_i-loop because the result is (nominally) updated by shifting and appending the next result digit.
- The decoding to determine s_i also changes: the determination will now be done on the basis of a U_i approximation that is obtained from assimilating leading bits of the partial-carry/partial-sum form.

If the result is produced in CS form, then at the end of the cycling a full carry–propagate addition is required for the conversion; on the other hand, with RSD form and on-the-fly conversion, no additional computations are necessary at the end of the cycling. The latter is therefore preferable for high-performance computation, and it is what we assume for the remainder of this discussion; otherwise, result arithmetic in CS form is easily accommodated.

In division, even if the result is generated in RSD form, that has no effect on the divisor–multiple that is subtracted at each step. On the other hand, with square root evaluation here, the "divisor multiple" is dependent on the "quotient" (result), and that introduces some complications.

With on-the-fly conversion (Section 2.1.2.2), the result will be generated in two forms:

$$Y_{i+1} = \begin{cases} Y_i \circ s_{i+1} & \text{if } s_{i+1} \geq 0 \\ Y_i^- \circ (r - |x_{i+1}|) & \text{otherwise} \end{cases}$$

$$Y_{i+1}^- = \begin{cases} Y_i \circ (s_{i+1} - 1) & \text{if } s_{i+1} > 0 \\ Y_i^- \circ ((r - 1) - |s_{i+1}|) & \text{otherwise} \end{cases}$$

where r is the radix, and $\circ$ denotes concatenation. Extending this to the present case, for $s_{i+1} > 0$, the "divisor–multiple" is

$$-s_{i+1}\left(2Y_i + s_{i+1} r^{-(i+1)}\right) = -s_{i+1}(2Y \circ s_{i+1})$$

and for $s_{i+1} < 0$, it is

$$|s_{i+1}| \left(2Y_i^- + (2r - |s_{i+1}|)r^{-(i+1)} \right) \; |s_{i+1}| \left(2Y_i^- \circ (2r - |s_{i+1}|) \right)$$

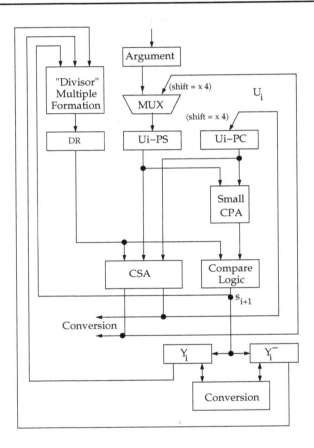

Figure 8.4: Hardware organization for radix-4 "SRT' computation of $\sqrt{x}$

The sketch of an architecture for the algorithm is shown in Figure 8.4. The similarities with the radix-4 SRT architecture (Figure 2.13) are apparent, and these extend to the operational aspects. Because of the similarities in algorithms and archirectures, it is common to have both square root and division on the same hardware. Detailed descriptions of such implementations will be found in [23, 29, 32, 33, 34, 41]

Higher performance, but also at higher cost, can be achieved by overlapping the computation of s_{i+1} with that of the next "partial remainder", U_{i+1}. A straightforward way to do this is to compute all the possible "partial remainders" concurrently with s_{i+1} and then immediately choose the correct one. This is depicted in the sketch of Figure 8.5, which is for the digit set $\{\bar{2}, \bar{1}, 0, 1, 2\}$. Descriptions of such implementations will be found in [32, 37, 41].

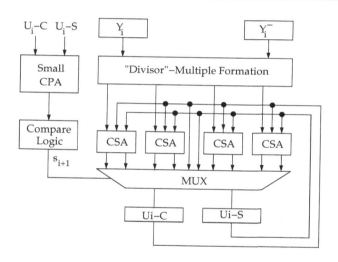

Figure 8.5: Overlapping radix-4 computations

8.3.7 *High-radix computation*

Most algorithms and implementations for non-binary radices use a minimally redundant radix-4 digit set, because of the difficulties in forming multiples of three (with the maximally redundant radix 4 and minimally redundant radix 8); multiples of three, five, and seven (with the maximally redundant radix 8); etc. Nevertheless, there are designs that use what are essentially larger radices, but in such a way as to avoid the need to directly compute the hard-to-form multiples: the multiples are formed indirectly, by cascading or overlapping computations that involve only "easy" multiples. Two of these are briefly described below; both are based on additive normalization of the SRT type. An alternative approach is digit selection by rounding (Section 2.3.4), in which the labour of computing hard-to-form multiples—by direct multiplication—is rewarded with a substantial reduction in the number of steps and, therefore, (one hopes) faster computation.

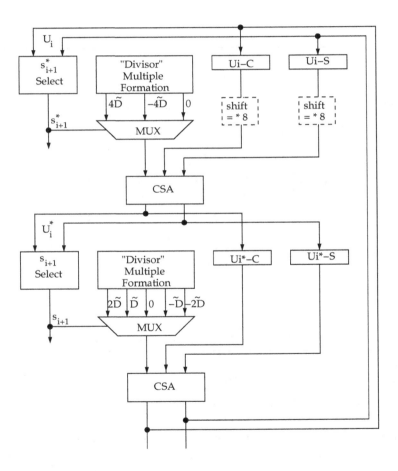

Figure 8.6: Radix 8 by cascading low-radix units

Cascading low-radix units

A radix-8 implementation for the combined evaluation of division and square root is described in [29]. The effective digit set is $\{\overline{6}, \overline{5}, \ldots, 0, \ldots, 5, 6\}$, which is obtained by cascading two stages: one that uses the digit set $\{\overline{4}, 0, 4\}$ and one that uses the digit set $\{\overline{2}, \overline{1}, 0, 1, 2\}$. The direct computation of difficult-to-form multiples is therefore avoided, and multiples of three and five are obtained indirectly, in two steps.

Using $\widetilde{D}$ to denote the divisor in division or the "divisor" in square root evaluation (as discussed above of Equations 8.46 and 8.47), the two stages are

$$U^*_{i+1} = 8U_i - s^*_{i+1}\widetilde{D} \qquad s^*_{i+1} \in \{\overline{4}, 0, 4\}$$

$$U_{i+1} = U^*_{i+1} - s_{i+1}\widetilde{D} \qquad s_{i+1} \in \{\overline{2}, \overline{1}, 0, 1, 2\}$$

which is equivalent to

$$U_{i+1} = 8U_i - (s^*_{i+1} + s_{i+1})\widetilde{D} \; .$$

So at the end of the cycle the radix-8 digit determined is $s_{i+1} + s^*_{i+1}$. The sketch of a hardware architecture is shown in Figure 8.6.

The use of digit selection by rounding (Section 2.3.4) takes a different approach. Although originally invented for computation with very large radices, [31] shows that the idea can be put to good use with radices as low as eight; one advantage of doing so with such modest radices is that maximally redundant digit sets can be used more easily. The design in [31] is for the radix-8 computation of reciprocals, square roots, and inverse square roots, and it is noteworthy for several optimizations that should lead to fast hardware without excessive costs.

Overlapping low-radix units

The use of non-binary radices can also be realized by overlapping— rather than cascading, as in the radix-8 case above—several low-radix units, thus, again, avoiding the difficult-to-form multiples: radix 4 from the overlap of two radix-2 units, radix 8 from the overlap of three radix-2 units or a radix-4 and a radix-2 unit, and so on. This is the basis of the radix-16 divider of [30] and of the combined radix-8 and radix-16 divider/square root-evaluator units of [32, 41].

A cycle in an "SRT" computation nominally consists of four phases: "quotient-digit" selection, "divisor–multiple" formation, "partial-remainder" computation, and quotient accumulation.[33] The last of these steps can easily be carried out in parallel with and separately from the first three (which, in principle, must be carried out in sequence) and so need not be of concern in the timing. The basis of the design in [30] is the observation that if carry–save arithmetic is used in the computation of the partial remainder, then the cycle time is dominated by the quotient-digit-selection phase, which on the other hand requires less hardware than the other phases. This suggests that replication of the digit-selection logic would be worthwhile if such logic could be used effectively—specifically, in reducing the "sequentiality" constraints in the first three phases. The design is for the production of two radix-4 digits in each cycle, effectively radix-16 computation.[34] This is done by overlapping the operations in a manner that we may imagine as the computation

$$U_{i+1}^* = 4U_i - s_{i+1}^* \widetilde{D} \tag{8.54}$$

$$U_{i+1} = 4U_{i+1}^* - s_{i+1} \widetilde{D} \tag{8.55}$$

where, as in the radix-8 case, $\widetilde{D}$ is the divisor in division or the "divisor" in square root evaluation.

These equations are similar to those for the radix-8 design of Figure 8.6; in particular, there is an implicit sequentiality in the computation of U_{i+1}^* and U_{i+1}. The difference between "overlapping" and "cascading" is that, relative to a design of the type shown in Figure 8.6, the sequentiality is substantially reduced by replicating the s_{i+1}-stage arithmetic elements, once for each possible value of s_{i+1}^*.

Equations 8.54 and 8.55 are equivalent to

$$U_{i+1} = 16U_i - (4s_{i+1}^* + s_{i+1})\widetilde{D}$$

That is, the two radix-4 digits, s_{i+1}^* and s_{i+1}, are equivalent to the single radix-16 digit $(4s_{i+1}^* + s_{i+1})$. So, if $s_{i+1}^* \in \{\overline{p}, \dots, p\}$ and $s_i \in \{\overline{m}, \dots, m\}$, then the nominal radix-16 digit set is $\{\overline{4p+m}, \dots, 0, \dots 4p+m\}$. Thus, for example, if the minimally redundant radix-4 digit set is used for both phases, i.e. $p = m = 2$, then the corresponding radix-16 digit set is $\{\overline{10}, \overline{9}, \dots, 9, 10\}$.

---

[33] The terms in quotation marks are to be interpreted according to whether the operation is division of square root evaluation.

[34] An implementation of such a divider will be found in the Intel Penryn processor.

Figure 8.7 shows a sketch of part of the corresponding datapath for Equations 8.54 and 8.55; the nominal multiplications by four will, as usual, be accomplished by wired shifts that are not explicitly indicated in the figure.

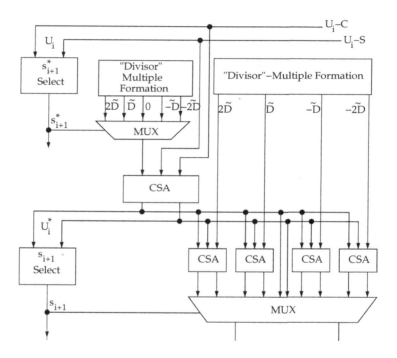

Figure 8.7: Overlapped radix-16 computation

A consideration of Figures 8.4–8.7 and the corresponding expressions immediately shows two things that are relevant for how the implementation is designed. The first is that different expressions can be usefully formulated and put to good use. Thus, for example, in [32], the implementations are based on "equivalents" of Equations 8.54 and 8.55 that have the general form

$$U_{i+1}^* = 4(4U_i - s_{i+1}^* \widetilde{D})$$

$$= 16U_i - s_{i+1}^*(4\widetilde{D})$$

$$U_{i+1} = U_{i+1}^* - s_{i+1}\widetilde{D}$$

And the second is that in cascaded/overlapped computation, there are several possibilities, of which the figures reflect just a subset. In Figure 8.7, for example, there is a sequentiality in the s-computations, and this too can be substantially reduced through "overlap by replication", as shown in Figure 8.8.

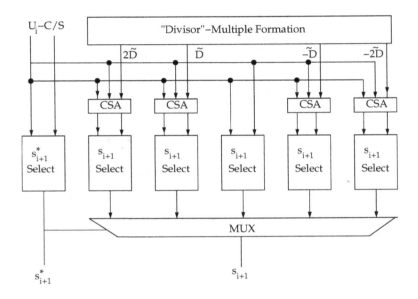

Figure 8.8: Overlapped s_i computation

Books! 'tis a dull and endless strife.

WILLIAM WORDSWORTH, *The Tables Turned*, 1798

References

Chapter 1

(1) S. M. Pizer w. V. L. Wallace. 1983. *To Compute Numerically: Concepts and Strateges*. Little, Brown & Company, Boston, USA.

(2) G. Dahlquist and A. Bjrck. 2008. *Numerical Methods in Scientific Computing, Vol. 1*. SIAM, USA.

(3) J. F. Hart, E. W. Cheney, C. L Lawson, H. J. Maehly, C. K. Mseztenyi, J. R. Rice, H. G. Thacher, and C. Witzgall. 1968. *Computer Approximations*. John Wiley & Sons, New York.

(4) J.-M. Muller, N. Brisebarre, F. de Dinechin, C.-P. Jeannerod, V. Lefèvre, G. Melquiond, N. Revol, D. Stehle, and S. Torres. 2009. *Handbook of Floating-Point Arithmetic*. Birkhauser, Boston, USA.

(5) J.-M. Muller. 1997. *Elementary Functions, Algorithms and Implementation*. Birkhauser, Boston, USA.

(6) W. J. Cody and M. Waite. 1980. *Software Manual for Elementary Functions*. Prentice Hall, Englewood Cliffs, USA.

(7) V. Lefevre and J. M. Muller. 2003. On-the-fly range reduction. *Journal of VLSI Signal Processing*, 33:31–35.

(8) D. Defour, P. Kornerup, J. M. Muller, and N. Revol. 2005. A new range reduction algorithm. *IEEE Transactions on Computers*, 54(3):331–339.

(9) M. Payne and R. Hanek. 1983. Range reduction for trigonometric functions. *SIGNUM Newsletter*, 18:19–24.

(10) V. Lefèvre, J.-M. Muller, and A. Tisserand. 1998. Towards correctly rounded transcendentals. *IEEE Transactions on Computers*, 47(11):1235–1243.

(11) M. J. Schulte and E. E. Swartzlander Jnr. 1993. Parallel designs for correctly rounded elementary functions. *Interval Computations*, 3:65–88.

(12) M. J. Schulte and E. E. Swartzlander Jnr. 1994. Hardware designs for exactly rounded elementary functions. *IEEE Transactions on Computers*, 43(8):964–973.

(13) A. Omondi and B. Premkumar. 2007. *Residue Number Systems: Theory and Implementation*. Imperial College Press, London, UK.

(14) J. Villalba, T. Lang, and M. A. Gonzalez. 2006. Double-residue modular range reduction for floating-point hardware implementations. *IEEE Transactions on Computers*, 55(3):254–267.

(15) F. J. Jaime, M. A. Sanchez, J. Hormigo, J. Villalba, and E. L. Zapata. 2011. High-speed algorithms and architectures for range reduction computation. *IEEE Transactions on VLSI Systems*, 19(3):512–516.

Chapter 2

(1) M. Ercegovac and T. Lang. 2004. *Digital Arithmetic*. Morgan Kaufmann, San Francisco, CA, USA.

(2) I. Koren. 2001. *Computer Arithmetic Algorithms*. A. K. Peters/CRC Press, Natick, MA, USA.

(3) A. Omondi. 1994. *Computer Arithmetic Systems: Algorithms, Architecture and Implementation*. Prentice Hall, Hemel Hempstead, UK.

(4) B. Parhami. 1999. *Computer Arithmetic: Algorithms and Hardware Designs*. Oxford University Press, New York, USA.

(5) A. Avizienis. 1961. Signed-digit number representations for fast parallel arithmetic. *IRE Transactions on Electronic Computers*, IRE-EC, 10:389–400.

(6) M. D. Ercegovac and T. Lang. 1987. On-the-fly conversion of redundant into conventional representations. *IEEE Transactions on Computers*, C-36(7):895–897.

(7) N. Takagi, Y. Yasuura, and S. Yajima. 1985. High speed VLSI multiplication algorithm with a redundant binary addition tree. *IEEE Transactions on Computers*, 34(9):789–796.

(8) M. D. Ercegovac. 1984. On-line arithmetic: an overview. *SPIE Real Time Signal Processing VII*, pp. 86–93.

(9) B. Parhami. 1990. Generalized signed-digit number systems: a unifying framework for redundant number representations. *IEEE Transactions on Computers*, 39(1):89–98.

(10) D. E. Atkins. 1968. Higher-radix division using estimates of the divisor and partial remainders. *IEEE Transactions on Computers*,

C-17(10):925–934.

(11) M. R. D. Rodrigues, J.H.P. Zurawski, and J. B. Gosling. 1981. Hardware evaluation of mathematical functions. *Proceedings of the IEE*, 128(E)(4):155–164.

(12) G. S. Taylor. 1985. Radix-16 SRT dividers with overlapped quotient selection stages. *Proceedings, 7th IEEE Symposium on Computer Arithmetic*, pp. 64–71.

(13) M. D. Ercegovac, T. Lang, and P. Montuschi. 1994. Very-high radix division with prescaling and selection by rounding. *IEEE Transactions on Computers*, 43(8):909–918.

(14) P. K. Tang and W. E. Ferguson. 2003. Narrow datapath for very high radix division. Patent 7,167,891 B2. United States Patent Office. (Google Patents.)

(15) J. H. P. Zurawski and J.B. Gosling. 1987. Design of a high-speed square root, multiply, and divide unit. *IEEE Transactions on Computers*, C-36(1):13–23.

(16) N. Burgess and C. N. Hinds. 2007. Design of the ARM VFP11 divide and square root synthesisable Macrocell. *Proceedings, 18th IEEE Symposium on Computer Arithmetic*, pp. 87–96.

(17) P. Kornerup. 2005. Digit selection for SRT division and square root. *IEEE Transactions on Computers*, 54(3):294–303.

(18) J. Fandrianto. 1987. Algorithm for high speed shared radix-4 division and radix-4 square root. *Proceedings, 8th IEEE Symposium on Computer Arithmetic*, pp. 73–79.

(19) J.-A. Piniero, S. F. Oberman, J.-M. Muller, and J. D. Brugera. 2005. High-speed function approximation using a minimax quadratic interpolator. *IEEE Transactions on Computers*, 54(3):304–316.

(20) L. Girard and Jonathan Sweedler. 1994. Methods and apparatus for subtraction with 3:2 carry-save adders. Patent 5351207 A. United States Patent Office. (Google Patents.)

(21) D. E. Knuth. 1998. *The Art of Computer Programming, Vol. 2.* Addison-Wesley, Reading, MA, USA.

Chapter 3

(1) J. E. Volder. 1959. The CORDIC trigonometric technique. *IRE Transactions on Electronic Computers*, EC-18(3):330–334.

(2) J. E. Volder. 2000. The evolution of CORDIC. *Journal of VSLI Signal Processing*, 25(2):101–105.

(3) J. S. Walther. 1971. A unified algorithm for elementary functions. *Proceedings, Spring Joint Computer Conference*, pp. 379–385.

(4) J. Walther. 2000. The story of unified CORDIC. *Journal of VSLI Signal Processing*, 25(2):107–112.

(5) *Journal of VSLI Signal Processing*, 25(2). Special Issue on CORDIC. 2000.

(6) C. W. Schelin. 1983. Calculator function approximation. *American Mathematical Monthly*, 90(5):317–325.

(7) C. Mazenc, X. Merrheim, and J.-M. Muller. 1993. Computing functions $\cos^{-1}$ and $\sin^{-1}$ using CORDIC. *IEEE Transactions on Computers*, 42(1):118–122.

(8) T. Lang and E. Antelo. 2000. CORDIC-based computation of ArcCos and $\sqrt{1-t^2}$. *Journal of VLSI Signal Processing*, 25(1):19–38.

(9) Y. H. Hu. 1992. The quantization effects of the CORDIC algorithm. *IEEE Transactions on Signal Processing*, 40(4):834-844.

(10) S. Wang, V. Piuri, and E. E. Swartzlander. 1997. Hybrid CORDIC algorithms. *IEEE Transactions on Computers*, 46(11):1202–1207.

(11) K. Kota and J. R. Cavallaro. 1993. Numerical accuracy and hardware tradeoffs for CORDIC arithmetic for special-purpose processor. *IEEE Transactions on Computers*, 42(7):769–779.

Chapter 4

(1) B. G. DeLugish. 1970. A class of algorithms for automatic evaluation of elementary functions in a binary Computer. Ph.D. thesis, Department of Computer Science, University of Illinois at Urbana-Champaign.

(2) M. D. Ercegovac and T. Lang. 1987. Fast sine/cosine implementation using on-line CORDIC. *Proceedings, 21st Asilomar Conference on Signals, Systems, and Computers*, pp. 222–226.

(3) N. Takagi, T. Asada, and S. Yajima. 1991. Redundant CORDIC methods with a constant scale factor for sine and cosine computation. *IEEE Transactions on Computers*, 40(9):989–995.

(4) J. Duprat and J.-M. Miller. 1993. The CORDIC algorithm: new results for fast VLSI implementation. *IEEE Transactions on Computers*, 42(2):168–178.

(5) D. S. Phatak. 1998. Comments on Duprat and Mullers branching CORDIC. *IEEE Transactions on Computers*, 47(9):1037–1040.

(6) D. S. Phatak. 1998. Double step branching CORDIC: a new algorithm for fast sine and cosine generation. *IEEE Transactions on Computers*, 47(5):587–602.

(7) A. Singh, D. S. Phatak, T. Goff, M. Riggs, J. F. Plusquellic, and C. Patel. 2003. Comparison of Branching CORDIC implementations. *14th IEEE International Conference on Application-Specific Systems, Architectures, and Processors*, pp. 215–225.

(8) H. Dawid and H. Meyr. 1996. The Differential CORDIC algorithm: constant scale factor redundant implementation without correcting iterations. *IEEE Transactions on Computers*, 45(3):307–328.

(9) M. R. D. Rodrigues, J. H. P. Zurawski, and J. B. Gosling. 1981. Hardware for evaluation of mathematical functions. *Proceedings of the IEE*, 128(E)(4):115–164.

(10) M. R. D. Rodrigues. 1978. Algorithms for the fast hardware evaluation of mathematical functions. M.Sc. thesis, Department of Computer Science, University of Manchester.

(11) J. H. P. Zurawski. 1980. High-performance evaluation of division and other elementary functions. Ph.D. thesis, Department of Computer Science, University of Manchester.

(12) J. H. P. Zurawski and J. B. Gosling. 1987. Design of a high-speed square root, multiply, and divide unit. *IEEE Transactions on Computers*, C-36(1):13–23.

(13) J.-A. Lee and T. Lang. 1992. Constant-factor redundant CORDIC for angle calculation and rotation. *IEEE Transactions on Computers*, 41(8):1016–1025.

(14) E. Antelo, J. Bruguera, and E. L. Zapata, 1996. Unified mixed-radix 2-4 redundant CORDIC processor. *IEEE Transactions on Computers*, 45(9):1068–1073.

(15) E. Antelo, J. Villalba, J, D. Bruguera, and E. L. Zapata. 1997. High-performance rotation architecture based on the radix-4 CORDIC algorithm. *IEEE Transactions on Computers*, 46(8):855–870.

(16) E. Antelo, J. D. Bruguera , T. Lang , E. L. Zapata. 1997. Error analysis and reduction for angle calculation using the CORDIC algorithms. *IEEE Transactions on Computers*, 46(11):1264–1271.

(17) E. Antelo, T. Lang, and J. D. Bruguera. 2000. Very-high radix CORDIC rotation based on selection by rounding. *Journal of VLSI Signal Processing*, 25:141–153.

Chapter 5

(1) J. E. Meggitt. 1962. Pseudo-division and pseudo-multiplication processes. *IBM Journal of Research and Development*, 6(2):210-226.

(2) W. H. Specker. 1965. A class of algorithms for ln x, exp x, sin x, cos x, $\tan^{-1}x$, and $\cot^{-1}x$. *IEEE Transactions on Electronic Computers*, EC-14:85–86.

(3) M. D. Perle. 1969. The dual logarithm algorithms. *Computer Design*, Dec:88–90.

(4) B. G. DeLugish. 1970. A class of algorithms for automatic evaluation of certain elementary functions in a binary computer. Ph.D thesis, University of Illinois, USA.

(5) T. C. Chen. 1972. Automatic computation of exponentials, logarithms, ratios, and square Roots. *IBM Journal of Research and Development*, 16:380–388.

(6) P. W. Baker. 1975. Parallel multiplicative algorithms for some elementary functions. *IEEE Transactions on Computers*, C-24(3):322–325.

(7) M. R. D. Rodrigues, J. H. P. Zurawski, and J. B. Gosling. 1981. Hardware evaluation of mathematical functions. *Proceedings of the IEE*, 128(E)(4):115–164.

(8) J. H. P. Zurawski. 1980. High-performance evaluation of division and other elementary functions. Ph.D. thesis, Department of Computer Science, University of Manchester.

(9) J. H. P. Zurawski and J.B. Gosling. 1987. Design of a high-speed square root, multiply, and divide unit. *IEEE Transactions on Computers*, C-36(1):13–23.

(10) M. R. D. Rodrigues. 1978. Algorithms for the fast hardware evaluation of mathematical functions. M.Sc. thesis, Department of Computer Science, University of Manchester.

(11) M. Ercegovac and T. Lang. 2004. *Digital Arithmetic*. Morgan Kaufmann, San Francisco, CA, USA.

(12) V. Kantabutra. 1996. On hardware for computing exponential and trigonometric functions. *IEEE Transactions on Computers*, 45(3):328–338.

(13) J. A. Pineiro, M. D. Ercegovac, and J. D. Bruguera. 2005. High-radix logarithm with selection by rounding: algorithm and implementation. *Journal of VLSI Signal Processing*, 40(1):109–123.

(14) J. A. Pineiro and J. D. Bruguera. 2003. On-line high-radix expo-

nential with selection by rounding. *Proceedings, IEEE International Symposium on Circuits and Systems (ISCAS 2003)*, vol. IV, pp. 121–124.

(15) M. D. Ercegovac. 1973. Radix-16 evaluation of certain elementary functions. *IEEE Transactions on Computers*, C-22(6):561–566.

Chapter 6

(1) P. M. Farmwal. 1981. On the design of high performance digital arithmetic units. Ph.D. thesis, Department of Computer Science, Stanford University.

(2) K. Hwang, H. C. Hwang, and Z. Hu. 1987. Evaluating elementary functions with Chebyshev polynomials on pipeline nets. *Proceedings, 8th IEEE Symposium on Computer Arithmetic*, pp. 121–128.

(3) I. Koren and O. Zinaty. 1990. Evaluating elementary functions in a numerical coprocessor based on rational approximations. *IEEE Transactions on Computers*, 39(9):1030–1036.

(4) A. Tisserand. 2007. High-performance hardware operators for polynomial evaluation. *International Journal of High Performance Systems Architecture*, 1(1):14–23.

(5) J. Duprat and J.-M. Muller. 1988. Hardwired polynomial Evaluation. *Journal of Parallel and Distributed Computing*, 5(3):291–309.

(6) W. Burleson. 1990. Polynomial evaluation in VLSI using distributed arithmetic. *IEEE Transactions on Circuits and Systems*, 37(10):1299–1304.

(7) J. C. Mason and D. C. Hanscomb. 2003. *Chebyshev Polynomials*. Chapman and Hall, London, UK.

(8) R.-C. Li. 2004. Near optimality of Chebyshev interpolation for elementary function computations. *IEEE Transactions on Computers*, 53(6):678–687.

(9) O. Mencer. 2000. Rational arithmetic units in computer systems. Ph.D. thesis, Department of Electrical Engineering, Stanford University.

(10) M. J. Flynn and S. F. Oberman. 2001. *Advanced Computer Arithmetic*. Wiley, New York.

(11) W. Fraser. 1965. A survey of methods of computing minimax and near-ninimax polynomial Approximations for Functions of a Single Independent Variable. *Journal of the ACM*, 12:295–314.

(12) R. C. Agarwal, F. G. Gustavson, and M. S. Schmookler. 1999. Series approximation methods for divide and square root in the Power3 processor. *Proceedings, 8th Symposium on Computer Arithmetic*, pp. 116–123.

(13) M. J. Schulte and E. E. Swartzlander Jnr. 1993. Parallel designs for correctly rounded elementary functions. *Interval Computations*, 3:65–88.

(14) M. D. Ercegovac, T. Lang, J.-M. Muller, and A. Tisserand. 2000. Reciprocation, square root, inverse square root, and some elementary functions unsing small multipliers. *IEEE Transactions on Computers*, 49(7):628–637.

(15) J. F. Hart, E. W. Cheney, C. L Lawson, H. J. Maehly, C. K. Mseztenyi, J. R. Rice, H. G. Thacher, and C. Witzgall. 1968. *Computer Approximations*. John Wiley & Sons, New York, USA.

(16) M. Abramowitz and I. A. Stegun, Eds. 1964. *Handbook of Mathematical Functions*. National Bureau of Standards, Washington, DC, USA.

(17) L. A. Lyusternik, O. Chervonenkis, and A. R. Yanpolskii. 1965. *Handbook for Computing Elementary Functions*. Pergamon Press, Oxford, UK.

(18) J. Cao, B. W. Y. Wei, and J. Cheng. 2001. High-performance architectures for elementary function generation. *Proceedings, 15th IEEE Symposium on Computer Arithmetic*, pp. 136-144.

(19) R. W. Hamming. 1987. *Numerical Methods for Scientists and Engineers*. Dover Publications, Mineola, New York, USA.

(20) M. Sadeghian, J. E. Stine, and E. G. Walters III. 2014. Optimized cubic Chebyshev interpolator for elementary function hardware implementations. *Proceedings, IEEE International Symposium on Circuits and Systems*, pp. 1536–1539.

(21) T. J. Rivlin. 1974. *The Chebyshev Polynomials*. John Wiley, New York.

Chapter 7

(1) D. Das Sarma and D. W. Matula. 1995. Faithful bipartite ROM reciprocal tables. *Proceedings, 12th IEEE Symposium on Computer Arithmetic*, pp. 17–27.

(2) M. J. Schulte and J. E. Stine. 1999. Approximating elementary functions using symmetric bipartite tables. *IEEE Transactions on Computers*, 48(9):842–847.

(3) F. de Dinechin and A. Tisserand, A. 2005. Multipartite table methods. *IEEE Transactions on Computers*, 54(3):19–33.

(4) J.-M. Muller. 1999. A few results on table-based methods. *Reliable Computing* 5(3):279–288.

(5) P. Kornerup and D. W. Matula. 2005. Single precision reciprocals by multipartite table lookup. *Proceedings, 17th IEEE Symposium on Computer Arithmetic*, pp. 240–248.

(6) J.-A. Piniero, S. F. Oberman, J.-M. Muller, and J. D. Brugera. 2005. High-speed function approximation using a minimax quadratic interpolator. *IEEE Transactions on Computers*, 54(3):304–316.

(7) C. I. Frenzen, T. Sasao, and J. T. Butler. 2010. On the number of segments needed in piecewise linear approximation. *Journal of Computational and Applied Mathematics*, 234:437–446.

(8) T. Sasao, S. Nagayama, and J. T. Butler. 2007. Numerical function generators using LUT cascades. *IEEE Transactions on Computers*, 56(6):826–838.

(9) S. Nagayama, T. Sasao, and J. T. Butler. 2006. Compact numerical function generators based on quadratic approximations: architecture and synthesis method. *IEICE Transactions on Fundamentals of Electronics, Communications and Computer Sciences*, vol. E89-A(12):3510–3518.

(10) D. Lee, W. Luk, J. Villasenor, and P. Y. K, Cheung. 2003. Non-uniform segmentation for hardware function evaluation. *Proceedings, 13th International Conference on Field Programmable Logic and Applications*, pp. 796–807.

(11) D. Lee , R. C. C. Cheung, W. Luk, and J. D. Villasenor. 2009. Hierarchical segmentation for function evaluation. *IEEE Transactions on VLSI Systems*, 17(1):103–116.

(12) M. J. Schulte and E. E. Swartzlander Jnr. 1993. Parallel designs for correctly rounded elementary functions. *Interval Computations*, 3:65–88.

(13) S.-F. Hsiao, H.-J. Ko, Y.-L. Tseng, W.-L. Huang, S.-H. Lin, and C.-S. Wen. 2013. Design of hardware function evaluators using low-overhead nonuniform segmentation with address remapping *IEEE Transactions on VLSI Systems*, 21(5):875–886.

(14) A. G. M. Strollo, D. Caro, and N. Petra. 2011. Elementary functions hardware implementation using constrained piecewise polynomial approximations, *IEEE Transactions on Computers*, 60(3):418–432.

(15) D.-U. Lee, R. Cheung, W. Lu, and J. Villasenor. 2008. Hardware implementation trade-offs of polynomial approximations and interpolations. *IEEE Transactions on Computers*, 57(5):686–701.

(16) D. H. Douglas and T. K. Packer. 1973. Algorithms for the reduction of the number of points required to represent a line or its caricature. *Canadian Cartographer*, 10(2):112–122.

(17) D. Lee, W. Luk, J. D. Villasenor, P. Y. K. Cheung. 2005. The effects of polynomial degrees on the hierarchical segmentation method. In: P. Lysaght and W. Rosenstiel, Eds., *New Algorithms, Architectures and Applications for Reconfigurable Computing*, Springer, Heidelberg, Germany, pp. 301–313.

(18) C. L. Lawson. 1964. Characteristics of the segmented rational minimax approximation problem. *Numerical Mathematics*, 6:293–301.

(19) T. P. Pavlidis and A. P. Maika. 1974. Uniform polynomial approximation with variable joints. *Journal of Approximation Theory*, 12:61–69.

(20) A. R. Omondi. 1994. *Computer Arithmetic Systems*. Prentice Hall, Hemel Hempstead, UK.

(21) J. F. Hart, E. W. Cheney, C. L Lawson, H. J. Maehly, C. K. Mseztenyi, J. R. Rice, H. G. Thacher, and C. Witzgall. 1968. *Computer Approximations*. John Wiley & Sons, New York.

(22) W. Fraser. 1965. A survey of methods of computing minimax and near-minimax polynomial approximations for functions of a single independent variable. *Journal of the ACM*, 12:295–314.

(23) M. D. Ercegovac, T. Lang, J.-M. Muller, and A. Tisserand. 2000. Reciprocation, square root, inverse square root, and some elementary functions using small multipliers. *IEEE Transactions on Computers*, 49(7):628–637.

(24) P. T. P. Tang. 1991. Table lookup algorithms for elementary functions and their error analysis. *Proceedings, 10th IEEE Symposium on Computer Arithmetic*, pp. 232–236.

(25) W. F. Wong and E. Goto. 1995. Fast evaluation of the elementary functions in single precision. *IEEE Transactions on Computers*, 44(3):453–457.

(26) J. Y. L. Low and C. C. Jong. 2013. A memory-efficient tables-and-additions method for accurate computations of elementary functions. *IEEE Transactions on Computers*, 62(5):858–872.

(27) J. E. Stine and M. J. Schulte. 1999. The symmetric table addition method for accurate function approximation. *Journal of VLSI Signal Processing*, 21(2):167–177.

(28) D. Defour, F. de Dinechin, and J.-M. Muller. 2002. A new scheme for table-based evaluation of functions. *Proceedings, 36th Asilomar Conference on Signals, Systems, and Computers*, pp. 1608–1613

(29) J. Detrey and F. de Dinechin. 2005. Table-based polynomials for fast hardware function evaluation. *Proceedings, 16th IEEE International Conference on Application-Specific Systems, Architecture and Processors*, pp. 328–333.

(30) S. Story and P. T. P. Tang. 1999. New algorithms for improved transcendental functions on IA-64. *Proceedings, 14th IEEE Symposium on Computer Arithmetic*, pp. 4–11.

(31) M. Sadeghian, J. E. Stine, and E. G. Walters III. 2014. Optimized cubic Chebyshev interpolator for elementary function hardware implementations. *Proceedings, IEEE International Symposium on Circuits and Systems*, pp. 1536–1539.

(32) J. Detrey and F. de Dinechin. 2004. Second order approximation using a single multiplication on FPGAs. *Proceedings, 14th International Conference on Field Programmable Logic and Applications*, pp. 221–230.

(33) S.-F. Hsiao, H.-J. Ko, and C.-S. Wen. 2012. Two-level hardware function evaluation based on correction of normalized piecewise difference equations. *IEEE Transactions on Circuits and Systems–II: Express Briefs*, 59(5):292–295.

Chapter 8

(1) D. Das Sarma and D. W. Matula. 1995. Faithful bipartite ROM reciprocal tables. *Proceedings, 12th IEEE Symposium on Computer Arithmetic*, pp. 17–27.

(2) R. P. Brent and P. Zimmermann. 2010. *Modern Computer Arithmetic*. Cambridge University Press, Cambride, UK.

(3) D. L. Fowler and J. E. Smith 1989. An accurate, high speed implementation of division by reciprocal approximation. *Proceedings, 9th IEEE Symposium on Computer Arithmetic*, pp. 60–67.

(4) S. F. Anderson, J. G. Earle, R. E. Goldschmidt, and D. M. Powers. 1967. The IBM System/360 model 91: floating-point execution unit. *IBM Journal of Research and Development*, 11:34–63.

(5) J.-A. Piniero and J. D. Brugera. 2002. High-speed double-precision computation of reciprocal, division, square root, and inverse square root. *IEEE Transactions on Computers*, 51(12):1377–1388.

(6) E. M. Schwarz and M. J. Flynn. 1996. Hardware starting approximation method and its application to square root operation. *IEEE Transactions on Computers*, 45(12):1356–1369.

(7) M. J. Schulte and K. E. Wires. 1999. High-speed inverse square roots. *Proceedings, 14th IEEE Symposium on Computer Arithmetic*, pp. 124–131.

(8) C. V. Ramamoorthy, J. R. Goodman, and K. H. Kim. 1972. Some properties of iterative square-rooting methods using high-speed multiplication. *IEEE Transactions on Computers*, C-21(8):737–847.

(9) M. D. Ercegovac, T. Lang, J.-M. Muller, and A. Tisserand. 2000. Reciprocation, square root, inverse square root, and some elementary functions using small, multipliers. *IEEE Transactions on Computers*, 49(7):628–637.

(10) M. D. Ercegovac, L. IImbert, D. W. Matula, J.-M. Muller, and G. Wei. 2000. Improving Goldschmidt division, square root, and square root recicprocals. *IEEE Transactions on Computers*, 49(7):759–762.

(11) P. Montuschi and M. Mezzalama. 1991. Optimal absolute error starting values for Newton–Raphson calculation of square root. *Computing*, 46:67–86.

(12) B. G. DeLugish. 1970. A class of algorithms for automatic evaluation of certain elementary functions in a binary computer. Ph.D thesis, University of Illinois.

(13) M. R. D. Rodrigues, J. H. P. Zurawski, and J. B. Gosling. 1981. Hardware for evaluation of mathematical functions. *Proceedings of the IEE*, 128(E)(4):115–164.

(14) J. H. P. Zurawski. 1980. High-performance evaluation of division and other elementary functions. Ph.D. thesis, Department of Computer Science, University of Manchester.

(15) J. H. P. Zurawski and J. B. Gosling. 1987. Design of a high-speed square root, multiply, and divide unit. *IEEE Transactions on Computers*, C-36(1):13–23.

(16) E. V. Krishnamurthy. 1970. On optimal iterative schemes for high-speed division. *IEEE Transactions on Computers*, C-19(3):227–231.

(17) J.-M. Muller, N. Brisebarre, F. de Dinechin, C.-P. Jeannerod, V. Lefèvre, G. Melquiond, N. Revol, D. Stehle, and S. Torres. 2009. *Handbook of Floating-Point Arithmetic*. Birkhauser, Boston, USA.

(18) R. C. Agarwal, F. G. Gustavson, and M. S. Schmookler. 1999. Series approximation methods for divide and square root in the Power3 processor. *Proceedings, 14th IEEE Symposium on Computer Arithmetic*, pp. 116–123.

(19) T.-J. Kwon and J. Draper. 2009. Floating-point division and square root using a Taylor-series expansion algorithm. *Microelectronics Journal*, 40(11):1601–1605.

(20) P. Markstein. 1990. Computation of elementary functions of the IBM RISC System/6000. *IBM Journal of Research and Development*, 34:111–119.

(21) C. Iordache and D. W. Matula. 1999. On infinitely precise rounding for division, square root, reciprocal and square root reciprocal. *Proceedings, 14th IEEE Symposium on Computer Arithmetic*, pp. 233–240.

(22) M. J. Schulte and E. E. Swartzlander Jnr. 1993. Parallel designs for correctly rounded elementary functions. *Interval Computations*, 3:65–88.

(23) J. Fandrianto. 1987. Algorithm for high speed shared radix-4 division and radix-4 square root. *Proceedings, 8th IEEE Symposium on Computer Arithmetic*, pp. 73–79.

(24) L. A. Lyusternik, O. O. Chervonenkis, and A. R. Yanpolskii. 1965. *Handbook for Computing Elementary Functions*. Pergamon Press, Oxford, UK.

(25) M. R. D. Rodrigues. 1978. M.Sc. thesis, Department of Computer Science, University of Manchester.

(26) P. Markstein. 2004. Software division and square root using Goldschmidts algorithms. *Proceedings, 6th Conference on Real Numbers and Computers*, pp. 146157.

(27) P. Kornerup and J.-M. Muller. 2006. Choosing starting values for certain Newton-Raphson iterations. *Theoretical Computer Science*, 351(1):101–110.

(28) M. J. Schulte, J. Omar, and E. E. Swartzlander Jr. 1994. Optimal initial approximations for the Newton–Raphson division algorithm. *Computing*, 53(3-4):233–242.

(29) J. Fandrianto. 1989. An algorithm for high speed shared radix-8 division and radix-8 square root. *Proceedings, 9th IEEE Symposium on Computer Arithmetic*, pp. 68–75.

(30) G. S. Taylor. 1985. Radix-16 SRT dividers with overlapped quotient selection stages. *Proceedings, 7th IEEE Symposium on Computer Arithmetic*, pp. 64–71.

(31) J. A. Butts, P. T. P. Tang, R. O. Dror, D. E. Shaw. 2011. Radix-8 digit-by-rounding: achieving high-performance reciprocals, square roots, and reciprocal square roots. *Proceedings, 20th IEEE Symposium on Computer Arithmetic*, pp. 149–158.

(32) A. Nannarelli. 2011. Radix-16 combined division and square root unit. *Proceedings, 20th IEEE Symposium on Computer Arithmetic*, pp. 169–176.

(33) M. Ercegovac and T. Lang. 2003. *Digital Arithmetic*. Morgan Kaufmann, San Francisco, CA, USA

(34) M. Ercegovac and T. Lang. 1999. Radix-4 square rot without initial PLA. *IEEE Transactions on Computers*, 39(8):1016–1024.

(35) J. F. Hart, E. W. Cheney, C. L Lawson, H. J. Maehly, C. K. Mseztenyi, J. R. Rice, H. G. Thacher, and C. Witzgall. 1968. *Computer Approximations*. John Wiley & Sons, New York, USA.

(36) T. C. Chen. 1972. Automatic computation of exponentials, logarithms, ratios, and square roots. *IBM Journal of Research and Development*, 16:380–388.

(37) N. Burgess and C. N. Hinds. 2007. Design of the ARM VFP11 divide and square root synthesisable Macrocell. *Proceedings, 18th IEEE Symposium on Computer Arithmetic*, pp. 87–96.

(38) P. Kornerup. 2005. Digit selection for SRT division and square root. *IEEE Transactions on Computers*, 54(3):294–303.

(39) S. Majerski. 1985. Square-rooting algorithms for high-speed digital circuits. *IEEE Transactions on Computers*, 34(8):724–733.

(40) J.-M. Muller, N. Brisebarre, F. de Dinechin, C.-P. Jeannerod, V. Lefèvre, G. Melquiond, N. Revol, D. Stehlè, and S. Torres. 2009. *Handbook of Floating-Point Arithmetic*. Birkhauser, Boston, USA.

(41) J. A. Prabhu and G. B. Zyner. 1995. 167 MHz radix-8 divide and square root using overlapped radix-2 stages. *Proceedings, 12th IEEE Symposium on Computer Arithmetic*, pp. 155–162.

Index